Britain's Europe

BRENDAN SIMMS

Britain's Europe

A Thousand Years of Conflict and Cooperation

ALLEN LANE
an imprint of
PENGUIN BOOKS

ALLEN LANE

UK | USA | Canada | Ireland | Australia
India | New Zealand | South Africa

Allen Lane is part of the Penguin Random House group of companies
whose addresses can be found at global.penguinrandomhouse.com

Penguin Random House UK

First published 2016
001

Set in 10.5/14 pt Sabon LT Std
Typeset by Jouve (UK), Milton Keynes
Printed in Great Britain by Clays Ltd, St Ives plc

A CIP catalogue record for this book is available from the British Library

ISBN: 978-0-241-27596-2

To Anita

Contents

List of Maps

I am deeply impressed with the melancholy and doubtful character of the prospects which hang before Europe . . . I think it would be rash on our part to indulge in too sanguine anticipations . . . If we look forward to the future, no doubt it is necessary for us to consider what is the position of this country with reference to Europe at large; and for my own part, separating the position of this country, ideally and for purposes of argument, for a moment from that of Europe, I cannot but feel that we have some reason to be thankful – thankful for the position of the country, and thankful for the union of the people . . .

But I admit, and am the first to assert that, whatever be that security, power, and independence, we have no right to wrap ourselves up in an absolute and selfish isolation. We have a history, we have traditions, we have living, constant, perpetual, multiplied intercourse and contact with every people in Europe. We should be unworthy of the recollections of our past, unworthy of our hopes of the future, unworthy of the greatness of the present, if we disowned the obligations which arise out of these relations to others more liable to suffer than ourselves.

– William Gladstone, speech to
House of Commons, 9 February 1871

Introduction: Our European Story

Michelet famously began his lectures on British history with the words 'England is an Island'. The Edwardian children's author H. E. Marshall spoke of the history of Britain as *Our Island Story* (1905). Likewise, Arthur Bryant drew on Shakespeare's iconic speech by John of Gaunt when he entitled the first volume of his *History of Britain and the British People* 'Set in a Silver Sea'. He entitled volume two, covering the period from the Tudors to the early nineteenth century, 'Freedom's Own Island'. More recently, Raphael Samuel, the radical founder of the History Workshop movement and a very different historian to Bryant in most ways, wrote *Island Stories*; there might be many stories, but he did not doubt that Britain's was primarily an *island* story. To underline the point, the jacket of the second volume, subtitled 'Theatres of Memory', features the white cliffs of Dover, as if they were a rampart to keep out foreign – that is, European – influences.[1] Christopher Lee's BBC Radio 4 broadcasts on British history were entitled *This Sceptred Isle* (1995),[2] another borrowing from John of Gaunt's speech. A recent collection by prominent historians speaks of the British Isles being *A World by Itself*,[3] taking its cue once again from the Bard, this time from *Cymbeline*. The former Conservative Secretary of State for Education Michael Gove, who has taken a particular interest in the teaching of history in schools, is very much part of this tradition. He has called for a return to the teaching of traditional topics to give 'children the ability to hear our island story'.[4] It is a powerful narrative, which is often much more nuanced than the summary above suggests and which, despite this author's reservations, deserves respect.

This book will argue the contrary view that the history of England,

and later of Britain, is primarily a continental story,[5] that her destiny was mainly determined by relations with the rest of Europe rather than with the wider world. It is not a systematic accounting of Britain's connections with the continent; that would have required a different and much longer book. This volume will concentrate on foreign policy and constitutional design. Economics and political thought will be relatively neglected; other dimensions such as migration, culture, 'national character'[6] and race will be practically ignored. The approach throughout will be relentlessly and unapologetically 'Whiggish', both in the insistence on the centrality of Europe and in the identification of a clear line leading from the past to the present, though not – necessarily – into the future.

We will begin with a short introduction showing how England was tied to the continent by the 'bonds of Christendom' and similar socio-political structures. We will note how England itself emerged in the struggle against the Vikings, and then developed a strong national identity and political focus in what came to be known as 'Parliament'. This will be followed by a chapter which shows how England lost her territorial link to Europe at the end of the Hundred Years War but rediscovered it at the start of the Hanoverian period. It will show how the continent nonetheless remained the principal reference point in British policy and politics, even more so after the onset of the Reformation. The chapter will also show how the United Kingdom itself was 'invented' as a parliamentary union in response to the pressures of the European system, and that it has 'punched above its weight' in the world ever since. Much of continental Europe, by contrast, had already lost its representative structures or was about to do so.

The following chapters attempt a thematic examination of Britain's highly sophisticated understanding of Europe in the eighteenth and early nineteenth centuries. Chapter 3, 'The bulwarks of Great Britain', shows how the continent was at the forefront of strategic and political debate in Britain throughout. The balance of power, and the connection between the central European balance and those of the peripheries, was crucial to the defence of British parliamentary freedoms. In the minds of contemporaries, the 'liberties of Europe' and those of the United Kingdom were closely connected. These preoccupations always far exceeded interest in the colonies, engagement with which was primarily motivated by a concern to mobilize resources in Europe or to deny them to rivals there. Chapter 4, 'There Goes the Neighbourhood', which focuses on the politician and political thinker Edmund Burke, shows how in the late eighteenth century the confessionally driven interest in the fate of the continent was overlain and then superseded by a sense that the ideological complexion of Europe, especially the growth of Revolutionary France, had serious implications for British security. Chapter 5 'The great bank of Europe', picks up these themes and explores how they carried forward into the Napoleonic Wars, when Britain used her vast resources to marshal continental coalitions in support of re-establishing the balance of power in Europe and thus the basis for her own prosperity and liberty.

In the nineteenth and early twentieth centuries, Europe was, as Winston Churchill suggested well before the First World War, 'Where the weather came from'. The next chapter, which takes the story from 1815 to 1914, shows that the continent remained important even at the height of the Victorian period, when the British empire surged and England became the 'workshop of the world'. British statesmen continued to see the European balance as vital, and they added to this a concern for the defence of liberalism, which was viewed as a bulwark against autocratic aggression. These preoccupations grew ever stronger as the continental balance shifted in the late nineteenth century in favour of Germany and Russia. By the outbreak of the First World War, this anxiety about the state of Europe far outweighed imperial ambitions; indeed, the latter were driven by the former. The following chapter, 'Under a single sway' reminds us how London was determined to prevent Eurasia and, in particular, Europe from being dominated by a single power, especially a totalitarian one. This centrality of Europe to British history during the era of the two world wars is too obvious to require much retelling.

'Our destiny has been to help shape Europe' (Chapter 8) deals with the period from 1945 to the present day, when the European question posed and poses itself in ways at once familiar and new. The security of Europe in the face of Soviet aggression remained the central preoccupation of British grand strategy and often had a profound influence on domestic politics. The project of western European integration was thus welcomed as a mobilization of the continent for the common defence, and the containment of centrifugal tendencies, not least German power. Integration was also, however, an existential threat to the integrity of the United Kingdom. For hundreds of years, Britons had repelled hostile takeovers; now they were being asked to contemplate a negotiated merger. Battle lines polarized not merely around questions of grand strategy but also around the nature of the UK itself, and even whether there should be a sovereign United Kingdom at all. The penultimate chapter suggests that, despite all the economic and political changes of the past seventy years, the UK remains a great power and the only European one at that. This is because her highly resilient social and political systems, which developed over centuries in response to European pressures, have enabled her to weather so many storms in the past, and will most likely do so in the future. The book concludes with a proposal of how to reconcile Britain's need for stability on the continent, which can be achieved only through the complete political integration of the eurozone, with the British people's desire to preserve the sovereignty of the United Kingdom. It suggests that what is required is not so much a European Britain as a British Europe.

MAPS

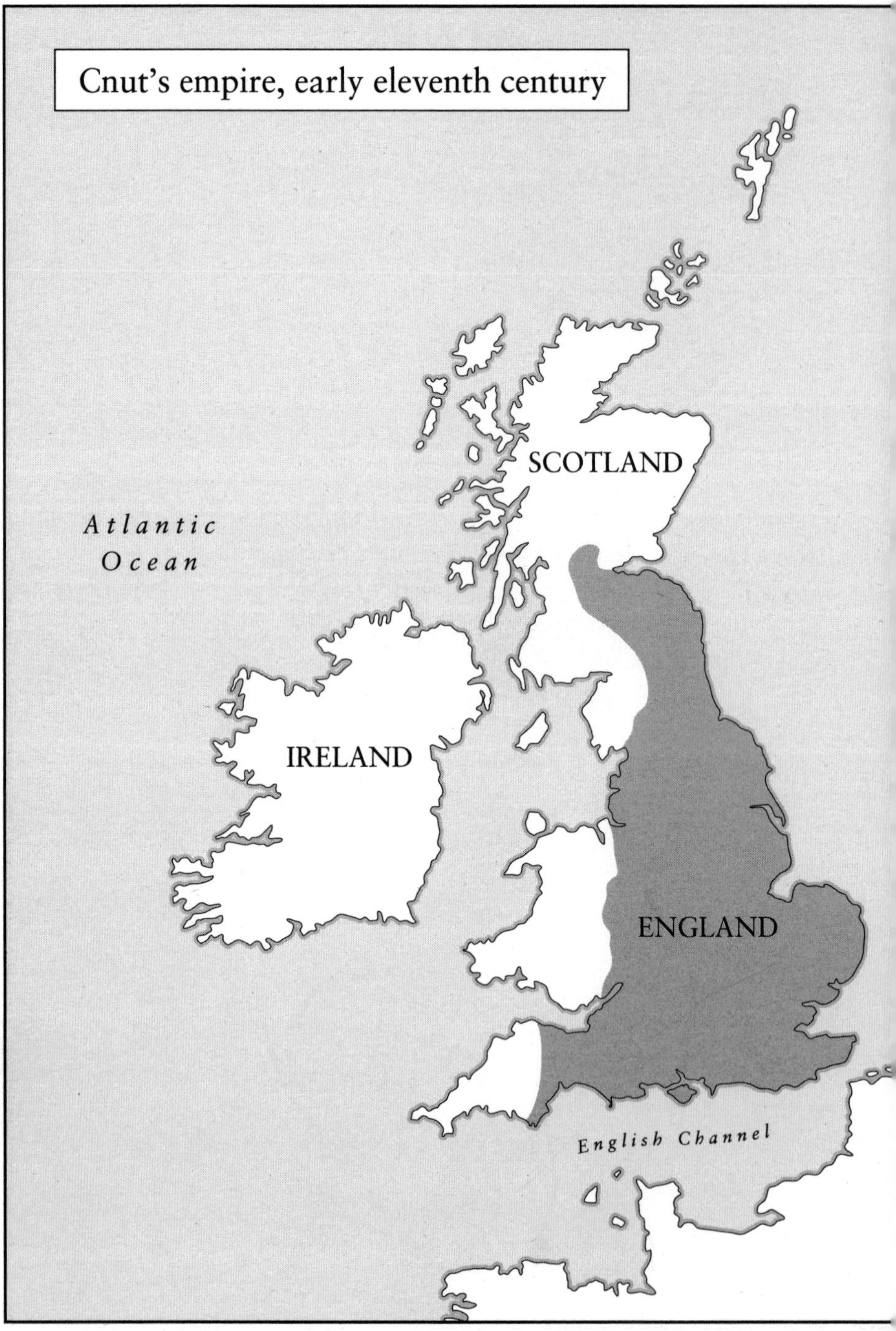
Cnut's empire, early eleventh century
SCOTLAND
Atlantic
Ocean
IRELAND
ENGLAND
English Channel

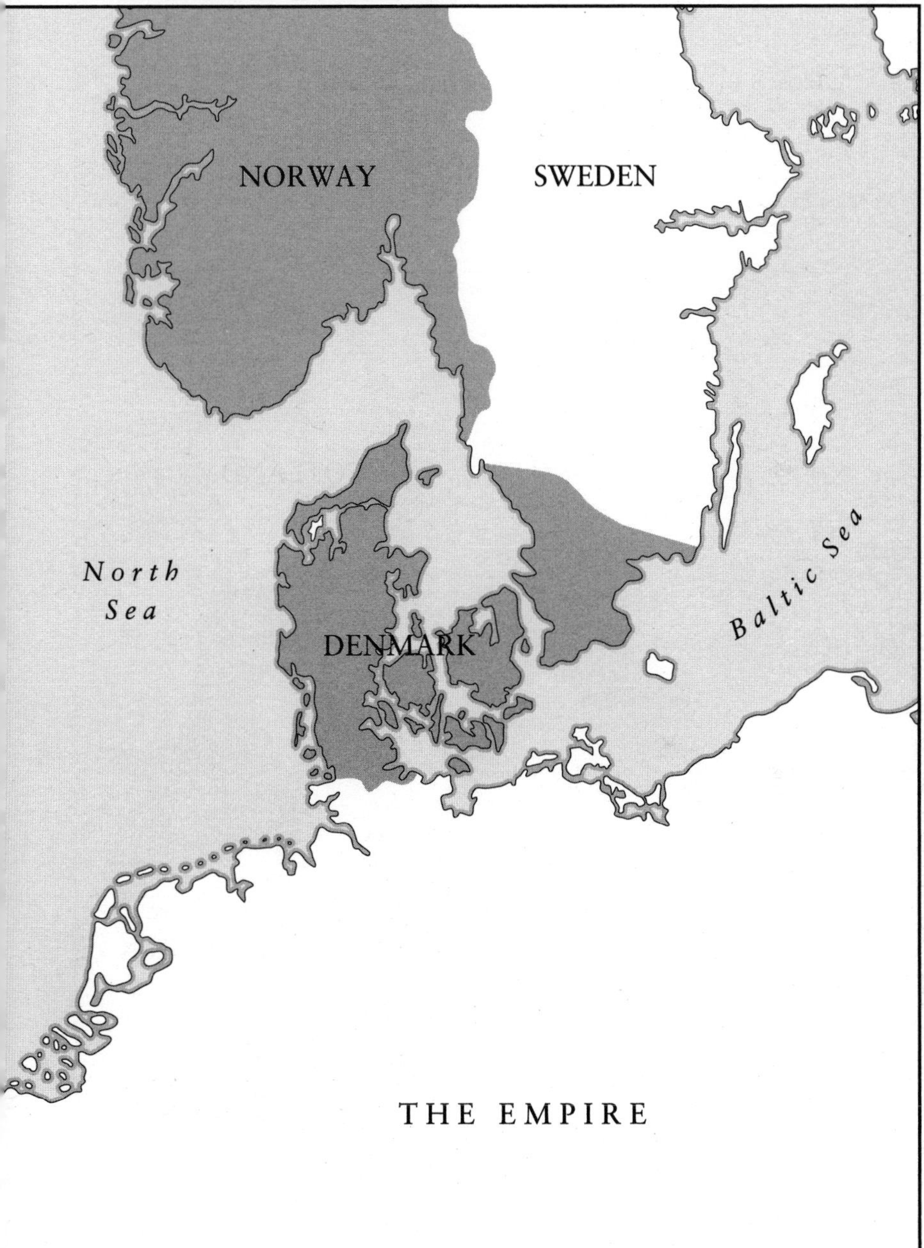
NORWAY
SWEDEN
North
Sea
DENMARK
Baltic Sea
THE EMPIRE

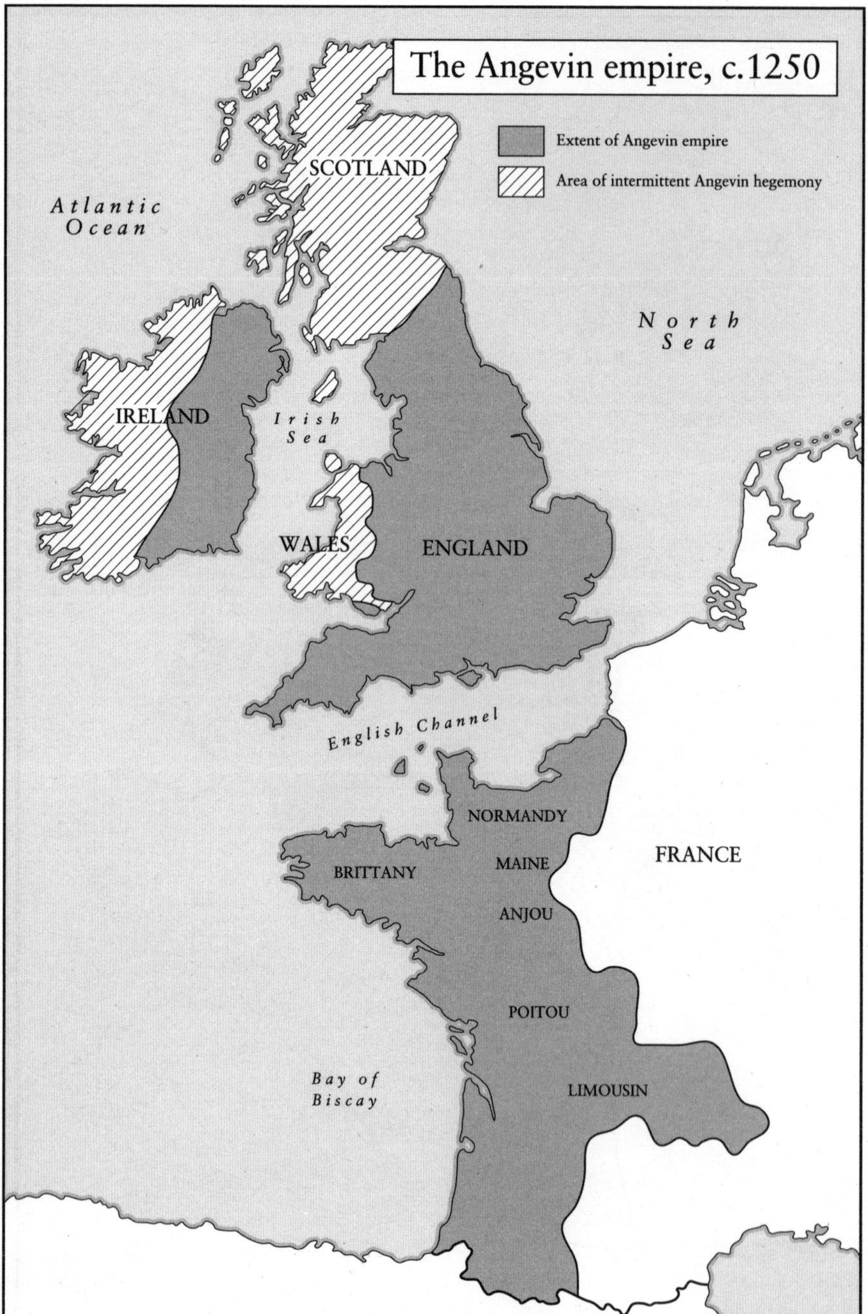

The Angevin empire, c.1250
Extent of Angevin empire
Area of intermittent Angevin hegemony
Atlantic Ocean
SCOTLAND
North Sea
IRELAND
Irish Sea
WALES
ENGLAND
English Channel
NORMANDY
BRITTANY
MAINE
FRANCE
ANJOU
POITOU
Bay of Biscay
LIMOUSIN

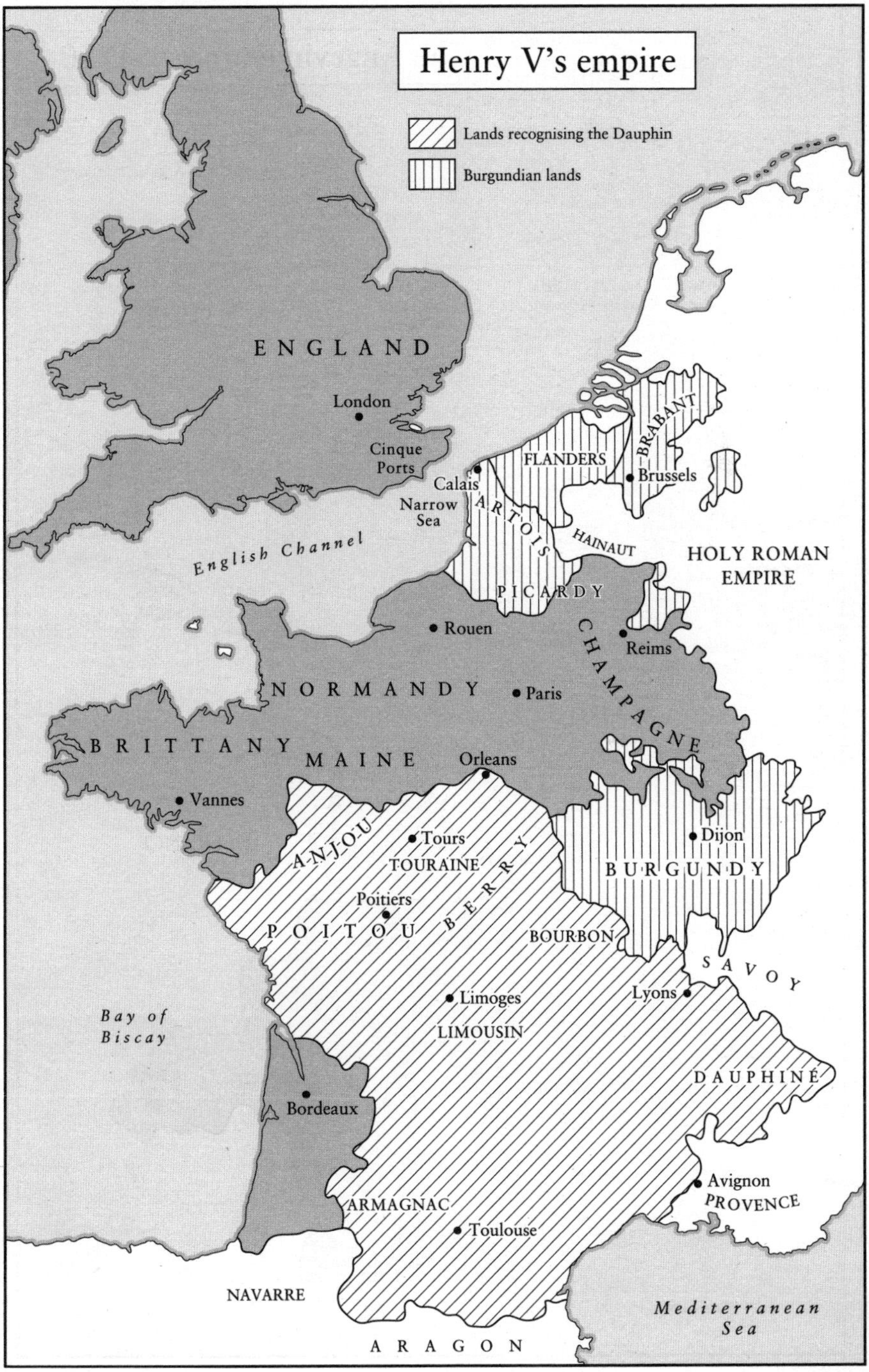
Henry V's empire
Lands recognising the Dauphin
Burgundian lands
ENGLAND
London
Cinque Ports
Calais
Narrow Sea
English Channel
FLANDERS
BRABANT
Brussels
ARTOIS
HAINAUT
HOLY ROMAN EMPIRE
PICARDY
Rouen
Reims
CHAMPAGNE
NORMANDY
Paris
BRITTANY
MAINE
Orleans
Vannes
ANJOU
Tours
TOURAINE
BERRY
Dijon
BURGUNDY
Poitiers
POITOU
BOURBON
SAVOY
Lyons
Limoges
LIMOUSIN
Bay of Biscay
DAUPHINÉ
Bordeaux
Avignon
PROVENCE
ARMAGNAC
Toulouse
NAVARRE
Mediterranean Sea
ARAGON

Tudors and the Continent
1: Henry VII's son Arthur marries Catherine of Aragon, daughter of Ferdinand and Isabella
2: Henry VII's daughter Margaret marries James IV of Scotland
3: Henry VII's daughter Mary marries Louis XII of France
4: Henry VII's son Henry VIII first marries Catherine of Aragon and then
5: fourthly marries Anne of Cleves
6: Henry VIII's son Edward VI is betrothed to Mary, Queen of Scots
7: Henry VIII's daughter Mary I marries Philip II, King of Spain, King of Naples, Duke of Milan, ruler of the Netherlands
8: Henry VIII's daughter Elizabeth I negotiates to marry first Henry III of France and then
9: Francis of Anjou, son of Henry II of France
SCOTLA
IRELAND
WALES
ENGLAN
Armada
1588
FRANC
Bay of
Biscay
Atlantic
Ocean
PORTUGAL
CASTILE AND ARAGON
SPAIN

NORWAY
SWEDEN
North Sea
DENMARK
Baltic Sea
UNITED PROVINCES
Pale of Calais
5
SPANISH NETHERLANDS
SILESIA
POLAND
HOLY ROMAN EMPIRE
BOHEMIA
8
9
AUSTRIA
HUNGARY
SAVOY
MILAN
FLORENCE
SIENA
PAPAL STATES
Adriatic Sea
OTTOMAN EMPIRE
NAPLES
SARDINIA

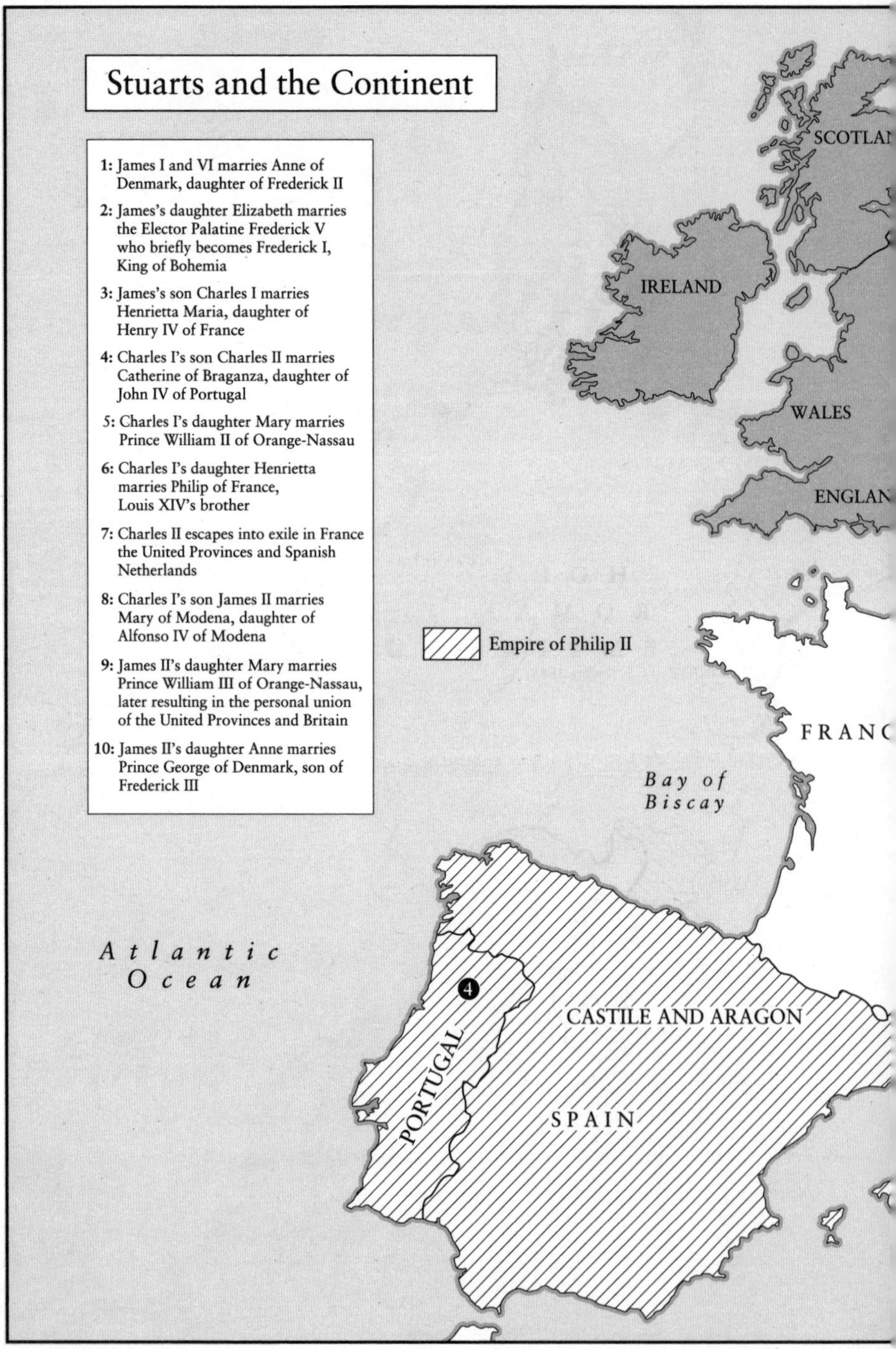
Stuarts and the Continent
1: James I and VI marries Anne of Denmark, daughter of Frederick II
2: James's daughter Elizabeth marries the Elector Palatine Frederick V who briefly becomes Frederick I, King of Bohemia
3: James's son Charles I marries Henrietta Maria, daughter of Henry IV of France
4: Charles I's son Charles II marries Catherine of Braganza, daughter of John IV of Portugal
5: Charles I's daughter Mary marries Prince William II of Orange-Nassau
6: Charles I's daughter Henrietta marries Philip of France, Louis XIV's brother
7: Charles II escapes into exile in France the United Provinces and Spanish Netherlands
8: Charles I's son James II marries Mary of Modena, daughter of Alfonso IV of Modena
9: James II's daughter Mary marries Prince William III of Orange-Nassau, later resulting in the personal union of the United Provinces and Britain
10: James II's daughter Anne marries Prince George of Denmark, son of Frederick III
Empire of Philip II
IRELAND
WALES
Bay of Biscay
Atlantic Ocean
4
PORTUGAL
CASTILE AND ARAGON
SPAIN

NORWAY
SWEDEN
Swedish Baltic Provinces
North Sea
DENMARK
1
10
Baltic Sea
5
9
UNITED PROVINCES
unkirk
SPANISH NETHERLANDS
7
POLAND
SILESIA
HOLY ROMAN EMPIRE
(before 1648)
BOHEMIA
2
PALATINATE
6
AUSTRIA
HUNGARY
SAVOY
MILAN
8
MODENA
FLORENCE
SIENA
PAPAL STATES
Adriatic Sea
OTTOMAN EMPIRE
NAPLES
SARDINIA

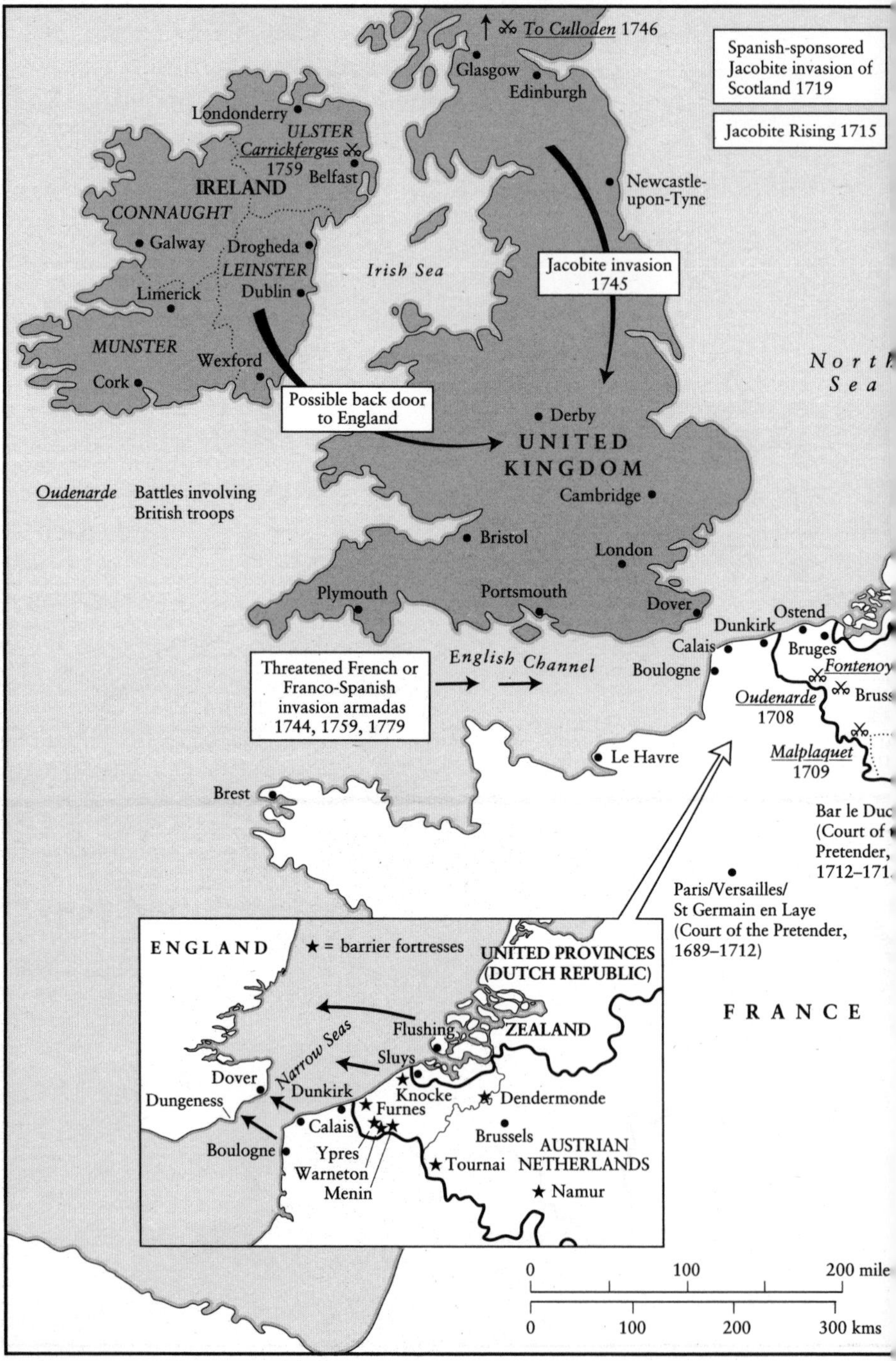

To Culloden 1746
Spanish-sponsored Jacobite invasion of Scotland 1719
Jacobite Rising 1715
Glasgow
Edinburgh
Londonderry
ULSTER
Carrickfergus 1759
Belfast
IRELAND
CONNAUGHT
Galway
Drogheda
LEINSTER
Dublin
Limerick
MUNSTER
Wexford
Cork
Irish Sea
Newcastle-upon-Tyne
Jacobite invasion 1745
North Sea
Possible back door to England
Derby
UNITED KINGDOM
Cambridge
Oudenarde Battles involving British troops
Bristol
London
Plymouth
Portsmouth
Dover
Ostend
Dunkirk
Calais
Bruges
Boulogne
Fontenoy
Bruss
Oudenarde 1708
Malplaquet 1709
English Channel
Threatened French or Franco-Spanish invasion armadas 1744, 1759, 1779
Le Havre
Brest
Bar le Duc (Court of Pretender, 1712–171
Paris/Versailles/ St Germain en Laye (Court of the Pretender, 1689–1712)
FRANCE
ENGLAND
★ = barrier fortresses
UNITED PROVINCES (DUTCH REPUBLIC)
ZEALAND
Flushing
Narrow Seas
Sluys
Dover
Dungeness
Dunkirk
Knocke
Furnes
Dendermonde
Calais
Brussels
Boulogne
Ypres
Warneton
Menin
Tournai
AUSTRIAN NETHERLANDS
Namur
0 100 200 mile
0 100 200 300 kms

Britain's security architecture in the eighteenth century
Copenhagen
Baltic Sea
DENMARK
Source of naval stores
Danzig
Elbing
Bremen and Verden (To Hanover 1719)
Electorate of Hanover
BRANDENBURG – PRUSSIA
Celle (British postal intercept station)
POLAND
Minden 1759
Hastenbeck 1757
Elbe
Weser
amillies 1706
iège
AUSTRIAN
THERLANDS
SILESIA (annexed from Austria by Prussia 1740)
Rhine
Dettingen 1743
HOLY ROMAN EMPIRE
ORRAINE
Blenheim 1704
HABSBURG MONARCHY (Austria)
(Under French influence from 1735; annexed by France, 1766)
Vienna
HUNGARY
SWITZERLAND
VENICE

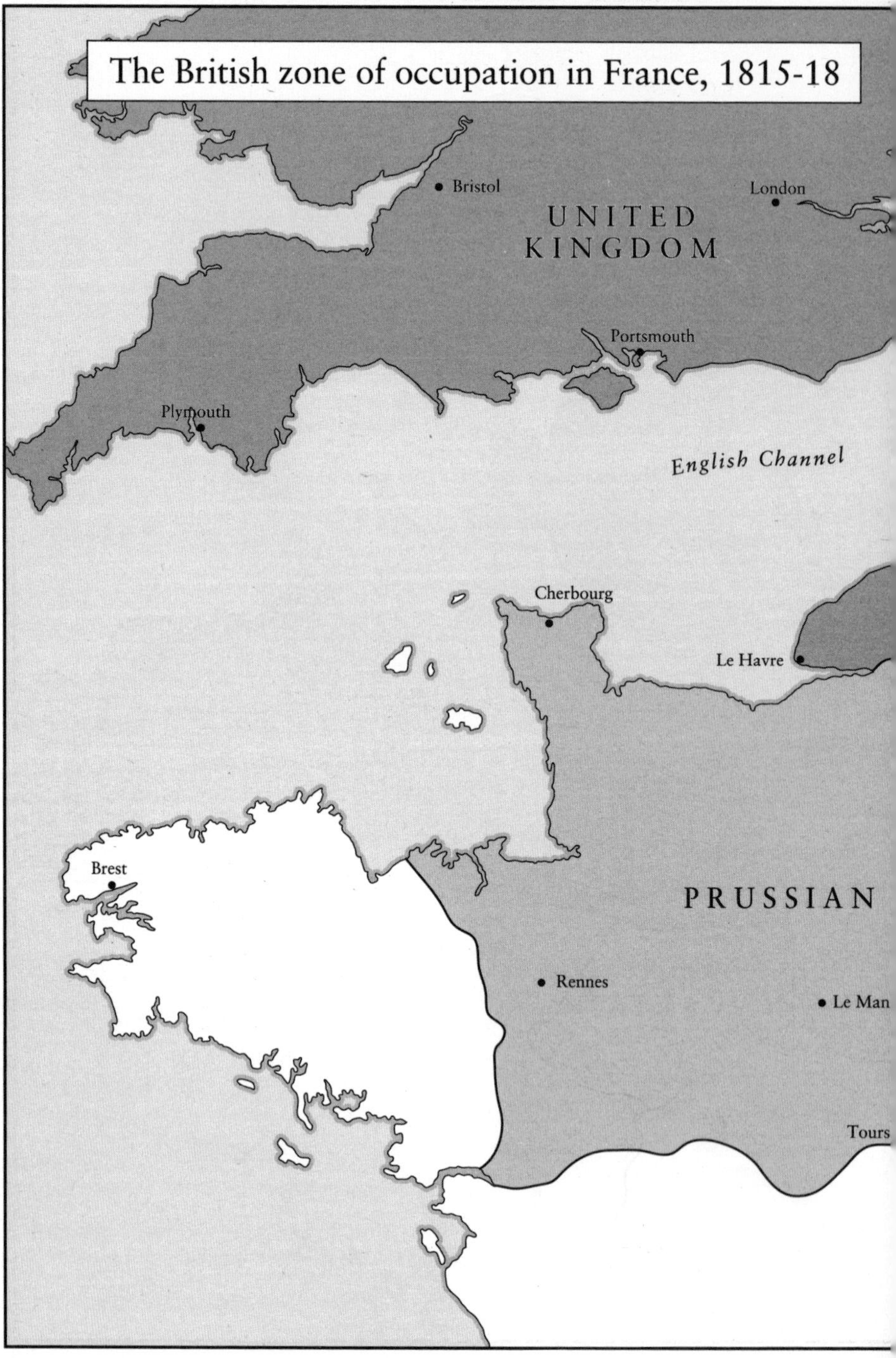

The British zone of occupation in France, 1815-18
Bristol
London
UNITED KINGDOM
Portsmouth
Plymouth
English Channel
Cherbourg
Le Havre
Brest
PRUSSIAN
Rennes
Le Man
Tours

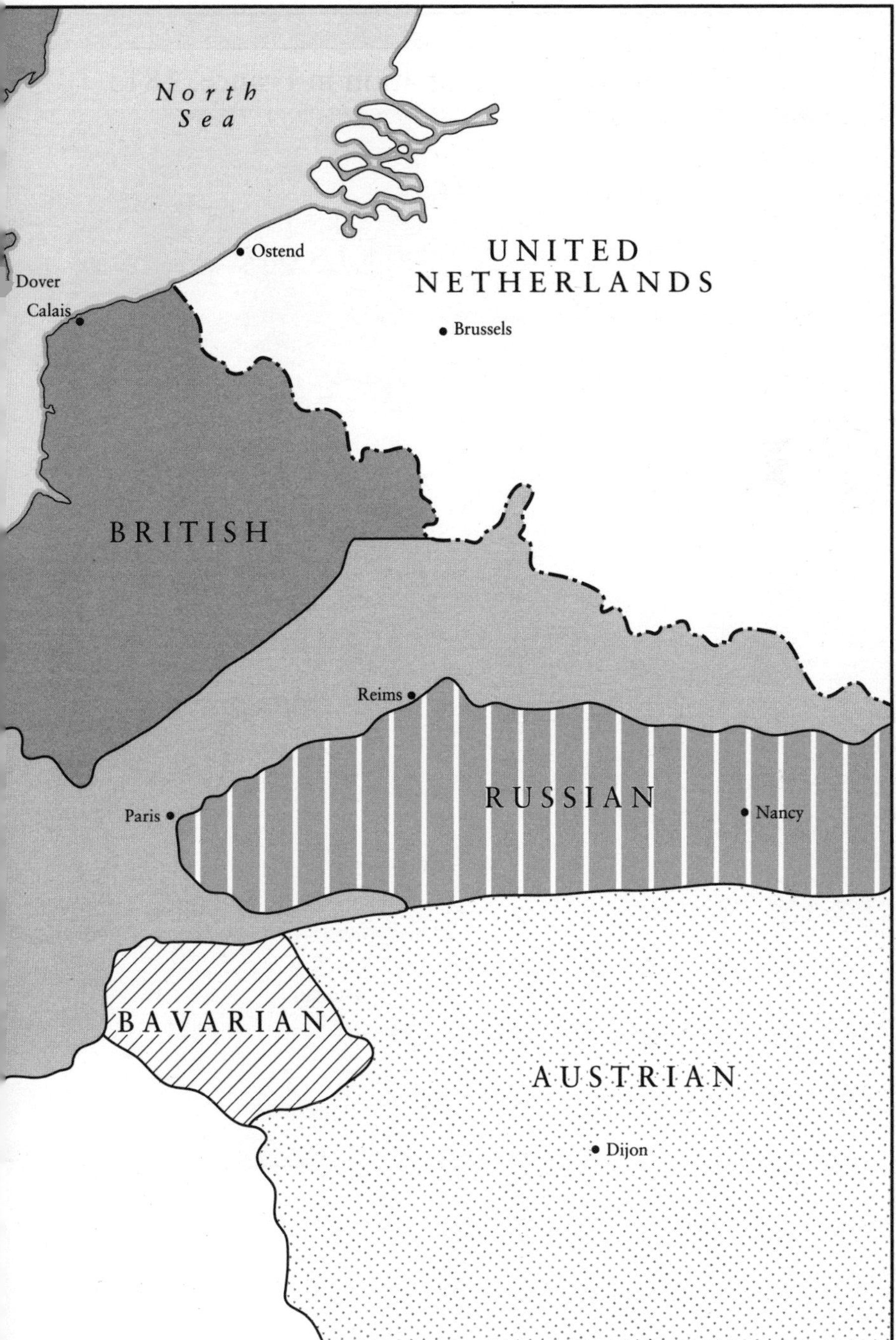
North Sea
Ostend
Dover
Calais
UNITED NETHERLANDS
Brussels
BRITISH
Reims
RUSSIAN
Paris
Nancy
BAVARIAN
AUSTRIAN
Dijon

UNITED
KINGDOM
TH
Dover
English Channel
Calais
Antwerp
Ypres
Bruss
BELGIUM
Lille
Etaples
Mons
Arras
Bapaume
Amiens
St-Quentin
FRANCE
Compiègne
Soissons
Reims

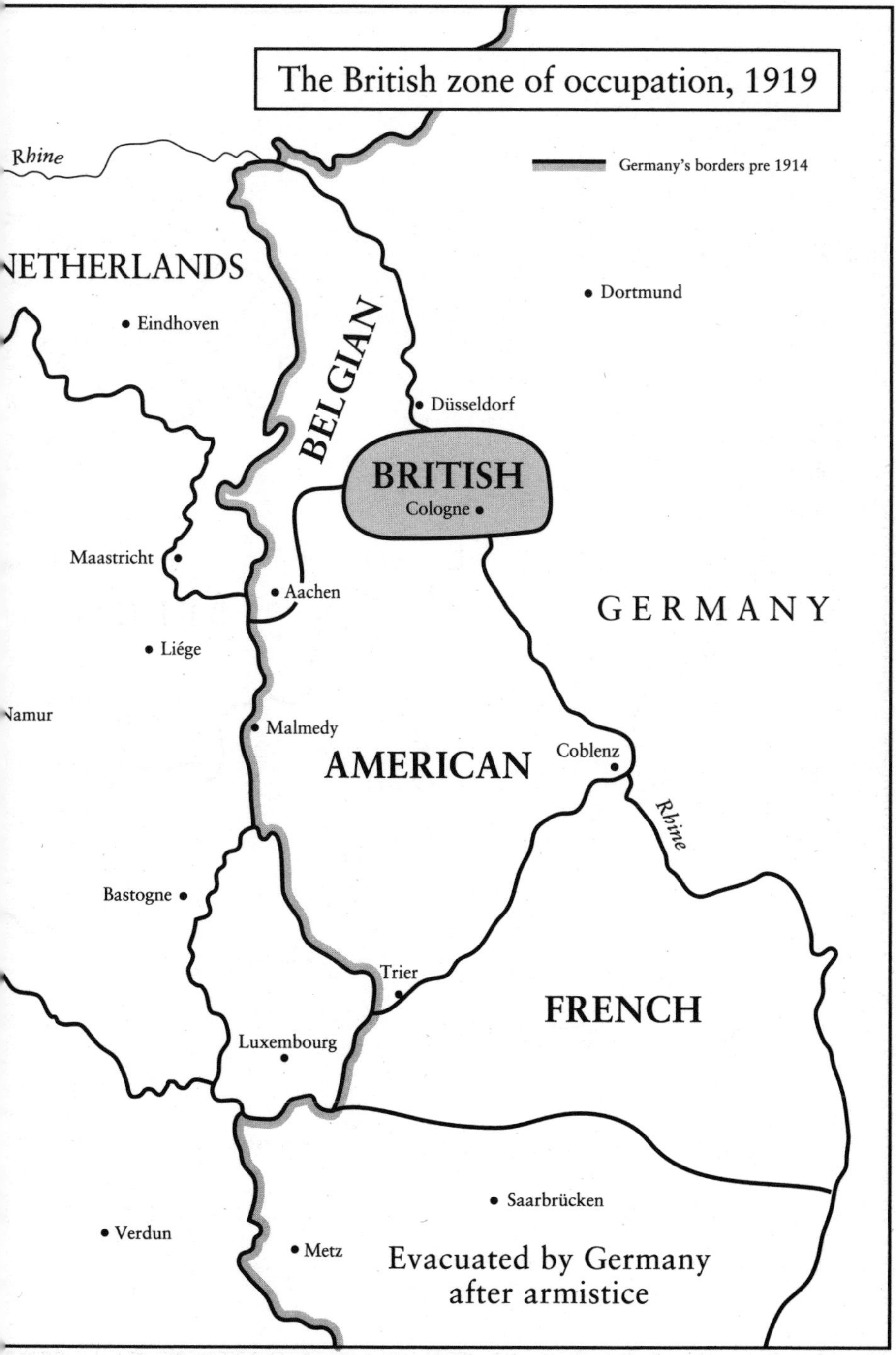

The British zone of occupation, 1919
Germany's borders pre 1914
Rhine
NETHERLANDS
Eindhoven
BELGIAN
Dortmund
Düsseldorf
BRITISH
Cologne
Maastricht
Aachen
GERMANY
Liége
Namur
Malmedy
AMERICAN
Coblenz
Rhine
Bastogne
Trier
FRENCH
Luxembourg
Saarbrücken
Verdun
Metz
Evacuated by Germany
after armistice

Berlin
FRENCH
BRITISH
SOVIET
AMERICAN
North Sea
NETHERLANDS
Amsterdam
American zone
Breme
BRITISH ZONE
Rhine
Münster
Essen
Düsseldorf
Cologne
Bonn
Aachen
Brussels
BELGIUM
FRENCH ZONE
FRANCE
Luxembourg

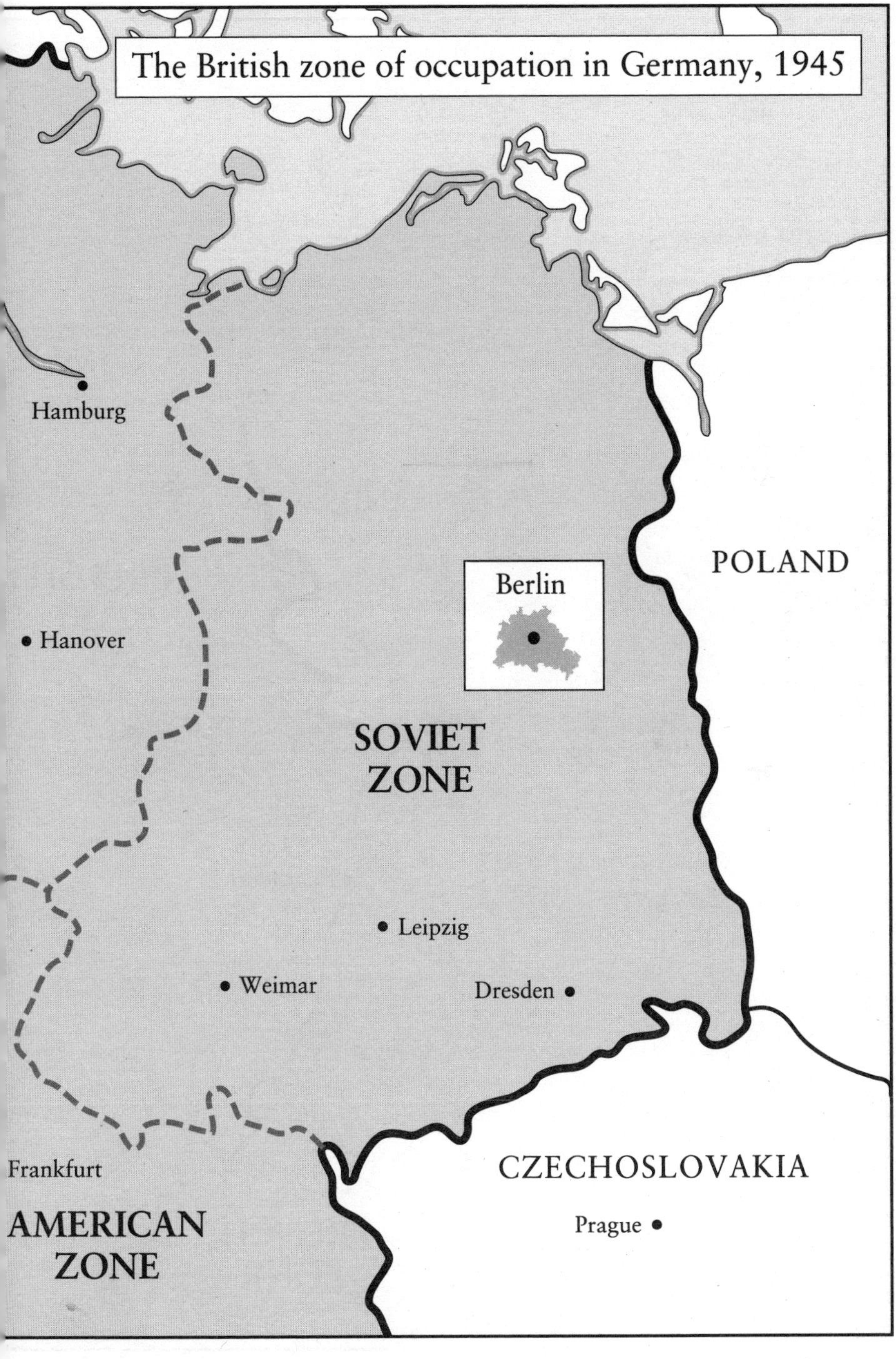
The British zone of occupation in Germany, 1945
Hamburg
Hanover
Berlin
POLAND
SOVIET
ZONE
Leipzig
Weimar
Dresden
Frankfurt
AMERICAN
ZONE
CZECHOSLOVAKIA
Prague

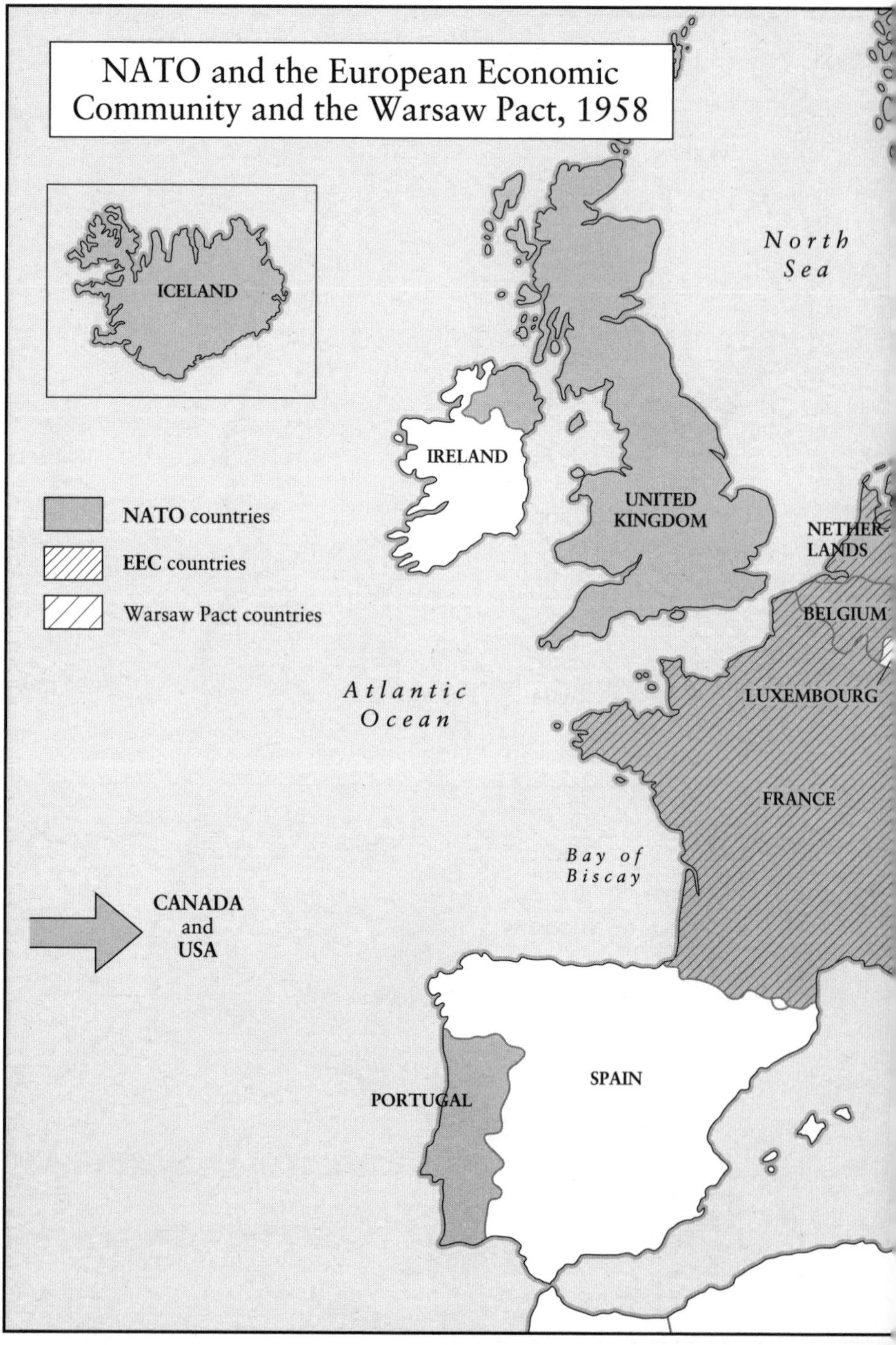
NATO and the European Economic Community and the Warsaw Pact, 1958
ICELAND
NATO countries
EEC countries
Warsaw Pact countries
IRELAND
UNITED KINGDOM
North Sea
NETHER-LANDS
BELGIUM
LUXEMBOURG
FRANCE
Atlantic Ocean
Bay of Biscay
CANADA and USA
SPAIN
PORTUGAL

FINLAND
NORWAY
SWEDEN
Baltic Sea
DENMARK
POLAND
U. S. S. R.
EAST GERMANY
WEST GERMANY
CZECHOSLOVAKIA
AUSTRIA
HUNGARY
WITZ.
ROMANIA
ITALY
YUGOSLAVIA
Black Sea
BULGARIA
ALBANIA
GREECE
TURKEY
Mediterranean Sea

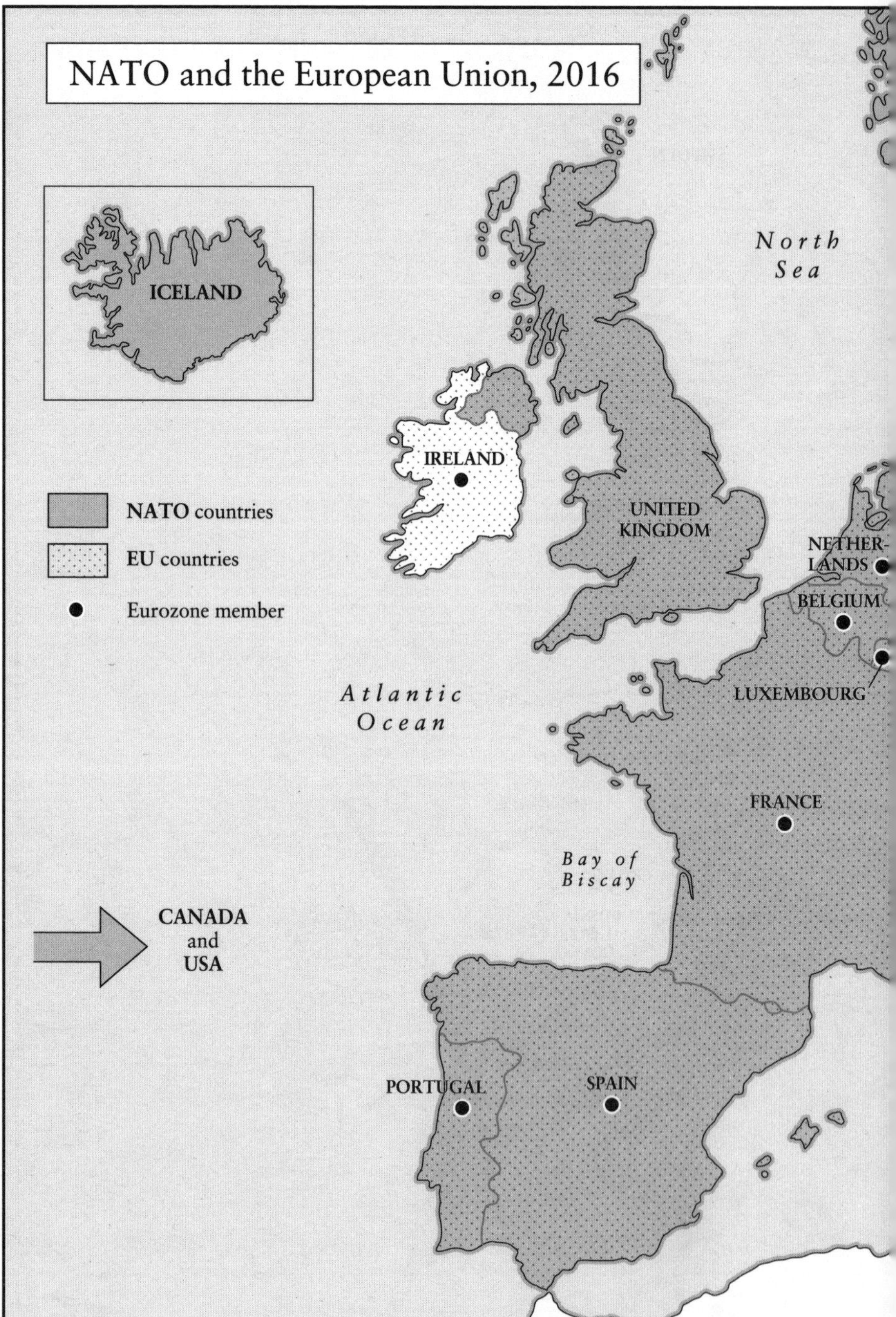
NATO and the European Union, 2016
ICELAND
IRELAND
NATO countries
EU countries
Eurozone member
UNITED KINGDOM
North Sea
NETHER-LANDS
BELGIUM
LUXEMBOURG
Atlantic Ocean
FRANCE
Bay of Biscay
CANADA and USA
PORTUGAL
SPAIN

FINLAND
NORWAY
ESTONIA
SWEDEN
Baltic Sea
LATVIA
RUSSIA
DENMARK
LITHUANIA
BELARUS
POLAND
GERMANY
UKRAINE
CZECH REP.
SLOVAKIA
AUSTRIA
MOLDOVA
WITZ.
HUNGARY
ROMANIA
SLOV.
CROATIA
ITALY
BOSNIA & HERZE-GOVINA
SERBIA
CRIMEA (currently under Russian occupation)
Black Sea
MONTE.
BULGARIA
MAC.
ALBANIA
GREECE
TURKEY
Mediterranean Sea
MALTA
CYPRUS

I

The Bonds of 'Christendom'. Europe and the Creation of England

In order that Christendom might be saved from the malice and evil onslaught of the infidels, who are attempting to destroy and annihilate it in various areas; and so that the king [of France], his adversary of England, and the princes of either side would be able to concern themselves with achieving good peace and true union in our Holy Mother Church, which has been so long divided and in Schism.

– French peace offer to England, 1396[1]

Calling to mind the great, inestimable, and well-nigh infinite cost and expenditure both of goods and blood that this land [England] has borne and suffered for the sake of that land [France]; the shameful loss of it, which God forever forbid, would not only be to the irreparable damage of the common benefit, but also an everlasting slur, and permanent denigration of the fame and renown of this noble realm.

– Edmund Beaufort, Commander of the English forces in France, 1449[2]

England was connected to Europe long before either existed. For millions of years, this was physically the case, as the land mass that was to become Britain was joined to the rest of the continent. Then the land bridge iced over and the subsequent thaw eventually created the English Channel. Strictly speaking, England still remained and remains geographically part of the continent of Europe: that is where you will find it in any atlas. Politically, in any case, England was always part of the larger whole. In the first century, the area was occupied by the Romans, making it a province of an empire which spanned the entire continent, and beyond, into Asia and Africa. After the Romans withdrew in the early fifth century, England was colonized by tribes from north Germany. Known as the Anglo-Saxons to distinguish them from the German kinsfolk they left behind,[3] they created the kingdoms of Northumbria, Mercia, Wessex, East Anglia, Essex, Kent and Sussex. In the seventh century, these areas were Christianized, making England part of another, wider European entity, namely the western 'Christendom' owing allegiance to the Pope in Rome, a constant for the next nine hundred years or so.[4] Their inhabitants spoke 'English' and were described as the *gens Anglorum*.[5] They maintained a lively communication with the continent, especially with what was to become Germany, and, thanks to the quality of the soil, their industriousness and their position at the junction of various European trade routes, they were exceptionally wealthy in Europe.[6] Despite their insular position, isolation was not an option for these early Englishmen, whose prosperity made them the target of attack from outside. Many years of Viking raids, followed by the seizure of land, soon showed that, even if the English had not been interested in Europe, Europe was interested in them.

The unification of the English kingdoms under Alfred the Great and his successors was primarily a reaction to these external pressures, and was largely complete before the year 1000.[7] 'England' did not always exist, nor did she simply emerge. She was created by force in order to deal with a European threat which remained the strongest argument for its continued existence. When two bitter rivals, Edward and Godwin, confronted each other in Gloucestershire in 1051, the chronicles record that observers 'thought it would be a great piece of folly if they joined battle, for in the two hosts there contained most of what was noblest in England, and they considered that they would be opening a way for our enemies to enter the country and cause much ruin among ourselves'.[8] England was distinctive within Europe by virtue of a universal land tax, part of it 'Danegeld', originally levied to buy off the Vikings, and an efficient bureaucracy to mobilize the country for common defence. Unlike in many continental states, there was a single recognized coinage across the realm, and a single system of justice and administration. The nature of royal authority did not vary much from region to region, as it often did in the rest of Europe. England had a strong state, certainly by the standards of the age, reaching deep into the lives of its inhabitants, and continuing to do so until the present day. There was an unusually widespread use of the vernacular language – that is, of English – in government and administration, and a strong sense of national pride. Though most European countries had representative structures of one sort or another, England was unusual in having a *national* assembly, which was sometimes attended by 'outsiders' from Wales and Scotland, and weak regional identities. These early English assemblies could be quite assertive and were capable of forcing a king to accept 'counsel', or advice.[9] The result was a remarkably coherent polity for its time: the first European nation state.[10]

At this time, England's strategic horizons were somewhat limited. To be sure, Englishmen were well aware of Europe more generally, partly in the form of the Universal Church and partly in the shape of the Holy Roman Empire, the successor to Rome in the political sense.[11] They spent most of their time, however, concentrating on events closer to home. The later Anglo-Saxon chronicle shows little concern with the continent as a whole but considerable interest in events in northern France and the Low Countries.[12] Above all, Englishmen looked over their shoulders to the Viking strongholds on the island itself, in Dublin, the Shetlands and in Scandinavia. In 1015, England became part of the lands of King Cnut, a composite monarchy which spanned the North Sea to include Denmark, Norway and even large tracts of southern Sweden.[13] Cnut was also interested in northern Germany, and attended the coronation of the Holy Roman Emperor Conrad II in Rome. Strategically, therefore, England faced east and north-east for the first two hundred years or so of her existence. It was from there that she perceived the most serious threat, and it was for this reason that, in 1066, faced with invasions from north and south, King Harold first turned north to deal with the king of Norway, Harald Hardrada, whom he defeated at the Battle of Stamford Bridge.

This strategic focus changed radically after the Norman Conquest, following William of Normandy's victory over the English at the Battle of Hastings. For the next five hundred years or so, the primary strategic focus switched south and south-east to the far side of the English Channel.[14] There were to be three distinct but overlapping English 'empires' in France; contemporaries did not use this term, but that is more or less what they were. The first was that of William the Conqueror and was centred on Normandy, which he and his successors used English resources to defend. This 'empire' was greatly extended by Henry II by inheritance from his father and through his marriage to Eleanor of Aquitaine in 1152, bringing him the provinces of Anjou, Maine and Touraine on the Loire, and from there stretching south through Aquitaine and Gascony to Bordeaux and the Pyrenees. The northern parts of this 'empire' were lost by King John in the early thirteenth century. In the aftermath, a second English 'empire' emerged in Gascony. This became the main focus of English activity in France after Henry III accepted the loss of Normandy in 1259 in the Treaty of Paris. Then, from the 1330s onwards, the Hundred Years War established a pattern of conquest across large parts of central and northern France, culminating in Henry V's conquests after Agincourt. For a while, through to the 1430s, Normandy, Maine, large parts of Flanders and even Paris itself were placed under English rule.

England acquired her French empire by dynastic happenstance, and her kings expanded it for reasons of ambition, but its retention soon acquired a strategic rationale. In the pre-modern age, sail was the fastest form of travel, making northern France and Flanders much closer to London than to northern England. The Channel was not a barrier but a conduit across the 'Narrow Sea'.[15] The 'Cinque Ports', often thought to be a form of coastal defence system, were intended just as much to supply a cross-Channel ferry service.[16] Proximity was good for trade, but bad for security. There was no way the infant navy could be sure of intercepting an invasion force once it had embarked.[17] Even with the English advantage of numbers and quality, existing navigational and shipbuilding techniques would not allow it. Whoever had access to the sea in the Middle Ages – and for long after – could cross if they had the ships to do so. This meant that England would either have to attack an enemy fleet before it left harbour, as she did with great success at Bruges in 1213 and Sluys in 1340 or, better still, to control the far shores to prevent embarkation in the first place. Channel ports such as Dover and Calais were thus understood as strategically interdependent, both as bastions against Europe and as sally ports into the continent. The closeness of the relationship is demonstrated by the fact that some governors of the southern English ports also served in the same capacity in Calais.

Nor was this the limit of England's engagement in Europe. She was deeply conscious of the need for allies there, an enduring theme in English history. France was 'leapfrogged' through a series of alliances with princes on her flanks. The most disastrous of these gambits was the alliance with the German emperor and Flanders, whose combined armies were smashed at the Battle of Bouvines in 1214. The most dramatic move was the Black Prince's expedition to Spain in the mid-fourteenth century in order to threaten France from the south. In political terms, the most spectacular coup was the election of Henry III's brother Richard of Cornwall as 'King of the Romans' in 1257, and thus claimant to the title Holy Roman Emperor. This move, achieved at vast cost (albeit paid largely from Richard's private fortune) by bribing a majority of the German Electors, who enjoyed the right of choosing the emperor, was intended to provide an outlet for a younger prince and to forestall the nightmare of a successful French candidacy. Though Richard never actually ruled as emperor in the end, it is an interesting counterfactual to speculate on what might have happened if he had. Henry III also attempted to have his second son, Edmund, placed on the Sicilian throne. The most effective English ally was long the Duchy of Burgundy, which menaced France from the east. The most enduring territorial connection, however, was with Flanders, an area of huge economic importance to England, and – even more vitally – the best ground for making an attack on Paris from the north. In short, England's strategic horizons throughout the Middle Ages stretched deep into the continent but always arched back to the security of the home island.

This European commitment shaped the way in which the kings of England looked at the British Isles. First, they regarded Scotland, Wales and Ireland as potential sources of men and money for continental campaigns. Ireland, for example, was a substantial contributor to English coffers in the thirteenth century. Second, they worried that their European enemies would use these peripheral polities as the 'back door' to England. The danger of such a pincer movement had been demonstrated by the events of 1066, when England had faced two enemies, Hardrada to the north and William the Conqueror to the south. There were Franco-Scottish invasions of England in 1174 and again in 1216. In 1295, the Scots and the French concluded a formal treaty, immortalized over time as the 'Auld Alliance' against England.[18] Thereafter, encirclement by Scots to the north and French to the south was a constant anxiety in English grand strategy. For example, in 1346, Scotland launched an invasion to help the embattled French. Likewise, in 1385, England was supposed to be gripped by the pincer movement of a Franco-Scottish army attacking across the Tweed and a French army across the Channel. In 1402, a French army invaded England via Wales. For all the sense of a common 'British' identity by virtue of geography and destiny,[19] the four peoples found it hard to coexist on their island archipelago.

To the medieval kings of England, there were only three ways of dealing with the problem of Scotland, Ireland and Wales. One was appeasement, but that tended to invite further demands, and risked the emergence of a vacuum which ran the risk of being filled by anarchy, foreign powers, or both. Another was deterrence, and that was the default option, condemning generations of Englishmen across the marches of Scotland, Ireland and Wales to bitter wars of attrition. The most effective solution was conquest. Ireland was invaded in the twelfth century, though English control there was limited to the east and south. Wales was conquered in the late thirteenth century and, although there were periodic large-scale rebellions until the early fifteenth century, from the 1280s it was colonized and administered on English lines. Scotland, likewise, was occupied for longer periods, but at great cost, since what was taken proved impossible to hold. This was partly the result of geography (with the most northerly parts of Scotland remaining impervious to conquest), partly of English misgovernment, and partly because the attempt of the English state to draw on the resources of neighbouring countries to support campaigns in Europe provoked resistance (for example, the revolt of William Wallace in the late thirteenth century). It was also because the peripheral peoples had, or developed, their own representative structures, with parliaments in Scotland and Ireland by the end of the Middle Ages, and distinct national identities. This was summed up for Scotland in the trenchant Declaration of Arbroath in 1320 in which it was vowed that '[w]e will never on any conditions be subjected to the lordship of the English. For we fight not for glory, nor riches, nor honours, but for freedom alone, which no good man gives up except with his life.' Until she could find some way of harnessing these sentiments to her own cause, or a common one, and similar ones among the Irish and Welsh, England would not only have to fear attack from the west and the north but was failing to draw on the full potential of the British Isles to defend her position on the continent.

Many Englishmen took a broad view of Europe, one which extended well beyond the narrow confines of the security of the realm. They thought of the continent as 'Christendom', a single space united by a common belief in Christianity. They shared the general European concern that the true faith was on the retreat around the world, particularly after the fall of Jerusalem to Saladin in 1187. In this view, Christendom was surrounded and outbred by fecund infidels.[20] Some, such as the thirteenth-century philosopher Roger Bacon, opposed military action against unbelievers. This only made such infidels even more anti-Christian, he claimed, and, in any case, 'Christian crusaders, even if sometimes victorious, make their expedition and then return to their own parts, while the indigenous population remains and multiplies.'[21] It was an argument we have heard in many forms since. Most, however, supported the idea of a crusade against the infidel, and in this respect they differed little from the rest of Christendom.[22] Sometimes, such expeditions were undertaken against targets within present-day Europe, such as the Albigensian Christian heretics in southern France or the heathen Prussians in the east. The young Henry IV took part in these Baltic Crusades. More usually, Englishmen were preoccupied with regaining the Holy Lands for Christianity. Like the rest of medieval Europe, they put Jerusalem at the centre not merely of their world view but – as contemporary maps such as the *Mappa Mundi* in Hereford Cathedral show – of their geographical understanding. Englishmen lived on the edge of Christendom, but they aspired to be at its heart. For this reason, many of them 'took up the cross', most dramatically Richard I, who led an army to the Holy Land in the 1190s, and Edward I, who learned of his succession to the crown of England while on crusade at Acre in 1272.

The Crusades had profound implications for England's place in Europe. They were by their very nature collaborative enterprises, whose success depended on working together with other Europeans.[23] The Crusades raised the question of whether it was right for Englishmen to fight Frenchmen, rather than uniting with them against the common infidel foe. This was an issue at the start of the Hundred Years War in the 1330s, when a planned Anglo-French crusade was called off after Philip VI of France and Edward III failed to agree its terms. The question returned to the agenda with the dramatic Turkish advances later in the century. In 1387, the Turks captured Salonica in northern Greece; in 1388, the Bulgarians were decisively beaten; and, a year later, the Serbs were shattered at the Battle of Kosovo. Sultan Bayazid I crowed that he would ride all the way to Paris, having fed his horse on the way at the altar of St Peter's in Rome. As one of Europe's leading nations, England felt honour-bound to join a crusade to recover the lost ground. Subsequently, English knights joined a holding force that had been sent to Hungary right away, while negotiations were started with France for a common effort. These, ultimately, led nowhere, and French and English ended up going to war with each other again rather than against the Turk.

The legacy of the Crusades endured, however. In 1398, only two years after the Turks had crushed a European crusade at Nicopolis on the Danube, John of Gaunt (himself previously a crusader in Spain and Portugal) announced that 'nothing substantial can be accomplished for the welfare of Christendom, unless the two [English and French] kings make a final peace together.'[24] When the distraught Byzantine emperor travelled to Europe to drum up support, Henry IV entertained him lavishly in London over Christmas 1400. Though Manuel II left with only money and goodwill, some Englishmen felt ashamed that they were not doing more for the defence of Christendom. 'I thought within myself,' the Welsh-born chronicler Adam of Usk wrote, 'what a grievous thing it was that this great Christian province from the farther east should perforce be driven by unbelievers to visit the distant lands of the west to seek aid against them. My God! What dost thou, ancient glory of Rome? Shorn is the greatness of thine empire this day.'[25] The idea that 'Christendom' – that is, Europe – should cohere in the face of an outside threat so great that it transcended petty quarrels with the French, Scots, Irish and Welsh continued to exercise a powerful hold on the minds of Englishmen.

Englishmen were linked to the continent not only by religion but also by family ties, commerce, education, the Latin language and a common culture more generally. They travelled back and forth across the Channel. One of the iconic Englishmen of the fourteenth century, Edward III's son John of Gaunt, was born in the Flemish town of Ghent, as his name suggested, to Philippa of Hainault, because his father was seeking Flemish allies there against France. English aristocratic culture, and all the paraphernalia of feudalism, such as manors, codes of chivalry, tournaments, troubadours, and much of the legal order (though the Common Law also had strong Anglo-Saxon roots), had been imported from France.[26] It differed little from arrangements on the other side of the Channel, and noblemen moved between the two worlds with ease. French was spoken on both sides of the water. Likewise, European influences – western and eastern – in architecture were ubiquitous. Edward I's principal 'castles' architect was the Savoyard Master James of St George. A Crusader himself, Edward began building Caernarfon Castle in 1283 in order to cow the Welsh. Its polygonal towers and banded masonry were raised in conscious imitation of the ramparts of Constantinople, and the main tower was to have three turrets mounted by imperial eagles.[27] What was being expressed here was a sense of solidarity with the continent and its challenges.

England was a European state, but she also stood out. Her wealth was considerable, long before empire and industrialization. A temperate climate and fertile soil made English agriculture highly productive. England was Europe's principal producer of wool for export to Flanders. London was a major trade entrepôt, and the English merchant marine was already very large. 'England is a strong land and a sturdy one, and the plenteoust corner of the world,' wrote the thirteenth-century encyclopaedist Friar Bartholomew, an Englishman based in Paris, 'so rich a land that scarcely it needeth help of any land.'[28] England was, in the famous words of the late-thirteenth-century chronicler Robert of Gloucester, a 'well good land' and, if it was later ravaged by the Black Death, it remained a place of great innate economic potential which could be tapped for warfare abroad. There were, of course, other prosperous countries in Europe. France, because it was considerably larger and more populous, was richer, at least in absolute if not in per capita terms.

Two things made England unique. First of all, the liberty of the subject, at least in theory, stood above the power of the king. The English ambassadors sent to France to negotiate peace in 1439 were instructed to tell the French king that 'God made not his people for the princes but he made the princes for his service and for the wele [welfare] of his people.'[29] Second, there was the impressive tax-gathering capacity of the state, which was facilitated not only by the most powerful secular bureaucracy anywhere on the continent but also by the cooperation of the national representative assembly which came to be known as Parliament. There were, of course, many other European assemblies of one sort and another, but that of England was unique. Unlike in many European monarchies, the kings of England had only limited demesne lands of their own and so were dependent on votes of money by their subjects. Because of this, and in contrast to the rest of Europe, the English nobility were not exempt from taxation, even if they tended to pass their fiscal burdens down the social ladder. Finally, by contrast with other European countries, the English parliament was a national rather than a regional institution from a very early stage.

Parliament grew primarily because of Europe. The kings of England needed money to fight wars in France and to protect their realm from attack by European powers, usually France and France's Scottish allies.[30] Unlike the French monarch, who had a small and 'closed' council, that of the kings of England was large and 'open'. Issues received the closest to a thorough and public airing possible, considering the time and place. Gradually, this council evolved into 'Parliament', a word first mentioned in 1236. Strictly speaking, Parliament could only offer 'counsel' but, given its ability to withhold or delay financial assistance, the dividing line between advice, persuasion and consent was a fluid one. The process was not linear or harmonious by any means, but with each war and royal concession in return for 'supply' of money, or its denial, the role of what we would today call Parliament was strengthened. In June 1177, for example, Henry II heeded the council's advice to delay his departure to Normandy.[31] One provision of Magna Carta in 1215, which partly reflected baronial unease at the failure and vast expense of King John's attempts to recover Normandy, was that the monarch agreed not to raise any tax 'except by the common counsel of our realm'. A statute of 1352 determined that soldiers were to be raised only with the consent of Parliament. In short, it was becoming increasingly clear that, when Parliament provided counsel, this was an offer the king could not easily refuse.

Something else happened which was to be of central importance in the development of England's relationship with Europe and the growth of English liberty – for the two are inseparably linked. To begin with, the King's Council and the nation at large tended to be sceptical of royal ambitions overseas. In the eleventh and early twelfth centuries, they paid grudgingly for the defence and attempted recovery of Normandy. In the late twelfth century, Richard I was heavily criticized for his campaigns abroad, partly because of their cost and partly because they entailed his absence from England.[32] In the thirteenth century, the cost of Henry III's vaulting ambitions in Europe, which went beyond the reconstruction of the cross-Channel empire to a role in the Holy Roman Empire, a presence in Sicily and even a crusade in Palestine, provoked a baronial revolt. In 1258, a number of barons, of whom Simon de Montfort would later emerge as leader, forced him to call a parliament in Oxford to bring him down to earth.[33] The rebellion was ultimately crushed, but Henry's hopes of European glory had been shattered. In Edward I's reign, a popular song proclaimed that 'A King ought not to go out of his kingdom to make war, unless the commons of his land will consent.'[34] Whether they liked it or not, the kings of England could be in no doubt that, if they wanted to make their mark on the continent, they would have to take the political public (what we would today call the nation) with them.

In the course of the fourteenth century, the national view of royal ambitions in France changed. Part of this was due to the opportunities for glory and enrichment. Some Englishmen, particularly under Henry V, became settlers there. Gascony, in particular, was economically very important, on account of the huge excise revenue the Crown gained from Gascon wines. The main reason for engaging in France, however, was security. Englishmen increasingly accepted the king's argument that the defence of England at home required a strong policy abroad to deny the enemy the bases from which to attack England's southern and eastern coasts. The nation experienced a traumatic French invasion in the early thirteenth century during the last years of King John. In 1295, the French raided Kent, no doubt boosting popular support for Edward I's war against them.[35] In 1338, Southampton was subjected to a devastating attack, and there was substantial damage elsewhere along the south coast. That same year, apparently, the French had intended to mount a major invasion. A written plan to that effect was discovered by English troops at Caen in 1346 and brought back to be read out publicly in the cemetery of St Paul's 'so as to rouse the people of the realm, that they might obediently show their esteem to the king, and pray devoutly for the prosperity and success of his expedition [to France]'.[36] In 1360, the French raided Winchelsea, and in 1377 there were even more extensive attacks, which caused widespread panic. The main damage, however, was political and psychological rather than physical and commercial. The country felt unsafe: fortifications were erected as far north as Bridlington Priory in the East Riding of Yorkshire. Whatever one thought of the king's claim to the French throne, which was the royal *casus belli*, it was clear to Englishmen, or so they believed, that only control of northern France and the Channel ports there would rid them of this scourge.

The support of nation and Parliament could not be taken for granted and remained contentious.[37] A poem written in 1339, shortly after the start of what was to become the Hundred Years War with France, attacked both the dispatch of troops to the Low Countries and the cost of the campaigns abroad. When asked in 1354 whether they wanted peace, the Commons are recorded as shouting, 'Yes!'[38] In 1378, the Gloucester parliament stated that it would pay only for the defence of the realm and not for aggressive war in France. It also announced, somewhat contradictorily, that it accepted that England was being defended in France. In 1381, the sheer cost of the wars led to a parliamentary poll tax to pay for them, and a massive peasants' revolt. A year later, Parliament refused money for an expedition to Ghent in the Low Countries. Medieval England, in other words, saw the beginnings of a great national debate, which continues to this day, on how best to protect and extend the realm at the least expense. Yet Parliament never pulled the plug on the French wars and, in the aftermath of enemy raids, such as that on Winchelsea, was apt to pay up with alacrity.

A steady stream of newsletters and dispatches from France kept the nation informed of events throughout the Hundred Years War. The spectacular military victories of the Black Prince in France, particularly those at Crécy and Poitiers, enthused Englishmen. Parliament came to see outposts in France as what they called 'barbicans of the realm', not only to hold the enemy on the far side of the sea but also as 'fine and noble entries and ports to grieve' the enemy.[39] The war in France was now 'owned' by the political nation, through parliamentary grants of money and men for military service. This was partly a matter of prestige and plunder, for English soldiers and settlers. It was mainly, however, a question of security, of keeping the enemy at bay on the far side of the water. 'Sire,' a grateful Parliament told Edward III, 'the commons thank their liege lord as far as they know how ... and from their hearts entirely thank God who has given them such a lord and governor, who has delivered them from servitude to other lands and delivered them from charges suffered by them in time past.'[40] The war and the conquered lands were exalted in popular ballads, songs and myths. Henry's victory at Agincourt in 1415 was celebrated throughout the land and entered the collective memory. The empire in France, in short, had become an English national project. This marked the shift from a purely dynastic royal interest to what we would today call an English 'national interest'.

The support of the nation through Parliament greatly increased the king's position in Europe and enabled England to 'punch above' her already considerable weight there.[41] It allowed the monarch to draw more quickly and extensively on the resources of the land for military purposes. The support of Parliament also increased the king's credit among moneylenders, an advantage which grew exponentially over the centuries to come. Moreover, debate in council or Parliament increased the quality of English decision-making in foreign policy. There was extensive discussion about which front to tackle first – Scotland, France, the Low Countries or Iberia – and in what strength. In 1344, for example, Parliament granted supply on condition that all the money was spent on the war, and that funds raised in the north would be used against the Scots. It also laid down that the king should go to France in person. In 1385, there was disagreement between the court, which wished to attack Scotland, and the opposition, who wanted to send more men to France. The latter were almost certainly right, because a French invasion by a huge fleet assembled at Sluys was only narrowly averted. And a decision, once made, was then backed by the political nation in Parliament and carried through to the end. Otherwise, the prolonged and, for a long time, victorious war in France would not have been possible. No other European state saw its external requirements and internal structure so well aligned so early.

There was, however, a crucial corollary to all this, which was fundamentally to shape the history of England. So long as the monarchy was competent and respected, Parliament and the people enhanced the power of the king. Where that was not the case, the monarch's authority was in danger. In the late fourteenth century, for example, Richard II was put on notice by his first parliament that England was effectively surrounded by enemies. His policy of appeasement against France after 1383 did not deliver security and was strongly criticized inside and outside of Parliament. Discontent mounted as England's allies collapsed, and when the French moved into Flanders and a Franco-Scottish army descended from the north it was the last straw. In 1386, as the French massed at Sluys, the Great Council sacked Chancellor Michael de la Pole, sidelined the king and demanded a more vigorous prosecution of the war against France. The Commons also objected to a 1392 plan to subject Aquitaine and Gascony to French overlordship on the grounds that it would be 'foolish and excessively injurious to the King and his crown to alienate forever such fine lordships, which had been ruled by hereditary right by the Kings of England for so long'.[42] Rumours of a permanent and shameful peace in France were enough to spark off a revolt by veterans in

Cheshire in 1393. If earlier kings, such as John and Henry III, had come under attack for doing too much in Europe, English monarchs were increasingly criticized for doing too little there. In keeping with the conventions of the time, these critiques were couched as an attack on 'evil advisors' rather than on the king himself, but their meaning was clear.

The Middle Ages saw a steady growth of England's military reputation in Europe. The crusading achievements of Richard I in the twelfth century were widely admired, and he was first given his sobriquet 'the Lionheart' – *Cœur de Lion* – by the French poet Ambroise, not by one his English subjects.[43] In the fourteenth century, the exploits of the English armies during the early stages of the Hundred Years War were legendary. 'When the noble Edward gained England in his youth,' the Flemish chronicler Jean le Bel wrote, 'nobody thought much of the English. Now they are the finest and most daring warriors known to man.'[44] The brutality of the *chevauchées* by which English raiders devastated large tracts of France was notorious. Henry V and, after his death, John Talbot, the 'English Achilles', were figures of continental renown. By the mid-fifteenth century, the English had acquired a reputation for extreme (though usually disciplined) violence in Europe. One way or the other, whatever metric one chose – economic potential, demography, military prowess, social resilience or political coherence – it was clear that England was a force to be reckoned with.

This was demonstrated not only to the French but also to the papacy, and the Church more generally, which, despite its divisions and abuses, was still the font of universal religious authority in most of Europe. There was widespread royal and elite unease with papal power, which led to the passing of various parliamentary measures, such as the Statute of Provisors (1351) and that of *Praemunire* (1353), which curbed the Pope's right to levy taxation and appoint to ecclesiastical office, and asserted royal supremacy. The Church was also fabulously wealthy, a fact which did not escape the notice of English rulers trying to fund their numerous wars. John of Gaunt, who dominated English politics during the late reign of his father, Edward III, wanted to seize at least some ecclesiastical revenues in England. John Wycliffe, Master of Balliol College in Oxford, was sent to Bruges in

1374 to argue the case, and his subsequent works all underlined the supremacy of royal or civil power over that of the Church. He was condemned by the papacy and a warrant was issued for his arrest, but Oxford stood by their man. Wycliffe lived out his days unharmed, protected by the civil power, even though he subsequently broadened his critique of the church into a full-blown theological and moral reform movement which, long after his death, became known as 'Lollardy'. None of this was unique in Europe, where criticism of the Church and designs on its property were routine. The followers of John Wycliffe, for example, were in communication with and had much in common with Czech dissidents on the far side of Europe led by Jan Huss. The English case was nonetheless unusual in that it involved the early translation of the Bible into the vernacular and a huge accompanying literature in English.[45] It also suggested that the demands of an English state defending its security in Europe had the potential to upend a religious order which linked the country with the rest of the continent.

The importance of England in Europe was also on display at the Council of the Church at Constance in southern Germany in 1414–18. This was called by Sigismund, soon to be emperor, and was intended to reform the papacy, not least by healing the schism between various anti-popes, and thus create the basis for Christian unity against the Turk. It was a pan-European conference, the nearest medieval equivalent to a modern EU summit. England and France were in bad odour because they were at war with each other, damaging the European commonweal and preventing their monarchs from attending. Nevertheless, England was represented by a substantial delegation. It worked together closely with the Germans for the reform of the Church. The problem lay in the voting rights, which tended to skew towards the large number of often corrupt Italian clergy. The English delegation suggested that voting should be by nation, with France, Italy, German and England herself all of equal standing. This was rejected by the French, who argued that their greater size and number of churches and dioceses rendered it 'absurd that the English should be considered as the equal of France, with a hundred and one dioceses'.[46] The English delegation shot back, on the basis of a reasoned exposition of the size and strength of the whole island of Britain, that 'the glorious realm of England' was very much the equal and probably the superior of France in the 'antiquity of its faith, dignity and honour'.

By the middle of the fifteenth century, however, things were not well in England. In Ireland, English control shrank to a perimeter around Dublin called the Pale. The Scots hovered north of the border. Henry V died before he could consolidate the vast English empire in France. His son and successor was an infant. Henry VI grew up to be feeble-minded. England became unstable, emboldening the French to resist. Parliament and people grew weary of the long war of attrition in France; they became disengaged from the great national project on the far side of the Channel. In 1431, Parliament candidly bewailed 'the burden of the war and how grievous and heavy' it bore on the country, making peace imperative.[47] By contrast, the tax-gathering power of the French monarchy increased, suggesting that a more absolutist rather than a representative system was better suited to mobilizing a nation for war.

In 1435, the strategic sky in Europe darkened further with the defection of the Duke of Burgundy following the Treaty of Arras. England was increasingly isolated. That same year saw an invasion scare on the Isle of Wight and along the entire south coast. Some, such as the author of the *Libelle of English Policy* (*c.* 1437) now argued that England should rely on the navy rather than on control of France for her security, perhaps the first 'blue water' manifesto in English history.[48] 'Cherish merchandise,' he wrote, 'that we may be masters of the Narrow Sea'. That was not the majority view, however, and even this author wanted to retain Calais. Over the next twenty years, the English lands in France were under more or less constant attack, punctuated by truces. One by one, the 'barbicans of the realm' fell to the French resurgence. In February 1449, Edmund Beaufort, the commander of the English armies in France, sent word to Parliament that the end of the latest truce would lead to a rapid military collapse. His warnings were ignored, and events took their course. In August 1450, John Paston's agent reported that 'this morning it was told that Cherbourg is gone and we have now not a foot of land in Normandy.'[49] England's relationship with Europe was about to enter a new phase.

2

'A piece of the continent'. Europe and the Making of the United Kingdom

Awake, awake English nobility!
Let not sloth dim your honours, new-begot
Cropp'd are the flowers-de-luces in your arms
Of England's coat one half is cut away.

–Messenger, in William Shakespeare, *Henry VI*, *Part I*, I.i

Our nation inhabits an island, and is one of the principal nations of Europe; but to maintain this rank, we must take advantages of this situation, which have been neglected by us for almost half a century: we must always remember that we are not part of the continent, but we must never forget that we are neighbors to it.

–Henry St John, 1st Viscount Bolingbroke,
defending the Treaty of Utrecht, concluded in 1713

In the mid-fifteenth century, England lost her empire in France. For a long time afterwards, she struggled to find a role in Europe. Her kings failed to reassert their claim to the French crown, which was effectively given up in the early sixteenth century. They occasionally toyed with the idea of a crusade against the Turks, but their main focus was on western and central Europe. A new strategic paradigm focussed on the Low Countries and Germany supplemented the old francocentric one. England also developed a much broader sense of the need to maintain the balance of power on the continent more generally. She became involved overseas, mostly for reasons to do with the European equilibrium. This was accompanied by a close ideological engagement in Europe after the Reformation, based on the assumption that the defence of Protestantism and parliamentary liberties in England required the defence of the 'liberties' of Europe on the continent. All this was the subject of furious debate among Englishmen, and by the end of the seventeenth century one could already see the contours of what was to become a familiar debate between Europhile Whigs committed to continental intervention and Eurosceptic Tories, who wanted to concentrate on maritime and commercial expansion instead. Moreover, England's involvement in Europe not only powered the emergence of the modern state but also led to the creation of the United Kingdom.

In July 1453, the Hundred Years War between England and France came to an end with the decisive French victory at the Battle of Castillon.[1] To all intents and purposes, what we would today call the English empire in France was destroyed;[2] only a small foothold around the 'Pale' of Calais remained. The magnitude of the catastrophe could not be disguised, especially on the south coast of England. Chroniclers spoke of the 'daily' influx of 'divers long carts with . . . armour and bedding and household [. . .] and men women and children . . . piteous to see driven out of Normandy'.[3] A sense of national humiliation and despair took root, as the nation struggled to understand how the great victories at Crécy, Poitiers and Agincourt had been reversed. Above all, the loss of the northern French coast greatly increased the vulnerability of England itself. The terrible precedent of the French raids of the 1370s suggested that it would not be long before the enemy appeared again on English shores, this time in strength. Already, as the Norfolk gentleman's daughter Margaret Paston lamented, the French were 'so bold that they come up to the land and play . . . as homely as they were Englishmen'.[4] In 1457, they raided the port of Sandwich in Kent. All this reinforced a long-standing belief that England would only be truly safe so long as she controlled both sides of the Channel coasts.

As the detritus of empire bobbed back across the water, furious Englishmen wanted to know what had gone wrong, and who was to blame.[5] There followed a prolonged inquest into the defeat, a sustained bout of national soul-searching which was eventually to reach into all parts of the body politic. The post-mortem had already begun in the final stages of the war following the loss of Normandy, and that of Gascony shortly after. In November 1449, the Lords and Commons met in a bad-tempered parliament in London to contemplate the waste of a hundred years of national effort, money and lives. There was general consensus across the country that the main fault lay with William de la Pole, the Duke of Suffolk, the Lord High Steward and King Henry VI's principal counsellor. Only treason at the highest level, so the thinking went, could explain the disaster. The articles of impeachment against Suffolk in February 1450, which led to his flight, capture, mock-trial and murder, were dominated by allegations of his betrayal of the English cause in France.[6] In Kent, a band of agrarian rebels under Jack Cade advanced on London, complaining not only of local grievances but that the king 'has had false counsel, for his lands are lost, his merchandise is lost, his commons destroyed, the sea is lost, France is lost'.[7]

Worse was to come. News of the fall of Bordeaux in August 1453 tipped King Henry VI – never the most mentally stable of men at the best of times – over the edge into a catatonic state, leaving a complete vacuum at the heart of government. More generally, the military collapse fatally undermined the Lancastrian monarchy. Partisans of the rival house of York charged that royal ineptitude had led to the fall of France, questioned the readiness of the remaining English bases such as Calais, and accused their rivals of planning to surrender them to the French.[8] The resulting Wars of the Roses, which roiled England in the second half of the fifteenth century, were thus very much a product of the failure of English grand strategy in Europe.[9] They also meant that England was too distracted to do more than bewail the fall of Constantinople to the Turks and the seemingly irresistible surge of Islam across the Balkans in the late fifteenth century. Henry VI proclaimed in one of his lucid moments in 1454 that he was willing 'to risk the whole strength of his realm in behalf of the catholic faith' to recover the city,[10] but this was just hot air. The reality was that England had ceased for the time being to count in Europe.

Englishmen now took a long, hard look at the national cause abroad and the domestic transformations needed to sustain it. The resulting debate raged well beyond the confines of Parliament in widely circulated handwritten texts.[11] Many looked to the examples of ancient empires for both comfort and warning. William of Worcester, for example, praised the way in which Roman senators 'attend[ed] to the common profit, setting aside singular avail', implicitly criticizing the petty bickering of English barons. Others were not too proud to learn from the enemy, with numerous manuscript translations into English of French reformist tracts. Some of those who followed these debates most attentively were women, such as the mother and daughter who read and annotated a translation of the thoughts of the French king's secretary Alain Chartier. Much of the discussion focussed on nuts and bolts: lack of provisions, pay, poor military discipline, and so on. But the most important points concerned broader problems with the English polity: the lack of consultation, the raising of taxes to support the war effort and, above all, the importance of 'good counsel'.[12]

By the end of the fifteenth century, something like a consensus had emerged. Most agreed that the English empire in France should be regained, not only to vindicate the king's historic rights but also to deny the enemy a base from which to attack England.[13] In order to do this, the mistakes of the Lancastrian dynasty would have to be rectified. Culturally, Englishmen would have to become less effeminate and more martial, perhaps the first instance of what was to become a long tradition of linking foreign-policy crises to domestic moral panic. Taxes would have to be paid on time – in other words, the nation as a whole should take responsibility for the reconquest of France – but in return the king would have to listen to the counsel of Parliament and seasoned advisors. Above all, the English would have to close ranks at home, not least through the act of confronting the enemy abroad. The best way of avoiding another War of the Roses, some influential voices argued, was to go to war with France again.

Meanwhile, in the rest of Europe, the general trend was in the other direction. Frenchmen came out of the Hundred Years War convinced that national salvation lay in the greater power of the Crown. Representative institutions continued to exist in France, but the divergence from the English case grew still larger. In Germany, attempts to turn the Reichstag, the imperial assembly, into a true national body responsible for the common defence and welfare petered out towards the end of the fifteenth century, though it remained an important political forum. Elsewhere on the continent, various estates, diets and other institutions survived, but they would be severely tested and in many cases destroyed by the challenges of war in the two centuries to come. Contemporaries were conscious of English exceptionalism. Sir John Fortescue wrote in his *Governance of England* around 1470 that, whereas France was governed only by a 'royal lordship', in which the monarch was supreme,[14] England uniquely enjoyed a 'public and royal lordship' in which the king could not raise taxes or make law without the consent of Parliament.

Over the next hundred years or so, the principal aim of what one might call English grand strategy was to regain control of the 'Narrow Sea', now once again disputed by France, to reassert the claim to the French throne, to regain territory in France, or at least to prevent the French from launching attacks on the south coast.[15] In June 1475, for example, Edward IV appeared at Calais with a view to putting pressure on France from the north, while Burgundy menaced her from the east; the French king managed to buy him off with difficulty. Likewise, Henry Tudor – who ruled England as Henry VII after his victory over Richard III on Bosworth Field in 1485 – sent expeditions to northern France in order to deny the French the bases from which to threaten the south coast. He also sought to keep the French and their old Scottish allies apart, and to prevent neighbouring Ireland from being used as a base to attack England from the west. Henry VII sent money to help embattled Christendom against Islam, but he made any active participation contingent on the mounting of a general European crusade, which never materialized. 'He had nothing more at heart,' Henry assured Pope Innocent VIII in January 1489, 'than when the preparations of Christendom itself shall be matured, to proceed against the infidels.' In the meantime, Henry averred that he was 'not meditating anything against the King of the French, but he is compelled at present to defend the Breton interests . . . for the defence of his own kingdom, the affairs of Brittany being so bound up with those of England'.[16] The Breton venture failed. Luckily for England, Charles VIII of France was preoccupied with expanding into Italy. He bought off Henry at the Treaty of

Étaples in 1491. This enabled the king to deal with internal challenges, such as that of the pretender Perkin Warbeck, without French interference.

Henry VIII's first priority when he came to the throne in 1509 was the reassertion of his claim to the French throne, or at least the recreation of a substantial English foothold in France.[17] This quest took him, or his armies, to Aquitaine, Brittany and Flanders.[18] In 1523, Henry appeared with an army at Calais to claim his 'true inheritance' of the French crown by 'just title'.[19] To this end, he sought alliances in the Holy Roman Empire, and periodically with the emperor, much as the medieval English kings had. Together with his chief minister, Cardinal Wolsey, Henry articulated an ever more ambitious vision for England in Europe. Wolsey spoke of 'exterminating the French out of Italy', while Henry saw himself as Europe's arbiter, no less. 'If I choose he will cross the Alps', he remarked of King Francis I of France, 'and if I choose he will not cross.'[20] Henry even wanted to make Wolsey Pope. It was this desire to lead Christendom and to keep the papacy well-disposed that motivated him in 1521 to write a book attacking the German reformer Martin Luther, or at least to authorize its publication under his name.[21]

Just how seriously Henry took his campaign for European standing was demonstrated by his bid for the German imperial crown. This was a long shot, but it was by no means quixotic. The king was deeply conscious of the traditional French argument from the Middle Ages that England was subject to the Pope, whereas the crown of France was subject to no one. If Henry wished to rearticulate his claim to the French throne, then imperial stature was essential. There was some support for the English monarch in Germany, not least in the person of the reigning emperor Maximilian, who was so desperate to keep the French out, and not yet confident that the Habsburg candidate was viable, that he repeatedly backed Henry's candidature. In truth, his prospects were slim. Henry's advisor Cuthbert Tunstall warned in 1517 that the winner 'must be of Germany [German] subject to empire, whereas your Grace is not'.[22] Yet the candidature remains one of the great 'might have beens' of English and European history. If Henry had won the imperial crown and his successors had kept it, then there would have been a very different British empire, and perhaps also a more 'British' – or 'English' – Europe. Representative government on the continent, already in retreat, might have revived. Calais enjoyed parliamentary representation, and even Tournai in Flanders, briefly held by Henry, sent a delegation to Westminster.[23] As it was, the failure of Henry's imperial bid, and the Pope's open support for his French rival's claims, made his turn away from the Roman Church much more likely. Put another way: could the English Reformation conceivably have been led by the German emperor?

Henry's ambitions to lead Christendom made at least a gesture towards the crusading ideal necessary. In 1511, he supported Thomas Darcy's expedition against the Moors in North Africa. It is likely that he planned a major campaign to push back the Turks after he had reasserted his claim to France, or perhaps secured election to the German imperial title. Henry never got that far, however. In 1518, he responded to Pope Leo X's requests for a crusade with the remark that he should be 'more apprehensive of a certain other person [Francis I] than the Great Turk, of one who devises worse things against Christendom than Sultan Selim'.[24] Cardinal Wolsey did secure a general peace treaty of the great powers based on the idea of common action against the Turks, but nothing happened. A year later, Henry told the pope that '[t]o strike a blow for Christendom has ever been the summit of our ambition,' but again, no action followed. Like many other European monarchs, he repeatedly used the general good of Christendom as a cloak for his selfish interests.

The king's refusal to lead Europe against the Turk did not mean that he had given up his ambition to lead Europe. It soon became clear, however, that he had a rival in the young Charles V, who was the successful candidate for the imperial throne and whose armies defeated Francis I at the Battle of Pavia in 1525. Henry toyed with the idea of supporting Habsburg hegemony in return for support in recovering the French crown, but the sheer extent of their domains made him nervous. A total victory of Charles over France, the king and his council noted, would make him 'monarch not only of Italy, but also all Christendom' and enable him 'to give laws to all the world'. For this reason, English diplomats helped to create the League of Cognac, which marshalled France, the papacy, Venice, Milan and Florence against Charles. England, however, had no plans to join the alliance herself but to help as and when appropriate, intervening militarily only in the last resort. In this way, Wolsey told Henry, 'Your Highness, God willing, shall have in your hands the conducing of universal peace of Christendom.'[25] These were perhaps the first elaborations of two themes which were to remain a constant in English, and later British, strategic debate: fear of the domination of the continent by a single power, and England's role as a balancer. The security of England, in other words, no longer rested just on a set of relationships on the far side of the Channel but on the state of Europe as a whole.

Henry's thirst for foreign glory cost a lot of money: 'the king's money goeth away in every corner,'[26] Wolsey remarked as early as 1511, only two years into Henry's long reign. The key here was cooperation with Parliament, which had to approve all past, current or imminent military expenditure. In the first decades of the reign, it was persuaded to agree to a 'subsidy' (tax) which was levied on land income and the value of goods. Approval was by no means automatic, as the English Parliament was unusually assertive by European standards.[27] There was serious disquiet voiced as early as 1523, and two years later the requested 'Amicable Grant' caused such discontent that Wolsey had to back down. By and large, however, the Lords and Commons stumped up, even if it was sometimes with bad grace.[28] This was because Parliament was in broad agreement with the king's grand strategy: the vindication of the monarchy's rights in France, or at least the control of the coastline, and the protection of the back doors to England via Ireland and Scotland. The radical programme of domestic transformation by Henry VIII and his reforming ministers Cardinal Wolsey and Thomas Cromwell was also driven by the need to fund Henry's extensive campaigns in Europe.[29] In the end, however, Henry managed neither to secure the imperial crown, nor to regain the English empire in France; by the end of his reign, all he had to show for the great national exertions was an expanded perimeter around the Pale of Calais (now including Boulogne).

Henry was also concerned with domestic affairs, which had profound implications for foreign policy. Already in 1517, Cuthbert Tunstall had tried to dissuade Henry from entering the imperial election with the argument that 'the crown of England is an empire of itself, much better than now the empire of Rome.'[30] More pressingly, Henry believed a male heir essential to pre-empt a challenge to the succession, and, when the Catholic Church would not allow him to divorce his wife Katherine – who had produced only a daughter, Mary – and marry Anne Boleyn, the king went his own way. Having initially backed the Pope and emperor against the German reformer Martin Luther, Henry broke with Rome himself. The Act of Supremacy in 1534 consequently reflects a concern with imperial kingship, a kind of 'caesaropapism'. The English Reformation began to take its course, the monasteries were dissolved, and England increasingly traded one set of religious affinities with the continent through the Universal Church for membership of what came to be known as the 'Protestant cause' in Europe. Of course, Henry's despoliation of Church lands not only enabled him to buttress his rule at home but provided a much-needed boost to war-financing.[31]

The European Reformation, and England's part in it, fundamentally shaped politics and security in the British Isles for the next two hundred years. England, Wales and Scotland embraced Protestantism of one sort or another, or had it forced upon them. Large pockets of the old faith survived across the British Isles, however, especially in Ireland, where Catholicism remained the majority religion and these communities were the focus of continental Counter-Reformation meddling. This meant that religious belief was never a purely domestic affair but was always linked to questions of external security and even national identity. England's relationship to Europe now acquired an ideological dimension which in some ways reinforced and in others expanded her traditional geopolitics. What happened in faraway places of which they had heard little now mattered to Englishmen in ways that had not been the case since the end of the Crusades.

If failures abroad spurred Henry on to greater efforts at home, they also sparked a fresh wave of national performance anxiety. Many were still smarting at the loss of the French empire one hundred years before – a wound inflamed by generations of Tudor chroniclers and which would be reopened at the end of the century by Shakespeare in his three historical plays about the reign of Henry VI – and history seemed to be repeating itself. Now, as Henry's war effort on the continent stagnated, they succumbed to moral panic and social malaise.

Englishmen, it was argued, had gone soft by neglecting their archery skills and spending too much money on fashion and gambling. Worse still, many were convinced that the overall population of England was steadily declining: the shrinking military muster rolls seemed to suggest this. All this mattered, as John Hales warned in 1548, because the king 'would lack people to defend us against our enemies'. As in the fifteenth century, the vulnerability of the southern maritime counties to French attack was much discussed. Many laid the blame for this state of affairs on the king's domestic policies, especially enclosure, which exalted sheep over men, and the Dissolution of the Monasteries, which allegedly undermined moral standards. There was also a general sense that the failure to engage in warfare abroad would lead to excess energies being consumed in domestic strife.[32]

Henry's sickly Protestant heir Edward VI made little impression in Europe. A failed war against Scotland and France forced England to abandon Boulogne. A rapprochement with France followed in order to deter intervention by the emperor. Edward died in 1553, bringing his Catholic half-sister Mary to the throne, which precipitated domestic unrest. In the following year, she married Philip of Spain. The marriage contract stipulated that Philip would be succeeded on his death by Carlos, his son by an earlier union, but that any son with Mary would inherit England, the Low Countries and Franche-Comté. English forces were sent to support Philip against the king of France in Flanders and played an important role in both the great victory over the French at Saint-Quentin in 1557 and at Gravelines a year later. France attempted to destabilize Mary Tudor by inciting the Scots on her northern border and marrying the Dauphin to Mary, Queen of Scots. The 'Auld Alliance' between Scotland and France once again sought the encirclement of England. Likewise, Sir Thomas Wyatt's forlorn insurrection was explicitly directed against the 'stranger', Philip.

Domestic politics polarized around foreign policy: many not only opposed English involvement in Philip's wars but saw the ambitious Spanish king as a far greater threat to their liberties than the traditional French enemy. This critique meshed with widespread discontent about 'Bloody Mary's' harsh treatment of English Protestants. The fall of Calais to the French in 1558, therefore, was a hammer blow to Mary's prestige. England had lost control of the Narrow Sea. In a coruscating speech to Parliament a year later, the Lord Keeper lamented that there had not been 'a greater loss in honour, strength and treasure, than to lose that place', which had 'bred throughout Europe an honourable opinion and report of our English nation'.[33] Once again, moral panic set in. 'What tenderlings the great part of our young gentlemen are,' one observer lamented, 'preferring fine clothes to lusty horsemanship.'[34] There were also furious allegations that Philip had not done enough to help the embattled garrison. To add insult to injury, Philip's chief minister, Cardinal de Granvelle, remarked that 'One would like to see more spirit, more resentment about Calais, and more memory of the ancient virtues of their fathers.'[35] The port, which Mary famously said would be 'lying in her heart' after death, had been England's last outpost on the continent, and vital to the defence of the south coast. Fairly or unfairly, its loss first established the fatal link in the minds of many Englishmen between popery and strategic incompetence.

In 1558, Mary died childless. Almost the first move of her successor, Elizabeth I, was to strike at Scotland, where the new land border with France now effectively ran. Taking up an invitation from the Scottish Protestant Lords of the Congregation to rescue them from French domination, she sent an army north which, though it did not perform well, did secure a treaty which effectively banished French influence on England's northern flank.[36] Elizabeth was also conscious of the loss of Calais, which she described as 'a matter of continual grief to this realm'.[37] She sent an expedition to Le Havre in 1562 in the hope of exchanging it for Calais, but soon gave up the attempt. This was partly because that country, which had descended into religious war by the 1560s, was no longer a threat. The main reason, though, was the emergence of a new threat to England's security. This was both ideological and territorial: the thwarted Philip II of Spain, no longer co-monarch of England, whose armies lay just across the Channel in the Low Countries and whose intention to reimpose Catholicism on England, and indeed most of Europe, was no secret. Elizabeth's interventions in France were therefore primarily designed to prevent the Spanish-backed Guise faction in the French religious wars from allowing English Catholics to use Normandy as a base for agitation in, and perhaps operations against, England herself. Thus William Cecil warned Elizabeth in July 1562, in the context of the English expedition to Le Havre, that a victory for the Guise would 'pleasure the King of Spain',[38] enable him to put Mary, Queen of Scots, on the English throne and seize Ireland for himself.

Once it became clear that French power would not revive for some time, and that Spain was the main threat, English attention shifted to the Habsburg Low Countries. Initially reluctant to offend Philip, Elizabeth began to give clandestine help to the Dutch Revolt against Habsburg rule when it started in earnest in 1572, but the Spanish advance was relentless. Philip's ships scattered the Turks at Lepanto, he annexed Portugal, he captured the Philippines, and he intervened at will on the Catholic side in the French religious wars. By the late 1580s, it seemed as if he was on the verge of finishing off the Dutch, too. His commander, the Duke of Parma, advanced inexorably in the Low Countries. Antwerp fell in 1585; Sluys, a strategically vital port on the other side of the Channel which had often served as the base for an attack on the south coast during the Middle Ages, succumbed in 1587, a traumatic moment for both English and Dutch. Boosted by success, Philip now began to speak more and more openly about his European and global ambitions. The back of a medal commemorating the union of crowns with Portugal was inscribed with the words *Non sufficit orbis* – 'The world is not enough.' A triumphal arch carried a legend suggesting that the king was 'lord of the world' and 'lord of everything in east and west'.[39]

All this convinced Englishmen, and Elizabeth, that their destiny was being shaped by a great struggle against the Counter-Reformation on the continent and its pretensions to create a 'universal monarchy', a system of domination, in the eyes of its opponents, of the Habsburgs over the other princes of 'Christendom'. The notion of Protestantism in one country – the theological and ecclesiological nub of Anglicanism – did not make much strategic sense. Sir Walter Mildmay, the Chancellor of the Exchequer, warned the House of Commons in 1576 that 'the tail of these storms which are so bitter and boisterous in other countries may reach us also before they be ended.' When the English freebooter Sir Francis Drake found Philip's *non sufficit orbis* medal when raiding the Spanish governor's palace in Santo

Domingo, it sent a further collective chill down English spines. In the 1580s, two of Elizabeth's most trusted advisors, the Earl of Leicester and Sir Francis Walsingham, warned that once Philip had defeated the Dutch he would turn his attention to England, using the resources of the Low Countries. The defence of Protestantism and liberty in England, it was generally believed, demanded the defence of Protestantism in the Dutch Republic and, ultimately, of the European balance everywhere.[40]

In short, Protestant geopolitics gave new impetus to England's continental policy. Now, the south coast was to be protected against Spanish rather than French attack. England's new national interest was to keep Philip out of the Low Countries, an area which Elizabeth's advisor William Cecil described as 'the very counter-scarp of England', that is, a defensive position just outside the inner perimeter.[41] This suggested that the real outworks of England were much further east, in the Holy Roman Empire. For this reason, Cecil called for 'a conjunction with all princes Protestants for defence', especially with 'the Protestant princes of the [German] Empire', such as John Casimir of the Palatinate, who held lands in the strategically crucial area of western Germany. In 1572, Elizabeth paid him to attack Spanish troops in Brabant and hoped to rally a Protestant League behind his banner.[42] So long as the empire did not fall into hostile hands – in other words, those of the Dutch rebels – England itself would be safe.[43]

Central to this strategy was a determination not to await the enemy attack passively. Preventive action was not only legitimate, but essential. Once the 'papists' in Europe and England had 'the upper hand', William Cecil warned Elizabeth in 1562, 'then it shall be too late . . . for then the matter shall be like a great rock of stone that in falling down from the top of a mountain, which when it is coming no force can stay.'[44] Likewise, Chancellor Mildmay implored the English Parliament to think 'aforehand [of] the dangers that may come by the malice of enemies and to provide in time how to resist them'. More concretely, Sir Francis Drake argued that 'these great preparations of the Spaniard may be speedily prevented,' by attacking him closer to home. Moreover, the new threat required Protestants to set aside reservations – of which Queen Elizabeth had plenty – about helping

Dutch and French rebels against their lawful sovereigns. The argument was not simply a religious one. Elizabeth, for example, inveighed against the tyrannical treatment of *both* Protestant and Catholic princes by Philip, for example his execution of the Catholics Egmont and Hoorn. Many Englishmen agreed with the authors of the tract *Vindiciae contra tyrannos*, which argued that princes who arbitrarily infringed the rights of their subjects could be deposed by outside intervention.[45]

It was against this background that Elizabeth finally intervened in the Netherlands with a land army, in the mid-1580s. As a surety for the money and troops committed to the Dutch, she took possession of the 'cautionary towns' of Brill and Vlissingen and nearby Rammekins fort. Though offered the crown by the Dutch rebels, she would accept nothing more than a rather nebulous 'overlordship' through the Treaty of Nonsuch in 1585. Elizabeth was driven not by territorial ambition but the assumption that the security of England depended on keeping the Low Countries and the Holy Roman Empire in friendly hands.[46] Not everybody agreed that an active land war was the way to deal with Philip. Even Cecil began to have second thoughts as the showdown with Spain approached. Philip might leave England alone so long as he was not provoked, he speculated. 'If the Queen would meddle no more in the matters of the Netherlands,' he claimed, 'but most strongly fortify her kingdom . . . gather money, furnish her navy with all provisions, strengthen her borders towards Scotland with garrisons, and maintain the ancient military discipline of England,' then all would be well. Others, such as the sailors Hawkins and Sir Francis Drake, believed that Spain could be defeated through a largely maritime strategy focussing on her overseas possessions and commerce, or by amphibious operations along the Spanish coast, such as those against Corunna, Lisbon and Cádiz.[47] This was the start of a long debate in English, and later British, grand strategy which continues to this day: whether the security and prosperity of the realm was better guaranteed by a continental or a maritime strategy.

What saved England was a combination of naval and ground forces working as part of a coordinated European strategy. The navy attacked the great Armada which Philip sent against England before it could rendezvous with the infantry and transports waiting in the Low Countries, but could not completely disperse it. Dutch ships operating from ports which would have fallen long previously without English support helped to blockade Parma's forces. Thereafter, a 'Protestant wind' drove the surviving ships of the Armada up the east coast of England, around the northern tip of Scotland and back down the west coast of Ireland to ports in Spain. So it was Elizabeth's infantry and the Dutch allies they had supported, as much as her English sailors, who saved England from invasion in 1588. All this was an object lesson in the importance of the Channel ports on the far side to the security of the realm and the need to rely on more than purely naval measures to repel an attack, or to prevent one from being mounted in the first place.

Moreover, England's programme of maritime expansion was rooted in a sense of its importance for the defence of her position in Europe. 'Whoever commands the sea,' Sir Walter Raleigh argued, 'commands the trade; whosoever commands the trade of the world commands the riches of the world, and consequently the world itself.' The prestige and fiscal muscle which Philip enjoyed as king of New Spain – which provided about 10 per cent of his revenues mid-century, rising to about one quarter by the end of his reign – was an important part of his European leverage. Richard Hakluyt, in his celebrated 'Discourse of Western Planting' (1584), noted that 'with this great treasure', Philip's father, Charles V, had 'got from the French King the Kingdom of Naples, the dukedom of Milan and all his other dominions in Italy, Lombardy, Piedmont and Savoy'. Elizabeth permitted Drake's voyages between 1577 and 1580, not as the first step towards an overseas empire of her own but to reduce the flow of bullion to pay Philip's armies in Flanders.[48] It was England's European strategic identity, not her supposed maritime destiny, which was being expressed here.

England's engagement in Europe drove her search for a sustainable constitutional order for the British Isles. Experience showed that in the hands of a hostile power, or of a Pretender, Scotland and Ireland would be the 'back door' to England, or at the very least contribute to her encirclement. In 1460, for example, Richard of York used Ireland as a base from which to mount his invasion of England. Another claimant to the English throne, Lambert Simnel, was crowned in Dublin in 1487. Four years later, Perkin Warbeck began his failed campaign to seize the throne in Ireland. It was to deal with these challenges, rather than to oppress the Irish, that London pushed through 'Poyning's Law', which asserted the supremacy of the Westminster over the Dublin parliament. Scotland, as we have seen, posed an even greater danger, at least until the success of the Reformation, and even periodically thereafter. She had her own parliament and long-established distinct commercial and dynastic links with Europe, particularly with France and the Low Countries, but also with Scandinavia and the Baltic. She was a European power in her own right. English forces defeated the Scots at Flodden in 1513, and Elizabeth contained them effectively enough, but they remained a concern, particularly in the context of their 'Auld Alliance' with France.

If Elizabeth's early intervention and the triumph of Presbyterianism solved the problem north of the border, at least for the time being, Ireland, where the bulk of the population remained Catholic, and where much of it bitterly resented English colonists of whatever religion, was a much thornier problem. For hundreds of years, London had left the Gaelic parts more or less to their own devices, paying particular attention only to the defence of the anglicized 'Pale' around Dublin and the retention of the southern and eastern ports from which an invasion of England could be mounted.[49] This changed in the course of the sixteenth century, during which the entire island became an arena of foreign intrigue, first by France and then the Habsburgs. This problem was much magnified by the attempted introduction of the Reformation in Ireland, which was furiously resisted not only by the Gaelic but also many of the 'Old English' settler population.[50] Spanish infiltration had to be stopped and the threat of Gaelic rebellion crushed for good. The brutal massacre of a papal-backed force of Italians and Spaniards – after surrendering at Smerwick in October 1580 – reflected this wider strategic unease among the English authorities. It came to the fore again with the revolt of the northern Irish lords O'Neill and O'Donnell in the 1590s. In 1596, a Spanish expedition was frustrated by adverse winds. Another attempt culminated in a failed Spanish expedition to Kinsale in 1601 but was a close-run thing. The English knew that, although they had been fortunate on these occasions, they would have to be lucky always, whereas the Spaniards would have to be lucky only once.[51]

A more durable solution would have to be found. Welding Scotland, Ireland and England together into a coherent whole would not just forestall enemy attacks, it would also make them collectively a more substantial actor on the European scene. London conceived this process primarily as an enlargement of England within Europe. Poyning's Law was an improvement, from London's point of view, as Ireland became a net contributor to the exchequer again, but the territory remained alienated. The Acts of Union with Wales under Henry VIII had shown the way, by incorporating the principality and giving it parliamentary representation in London. For various reasons, this was not yet possible in Scotland or Ireland. Some form of closer bond was particularly important, however, in a context where rival states were expanding, or forming ever larger unions with other states, to remain competitive. In 1526, Hungary, Croatia and Bohemia were added to the Habsburg conglomerate; Poland and Lithuania combined in 1569; and Philip acceded to the Portuguese throne in 1580. Elizabeth's chief minister, Cecil, in 1560, looking out at Europe, especially at the Habsburg behemoth, noted that England's enemies 'have of late so increased their estates that now they are nothing like what they were, and yet England remains always one, without accession of any new force'. For this reason, he recommended that 'united strength, by joining the two kingdoms [England and Scotland], having also Ireland knit thereto, is a worthy consideration'. In the end, dynastic happenstance after the death of Elizabeth brought the Scottish and English crowns, but not their representative assemblies, together under James I in 1603.[52] This solved the problem for the moment, greatly increasing the security of England, but proved to be a brittle arrangement in the long run.

In the early seventeenth century, James VI tried to revive the idea of a religious reconciliation between all the major Christian faiths: Anglicanism, Lutheranism, Calvinism, Roman Catholicism and Greek Orthodoxy. Before ascending the English throne, as King of Scotland he bewailed 'the discords of Christian princes' which had endangered the 'common cause' against the Turks, suggesting instead a general European alliance against the Ottomans. In 1604, James proclaimed his desire 'to live peaceably with all states and princes or Christendom' and his hope that 'such a settled amity might (by a union in religion) be established among Christian princes as might enable us all to resist the common enemy [the Turks].'[53] It is likely that James also saw this policy as a device to unite Catholics and Protestants at home, by steering the site of contestation away from Europe, where agreement was impossible, towards the Muslim 'other', as we would call it today. These plans and the continued popular interest in containing 'the Turk' showed that the Reformation did not completely destroy English belief in the essential unity of 'Christendom'.[54] They never came to anything, however, partly because James could find no takers in Europe itself and partly because other threats loomed larger in the minds of the political nation.

English concerns now shifted. The survival of the Dutch rebels (thanks to Elizabeth's intervention), the establishment of the United Provinces and the conclusion of an Anglo-Spanish peace in 1604 took the Low Countries out of the immediate firing line. The focus moved to Germany. This was because the Holy Roman Empire had become the fulcrum of the Catholic–Protestant struggle on the continent and the alleged Habsburg ambitions of 'universal monarchy'. Here matters came to a head over the little north-west German principality of Cleves-Jülich. If it fell into Spanish or Austrian hands, either directly or by proxy, the United Provinces would be directly threatened, as would the confessional balance within the empire, thus exposing England herself to attack from Habsburg and Counter-Reformation Catholicism. The Netherlands and the Protestant German principalities were seen as the crucial outworks of European Protestantism, and thus of England herself. It was there, rather than on the high seas, that England would be defended. Small wonder that Robert Cecil, the Lord High Treasurer, told the parliament of 1610 that '[t]he war of Cleves doth threaten a general altercation in Christendom.' A substantial English force was duly sent to the region, where it participated in the siege of the Habsburg garrison in the city of Cleves, alongside troops from France, Brandenburg and the Dutch Republic.[55]

Europe drew back from the brink, but only for a few years. The German Reichstag, paralysed by confessional bickering, did not meet after 1613. The Protestant Elector Palatine Frederick, who was married to a daughter of James I, became the focus of Protestant, especially Calvinist, hopes in England and Germany. It was the perceived failure of the king to defend him and the 'Protestant cause' in Germany which eventually destroyed the relationship between Parliament and the Stuarts. In the Addled Parliament of 1614, James demanded money for the costs of the Cleves War, the Palatine wedding and other government expenditures. The king's ministers asked Parliament to fund the navy, to pay the garrisons of the cautionary towns in the Low Countries, to prevent Ireland from becoming 'a thorn in our side', to cover 'His Majesty's Charge in Germany for settling the right Inheritors there [in Cleves]', to contain France and, of course, Spain, which was wont to 'fish in troubled water'.[56] Parliament, however, was unconvinced that James had the best strategy for dealing with the danger and authorized only limited payments. Many Members of Parliament also opposed James's plan to hedge England's diplomatic bets through a Habsburg marriage for his heir, Charles. This 'Spanish match' never came off but, in the context of the controversy over royal failure to support European Protestantism, it deepened the divide between the Crown and the political nation.

Matters boiled over after the outbreak of the Thirty Years War in Germany in 1618.[57] The rapid advances of the Spanish-imperialist Catholic party there and the failure of the Stuarts to do anything much about them,[58] outraged many Protestants throughout the conflict. Well informed by a burgeoning press, the development of which was largely driven by events in Europe,[59] they watched in despair as the Protestant Elector Palatine was deposed as king of Bohemia and soon as Elector as well. There was an air of unreality about this critique, as it did not account for Frederick's incompetence and the many practical constraints on military intervention deep inside the continent. Be that as it may, to many Englishmen the contest over Bohemia was not taking place in a far-off country between people of whom they knew nothing. As Sir John Davies told the House of Commons in 1620, 'the Palatinate is on Fire; Religion is on Fire; and all other Countries [are] on Fire . . . this is dangerous to the Low Countries, the United Princes and the whole Protestant Interest.' This was the context in which John Donne, a soldier, a diplomat and an enthusiast for Elizabeth Stuart's marriage to the Elector Palatine, penned his legendary lines that 'No man is an island entire of itself; every man is a piece of the continent . . . If a clod be washed away by the sea, Europe is the less. As well as if a promontory were. As well as if a manor of thy friend's or of thine own were.' Across Europe, it seemed, the dominoes were falling: Bohemia, the Palatinate and the whole 'Protestant cause' in the empire itself.[60]

The great European struggle sparked off a new wave of moral panic and domestic unrest at home. Throughout the 1620s and 1630s, English Puritans had recoiled from what they regarded as the crypto-'popery' of Anglicanism and the effeminacy of the court with its overdressed toadies,[61] not to mention the overwrought homoeroticism they saw in the relationship between monarch, ministers and favourite. To them, there was something rank about this opulence and sensuality at a time when the Protestant cause was being sold down the river in Germany.[62] The Duke of Buckingham, whose closeness to James had been as notorious as his failure to relieve the Huguenot stronghold of La Rochelle, was impeached in 1626; he was neither the first nor the last English minister to pay that price for perceived incompetence in Europe. Two years later, when things did not look up strategically under Charles despite his obvious personal probity, the king's parliamentary critics passed a series of condemnatory Commons resolutions. Looking across to the continent, they saw 'a mighty and prevalent party . . . aiming at the subversion of all the Protestant churches of Christendom', and noted 'the weak resistance that is made against them'.[63]

England's absence in Europe mattered because the strategic potential of the country was vast. She was already in the throes of a huge demographic and economic transformation, which would eventually turn an already prosperous realm into the powerhouse of Europe.[64] Her population was rising substantially, more quickly than those in most other parts of the continent, and it was far more mobile than was the case elsewhere. This benefited commerce and agriculture. London was rapidly becoming a metropolis, the second city in Christian Europe, and fast gaining on Paris. English merchants were prominent, and often dominant, not merely in the Channel and the Atlantic but also in the Baltic and the Mediterranean.[65] The Dutch Republic was economically strong and politically sophisticated, with a far greater share of global commerce, a bigger merchant marine and a formidable navy, but much weaker demographically and militarily. France was substantially larger, but England was nimbler. The problem for the Stuarts was that any attempt to mobilize this immense latent power foundered not so much on the unwillingness of Englishmen to pay, but on their increasing conviction that the monarchy was strategically incompetent at best and malevolent at worst.

Charles's attempts to restore his authority at home in order to project power abroad soon brought him into conflict with the Scots, provoked a rising in Ireland and, ultimately, led to confrontation with Parliament. In 1642, England was convulsed by civil war, leading to the defeat of the king in 1646, his execution in 1649 and the replacement of the monarchy by a Protectorate under Oliver Cromwell. By then, the dispute between the two sides had outgrown the original questions of foreign policy with which the fatal misunderstanding between king and Parliament had begun. Throughout this period, however, the underlying argument over Germany was never lost from sight. The failure to support the Palatinate and European Protestantism featured highly in all of Parliament's major statements (the content of which is otherwise of no concern to us here): the Grand Remonstrance and, once conflict was under way, the Nineteen Propositions in 1642 and the subsequent Propositions of Uxbridge. The prosecutor's undelivered draft speech at the trial of Charles I began with the king's alleged failure to come to the aid of continental Protestants. In short, the revolt against Charles had begun as, and in many ways remained, a protest against Stuart policy in Europe.

Just as the Elizabethans had looked overseas for fundamentally European reasons, so did seventeenth-century Englishmen, in both cases in order to contain continental aggressors. Sir Benjamin Rudyerd warned the House of Commons in 1624 that it was the Spanish mines in America which fuelled their 'vast ambitious desire of universal monarchy'. No better way of helping the embattled Palatines, another argued, than to 'wast the Kinge of Spaines Shipping upon his coast, [and] interrupt the retornes of his Plate'.[66] English colonization of the New World was also very much an extension of the European conflict, though it also developed a dynamic of its own.[67] The

Puritans who left England in the 1620s and eventually arrived in Massachusetts were not turning their back on the Old World, far from it. Despairing of England, and then of the increasingly exposed Dutch Republic, they saw America not as a promised land but as a springboard from which they would prepare the defeat of the 'Antichrist', that is, the Habsburgs in Europe. They prayed for reform in England, for 'the miserable state of the churches in Germany' and the victory of the Protestant cause there. The colonists followed the news from the continent closely, particularly that from the Protestant redoubts of Geneva, Frankfurt, Leiden, Heidelberg and Strasbourg, as well as from England itself; they trembled for the Palatinate and rejoiced at the successes of the Swedish king Gustavus Adolphus, who helped to restore the fortunes of the 'Protestant cause' in Germany.[68] Some even returned to fight in the wars on the other side of the Atlantic.

Because the security of England depended so much on the balance of power, especially in Germany, and because that in turn rested so much on the domestic equilibrium in the various principalities, English statesmen were compelled to overcome any inhibitions they might have had about subverting legitimate authority. They believed that their freedom within the state system depended on the preservation of 'liberty' within certain states. At one level, of course, the 'liberty' that these sixteenth-, seventeenth- and eighteenth-century protagonists had in mind was very different from our twenty-first-century understanding of the term. They were referring to the legal or socio-economic 'privileges' which aristocrats or townspeople enjoyed either by contract or custom, on which the unequal and stratified European society of orders rested. In other respects, however, their conception of 'liberty' and 'freedoms' was more modern, including an insistence on the limits of monarchical power, the defence of property, and taxation by consent only. One way or the other, Englishmen made a direct connection between the dynamics of the struggle for mastery among European states and the battle for 'liberty' within them. Thus Elizabeth I – albeit with considerable reluctance – adopted the cause of both Catholic and Protestant Dutch nobles because she wanted to deny Spain absolute control of the Low Countries and thus the base for a descent on England.

No thanks to the Stuarts, the Protestant cause in Germany survived. Paradoxically, it was rescued not only by the Protestant Swedes but also the Catholic French, who wished to curb the power of the Habsburgs. Both sides fought each other to a standstill. The resulting treaties of Westphalia laid down the toleration of the three major confessions: Roman Catholic, Lutheran and Reformed (Calvinist).[69] The political structure of the new Holy Roman Empire, though hierarchic, with an emperor at the head, was a sophisticated form of early modern consociationalism, in which confessional matters – which was almost everything of substance – had to be settled by compromise rather than majority vote. Within territories, rulers were bound to respect certain rights, including the right to convert. Those religious minorities who had enjoyed toleration in 1624 were not only guaranteed it for the future but could not be excluded from certain civic offices. These arrangements, and the imperial constitution as a whole, were guaranteed by two outside powers, France and Sweden, and in time Russia became a formal guarantor, and England (later, Great Britain), a very active informal one.

The German war ended in 1648, before the victorious parliamentarian side could intervene, but the Franco-Spanish contest continued just across the Channel. It was decided by the intervention of England. First, Oliver Cromwell subdued Ireland, where the papacy and the Habsburgs were supporting the Catholic Confederation of Kilkenny. Then he crushed the Scots. Thereafter, he made his first priority the pursuit of the Protestant crusade in Europe which Parliament had so long demanded. Contrary to expectations, however, the Dutch refused to sink their colonial and commercial differences with London in the common cause. They even rejected England's offer to drop the Navigation Act of 1651, which stipulated that all commerce with the island should be carried by English ships, in return for an anti-Habsburg alliance. Some felt that Dutch pretensions to commercial dominance were a form of 'universal monarchy'. Cromwell therefore defeated them militarily in 1653–4. In 1654, he became Lord Protector, a quasi-monarchical position.

For the Commonwealth and the Protectorate, the Protestant cause was thus not simply a front for commercial interests, nor was it completely synonymous with realpolitik. In perhaps the most striking example of 'selfless' diplomatic engagement, Cromwell confronted the Duke of Savoy over his persecution of the Vaudois Protestants. Not only did he organize the collection of a large sum for their relief, contributing a substantial amount of his own money, but he sent an extraordinary envoy to Turin, and a fleet with instructions to disrupt Savoyard shipping, and even to attack Nice as a last resort. In terms purely of state interest, Cromwell was shooting himself in the foot here: the Duke of Savoy was a potentially valuable ally against the Habsburgs, whose territories lay astride the 'Spanish Road', the Habsburg line of communications between the Low Countries and the Iberian Peninsula. Cromwell saw ideology and security as inseparable: defending his co-religionists abroad always contributed to the protection of the realm itself, even if it cut across some traditional or opportune diplomatic relationships.[70]

In 1655, Cromwell started his crusade against Spain. Expeditions were dispatched to the Caribbean, in part to secure the riches there for England and in part to deprive the Spaniards of the colonial resources to support a European hegemony. As the former West Indian planter Thomas Gage observed, 'the flourishing condition of and strength of the House of Austria (Rome's chief strength and pillar)' was attributable to the 'American [silver] mines; which being taken away from Austria [meaning the Habsburgs more generally], Rome's triple crown would soon fight away and decay'.[71] This was the same Eurocentric argument for engagement overseas which had begun in Elizabeth's time and was taken up by the parliamentarian side under the early Stuarts. The main blow, however, would be struck in Europe itself. To this end, Cromwell concluded an alliance with France in 1657. At his insistence, the French chief minister Cardinal Mazarin agreed to ease restrictions on the Huguenots. A year later, the joint armies inflicted a decisive defeat on the Spaniards at the Battle of the Dunes. Madrid came to terms with London and Paris at the Peace of the Pyrenees in 1659. England annexed Dunkirk, just over a hundred years after the traumatic loss of Calais as a continental bridgehead through which she could pursue her interests in Europe. The return to Europe, it seemed, had begun.

Across much of Europe, the seventeenth-century struggles had generally served to strengthen princely absolutism, partly as a barrier against internal strife and partly as the best form of defence against outside interference. The Estates General of France, who were not really comparable to Parliament anyway, were not summoned after 1614. In Prussia, the Great Elector entered into a 'grand bargain' with his Estates, which gave them greater control over their peasantry but largely stripped them of their participatory rights. This proved to be the basis of Prussia's subsequent rise to great-power status. In England, on the other hand, the mid-seventeenth-century path to extraction and mobilization ran via increased participation. The parliamentarian side in the Civil War showed that representative assemblies were not only as good as but actually better than monarchical systems at agreeing an effective grand strategy and raising the resources to implement it. A new type of state was taking shape: extractive, consultative (though Cromwell's relations with Parliament were fraught), resilient, creditworthy and utterly lethal.[72] Cromwellian England, in short, had found what had so long eluded the Stuarts: a domestic structure capable of sustaining the European effort which the national interest required.

Shortly after, Cromwell died and, after a brief interlude, Englishmen tired of internal strife and foreign war and restored the Stuart monarchy, under Charles II. Like his father and grandfather, however, Charles struggled to make his voice heard on the continent. He sold Dunkirk to France and was complicit in the growth of a new threat to the European balance of power and English liberties in the shape of Louis XIV of France. By the end of the decade, Charles was firmly in Louis's pocket, concluding the secret Treaty of Dover in June 1670, in which he undertook to support the French king against the Dutch in return for his military assistance in restoring Catholicism and monarchic power in England. Englishmen were particularly concerned about the integrity of the Holy Roman Empire.[73] In 1670, Louis annexed the imperial fief of Lorraine, which cut the link between the Free Duchy of Burgundy (Franche-Comté) and the Habsburg Netherlands. Spanish power was now buckling all along the line: a Hispano-Dutch alliance underlined the extent to which the European scene had changed. In 1672, the French king launched a ferocious attack on the United Provinces. Louis seemed unstoppable.[74] England's absence in Europe was much lamented by Europeans, who feared the suspected ambitions of Louis XIV to erect a Catholic 'universal monarchy'. One of his French noble opponents penned a tract entitled *L'Europe esclave si l'Angleterre ne rompt ses fers* ['Europe a slave, if England does not break its chains'] (1669), a view which was widely shared across the continent.[75]

England herself was deeply divided on how to proceed in Europe and, by extension, elsewhere in the world. Many English Tories, for example, felt that the Dutch were a greater commercial and ideological threat. Some also believed that the nation's real destiny lay in commercial expansion overseas, either in North America or in the North African enclave of Tangier, which Charles II had inherited through his marriage to Catherine of Braganza, along with Bombay. But to those we have come to know as the 'Whigs', the notion that the European balance and English liberties should be defended in the Low Countries and the empire was as axiomatic as it had been to parliamentarians in the 1620s.[76] Thus Sir Thomas Littleton warned Parliament in April 1675 of the mortal danger stemming from the 'enlargement' which Louis 'had made of his empire in Flanders, Germany, the Franche-Comté and elsewhere'.[77] These critics hammered overseas commitment, especially the Tangier colony, partly as sinkholes of popery and moral corruption, but mainly as a distraction from the real front in Europe. The Earl of Shaftesbury stated that 'foreign [that is, European] protestants' should have priority over any imperial ventures because they were 'the only wall and defence to England; upon it you may build palaces of silver'. The 1st Duke of Montagu put it more succinctly: 'I had rather see the Moors in Tangier, than the Pope in England.'[78]

The anti-monarchical critique of English foreign policy reached new heights with the fall of further bastions in Germany, especially in Strasbourg, which Whig pamphleteers described as a 'rampart' of German Protestantism and thus of English liberty. Even some Tory pamphleteers lamented the loss of 'the Keys into Germany'.[79] Things got even worse under James II, who succeeded to the throne in 1685 and was openly Catholic, espousing a more colonial and maritime policy rather than continental engagement. The considerable commercial growth and colonial expansion under Charles II and James II cut no ice with their critics, however, for whom European affairs had primacy. Their concern with the possibility of a Catholic Succession to James via any children with his second wife, the Catholic Mary of Modena, was at root an anxiety about a cross-Channel Catholic axis with Louis which would ruin English liberties as surely as that between Mary and Philip had (or was believed to have) done. For the second time in a century, therefore, the Stuart monarchy found itself at odds with the political nation over Europe.

When Louis moved against the Palatinate in the late 1680s, he touched a strategic and emotional raw nerve in England. His inexorable advance in Europe also drove William of Orange to invade England in November 1688. Only by restoring constitutional government in England, the Dutchman believed, could he hope to see the country participate in the defence of European liberties against Louis. A month after the invasion, he announced his expectation 'that through a parliament these realms may be made useful in order to assist our state [the United Provinces] and our allies'. William's confidant Bentinck described the invasion as having been undertaken for 'the service of God, the defence of the laws of England and the liberty of that state and the interest of the whole of Europe'.[80] The new king saw himself as the leader of God's international forces on earth, and his English supporters such as Bishop Burnet called upon their countrymen not to skulk in their island but to act as a Protestant 'Israel': 'a light to the Gentiles' in defence of liberty and true religion in Europe.[81] The English 'Glorious Revolution' of 1688, in other words, was a product of the state system, undertaken in order to restore England's weight in the councils of Europe.

Two decades of intense English involvement in European affairs followed. The Nine Years War, which pitched England together with her Dutch, Habsburg and other allies against Louis XIV, was fought mainly in Flanders, with some sideshows in Ireland and elsewhere. Its aim was to keep the French out of Germany and the Low Countries. It ended with the Treaty of Ryswick in 1697 but, within a few years, the question of the succession to the Spanish crown led to a new conflagration. Here the issue was not so much Louis's claim to the Spanish colonial empire as his occupation of the Spanish Netherlands. In 1701, England, the Dutch and the Austrian Habsburgs concluded a 'Grand Alliance' specifically designed to maintain the 'balance of power' in Europe against France. Over the next ten years or so, English armies battled across the continent, in Spain, Flanders and Germany. Their commander, the Duke of Marlborough, repeatedly crushed the French in iconic battles: at Blenheim in deepest Bavaria, at Ramillies and Oudenaarde. The inscription on his victory column at Blenheim Palace in Oxfordshire proclaims him the man who 'rescued the [German] Empire from desolation, asserted and confirmed the liberties of Europe'.[82] The Whig Duke of Devonshire remarked in 1706 that Britain was now the island of 'liberty' and had the 'right to set all Europe free'.[83]

Once again, the overseas and the home fronts were conceived through a European prism. Throughout the war, Anglo-Dutch fleets relentlessly hammered Franco-Spanish commerce in order, as one set of Admiralty instructions from London made clear, 'to depriv[e] them of the supply of money and plate which they seem to rely on for the support of the war'. In 1703, for example, the orders for an attack on Havana stressed the need to 'prejudice the family of Bourbon and advance the interest of the house of Austria', that is, England's Habsburg allies against France.[84] A blow struck in the New World was thus really aimed at the Old. Likewise, the struggle against domestic dissent was inseparable from the European contest. English suspicion of local Catholicism was greatly increased by its association with the Stuart Pretender and his French absolutist backers. How to balance these anxieties with the maintenance of the constitutional liberties upon which England's freedoms and her strength rested remained a difficult issue into the next century and, in different ways, has remained one all the way up to the present.

These European contests fundamentally shaped the English state and society, and completed the work begun under Cromwell. In the 1690s, the English overtook the Dutch pioneers and established the strongest and most 'modern' state in Europe.[85] A funded national debt was created, supported by the new Bank of England (1694) and a sophisticated stock and money market. Underpinning all this was a broad political consensus in favour of parliamentary government and resisting tyranny, at home and abroad. The Triennial Act of 1694 stipulated that parliamentary elections were to take place every three years, and the abandonment of pre-publication censorship allowed political and commercial matters to be discussed freely in and outside Parliament. A largely independent newspaper press catered for the public's insatiable demand for news about the continent.[86]

English politics throughout the 1690s and the 1700s were dominated by how best to wage the war. What we would today call Eurosceptics argued with Europhiles. The Whigs supported William, and later his successor, Queen Anne, in their call for direct military intervention on the continent. The Tories preferred a more indirect maritime and colonial strategy. There was little disagreement, however, about the fact that Louis had to be stopped, or that a free people required a strong, and thus expensive, state to protect them.[87] Shortly after the Glorious Revolution, the Tory Sir Edward Seymour said that 'the King of France has been the devil and walking ghost in every parliament'.[88] 'Do what is necessary to carry on the war,' the Commons proclaimed in the 1690s, 'but do nothing which may destroy the constitution.'[89] This enabled England to raise the staggering sums needed to fight Louis, funding a huge proportion of the war – at least a third – out of long-term loans rather than income. 'Holding the balance of Europe,' the political economist Charles Davenant wrote in his *Essay upon the Balance of Power* (1701), 'will make us patiently endure the bloodshed, hazards, losses and expenses of Treasure' necessary to maintain it.[90] Englishmen thus lived not only in the freest of the larger European states but also the most powerful in relation to its size and population, and perhaps even the strongest in absolute terms as well.

The war also led to profound constitutional change in the British Isles. It spurred the completion of the modern British state.[91] In 1701, the Act of Settlement laid down that the Crown would pass to the House of Hanover, 'being Protestants'. Parliament was also determined to ensure that the succession in Scotland be regulated for all time in order to pre-empt Jacobitism and prevent France from re-encircling England. More generally, the war effort against France required ever greater coordination between north and south. It made no sense at all to have two separate commercial and colonial policies, for example. Just before the war, the two countries had nearly come to blows over the Scottish colony at Darien on the Isthmus of Panama, while Scotland continued to trade normally with France even as her regiments served in Germany and Flanders. Many Tories opposed the Union project, but Whig elites on both sides of the border agreed that, whatever their differences, the containment of Louis XIV came first. So, in 1707, they concluded an Act of Union, in which Scotland received generous representation at Westminster, retaining her legal system and national church while relinquishing her separate foreign and security policy. As the British pamphleteer Daniel Defoe remarked two years later, England's 'considerations for uniting' were 'peace, strength and shutting a back door of continual war, and confusion from the North'.[92] In some ways, the union was a strategic enlargement of England and the Westminster parliament, but it also created something entirely new. The Union was made in order to prosecute the war, and the war deepened the Union through the prosecution of the common cause.[93] Just as Europe had made England, it made the United Kingdom, which has remained a force to be reckoned with on the continent and in the wider world ever since.

Meanwhile, the war effort stagnated. Marlborough failed to deliver a 'knock-out' blow against Louis. In the face of continued expense and bloodshed, sceptical voices in the British public sphere and in Parliament grew ever louder. In November 1709, a mob demanding peace attacked Dissenting meeting houses and the Bank of England. A year later, the British expeditionary force in Spain was crushed at Brihuega, the Austrian-backed one at Villaviciosa. French troops advanced deep into Spain. With the Whig policy of continental engagement now comprehensively discredited, Queen Anne dismissed her ministers and replaced them with a Tory administration committed to a more maritime and colonial approach. Not long after, the Whigs were thrashed at the general election, primarily because the public had lost patience with their grand strategy. The dominant figure in the new British government, Henry St John – soon to be Viscount Bolingbroke – hated both the Dutch and the Austrians. He immediately set about winding down the land war in Flanders and switched priority towards the naval effort against France in the colonies and on the high seas. In a bestselling tract, *The Conduct of the Allies*, the Tory writer and propagandist Jonathan Swift not only lampooned the Whig strategy of continental engagement but also targeted the fiscal-military complex, which he accused of prolonging the war for personal financial gain: 'that set of people who are called the moneyed men; such as had raised vast sums by trading with stocks and funds . . . whose perpetual harvest is war, and whose beneficial way of traffic must very much decline by a peace'.[94]

In mid-April 1711, Emperor Joseph I died suddenly. Six months later, he was succeeded by his younger brother, Charles, the candidate of the Grand Alliance for the Spanish throne. This raised the spectre of a return of the empire of Charles V. As St John remarked, 'If the Empire and the dominions of Spain are to unite in the person of this prince [Charles], the system of the war is essentially altered.' The Whigs still argued that French power was so great that it required a united Habsburg bloc to balance it; but the argument was being lost. Support for the land war in Europe ebbed away. British generals were openly censored by the House of Lords. Marlborough himself was sacked in December 1711. Flanders was progressively starved of men and money; resources were diverted overseas. By the beginning of 1712, British forces in Europe had effectively ended operations, while the other belligerents were equally exhausted.[95] The British and Dutch came to terms with France at the Treaty of Utrecht in April 1713, and the emperor did so at the Treaty of Rastatt in March the following year.

The Utrecht settlement was designed to contain France; it was largely shut out of Germany. The Spanish Netherlands passed to Austria and constituted a powerful 'barrier' to French ambitions. Britain and the Dutch were expressly committed to their defence. Britain's European position was reinforced by the Hanoverian succession, which took place in 1714 after the death of the last Stuart, Queen Anne, in 1714. The new king, George Ludwig of Hanover, was a firm Francophobe determined to deliver on all continental commitments. His own somewhat precarious position on the throne was in turn guaranteed by the Dutch. British constitutional freedoms were thus explicitly linked to the maintenance of the European balance. This was to be safeguarded through a series of geopolitical measures. In Italy, Louis was to be boxed in by Habsburg gains in Lombardy. The French position in the western Mediterranean was seriously weakened by Britain's retention of Gibraltar (captured in 1704), which controlled the passage in and out of the Mediterranean, and the still more vital Minorca, whence it was supplied and the French Toulon squadron could be monitored. Philip was recognized as king of Spain – and the Grand Alliance abandoned its Catalan allies – but he was forced to renounce all claims to the French throne. Above all, the crucial Spanish Netherlands passed to Austria, locking the country more directly into the containment of France.

The commercial and colonial aspects of the peace were also very significant, but more because of their strategic importance than for any purely economic reasons. Britain annexed Newfoundland and most of Nova Scotia in present-day Canada, and their fisheries, which were vital not just for food but for the training of seamen. She also secured the coveted Asiento, the monopoly right to trade with South America, especially in slaves. This was now placed in the hands of the British South Sea Company, which the Tories had set up in 1711 as a counterweight to the Whig-dominated Bank of England and the East India Company. Its purpose was to generate not merely personal profits for shareholders but also capital for governmental loans to pursue a vigorous foreign policy. The River Scheldt, at whose mouth lay Antwerp, formerly northern Europe's largest port, was to remain closed to shipping in order to preserve the pre-eminence of Amsterdam; Dutch economic success was based at least as much on diplomatic coercion as competitiveness. The resulting economic gain was supposed to help the Dutch to garrison the barrier fortresses. Likewise, Bolingbroke sought a commercial treaty with France not for pecuniary gain or to 'engage' the Bourbons but because he thought that Britain would prevail in open economic competition. In this way, for both the Dutch and the British, the European commercial and strategic balances were closely connected.[96]

Domestically, the accession of George Ludwig of Hanover epitomized the triumph of Parliament in the United Kingdom in a Europe where representative government was in retreat.[97] As we have seen, the French Estates General, much weaker than their London counterparts to start with, were not even called after 1614. Those of Brandenburg were neutered shortly after the end of the Thirty Years War. The Danish estates met for the last time in 1660; the Crown became hereditary rather than elective. Elsewhere – for example in Poland, Sweden, Venice and the Habsburg monarchy – representative structures survived but were under constant threat. In all cases, the argument for absolutism, or at least increased princely authority, was made on the basis of the need for domestic coherence in the face of external challenges. In England, unusually, the argument went the other way. There, the political nation was convinced that the United Kingdom was strong in Europe not in spite of her parliamentary system, with all its faults and corruptions, but because of it.

The Hanoverian succession was also important in another respect. In the mid-fifteenth century, England had suffered the traumatic loss of most of her French empire in Europe, followed over the next two hundred years by that of the last enclaves in Boulogne, Calais and (briefly) Dunkirk. Towards the end of the seventeenth century and the start of the eighteenth, however, permanent dynastic and military links with Europe had been re-established: first, with the short-lived Personal Union with the Dutch Republic under William III, and then through the much longer-lasting Personal Union with Hanover, which – as we shall see – turned Britain into a north German power. Her borders now effectively ran along the Elbe and the Weser, rather than the English Channel. England – or the United Kingdom she was now the dominant part of – was now very much a 'piece of the continent' again.

3

'The bulwarks of Great Britain'. The United Kingdom and the Continent in the Age of Absolutism[1]

The [Holy Roman] Empire may be considered as the bulwark of Great Britain, which if it be thrown down, leaves us naked and defenceless.

– Henry Pelham, soon-to-be prime minister, 1741[2]

Whenever you leave France to do whatever she pleases upon the continent, you will leave her hands at liberty and then an invasion of this country may be no chimerical project. All the world knows how soon France established a very formidable marine in the time of Louis XIV. She may as readily re-establish that which she has now lost when she shall be at liberty to employ all her measures and men for that purpose.

– William Pitt the Elder, 1761[3]

Britain had shaped Europe in her interests at the Treaty of Utrecht in 1713. It soon became clear, however, that she had designed a system to deal with past threats, principally from France, rather than those of the future. The new challenges came first from Spain, which was unreconciled to the loss of its Mediterranean lands; then in the 1720s from the ambitions of Emperor Charles VI; then from the 1730s from a revived France; and from the rising powers of the East, Prussia and Russia. The Dutch Republic, an old ally, declined rapidly and proved unable to fulfil its former 'barrier' function in the Low Countries. Britain adapted quickly. Over the next fifty years, she threatened war or waged it on numerous occasions. She embarked on a fresh round of alliance building, which for a time embraced even France. Spain was contained in the first two decades of the century, and defeated in two major wars mid-century. Russia was deterred. Charles VI was seen off without war. Prussia was co-opted. France was prevented from dismembering the Habsburg lands in the War of the Austrian Succession (1740–48) and utterly crushed in the Seven Years War (1756–63). In all cases, Britain worked closely with her allies. She also built a new empire overseas, designed to contribute to her weight in Europe. As always, Britain's engagement on the continent was controversial and there was a vocal group of what we would today call 'Eurosceptics' who demanded a more maritime and colonial policy. The consensus, however, remained very much in favour of the vigorous defence of the 'liberty and repose of Europe' upon which the security and freedom of the United Kingdom rested.

The British elite knew about Europe, and knew more as the eighteenth century progressed. A considerable number had fought there during the war of Grand Alliance against Louis XIV, and were to do so again in the 1740s and 1750s.[4] Some of them studied there, including William Pitt the Elder, who spent time at the University of Utrecht. Many more went on the Grand Tour.[5] British statesmen frequently accompanied the king to Hanover.[6] British newspapers and imported foreign gazettes reported in great detail on European developments.[7] As a result, the British elite was remarkably well informed. This comes across very clearly in the parliamentary sphere, where embarrassing gaffes or manifest geographical ignorance were rare, at least before 1760.[8] At the same time, the early-eighteenth-century British foreign policy establishment was in many respects part of a broader European elite. Two of the most prominent experts of the time, Luke Schaub and François Saint-Saphorin, were foreign born and routinely reported to London in French from their diplomatic posts; in the latter case, English documents had to be translated into French before he could read them.[9] Few British statesmen picked up as much European language and culture as Lord Carteret did at Westminster School,[10] but most could get by in French.[11]

Contemporary vocabulary reflected the centrality of Europe, most strikingly in the use of the words 'empire' and 'electorate'. These terms had acquired their present-day meaning in the nineteenth century. To eighteenth-century protagonists, however, the empire meant the Holy Roman Empire'[12] rather than a global domain on which the sun had yet to set. Likewise, the 'Electorate' was in most contexts not something whose votes British statesmen periodically sought; they were more interested in the north German Electorate of Hanover (the title of 'Elector' referring to the right to elect the Holy Roman Emperor), to which Britain was bound by dynastic union and to which her monarch regularly repaired. When Lord Hervey, the diarist and courtier, said of Queen Caroline that 'whenever the interests of Germany and the honour of the Empire were concerned, her thoughts and reasonings were often as imperial as if England had been out of the question',[13] he was clearly referring to central Europe, not overseas. Likewise, when the Duke of Newcastle spoke of the '[t]he liberties of the Empire, in opposition to France',[14] it was the German princes he was concerned with. In short, the world eighteenth-century British statesmen inhabited – certainly before 1760 – was still a firmly Eurocentric one.

Of course, there were those who attacked the British strategic consensus on Europe and espoused a naval and insular destiny in its stead.[15] As we have seen, this discourse had a long pedigree, but it exploded with renewed force in the 1730s in the popular and parliamentary clamour for a maritime war against Spain.[16] The immediate demand here was for revenge for the mutilation of the British seaman Jenkins by the Spanish coastguard, for the despoliation of the Spanish overseas empire and the liberation of the oppressed Indians, but the real driver was the desire to express Britain's maritime destiny. These currents were famously summed up by the former secretary of state and arch-Tory Bolingbroke in his tract on *The Idea of a Patriot King*, which was penned in 1738. 'The situation of Great Britain,' Bolingbroke wrote, 'the character of her people, and the nature of her government, fit her for trade and commerce . . . The sea is our barrier, ships are our fortresses, and the mariners, that trade and commerce alone can furnish, are the garrisons to defend them.' 'Great Britain,' he continued, 'is an island.' She should avoid continental wars and devote 'a continual attention to improve her natural, that is her maritime strength'. He concluded that '[l]ike other amphibious animals, we must come occasionally on shore: but the water is more properly our element, and in it, like them, as we find our greatest security, so we exert our greatest force.'[17] Throughout the post-1714 period, these themes formed the staple of opposition attacks on British involvement in Europe. Continuing the 'Eurosceptic' tradition first elaborated in the late seventeenth century, these critics dismissed continental engagement as futile and unBritish.[18]

It is hardly surprising, therefore, that the very notion of a European balance and Britain's supposed role in it should have been so controversial. As Walpole remarked with some exasperation in January 1734:

> [R]eally by some gentleman's way of talking, one would imagine that the ministers of England were the ministers of Europe; . . . If any unforeseen accidents abroad, if the ambitions of any foreign prince or the misconduct of any foreign court, produce any untoward effects or occasion any troubles or commotions in Europe, the ministers of England are immediately loaded with the whole; it is they who have done the mischief and they must answer for it.

'The balance of power,' the anti-Walpolean Whig courtier and colonial enthusiast the Earl of Halifax announced in late January 1744, 'has a powerful sound, which many who never appeared to know or to consider its meaning, have employed to subject this unhappy nation to plunder, and to exact subsidies for the neighbouring powers.'[19] William Pitt the Elder expressed himself in similar terms while in opposition.[20]

All the same, the prevailing elite sense was that Britain was an integral part of Europe, and could and should not cut herself off from developments there. This was partly a question of economic interest, as trade with Europe far exceeded that with any other part of the world. In November 1755, the Lord Chancellor the Earl of Hardwicke observed that 'No man of sense or integrity will say that you can quite separate yourselves from the continent. A commercial kingdom must have connections there.'[21] The main reason for the preoccupation with the continent, however, was strategic.[22] They had come to that view during the Wars of the Grand Alliance (1688–1713), when England – after 1707, Great Britain – had been the lynchpin of the European effort against France. In 1716, for example, the Earl of Sunderland attacked the 'old Tory notion that England can subsist by itself whatever becomes of the rest of Europe', as one 'so justly exploded ever since the revolution [of 1688]'.[23] In 1752, the Duke of Newcastle justified the payment of subsidies to the Elector of Saxony on the grounds that Britain should not rely only on the 'wooden walls' of the navy.[24] A year later, William Pitt, now in government, told Parliament that it 'must go as far as the interests of this country were combined with those of the powers of the continent, for combined they were'.[25]

On this view, island status and the 'wooden walls' of the navy were not enough to shield Britain from shifts in the European balance. In 1742, the MP John Perceval dismissed the 'new doctrine [which] has been taught and inculcated for some months past, that it is of no importance to this nation what may happen on the continent; that this country is an island intrenched within its own natural boundaries, that it may stand secure and unconcerned in all the storms of the rest of the world'. Two years later he warned that if France succeeded in putting 'all Europe' into 'universal bondage', then 'our situation as an island will never balance our situation in such a neighbourhood'.[26] Likewise, Carteret lampooned those who called on Britons to 'disregard all the troubles and commotions of the continent, not to leave our own island in search of enemies, but to attend our commerce and our pleasures'. In fact, he argued, 'our own independence', was closely linked to the 'liberties of the continent'.[27]

This was because eighteenth-century Britain was not, *pace* her naval enthusiasts, generally believed to be an island in geopolitical terms. Naval technology still made it impossible to guarantee interception of an invading force by sea.[28] Moreover, thanks to the personal union with Hanover, it had been a composite state since 1714, whose borders lay in north Germany as much as on the Channel, the Atlantic or the North Sea. Hanover, as the opposition Whig peer the Earl of Chesterfield complained in a famous pamphlet, 'robbed us of the benefit of being an island'.[29] Indeed, during this period Britain should more properly be called 'Hanover-Britain'.[30] The relationship was a symbiotic one, in which the king and often his ministers tended to see British and Hanoverian interests as one and the same.

A glance at both confidential correspondence and public rhetoric bears this out. Viscount Townshend, then Secretary of State for the

Northern Department, argued in the early 1720s that there was nobody who did not see that 'the interests of His Majesty as King and Elector were inseparable and that his German affairs could not suffer without weakening his government here'. Even if 'His Majesty had two characters/identities, He was the same person and consequently had the same interest'. Three years later, Townshend reminded his correspondent that 'we all serve one master and the British as well as the German minister must obey his orders as they see fit to give us.'[31] In the early 1740s, Lord Carteret warned that 'all the weight and power' of Great Britain would be exerted in defence of the king's 'German dominions . . . whenever they shall be involved with England in the great and general cause'.[32] Likewise, in the Seven Years War, the Earl of Hardwicke argued that '[t]he case of Great Britain and Hanover [was] mixed and entangled.'[33] Indeed, when British statesmen had the opportunity to neutralize Hanover, as they did in 1726, 1741 and 1757, they declined to do so, mainly for strategic reasons. Hanover was integrated into – some claimed subordinated to – a common European strategy.[34] British and Hanoverian diplomats worked together closely, if not without friction, throughout the period, particularly under Townshend in the 1720s and the Newcastle–Münchhausen partnership in the late 1740s and early 1750s.[35] In short, as the Tory Baron Bathurst put it in a mid-century pamphlet, Britain had a 'naturalized tenure among the Germanic body on the continent'.[36] Britain was perceived geographically and strategically not as an island but as a European state.

To most, the idea that Britain had the principal role to play in the maintenance of the balance of power was axiomatic.[37] Moreover, the balance was not self-perpetuating: it required active British management. As one parliamentarian observed in the mid-1730s, 'though all the nations of Europe are equally concerned with us in preserving the balance of power, yet some of them may be blind to their own interest; nay it is very probable some of them always will.' Therefore, he argued, Britain should not 'neglect what is necessary for our own security' or refuse to contribute to maintaining the balance. It was her task to make Europe see its own interest. One peer, Lord Cholmondeley, remarked in the House of Lords in April 1741 that it was up to Britain to rally Europe: '[T]ill we take the lead, other powers will not stir.' Likewise, the Whig MP Thomas Winnington justified the dispatch of troops to Flanders in April 1742 'because it will shew that we are not only willing but ready to join with those other powers of Europe, who ought to have as great an interest, and ought to have an equal concern for preserving a balance of power in Europe'.[38]

But Britain had not merely a calling to maintain the balance, it also had a clear interest in doing so. It was only the European balance, British diplomats, statesmen and Members of Parliament believed, that stood between Britain and the threat of 'universal monarchy', which would not only destroy British commerce but would bring in its train the return of the Stuarts and the subversion of the Revolution Settlement of 1688. Jacobitism could and should be fought at home, but the best way of containing it was to maintain the overall balance of power. As Carteret argued in December 1741, at the height of the revival of French power in Europe, '[t]he liberty and repose of Europe is almost lost; after which we shall not keep ours long.' It was for this reason that the 'liberties of Europe' and the 'Protestant cause' were often spoken of in the same breath. Concern for the European balance persuaded Britons, albeit grudgingly, to overcome their inhibitions about standing armies, to dig into their pockets and endorse the annual Mutiny Bill, which paid for the standing army, as well as subsidies to continental powers.[39]

Sir Robert Walpole, who dominated British politics in the two decades before 1740, was a rather important exception. He was as much of a Tory in foreign policy as he was a Whig at home; he famously kept Britain out of the War of the Polish Succession. Yet throughout his long ascendancy, foreign policy tended to be dominated by the more interventionist secretaries of state, especially the Duke of Newcastle, Townshend and Carteret, and the monarch himself. This was certainly true of the 1720s, though in the 1730s Walpole did assert himself more effectively. But even Walpole was less hostile to Hanover and less ignorant of European affairs than is sometimes supposed.[40]

The defence of the balance of power was a central and often the dominating issue in eighteenth-century British domestic politics. Failure to deliver it, and to maintain Britain's continental alliances, cost Bolingbroke office after the Treaty of Utrecht. Throughout the 1730s, popular and parliamentary opposition to Walpole's policy of appeasement in Europe mounted. Failures in the overseas war against Spain seriously damaged his administration, but it was the mismanagement of the European balance of power which proved fatal. In February 1741, Parliament debated a 'Motion for the removal of Sir Robert Walpole', which charged that 'during the course of [his] administration, the balance of power in Europe has been destroyed; the House of Bourbon has been aggrandized . . . and the House of Austria has been depressed'. This mattered because, as one critic – Lord Carteret, himself a former secretary of state and future chief minister – explained, 'errors in foreign affairs are worse than in domestic, for you cannot correct them.' Over the course of the next two years, Walpole was battered by a series of such attacks, many of them designed not merely to depose him but to pave the way for his impeachment, possible imprisonment and even execution. After all, the young Whig firebrand William Pitt argued, 'he who has doomed thousands to the grave, who has cooperated with foreign powers against this country' should be not merely 'stripped' of office and honours but also 'of his life'. Once the imperial crown had fallen to the French-sponsored Charles Albert, the Elector of Bavaria, Walpole's position became untenable and in March 1742 he resigned, escaping an official enquiry and likely legal sanction only by a tiny margin of votes.[41] The culture of intervention in Europe had done for him in the end.

Indeed, the rise and fall of most eighteenth-century British administrations was determined by their relationship with Europe. Walpole's successor, Lord Carteret, also fell over German policy, partly because of controversial payments made to Hanoverian troops in British service and partly for his failure to contain Frederick. The same pattern was repeated a decade later during the Seven Years War, which went very badly for Britain at the outset. Criticism of the Duke of Newcastle's administration mounted with every defeat in 1756. The loss of Minorca unleashed a cascade of pamphlets and other broadsides accusing the government of neglecting the European balance of power. By the end of the year, this disquiet had led to the formation of a new government including the opposition stalwart, William Pitt, whose long ascendancy was based on his skilful synthesis of continental and colonial strategy.

As in centuries past, the fortunes of war also triggered moral panics. Concerns about the advance of French power in the 1730s spawned anxiety about continental wines and opera, which many deemed an unmanly and unBritish art form. There was another round of soul-searching during the calamitous opening phase of the Seven Years War. According to *Harrop's Manchester Mercury* in August 1756, the 'immediate loss we have met with in the Mediterranean [the loss of Minorca] is a loud call to awake from Luxury and Selfishness, Extravagance and Indolence'.[42] A year later, Jonas Hanway inveighed against tea as an oriental vice sapping the vitality of Englishmen: 'Were they the sons of tea-sippers,' he asked, 'who won the fields of Cressy [Crécy] and Agincourt, or dyed the Danube's streams with Gallic blood [at Blenheim]?'[43] Others linked Britain's poor performance to the inequality between classes: Henry Home, Lord Kames, condemned the public school system for its failure to teach boys 'patriotism'.[44] In a widely read tract, the Reverend John Brown even attributed Britain's humiliation in Europe to a 'vain, luxurious and selfish EFFEMINACY'.[45] The road to salvation, these critics argued, was a thoroughgoing moral regeneration and the creation of a truly inclusive national militia to give expression to the new manly spirit. This military commitment was then parlayed into a claim for greater (male) political participation. 'Every subject, every Man,' William Williams sermonized in 1757, 'is a soldier.'[46] The Militia Bill passed in 1757 reflected this thinking. There was also an increasing sense that the state should take a closer interest in the medical welfare of scarce manpower, which suffered badly from disease in the campaigns overseas and 'rott[ed] piecemeal in the wilds of Germany'.[47]

For much of the eighteenth century, certainly from the 1730s to the 1770s, British statesmen deemed the principal threat to the European balance of power and to their domestic liberties to be France. In the 1720s, however, there were widespread fears of Austrian, Spanish and even Russian pretensions to 'universal monarchy', or at least regional hegemony in key areas such as the Baltic and the Mediterranean. In every case, with the single exception of Orthodox Russia, the antagonist was Roman Catholic. It is also true that in contemporary rhetoric, anti-popery, the Protestant cause and the balance of power were closely connected. But 'universal monarchy' was essentially a political, not a confessional, term. It had, after all, been applied to the Protestant Dutch in the seventeenth century, and it never prevented alliances with Catholic great powers, primarily Austria, but also France.[48] The British national interest was by now essentially a secular concept in which the religious connotations of previous centuries had been replaced by an emphasis on political liberty.

As in the seventeenth century, when Cromwell supported the Vaudois Protestants against his Savoyard ally, British foreign policy sometimes privileged ideology over pure reason of state. During the War of the Austrian Succession, the Empress Maria Theresa accused Bohemian Jews of collaborating with the Prussians, and ordered the expulsion of the Prague Jews as a potential fifth column in 1744. This provoked the first general mobilization of trans-state Jewish opinion, producing a flood of petitions and protests from merchants and communities across Europe directed not only at the empress herself but at the powers capable of influencing her. Despite the Anglo-Austrian alliance, the secretary of state Lord Harrington condemned the expulsions to her ambassador as 'detrimental and prejudicial to the true interest of the common cause' against France. These pleas initially fell on deaf ears, but Maria Theresa soon relented and the Jews ultimately returned home. Britain had thus undertaken its first – albeit only partially successful – humanitarian intervention on behalf of a non-Christian grouping.[49]

All this required a very high level of conceptual flexibility from British statesmen and diplomats. Most of the time, it made sense to view the territorial configuration of Europe as a system of barriers designed to contain France. The two Bourbon courts of Madrid and Versailles had to be kept apart at all costs; never again should a French king be able to proclaim, as Louis XIV once had, that there were 'no more Pyrenees'. Piedmont-Savoy had to be bolstered to keep the French out of Italy; the Austrian presence there was to be nurtured. The British presence in Gibraltar and especially Minorca served to curb Spain and, after the breakdown of the entente in 1731, France as well. The loss of Naples and Sicily to the Spanish Bourbons after the Habsburg defeats in the War of the Polish Succession was therefore a major blow to Britain's European policy. First of all, because it made the containment of French thrusts into Italy more difficult. Secondly, because it subverted Austrian power more generally and thus the balance of power as a whole.

Central Europe was equally, if not more, important. At first sight, this may seem surprising. Britain had continuous diplomatic accreditation only to the two largest German states, Austria and Prussia,[50] and the level of representation was uneven.[51] In fact, the Holy Roman Empire was an important pillar of the European system; maintaining its integrity against French encroachments was a high priority in Whitehall. 'The Empire,' the soon-to-be chief minister Henry Pelham claimed in April 1741, 'may be considered as the bulwark of Great Britain, which if it be thrown down, leaves us naked and defenceless'; he was using the term in its non-colonial sense, of course. Similarly, the MP George Doddington claimed that 'France knows very well, that the German Empire, when united, is a body too mighty for her to encounter.'[52] Critical to this unity was strong leadership from the emperor.[53] 'It is for the general interest of Europe,' the Duke of Newcastle, who served both as a foreign secretary and as chief minister, wrote in the mid-1740s, 'that the Imperial Crown should be fixed in the House of Austria, late experience has, I think, sufficiently shewd. A weak emperor will be (and sooner or later must be) a French emperor.'[54] British elite opinion was correspondingly aghast when the territory of Lorraine, which many regarded as an outer rampart or 'barrier' for the empire, was lost to France.[55]

The resulting familiarity of British politicians with the complexities of the Holy Roman Empire is well documented. Thus Lord Townshend, who served as foreign secretary, was forced into the highways and byways of the *droit de non appellando*' (the right of an estate of the empire not to have judicial decisions appealed to a higher court) and other imperial arcana in the 1720s. On other occasions, even Townshend had to admit defeat. 'I confess,' he remarked vis-à-vis George I's obsession with the imperial investitures of Bremen and Verden, 'that I am not sufficiently familiar with the laws of the Empire and its particular constitutional structure.'[56] Townshend did know enough, however, to recognize his own ignorance; he may, of course, merely have been tactfully suggesting to his master that this was a Hanoverian, not a British, matter. To the elder William Pitt, recommending the imperial jurist Samuel von Pufendorf to his nephew at Cambridge came quite naturally; he praised another learned tome 'relating to the Empire of Germany' as 'an admirable book in its kind, and esteemed of the best authority in matters much controverted'.[57] Pitt also showed a familiarity with German politics during the relevant parliamentary debates, at least when it suited him.[58]

Just across the Channel lay the 'barrier', a ring of Dutch-garrisoned fortresses backed up by the Austrian Habsburgs in present-day Belgium to prevent French troops from flooding into Flanders and towards the Dutch Republic. The progressive decline of the Dutch in the early and mid-eighteenth century, and the steady loss of Austrian interest in maintaining the 'barrier' profoundly affected the way in which the British elite thought about Europe from the mid-1730s onwards.[59] As one ministerial pamphleteer argued towards the end of the War of the Austrian Succession, 'this island would be the seat of the war, if once our out-works on the continent were entirely in the possession of the enemy.'[60] The choice of words here was significant: the first line of defence was not the Channel – the 'moat defensive to a house' of Shakespearean and navalist rhetoric – but the mainland itself. Ten years later, Newcastle lamented that he saw 'the great system upon the point of being dissolved – the court of Vienna is driving the Republic, and with her this country, from them as fast as they can.' If the Dutch withdrew their garrisons from the barrier towns, Newcastle continued, 'the system founded upon the Grand Alliance is at an end.'[61]

The greatest hindrance to the British strategic conceptualization of Europe, however, was not the decrepitude of the barrier but its redundance. This was most obviously the case in the two decades after the Utrecht Treaty, when the elaborate system devised to contain France proved – rather like the guns at Singapore in 1942 – to be pointing the wrong way. During this period, British interests were threatened in the Baltic by Russia, in the Mediterranean by Spain, and in central Europe by the growing ambition of Emperor Charles VI. In these circumstances, British policy had to be thrown into reverse. During the years immediately after the Treaty of Utrecht, Stanhope concluded an alliance with France (1716–31), boxed in Spain to the south through the Quadruple Alliance and, less successfully, sought to contain Peter the Great in the north.[62]

In order to master the challenges thrown up by the state system, the British elite conceived of Europe in the round. This meant keeping an eye on several evolving local balances simultaneously. Some areas mattered much more than others, but each part of Europe was believed to be connected. Thus the Duke of Newcastle, the Secretary of State for the South, remarked in February 1725 that 'the affairs of the North and South are so interwoven together, that any stand or rub that happens in either place must in consequence affect the other.'[63] Soon afterwards, Townshend highlighted the link between the Mediterranean and the Baltic balances by observing that 'though the fire begins so far off as Gibraltar, yet the train is so laid that the flame would soon reach to the north.'[64] In the same spirit, a decade later, Newcastle reported that George II had responded to French attempts to bring Sweden into the War of the Polish Succession with the observation that 'if Sweden was to take part in the war in the north that could not but influence the general affairs of Europe.'[65] Twenty years after that, the Secretary of State for the Southern Department, Thomas Robinson, articulated the complexity of the balance when he remarked that '[w]e can do nothing without the Dutch, the Dutch nothing without the Austrians, nor the Austrians anything without the Russians.'[66]

Nowhere was the interconnectedness of Europe more evident than on the dynastic front. Here Britain's assets were limited. As a Protestant power in a world dominated by the larger Catholic dynasties, there were relatively few options, and the conversion of the Saxon elector to become King of Poland narrowed them still further. An Anglo-French marriage project was broached by Paris in the early 1720s but turned down by George I, largely for confessional reasons. A match with the Stadtholder in the mid-1730s was in part designed to shore up the increasingly moribund Dutch.[67] Apart from Scandinavia, Britain was for the most part limited to unions with the middling and smaller German states. In the mid-1750s, for example, several marriages were mooted to bolster the defence of Hanover and – especially – the alliance with Prussia.[68] Of course, the traction provided by marriage should not be overestimated: the dismal state of Anglo-Prussian relations in the 1720s was caused by the mutual hatred between George I and his son-in-law Frederick William I.

The potential threat from dynastic marriages on the continent was enormous. In this period more than any other since, British statesmen and diplomats lived figuratively with almanacs, Court calendars and royal genealogies in one hand and a map of Europe in the other. The greatest continuous dynastic headache facing Britain in the early eighteenth century was the Austrian Succession. Ever since the early 1720s, it was probable that Emperor Charles VI would die without a male heir. Whether or not the daughters of his deceased elder brother, or – as Charles himself laid down in the Pragmatic Sanction – his own eldest daughter, Maria Theresa, succeeded was not important in itself. What was immensely significant was whether and under which circumstances the Habsburg inheritance would be passed on, undivided or partitioned. In the 1720s, when relations with Austria were abysmal and a dynastic union with Spain was in the offing, Britain was reluctant to endorse the Pragmatic Sanction and thus an immense Austro-Spanish conglomerate. By the 1730s, when it became imperative to shore up Austrian power in central Europe as a bulwark to France, there was no keener advocate of the Pragmatic Sanction. Some deaths and marriages mattered much more than others, depending largely on whether they changed the nature of the strategic map.

Looking at Europe in the round brought opportunities as well as challenges: one of the standard tactics of British statesmen in the 1720s was to attempt to mobilize the Ottoman Turks against the Russians. Thus Townshend instructed the British envoy to Constantinople, Abraham Stanyan, in November 1725 that the Russians should be pinned down in Asia to make them 'less attentive and less enterprising to create trouble and uneasiness to the King on this side'.[69] Likewise in the mid-1750s, Russia was mobilized to deter Prussia from attacking Hanover. These examples show not so much that these strategies were subtle or well-founded but that British statesmen explicitly conceived of Europe and Britain's place in very broad terms.

There was, however, one serious barrier to integrated thinking in foreign policy: the division between the Southern and Northern Secretaryships of State. The Northern Secretary dealt with Austria, the

United Provinces, Prussia, Poland, the Holy Roman Empire, Denmark, Sweden and Russia. The Southern Secretary was responsible for France, Spain, the Italian states, Portugal, Switzerland and the Ottoman empire. This could lead to a bifurcation in strategic vision, with the inevitable friction that entailed. Strictly speaking neither of the secretaries was subordinated to the other, and the balance between them fluctuated. In some cases, the division of responsibility was clear: bilateral relations with Prussia were always likely to be handled by the Northern Secretary; those with Portugal by the Southern Secretary. France, which was diplomatically heavily committed across Europe, was a less straightforward case but generally fell within the purview of the Southern Secretary. Russia, however, posed particular difficulties. Baltic issues were obviously the remit of the Northern Secretary, and most dealings with St Petersburg took place within a broadly north German or north European context. Yet, as we have seen, British statesmen also tried to use the Ottoman empire – the responsibility of the Southern Secretary – against Russia.

The same blurring of competencies was also to be seen, in slightly less extreme form, with regard to Austria, which was at the time a central, western and southern European power. The resulting confusion was summed up in August 1736 by the veteran diplomat Horace Walpole. 'I do not wonder,' he wrote:

> at [our] embarrass in . . . negotiations; consultations and orders are carried on in England with such confusion and in so undigested a manner; the affairs of Turkey are in the province of one Secretary [of State], the directions to be sent to the Hague belong to the department of another, these two I believe see one another but little, and I perceive that one [Harrington] writing nothing at all and the other [Newcastle] will not suffer nobody but himself to think or write anything that may concern his province.[70]

Nowadays, one would say that eighteenth-century Britain suffered from a lack of 'joined-up' government.

Some believed that the danger of hasty and unreflective engagement in Europe was that Britain might become the 'Don Quixote' of Europe, tilting at imaginary threats to the balance. In March 1734, at the height of the War of the Polish Succession, in which Britain remained neutral, one parliamentarian exclaimed:

> For God's sake, Sir, are we thus to be eternally the dupes of Europe? If the emperor, or any other power, neglects to keep their fortified places in a proper posture of defence, must we answer for that neglect? Are we, for the sake of preserving the balance of power to undertake, at our own charges, to defend every power in Europe, and to prevent their being invaded or conquered by any of their neighbours.

Ten years later, the MP Edmund Waller warned that:

> we have of late got into a ridiculous custom, of making ourselves the Don Quixotes of Europe; and sometimes under the pretence of preserving a balance of power in Europe, at other times under the pretence of preserving a balance of power in the north, we have engaged . . . in the quarrel of almost every state in Europe, that has, by its impudence or ambition, brought itself into any distress. The consequence is, that whilst we take upon ourselves the burden of defending our allies, they give themselves very little trouble about defending themselves.

Britain thus risked, as the parliamentarian John Philipps warned in December 1741, becoming a 'knight errant', wasting the nation's blood and treasure on selfless quests which European powers should be undertaking themselves.[71] Today, we would speak of the danger of 'free-riding'.

The instruments which British statesmen could bring to bear in support of their European policy were varied, but also problematic. One option was pre-emption, or unilateral military intervention. Here the Royal Navy proved itself a useful instrument of British European policy. In 1718, for example, Admiral Byng destroyed the Spanish fleet off Cape Passaro before the declaration of war, and thus wrecked Madrid's attempt to dominate the western and central Mediterranean. Pre-emptive strikes were also widely canvassed as tension mounted with Spain in the late 1730s. In 1742, Commodore Martin appeared in the Bay of Naples and threatened to level the royal palace if its ruler did not come to heel. Pre-emptive strikes were actually carried out against French shipping in 1755, well before the formal outbreak of hostilities. The lessons of Frederick the Great's surprise attack on Silesia were also taken to heart. In October 1761, for example, the parliamentarian George Lyttelton demanded that Britain should act '*à la Prussienne* and strike first, while the enemy was unguarded'.[72]

Unilateral military – principally, naval – intervention, was however a very limited and imprecise instrument.[73] It sufficed neither to intimidate Peter the Great in the Baltic between 1716 and 1720, not least because the Royal Navy could not follow his galleys into shallow waters, nor to master Spain in 1739–41, nor to compensate for Britain's weakness on land in the final years (1746–7) of the War of the Austrian Succession. Moreover, Britain was simply not strong enough to right the European balance on her own. Her peacetime regular army was larger than that of a middling German state but substantially smaller than the Prussian and Austrian armed forces, not to mention those of France. Between 1714 and 1740, there were on average some thirty-five thousand men available for service around the world.[74]

Central to the culture of intervention, therefore, was a realization that British power was limited and that British interests could be achieved only in cooperation with other states. There was a resulting reliance on diplomacy and European alliances, often backed up with Britain's formidable fiscal power, in the shape of subsidies. It was for this reason that the former arch-unilateralist William Pitt announced in late 1759 that he had 'unlearned his juvenile errors, and thought no longer that England could do it all by herself'.[75]

If much of the public sphere, the louder parliamentary voices and some of the more raffish politicians wrapped themselves in the naval flag at the expense of the European connection, the anti-unilateral reflex among the elite was stronger. Here the traumatic experience of the Treaty of Utrecht, when Britain had abandoned her continental allies, resonated throughout the first half of the century.[76] It made British statesmen cautious of courting popularity at the expense of the true national interest. 'I remember the great approbation given to the Treaty of Utrecht,' Carteret remarked in February 1741, 'and in a little time the makers of it impeached. The capital fault of it was making France too strong, and Germany too weak.'[77] Pulling out of Europe, another parliamentarian argued not long after, 'will be a more unjustifiable measure than the desertion of the Grand Alliance in 1712'.[78] It was this same reflex that caused William Pitt to announce at the height of the Seven Years War – December 1758 – that 'he would not give up an iota of our allies for any British consideration.'[79] Indeed, after Pitt's resignation in 1761, ostensibly over Spain but really because of the abandonment of the Prussians, one friend conjured up the spectre of 'Gertrudenberg and Utrecht'.[80] Pitt himself referred to the 'treaty of Utrecht, the indelible reproach of the last generation'.[81]

All this contributed to a culture of strategic restraint. Ministers differed from the militant pamphleteers, and hawkish parliamentarians determined on colonial despoliation. They knew that unilateral action could jeopardize Britain's defence of the European balance and indeed provoke an anti-hegemonic reflex against her. It was for this reason that British statesmen hesitated to push home their maritime advantage against France towards the end of the Seven Years War. Newcastle observed that 'to think of being able to extirpate the French from north America, or if we could, that our business was done by doing so, or that such a nation as France would sit down tamely under it, is to me the idlest of all imaginings.'[82] The Duke of Bedford, a former secretary of state, claimed that 'the endeavouring to drive France entirely out of any naval power is fighting against nature and . . . must excite all the naval powers of Europe to enter into a confederacy against us as adopting a system.'[83] Even Pitt conceded the force of these arguments. 'He sees,' as one observer noted, 'that in order to obtain peace, so much of our acquisitions must be given up.'[84]

This shows that the European balance of power was explicitly accorded a much higher priority than colonial or commercial concerns.[85] Thus British statesmen were slow to anger over colonial 'depredations' in the 1730s, for fear of driving Spain further into the French camp in Europe, where Britain was temporarily isolated. It was the failure of Walpole to stop the threatened partition of the Habsburg lands in 1740–41 which holed his administration below the waterline, not the much criticized handling of the war with Spain. Similarly, in the Treaty of Aix-la-Chapelle, the Canadian fortress of Louisburg, wrested with such fanfare from the French three years earlier, was exchanged for a French withdrawal from the Low Countries, a much more vital area of British interest.[86] Truly, 'the New World had redressed the balance of the old.'[87]

It is significant that in the early stages of the Seven Years War Pitt initially asked not for the Southern Secretaryship, with its colonial responsibilities, but for the Northern Department. Whatever his public rhetoric and later myth, therefore, Europe remained his principal preoccupation throughout. In June and July 1757, at the height of the war, there were many more ships and men deployed on the near side of the Atlantic.[88] The famous coastal expeditions against Saint-Malo, Brest and Rochefort were not so much expressions of naval virtue as a desperate attempt to draw off French resources and thus ease the pressure on Britain's only continental ally, Frederick the Great. Even at the height of the conflict, the imperial apotheosis of 1759, the year of victories, most British regular forces were to be found in Europe rather than overseas, and the contingent in Germany was actually increased in 1760.[89] For most of the war, which is now remembered very much as an imperial venture, British officers – including General Wolfe, the hero of Quebec – longed for European rather than colonial postings. In December 1758, Wolfe, as yet unaware of his impending rendezvous with imperial destiny, lamented that 'it is my misfortune to be cursed with American services,' whereas his friend was lucky enough 'to serve in an army commanded by a great and able Prince', that is, the Duke of Brunswick.[90]

The Seven Years War saw the apotheosis of a British grand strategy which combined diplomatic, military and naval instruments. Maintaining the European balance was not an alternative to the maintenance of naval supremacy but its precondition, or so many British statesmen believed. If one European power achieved continental hegemony, they would not only control the Channel ports from which to attack England but would also be able to devote their entire resources to outbuilding the Royal Navy. The Duke of Newcastle famously pronounced in 1749 that France would overawe Britain at sea if it were not distracted by Britain's allies on the continent.[91] Pitt went further, arguing that not merely naval but colonial dominance depended on upholding a land front against the enemy in Europe. 'Had the armies of France not been employed in Germany,' he told Parliament, 'they would have been transported to America . . . America had been conquered in Germany.'[92] 'However inconvenient and expensive the German war is for England,' he now argued, 'it is more inconvenient and more expensive for France.'

In short, by mid-century, a coherent British strategic culture had emerged. It was firmly Eurocentric: it gave absolute priority to preventing the growth of a hegemony on the continent, from the 1730s a role taken by France after a generation when Spain, Russia and Austria had all played that part. This culture was mainly, though not exclusively, Whig. In this culture, political and diplomatic instruments counted as much as military or naval ones; sometimes more so. It was restrained and conscious of the limits of British power. It generally subordinated narrowly naval and colonial interests to continental European concerns, but it also mobilized these resources in support of the balance of power on the mainland. Underpinning everything was a powerful sense of structure: Europe was conceived as an overall balance with a combination of regional balances. The British elite were generally well informed about Europe, and at all times sensitive, perhaps overly so, to potential dynastic permutations and geopolitical revolutions. British statesmen thought and spoke of Europe in terms of 'systems', 'barriers' and 'natural' allies, such as the Habsburgs. Rather than being fixated on the 'moat' of the surrounding silver sea, they conceived of the European mainland itself as an integral part of Britain's defences – a 'rampart'. *Pace* Walpole, they were expected to be, and often perforce were, 'ministers for Europe'.

All this was about to change. In November 1760, the dissenting minister and wool merchant Israel Mauduit published a devastating pamphlet entitled *Considerations on the Present German War*. The author rehearsed a range of familiar themes and arguments with new vigour: that Britain was in her element at sea, hence land warfare should be avoided; and that only a united Germany was any use as a barrier against France, hence interference in what was essentially an Austro-Prussian 'German civil war' was redundant.[93] The impact of the *Considerations* was massive, and instantaneous. Some five thousand copies were printed in five editions, which were read, and read out, in taverns, inns, newspapers and journals throughout London and the country. His arguments resonated not only among an increasing number of MPs but also with the new king, George III, who acceded to the throne in 1760 and did not share his grandfather's preoccupation with the Holy Roman Empire. In particular, they persuaded his new chief minister, Lord Bute. Two years later, Britain abandoned Frederick the Great and withdrew from the war in Europe. Shortly after that, in 1763, she forced France and Spain into a humiliating peace in which she carried off large swathes of the globe, including Quebec and other contested areas in North America.

Domestically, the end of the Seven Years War, and particularly the way in which it ended, had immediate political repercussions. Prime Minister Bute was so viciously attacked in the public sphere for his abandonment of the Prussian alliance that he resigned in early April 1763. The radical Whig MP and pamphleteer John Wilkes accused him of betraying British interests by 'deserting' Prussia and her 'magnanimous' King Frederick and concluding an 'ignominious' peace.[94] At the same time, the sheer scale of the triumph in 1763 unleashed a wave of national self-satisfaction. Victory was attributed to the superiority of British commerce and virtue. This hubris was soon reflected in the new direction of British foreign policy.

Of course, the accession of George III in 1760 and the triumphant end to the Seven Years War in 1763 did not change British strategic culture overnight. Statesmen continued to see Europe as their primary focus,[95] but they were now working within a context that was more stridently colonial and maritime than anything they had previously known. Unlike the first forty-odd years after 1714, they found themselves working with a monarch – George III – who was firmly opposed to the 'German War'; he sought to safeguard Hanover primarily through the structures of the Holy Roman Empire rather than European alliances. Moreover, British statesmen were themselves not immune from the naval exuberance that had accompanied victory in the Seven Years War; and they were less willing than an earlier generation to make concessions in support of a continental alliance. The habit of intervention in Europe receded.[96] In this new conception of the world, the colonial empire now loomed much larger.

Unilateral displays of naval muscle against France and Spain now became routine. In 1763, for example, a naval force was dispatched to intimidate the French over the Turks and Caicos Islands, near the

Bahamas, and the Spaniards in the Bay of Honduras. These measures were seductive because they offered gratification without commitment, but they also gave Britain an international reputation for arrogance. More particularly, the new 'naval' approach allowed London to reduce its diplomatic and military presence in Europe, especially the Holy Roman Empire, leaving her dangerously isolated.[97] Attempts to secure a continental alliance with Austria, Prussia or Russia in the late 1760s failed completely, not least because Britain was unwilling to promise St Petersburg support against the Turks, or indeed anybody else, in return for Russian help in Europe. To make matters worse, London was plagued by naval confrontations in the Mediterranean and South Atlantic. In 1768, France bought Corsica from Genoa, occupied the island and quickly suppressed a separatist insurgency under the leadership of the charismatic Pasquale Paoli. This was a severe blow to Britain's European position generally, and a direct threat to her bases in Minorca and Gibraltar. Taken entirely by surprise, London failed to react effectively.

It rapidly became apparent, moreover, that the triumphs of the Seven Years War had not banished the Bourbon spectre for good, quite the reverse. Instead of a largely commercial agglomeration of trading posts and colonies, Britain was now responsible for a sprawling territorial empire with a new and even more vulnerable perimeter line. It was threatened by Native American revolts, unrest in Ireland and India, and the revival of Bourbon power.[98] London now attempted to make the empire contribute more effectively to its own defence. In October 1763, the ministry issued a proclamation that there should be no settlement west of the Appalachians, beyond what came to be known as the 'proclamation line'.[99] This shortened the defence perimeter in North America and was a gesture towards Bourbon and Indian sensitivities. Around the same time, London brought in a Sugar Act, and then a Stamp Duty on property, to force the American settlers to pay for their own defence.[100] Both measures caused widespread outrage among the colonists, who resented any restrictions on their territorial expansion and any suggestion that they should be taxed into the bargain. The scene was set for a confrontation which would have profound implications for Britain's position in Europe.

4
There Goes the Neighbourhood. Britain and Europe in the Age of Revolution[1]

A more mischievous idea cannot exist than that any degree of wickedness, violence and oppression may prevail in a country, that the most abominable, murderous and exterminatory rebellions may rage in it, or the most atrocious and bloody tyranny may domineer, and that no neighbouring power can take cognizance of either or afford succour to the miserable sufferers.

– Edmund Burke to Lord Grenville,
Beaconsfield, 18 August 1792[2]

[T]he vicinage [neighbourhood] of Europe had not a right, but an indispensable duty, and an exigent interest, to denunciate this new work [the French Revolution] before it had produced the danger we have so sorely felt, and which we shall long feel.

– Edmund Burke, 'Thoughts on French Affairs', 1791

Britain won an empire in America in the first two thirds of the eighteenth century, but she soon nearly lost her role in Europe. Preoccupied by her overseas possessions and puffed up with pride after the glories of the Seven Years War, she allowed the continental balance to slide. Britain's alliances lapsed. The eastern powers rose unchecked. Poland was partitioned, threatening the security of the Holy Roman Empire. The Bourbon powers, France and Spain, plotted revenge. Then Britain's world was then rocked by two epic revolutions. First, the American colonists, scandalized by the global retreat of British power, revolted against the metropolis. The resulting war of independence drew in all the main European powers and resulted in the partition of the first British Empire. The loss of America was almost as traumatic as that of France three hundred years before. Britain's European recovery was unexpectedly swift, but it was soon challenged once more by Revolution in France. Both of these challenges are best examined through the eyes of Britain's most illustrious political thinker, the Irishman (and enthusiast for England) Edmund Burke. It was he who refined the Whig doctrine of European intervention into a general principle linking the security of Britain to not merely the geopolitical but also the ideological state of the European neighbourhood ('vicinage').

It has often been remarked that Edmund Burke was many things: Irishman, Briton, and a critical supporter of overseas empire but, above all, Burke was a *European*.[3] He invoked the solidarity of medieval Christendom in ways that would have seemed familiar to earlier generations of Englishmen.[4] By the end of the century, his principal preoccupation was the 'Commonwealth of Europe'.[5] It became the increasingly dominant theme in his 'Great Melody',[6] which began when Burke came of age as a political polemicist in the context of three successive perceived blows to European liberty and the balance of power. First, there was the French occupation of Corsica. France completed the purchase of the island from Genoa in May 1768, rapidly crushed the resistance of Corsican patriots under Pascale Paoli and, by mid-1769, was in full effective control of the island.[7] British public opinion was outraged, and James Boswell not only edited *British Essays in Favour of the Brave Corsicans* later that same year but also raised enough in subscriptions to buy thirty artillery pieces for Paoli.[8] Burke's initial response stressed the strategic implications for Britain.[9] Later, however, in his coruscating attack on the administration, in the 'Thoughts on the Present Discontents' (1770), Burke condemned 'the conquest of Corsica, by the professed enemies of the freedom of mankind, in defiance of those who were formerly its professed defenders'.[10] Then, in August 1772, King Gustavus of Sweden launched a French-backed coup against his parliament. Burke saw this as a threat to European and British freedoms more generally, which could be linked, more or less opportunistically, back to his own struggle against the allegedly despotic tendencies of George III. The following month he told one correspondent that he feared 'the Court may assume as uncontrolled a power in this country as the King of Sweden has done in his.'[11]

At around the same time, Russia, Austria and Prussia announced that the old Polish Commonwealth would be partitioned between them. The eastern powers justified their move at least in part as an intervention to curb Polish mistreatment of religious minorities such as Protestants and Orthodox Christians. To Burke, however, the Polish partition was an affront to European freedoms. He spoke of 'the utter subversion of almost all the remaining monuments of public liberty', which did 'violence to humanity and justice'. Burke also regarded the partition as 'the first very great breach in the modern political system of Europe'. The unprovoked dismemberment of a large European state by a coalition of predators seemed to create an ominous precedent for 'Europe as a vast commonwealth', an early use of this term by him. Here Burke was not simply enunciating a principle of abstract international law but rather a direct geopolitical threat to British security. He doubted that 'the insular situation of Great Britain weaken[ed] the application' of the principles of the balance of power as much as some claimed. Burke pointed out that no 'single state, in the present political and physical state of Europe could expect independence and safety, unconnected with all the others'.[12] In other words, the violence offered to 'liberty' and 'mankind' in Poland would eventually beat a path to England's door, because she was geopolitically part of the continent.

This was because the resulting territorial shifts had weakened the Holy Roman Empire and its barrier function, the neuralgic spot of traditional Whig strategic thinking. Hitherto, Burke argued, 'Poland was the natural barrier of Germany, as well as of the northern crowns, against the overwhelming power and ambition of Russia.' The partition now threatened 'totally to unhinge the ancient system of Germany and the north'. Poland might now be 'the road by which the Russians will enter Germany'. Moreover, Burke feared that the partitions would set off a chain reaction of other partitions or 'exchanges', for example between the Duke of Mecklenburg-Schwerin and Prussia.

This might 'prepare the way for a total change of system in Germany'. Besides, Burke continued, the failure of noble liberty in Poland cast a harsh light on the viability of princely freedoms in a Germany surrounded by an unforgiving international environment. 'That empire,' he wrote, 'seems to be in as precarious a situation as it has been at any time since its foundation. The equilibrium has been entirely overthrown.'[13] All this mattered, because the integrity of the German empire was the foundation upon which the security of the Low Countries, Britain's strategic Achilles heel, rested.

In short, the partition of Poland and the revolution in Sweden were not only devastating blows to European liberty *and* to the European balance: they were a threat to the balance *because* they were a threat to liberty, and vice versa. 'No equal portion of time,' Burke wrote, 'has been so fatal to public liberty, and the rights of mankind, as that which comprehends the overthrow of the constitution' in Sweden and Poland. Military action to reverse these coups, to restore the rights of mankind, he implied, would be fully justified. 'Wars may be deferred,' he wrote, 'but they cannot be wholly avoided; and to purchase present quiet, at the price of future security, is undoubtedly a cowardice of the most degrading and basest nature'.[14] In other words, the defence of liberty in Europe and the defence of the European balance were inextricably interconnected in Burke's mind well before the French Revolution, a connection which had already been made previously by generations of Englishmen and Britons.

Britain, however, did not intervene, either to support the Corsicans or to restore Swedish liberties, or to defend the integrity of Poland. In the latter case, there were practical obstacles to doing so: one could not simply, as one wag remarked, 'tow the fleet overland to Warsaw and restore the constitution'.[15] Nevertheless, the international turbulence of the late 1760s and 1770s led to the revival of interventionist sentiment in Britain. At one level, this was nothing new. The largely Protestant public sphere had long sympathized with and demanded intervention on behalf of embattled co-religionists. The emerging British humanitarian sensibility of the period took these discourses a step further, however. Prominent writers and parliamentarians such as James Boswell and Burke championed the cause of 'liberty' in Corsica and Poland in a way that transcended confessional allegiance.[16]

Many such interventions, of course, were recommended and carried out for self-interested motives. Indeed, the effective defence of minority rights *depended* on a synergy between sentiment and strategy; the two were not always easy to separate. Sympathy for the cause of 'liberty' in Corsica, for example, was part of a broader concern for British freedoms and the containment of France, on which these ultimately depended.

In 1775, the North American colonies revolted, partly in protest at the failure of the British state to deliver security in the New and Old Worlds, and partly in opposition to London attempts to make them pay for that security. For London, nothing less than the balance of power in Europe was at stake. Without America – so the consensus in London ran – Britain would be unable to face France and Spain on the near side of the Atlantic. The British secretary of state Lord Stormont feared that if the 'resources that [fed] and maintain[ed]' Britain's power 'in support of the general interest in Europe' were no longer available, the country would lose her 'weight in the general scale',[17] by which he meant the balance of power. Conversely, many European powers were convinced that if the British prevailed in America they would gain such an accretion of power as to become insufferable. Victory for the colonists, the French chief minister Vergennes observed in late 1775, would mean that '[t]he power of England will diminish and our power will increase to the same degree.'[18] France, long a covert supporter of the Americans, and cheered by the US victory at Saratoga in 1777, finally entered the war openly in 1778, followed by Spain in 1779. Britain was totally isolated. She narrowly escaped a joint Bourbon invasion. A year later, the Dutch were so maddened by Britain's naval high-handedness and general arrogance that they entered the lists, too. At around the same time, Catherine the Great, herself offended by the Royal Navy's treatment of non-belligerent shipping, founded the League of Armed Neutrality. Now Britain was, in the mortified expression of the head of the Admiralty, Lord Sandwich, practically 'at . . . war with the whole world . . . The powers united will dismember our state and make such partition among them as they see fit.'[19]

A substantial minority in Britain, including the elder Pitt and Edmund Burke, did not see things that way. They sympathized with the colonists and their Whiggish love of liberty and limited government. To be sure, these critics were anxious about the revival of Bourbon power, but they reproached the administration for bringing this about through the alienation of the Americans. They despaired at the effusion of English blood on both sides of the Atlantic. In Parliament, Pitt (now Lord Chatham) contrasted the patriotic virtue of the colonist with the unBritish absolutist pretensions of Lord North and George III, who had had to resort to foreign mercenaries in order to pursue the war against the American colonists. In late May 1777, he accused the government of 'ransack[ing] every corner of Lower Saxony; but 40 000 German boors never can conquer ten times that number of British freemen'. Soon after, he demanded that government should 'conciliate to gain the confidence of those who have survived the Indian tomahawk, and the German bayonet'.[20] His motivation was to rally Britons on both sides of the Atlantic against the common enemy in Europe.

In the face of these new naval, military and subversive challenges, the British state embarked on its most intense programme of mobilization so far. The reach of the state was extended. In the case of the army, the 1778 and 1779 Recruitment Acts permitted the conscription of healthy unemployed men and criminals. A 1779 Act increased forcible impressments into the navy. It brought into the armed forces not merely the usual aristocratic and deadbeat suspects at either end of the social spectrum but also many from middling and artisan backgrounds. The achievements of this unprecedented mobilization drive were impressive: the Royal Navy increased its number of ships of the line by 50 per cent over the three years from 1778 to 1780; the number of seamen jumped by more than half in the same period. The British government also began to think about ways of tapping the vast manpower potential of Catholic Ireland and overcoming the objections of the local Protestant Ascendancy to their recruitment.[21] But the colossal efforts of the nation and the stupendous performance of the 'fiscal-military' state did not suffice to turn the tide in America, or to uphold British naval supremacy when it was most needed. Britain's European isolation proved fatal. Undisturbed by a land war in Europe, the Bourbon powers out-built Britain at sea, as the Whigs had always feared they would. France not only gained temporary control of the waters around North America but also succeeded in putting a land force ashore to support Washington. In 1781, a joint Franco-American effort surrounded a large British force at Yorktown and forced it to surrender. In London, Lord North's government did not survive the blow for long. The new administration soon sued for peace.

The Treaty of Paris, which brought the American War to an end in 1783, marked a revolution in the international state system. Britain's empire was partitioned between France, Spain and the colonists. She was forced to recognize the thirteen colonies as independent states. Britain kept Gibraltar, but Florida and Minorca were surrendered to Spain, and France recovered Louisiana. France, in the triumphant words of Vergennes, had 'erased the stain of 1763'. Moreover, a new power had arisen in the western hemisphere, and far-sighted observers were already predicting that the imperial baton would soon pass from Britain to the United States. 'This little island [England],' Horace Walpole had remarked on hearing of the Declaration of Independence in 1776, 'will be ridiculously proud some ages hence of its former brave days, and swear its capital was once as big as Paris, or – what is to be the name of the city that will then give laws to Europe – perhaps New York or Philadelphia'. When one Frenchman predicted that the thirteen states would become 'the greatest empire in the world', a member of the British delegation in Paris shot back: 'Yes, sir, and they will all speak English, every one of 'em.'[22] So it eventually proved, vindicating the Whig argument that the American claim to liberty should not be resisted. The emergence of another 'British' state on the far side of the Atlantic ultimately increased the security of Great Britain.

Very quickly, the United States turned itself into a larger and stronger United Kingdom, with a view to defending its position among the European great powers. This was initially a matter of urgent self-defence. The withdrawal of British naval protection after the Revolution immediately exposed US merchant shipping to vicious attacks by the Barbary Corsairs operating out of North Africa. There were also numerous threats to the new republic closer to home. Spain had closed the Mississippi to navigation in 1784 and maintained a menacing presence in Florida to the south. Britain had held on to Canada and remained hostile. Unfortunately, the constitutional arrangements inherited from the Revolutionary War were completely unsuited to deal with the challenges of the 1780s. There was no real executive to speak of, Congress had no power to raise taxes to pay for national projects, and all international treaties had to be ratified by each and every one of the states before they came into force. Moreover, the costs of the War of Independence had left the individual states with huge debts. As a result, the United States lacked a proper army and navy, because the states could not agree on how it should be paid for and were fearful that it might be used to undermine their liberties. Indeed, so loose were the bonds which held the confederation together that many Americans feared the United States might fragment into its component parts, or even succumb to civil strife, arguing over the western territories. The choice was stark: either Americans moved closer together to create a state capable of waging war and conducting territorial expansion, or they would go to war against each other and eventually become victims of expansion by an outside power.[23]

It was for this reason that the representatives of the thirteen colonies came together at Philadelphia in 1787 in order to agree a constitution. They were immediately confronted by the question of which European union model they should follow. James Madison and Alexander Hamilton looked at the 'federal system' of the 'Germanic empire' and found it to be 'a nerveless body, incapable of regulating its own members, insecure against external dangers, and agitated with unceasing fermentations in its own bowels'. As for Poland, they argued that it was 'equally unfit for self-government and self-defence [and] has long been at the mercy of its powerful neighbours who have lately had the mercy to disburden it of one third of its people and territories'.[24] Of all the European precedents, the only one which found any favour among the Federalists was the Anglo-Scottish Union of 1707, by which the two parties, formerly so divided, had come together to 'resist all [their] enemies'.[25] The constitution agreed at Philadelphia in 1787–8 showed that Americans had learned from the British, German and Polish experiences. Like the Scots and English, they determined, as the preamble put it, to 'form a more perfect union'. A strong executive was established in the shape of a presidency empowered to conduct foreign policy and conclude treaties, which were subject, however, to ratification by the two Houses of Congress. Like the English and later the British, Americans had given themselves a domestic constitution which corresponded to the external needs of the state. In due course, this process created a uniquely powerful actor which was to come to Britain's aid in Europe on at least three occasions.

The American War produced a searching inquest into the cause of the disaster in Britain. It was clear that the 'free' polities of Poland, Sweden and the United Provinces were in terminal decline. The future seemed to lie with the central and eastern European autocracies, which had streamlined their societies for military mobilization and expansion. As the British under-secretary of state for war pointed out at the height of the war, 'the great military powers in the interior parts of Europe, who have amassed together their great treasures, and have modelled their subjects into great armies, will, in the next and succeeding period of time, become the predominant powers.'[26] If the British parliamentary system was to regain its capacity to punch above its weight in Europe, fundamental domestic reform would be needed, and perhaps also a change of strategy. The resulting transformations and learning curve showed both the exceptional capacity of the United Kingdom to recognize and correct error and the resilience of her institutions.

Defeat brought reform across the board. Many agreed that the path to recovery would involve fundamental domestic transformation. Some believed that spiritual and moral renewal would be enough. Others argued that a broadening of the franchise was necessary to mobilize all the national energies in support of the common cause. Many supported the idea of 'economical reform' to put the finances back in order. Meanwhile, a 'second' and geographically even more extensive empire was established, using the demographic reserve of American loyalists, some of them freed black slaves.[27] In 1788, the first settlers were put ashore in Australia, and new colonies were soon established or old ones developed in Africa, Asia and the Americas, especially Canada. The main task, however, was the rebuilding of Britain's European alliances. Structurally, this involved the amalgamation of the Southern and Northern Secretaryships of State into a single 'Foreign Office' in 1783, in the hope of producing a more coherent policy. Conceptually, it meant a reconsideration of the policy pursued after 1760. The Tory 'blue water' approach, with its contempt for European 'entanglements', was widely regarded as discredited. 'To recover our weight on the continent by judicious alliances,' the seasoned diplomat and MP Sir James Harris remarked in December 1783, 'is the general wish of every man the least acquainted with the interests of this country.'[28] Never again should Britain find herself isolated in Europe.

The United Kingdom recovered her European position much more quickly than anybody imagined. Pitt the Younger succeeded in getting the national debt under control. Ireland was conciliated, at least for the time being. In 1787, Britain and Prussia combined to see off a French attempt to subvert the House of Orange in the Dutch Republic. A year later, Britain was back in the diplomatic game in Europe with the conclusion of a Triple Alliance with Prussia and the Dutch. France, by contrast, had been so bankrupted by her military efforts during the century and so unsuccessful in defending her interests in central and eastern Europe, especially to advance Austrian and Russian power, that the monarchy was in terminal decline. In 1789, the country erupted in revolution, largely for the same reasons that had twice brought down the Stuart dynasty in England.

In London, the immediate impact was limited. There was general agreement only that the revolution had finally destroyed all French influence within the state system. 'I defy the ablest heads in England, to have planned, or its whole wealth to have purchased', the British foreign secretary the Duke of Leeds remarked shortly after the Bastille fell, 'a situation so fatal to its rival, as that to which France is now reduced by her own intestine commotions.'[29] Britain had, in fact, other matters on her mind. In May 1790, she was plunged into a confrontation with Spain over Nootka Sound on the west coast of Canada which brought the two powers to the verge of war. Above all, Britain looked with increasing alarm at the Russian advance in eastern Europe, fearing that Catherine the Great had 'conceived the project of securing the exclusive command of the Baltic', from which the Royal Navy still sourced vital masts, tar and hemp. London was also deeply concerned about Russian penetration of Poland, which, as one memorandum put it, 'would serve her for a road to invade at pleasure and disturb the peace of Europe'. As if all this were not bad enough, Britain feared, as the British envoy to Vienna put it, that the tsarina would 'seize some unlucky moment, when the rest of Europe was unable to assist [Turkey], and erect her standard in Constantinople', while Pitt himself fretted that Russia would use the Ottoman empire as a base from which to stake a 'rivalship with our interests in the East Indies'. When the Russians captured the strategically vital fortress of Ochakov on the northern shore of the Black Sea, London decided to act. The Cabinet agreed to take military measures in March 1791, but the enterprise foundered not only on the impracticality of using naval power to coerce Catherine but also on massive opposition from a Parliament and public sphere utterly unpersuaded of the case for war on the far side of Europe over a town few Britons had previously heard of.[30] So in 1789–91 it looked very likely that Britain would go to war not over France but either over North America or eastern Europe.

Within a short period, all this had changed. Britain might refuse to engage in Europe, but that did not mean that Europe would not engage with her. Austria and Prussia intervened to crush the Revolution in 1792 and received a bloody nose at the Battle of Valmy. The resurgent French forces poured into the Low Countries, threatening the south coast of England. After stern warnings from London, the French declared war on Britain and the Dutch Republic. Not long after, they burst into Holland and Germany, and then into Italy. Across Europe, established governments folded in the face of the onslaught. By the end of the decade, much of western and southern Europe was under direct French control or that of 'sister republics' affiliated to the Revolution. Britain still prevailed at sea and in the New World, but repeated attempts to regain the initiative in Europe through expeditionary forces or the support of rebellion inside France failed miserably. Worse still, there was every chance the French would not only take over the rest of the continent but would mount an assault on the home island itself.

The question of how to respond to this threat completely dominated British politics and policy in the 1790s. It tore the Whigs apart. Some, such as Charles James Fox, sympathized openly with the Revolution. A substantial number under the Duke of Portland, by contrast, were appalled by its violence and supported the war effort. Passions ran so high that Fox and his followers eventually seceded – for a while – from the House of Commons. Pitt profited from these divisions among the opposition, but he was damaged by his failure to uphold the European balance in the face of the French threat and, in particular, to keep the Revolutionaries out of the Low Countries. He was also plagued by two fundamental strategic disagreements within his own camp. The first reprised a long-standing debate in English and British geopolitics, which was whether the war against France should be waged primarily at sea, as the secretary at war Henry Dundas believed, or on the mainland of Europe, as the foreign secretary Lord Grenville argued. The second divide was a new version of an old theme, which was whether a deal could be reached with the Revolutionaries on the basis of mutual coexistence, as Pitt hoped, or whether, as another secretary at war, William Windham, contended, Revolutionary France posed such an ideological threat that only its destruction would guarantee Britain's security. These issues absorbed all those politically active in the United Kingdom and many who were not, but there was nobody more prominent in these debates than Edmund Burke.

Edmund Burke took from the Glorious Revolution of 1688 a Whiggish love of liberty and limited government, which found expression in his support for the American colonists.[31] He took from the Enlightenment a 'peculiar universalism', which was reflected in his concern for the rights of Indians in Bengal and his opposition to the slave trade.[32] During the trial of Warren Hastings, Burke pointedly condemned 'the geographical morality by which the duties of men in public and private situations are not to be governed by their relations to the Great Governor of the universe, or by their relations to men, but by climates . . . parallels not of life but of latitudes.'[33] Yet he was also temperamentally and in some ways ideologically conservative, in that he was sceptical of any grand schemes to make society anew in disregard of history and tradition. This put him almost immediately at odds with the French Revolution.[34] More important still to explaining Burke's passionate engagement in European affairs was his rootedness within the Whig interventionist tradition, which hinged on the assumption that Britain should not only actively defend European 'liberties' but that British liberties in turn had once been saved by outside intervention in 1688. 'An abstract principle of public law,' he later wrote, 'forbidding such interference, is not supported . . . by the practice of this kingdom, nor by that of any civilized nation in the world. This nation owes its laws and liberties, his Majesty owes the throne on which he sits, to the contrary principle.'[35]

Of course, Burke's idea of 'liberty' differed in many respects from modern conceptions of the term. It was explicitly opposed to 'democracy', at least in the Jacobin sense of the word. Though he was far from intolerant, Burke's fervent defence of 'religion' placed him at odds with the 'atheistical' French Revolutionaries. Moreover, his 'liberty', like that of other Europeans, was based on an unequal society of orders. That said, Burke's opposition to 'tyranny', his support for limited government, his passionate defence of property rights, his insistence on consensual taxation and other constitutional freedoms are recognizably modern. His concern for the rights of 'millions' of Indians, whom he wished to save from 'oppression and tyranny',[36] went well beyond a narrowly conservative defence of the caste system. More importantly for our purposes, Burke's conception of liberty and liberties profoundly shaped his approach to international affairs and the doctrine of intervention.

In the very early stages, Burke was ambivalent about the French Revolution, 'not knowing [in August 1789] whether to blame or applaud'.[37] Though he never shared the *Schadenfreude* with which many celebrated the apparent decline of French power in 1789, Burke did not at first completely reject the widespread belief that events in France were inspired by England's own Glorious Revolution of 1688.[38] Within a year, however, Burke had tilted decisively against the Revolution in his *Reflections on the Revolution in France* (1790).[39] The book was not merely a literary and political landmark but also a publishing sensation, selling well over seventeen thousand copies (with a much greater readership) and provoking about another hundred pamphlets in turn. Many hated the 'Reflections', and most admired its 'eloquence' rather than its content, but almost everybody read it.[40] Not since Israel Mauduit's *Considerations on the Present German War* in 1760, and before that Jonathan's Swift's *The Conduct of the Allies* in 1711, had the British public been engaged in such lively debate about a single work.[41]

Burke condemned the Revolution as an attack on tradition, religion, property and 'chivalry', 'a revolution in sentiments, manners and moral opinions'.[42] The insults offered to the French Royal family and especially Marie Antoinette, he argued, were really assaults on the institution of monarchy more generally. 'It appears to me as if I were in a great crisis,' Burke writes towards the beginning of the *Reflections*, 'not of the affairs of France alone but of all Europe, perhaps of more than Europe. All circumstances taken together, the French Revolution is the most astonishing that has hitherto happened in the world.' 'The age of chivalry is gone,' Burke later warned, 'That of sophisters, economists, and calculators has succeeded . . . ancient chivalry . . . which has given its character to modern Europe'.[43] What is striking about these passages is not just their prescience – all this was written well before the execution of the king and the outbreak of the Terror – but the way in which Burke defined the problem from the beginning not in narrowly French, or even British, but very much in European terms.

The explicitly ideological nature of Burke's hostility to Revolutionary France did not place him outside the traditional British balance of power discourse, however. It is true, of course, that his doctrines ran directly contrary to the prevailing view of William Pitt's administration.[44] It is also true that London was uneasy about the French émigrés whom Burke championed, partly because it entertained grave doubts as to their military value, but primarily because any commitments to them might get in the way of a compromise peace with Revolutionary France. Containing French power, in particular by restoring the integrity of the Low Countries, not reversing the Revolution, was Britain's war aim. All the same, Burke's response to the Revolution should be understood not as a simple repudiation of balance-of-power thinking – and thus of what we would today call 'realism' – but as a variation on it.

Burke believed that the Revolution posed a mortal threat to British liberty and security for three interconnected reasons. First, he feared the subversive example of the Revolution. In the *Reflections*, Burke pointed to the danger of Revolutionary ideas. 'France has always more or less influenced manners in England,' he wrote, 'and when your fountain is choked up and polluted, the stream will not run long, or will not run clear with us, or perhaps with any nation. This gives all Europe, in my opinion, but too close and connected a concern in what is done in France.' Burke therefore spoke of the 'rights of men' as a 'grand magazine of offensive weapons'. 'Formerly your affairs were your own concern only,' he wrote. 'We felt for them as men; but we kept aloof from them, because we were not citizens of France. But when we see the model held up to ourselves, we must feel as Englishmen, and feeling, we must provide as Englishmen.' The answer, he said, was to 'keep at a distance' the Revolutionary 'plague', against which 'the precautions of the most severe quarantine ought to be established'.[45] At this point, Burke was not yet making a plea for military intervention but rather for placing the Revolution in an ideological quarantine.

Soon after, however, Burke became convinced that containment was not enough. In the course of the following year, his 'Letter to a Member of the National Assembly' (1791) argued that only power 'from *without* [his italics]' would be sufficient to dislodge the Revolution. This, he continued, 'may be given . . . in pity; for surely no nation ever called so pathetically on the compassion of all its neighbours'.[46] In speaking of 'compassion', Burke was expressing a humanitarian obligation towards France. For although his objections to the Revolution ranged across 'religion', 'property' and 'chivalry', they could all be subsumed under the single heading of 'tyranny'. The Revolution, Burke argued, 'oppressed' the 'small reliques of the persecuted landed interest', the 'burghers' and the 'farmers . . . Two persons cannot meet and confer without hazard to their liberty . . . numbers scarcely credible have been executed, and their property confiscated.'[47]

Burke was clearly demonstrating a secular and universal concern for liberty. The Revolution's war on the domestic freedoms of Frenchmen grieved Burke as much as the (alleged) threats to British freedoms had in the 1770s, or the rights of Indians in the 1780s. He thought that 'all men who desire [Liberty] deserve it.' Far from seeing it as a geographically, historically or culturally contingent phenomenon, therefore, Burke regarded liberty as 'our inheritance, it is the birthright of our species.'[48] In early December 1794, Burke wrote that the re-establishment of order in France was not merely in the 'interest of this kingdom [Britain] but also of 'mankind in general' (*du genre humain en général*).[49] In the following year, he referred to the Revolution as 'the most infernal Tyranny and oppression that ever vexed or menaced the race of man'.[50] And the year after that, Burke wrote 'We cannot arrange with our enemy in the present conjuncture, without abandoning the interest of mankind.'[51] And here the context clearly shows that the words 'humanity' and 'mankind' are surely no mere appeal to sentimental moral principle but refer to values and rights which are the birthright of all (or most) men of property.

In such situations, Burke claimed, intervention was not only justifiable but imperative, because there was no other way of helping the victims. Right at the beginning of 1791, Burke wrote that he had 'no opinion at all of internal remedies . . . I cannot persuade myself that any thing whatsoever can be effected without great force from abroad.'[52] In his *Thoughts on French Affairs*, published later that year, he noted simply that 'no counter-revolution is to be expected in France from internal causes solely.'[53] He was therefore sympathetic to the arguments of French émigrés such as Pierre-Gaeton Dupont, who told Burke in May 1791 'that in cases where the oppression is so great that the oppressed cannot even ask for help, it is enough that there is public and unequivocal notoriety of this to require the intervention of a foreign power'.[54]

Burke brought together all these themes in his broadside 'Heads for Consideration on the Present State of Affairs' (1792). He rebuked the courts of Austria and Prussia for suggesting 'that they had nothing to do with the interior arrangements of France', and he did so in terms which suggested that Burke fully understood the latitude which the true spirit of Westphalia gave to the counter-revolutionary powers. 'In this particular,' Burke lamented, 'the two German courts seem to have as little consulted the publicists of Germany, as their own true interests, and those of all the Sovereigns of Germany and Europe.' Small wonder, then, that in the same document Burke dismissed the doctrine of non-intervention in the internal affairs of a sovereign state as 'a false principle in the Law of Nations'.[55]

What Burke was proposing was not mere benevolence, of course. 'Help,' he wrote, 'may be given by those neighbours on motives of safety to themselves. Never shall I think any country in Europe to be secure, whilst there is established, in the very centre of it, a state (if so it may be called) founded on principles of anarchy, and which is in reality, a college of armed fanatics, for the propagation of the principles of assassination, robbery, rebellion, fraud, faction, oppression and impiety.'[56] 'How could we possibly avoid war,' Burke asked Parliament in 1792, 'when France had denounced [*sic*] destruction against all the Kings of Europe. We were forced, on principle of self-defence, into a confederacy with all the sovereigns of Europe.'[57] Later, in 1796, Burke described the Revolution as 'an armed doctrine', a 'system, which, by its essence, is inimical to all other governments, and which makes peace or war, as peace or war may best contribute to their subversion'.[58] It therefore had to be confronted at both levels: that of 'compassion' as well as 'safety'.

The chief reason for this was that France was 'so powerful and so close'.[59] The very proximity – or 'vicinity',[60] as he put it – not merely of French power but of French ideas, 'a country but twenty-four miles from the shore of this island',[61] entitled Britain to move decisively against the source of the 'contagion'. Otherwise, he wrote, 'They who are to live in the vicinity of this new fabrick, are to prepare to live in perpetual conspiracies and seditions; and to end at last in being conquered, if not to her dominions, to her resemblance.'[62] Indeed, Burke warned of France creating 'an universal empire, by producing a universal revolution'; Britain faced 'a sect aiming at universal empire, and beginning with the conquest of France'.[63] At one level, 'vicinity' referred to the fact that France lay only a short distance away across the Channel. But Burke was also referring to a more general European 'neighbourhood', or the 'grand vicinage of Europe'. He claimed that, in Europe as a whole, no 'new erection' or 'nuisance' was permitted which 'may redound, even secondarily, to the prejudice of a neighbour'. For the Revolution 'violates the rights upon which not only the community of France, but those on which all communities are founded'.[64] And when Burke's critics argued that 'our insular situation . . . is proof against every innovation,' he responded that 'They talk as if England were not in Europe.'[65]

Burke argued that to 'abandon Austria' was to 'abandon Holland' and thus allow the French a staging post to attack Britain (1793). Burke condemned 'the direct, or indirect annexation to France of all the parts of the continent, from Dunkirk to Hamburg; and immense accretion of territory; and in one word, *THE ABANDONMENT OF THE INDEPENDENCE OF EUROPE* [emphasis in the original]'.[66] Burke, on the other hand, argued that all the West Indies could 'never amount in any fair estimation to a fair equivalent for Holland, for the Austrian Netherlands, for the lower Germany' and all the other parts of the continent 'now under the yoke of regicide'.[67] Indeed, in 1797, Burke – who constantly insisted that Britain, far from being an island, was part of Europe – described the emperor as not only an 'ally' but 'an integral part of the strength of Great Britain . . . and in a manner part of Great Britain itself'.[68] The connection between the United Kingdom and the continent could not have been more forcefully expressed.

For all these reasons, Burke claimed that French sovereignty needed to be set aside for the greater good. 'A positively vicious and abusive government,' he wrote even before the excesses of the Revolution had become clear, 'ought to be changed and, if necessary, by violence, if it cannot be (as it is sometimes the case) Reformed.'[69] After all, as we have seen, William of Orange had rescued English liberties in 1688. Burke therefore dismissed as 'mischievous' the idea 'that no neighbouring power can . . . afford succour to' a population subjected to 'the most abominable, murderous and exterminatory rebellions' and 'the most atrocious and bloody tyranny'.[70] Indeed, Burke argued that the Revolutionary regime had to be not merely contained, if necessary by intervention, but toppled. He was proposing what we would today call 'regime change'.[71] The right to intervene in the internal affairs of an independent state was conferred by neighbourhood: 'the vicinage itself is the natural judge. It is . . . the assertor of its own rights.' Moreover, Burke argued, the 'Law of Neighbourhood' permitted Britain and her allies to undertake pre-emptive action to 'anticipate . . . a damage justly apprehended but not actually done'. For this reason, he continued, 'the vicinage of Europe had not a right, but an indispensable duty, and an exigent interest, to denunciate this new work before it had produced the danger we have so sorely felt, and which we shall long feel.'[72]

This broader European 'vicinity' was crucial to Burke's interventionism, because it enabled him to resolve the tension between universal principles and practical limitations.[73] 'Men,' he said, 'are rarely without some sympathy in the sufferings of others.' However, Burke continued, 'in the immense and diversified mass of human misery, which may be pitied, but cannot be relieved, in the gross, the mind must make a choice.' This being so, he went on, 'our sympathy is always more forcibly attracted towards the misfortunes of certain persons, and in certain descriptions: and this sympathetic attraction discovers, beyond a possibility of mistake, our mental affinities, and elective affections.'[74] This choice would be made on two grounds: practicality and necessity. Thus, when challenged as to why he did not urge intervention against the second partition of Poland in 1793, Burke responded that 'let our opinions on that partition be what they will, England, by itself, is not in a situation to afford to Poland any assistance whatsoever.'[75] He swatted back objections that the terrible crimes of the Barbary corsairs were going unpunished with the following statement: 'Algiers is not near; Algiers is not powerful; Algiers is not our neighbour; Algiers is not infectious. When I find Algiers transferred to Calais, I will tell you what I think of that point.'[76] Confronting tyranny in France was thus no precedent for a crusade without end. The principles of liberty were universal, but Britain's ability to vindicate them was limited. Burke therefore thought that while Britain should speak up for freedoms wherever they were endangered, it should pay particular attention to threats close to home. Intervention was essential to extirpate Jacobinism and restore both religion and the social difference on which liberty rested. In practice, this meant that Britain should halt the abuses of the East India Company because it could, and those of the French Revolution because it had to.

Secondly, Burke saw the Revolution as a specific geopolitical threat to British interests in the Holy Roman Empire. He boasted an expert knowledge on the imperial constitution, which he paraded throughout the 1790s.[77] Burke argued that, whereas the *ancien régime* had been the 'author and natural support of the treaty of Westphalia', 'the natural guardian of the independence and balance of Germany', the new ideas were 'utterly irreconcilable with' the German imperial constitution. 'The treaty of Westphalia,' he wrote, 'is, with France, an antiquated fable.' Not, as one might imagine because it had broken with traditional notions of state sovereignty, but because '[t]he rights and liberties [France] was bound to maintain [in the Holy Roman Empire] are now a system of wrong and tyranny which she is bound to destroy.'[78] Right at the top of the demonology of the Revolutionaries were the petty German princes, who sheltered the hated émigrés in their residences just beyond the Rhine (particularly, in Koblenz), and the despised imperial constitution, which stood between the Revolutionaries and the realization of their ideological and strategic goals.[79] The *liberté* of 1789 clashed with German liberties, and in so doing infringed the 'Liberties of Europe', the balance of power on the continent, upon which British freedoms depended.

Burke believed this mattered because 'all the politics of Europe for more than two centuries' had shown 'the independence and the equilibrium of the empire to be . . . the very essence of the system of balanced power in Europe, and the scheme of public law, or mass of laws, upon which that independence and equilibrium are founded'.[80] Echoing the ambivalence of an earlier generation of Whigs, Burke thought that the equilibrium was jeopardized by events in France in a double sense. French weakness would lead to a partition of Germany between Austria and Prussia: 'it is through her alone that the common liberty of Germany can be secured against the single or the combined ambition of any other power.'[81] At the same time, French subversion threatened 'to throw the empire into confusion'. Worse still, the French were known to 'hold out from time to time the idea of uniting all the other provinces of which Gaul was anciently composed, including Savoy on the other side, and on this side bounding themselves by the Rhine'.[82] For all these reasons, Burke predicted that it would, 'on the side of the ecclesiastical electorates [in western Germany] that the dykes, raised to support the German liberty will [first] give way'.[83]

If that happened, the barrier system in the Low Countries would be in jeopardy. This, Burke knew, was the rampart of British liberties, 'those outworks, which ever till now we so strenuously maintained, as the strong frontier of our own dignity and safety, no less than the liberties of Europe'.[84] Their loss would 'cut off all political communication between England and the continent'.[85] 'Holland,' he told the House of Commons in 1791, 'might justly be considered as necessary [a] part of this country as Kent.'[86] Later, he wrote that the

German emperor – to whom the defence of the Austrian Netherlands fell – was 'an integrant [*sic*] part of the strength of Great Britain, and in manner part of Great Britain itself'.[87] So France was in Burke's sights as a threat to the barrier as early as December 1791, long before French Revolutionary armies had entered the Low Countries in 1793.[88] All this, of course, was classic Whig geopolitics stretching back to the Glorious Revolution, and further: the crucial role of the Low Countries; the consequent centrality of the Holy Roman 'Empire' and 'the common liberty of Germany'; the interplay of 'safety' and solidarity or 'compassion'; the language of 'dykes', 'balanced power' and 'equilibrium'.[89] The ideological and the strategic here cannot be usefully separated.

To conclude, Burke's interventionist doctrine was no new departure but an elaboration of traditional Whig thinking about British liberty, German freedoms, the liberties of Europe and the reciprocal right of intervention in the internal affairs of another state within the European 'neighbourhood'. That said, Burke carried the concept of intervention a whole stage further, and put it on a firm intellectual footing. European notions of what or who deserved protection had already evolved from a narrow confessional solidarity to embrace (some of) those suffering arbitrary rule; now Burke had brought the much broader category of 'humanity' into play. There was also a powerful strategic imperative behind all this. The elimination of the Revolution, was vital to the preservation of the German balance, and thus of the whole European equilibrium and was not just essential to safeguard British security, but necessary for the protection of the universal rights of all 'humanity', without which the survival of individual members of the European Commonwealth would be meaningless.

5
'The great bank of Europe'. Britain and the Continent in the Age of Napoleon[1]

I see various and opposite qualities – all the great and the little passions unfavourable to public tranquillity – united in the breast of one man [Napoleon], unhappily whose personal caprice can scarce fluctuate for one hour without affecting the destiny of Europe.

– William Pitt, *c.* 1804[2]

Our interest is that till there can be a final settlement that shall last, every thing should remain as unsettled as possible: that no usurper should feel sure of acknowledgement; no people confident of their new masters; no kingdom sure of its existence; no spoliator secure of his spoil; and even the plundered not acquiescent in their losses.

– George Canning, 1807[3]

The United Kingdom failed to get to grips with the French Revolution and for a long time it struggled to defeat the subsequent Napoleonic regime. Time and again, Britain sent an army to Europe, subsidized European coalitions or backed rebel movements; and, time and again, her hopes of breaking French hegemony were dashed. It seemed possible that Napoleon would parlay his vast continental European resources into naval strength and colonial ambition. On several occasions, the British Isles themselves were threatened. There were times when the ideologically and strategically objectionable new order on the continent appeared there to stay. Despite this, London and the nation never really faltered. Once the threat of invasion had been seen off, Prime Minister William Pitt memorably pronounced that 'England had saved itself by her efforts' and hoped that she might save 'Europe by her example', and so it proved, eventually. Sustained by generations of engagement with the continent, more convinced than ever that her security depended on the balance of power there, drawing on the immense commercial strength and creditworthiness of the fiscal-military state, relying on the resilience of their political institutions, Britons stayed the course and eventually prevailed at the head of a mighty coalition of European powers.

Some seventy-five years ago, when the British faced an overwhelming continental adversary across the straits of Dover in the summer of 1940, it seemed natural to turn for inspiration to the great struggle with Napoleon one hundred and fifty years earlier. Already in 1938, the refugee Paul Frischauer had published *England's Years of Danger. A New History of the World War 1792–1815*, dramatizing the events with obvious presentist intent.[4] In 1943, Carola Oman penned *Britain against Napoleon.*[5] Across the ocean, Frank J. Klingberg and Sigurd B. Hustvedt published *The Warning Drum*, a collected edition of British popular broadsides against the 'totalitarian' Napoleonic invasion scare of 1803.[6] Even Arthur Bryant, once susceptible to more modern Bonapartist sirens, contributed *The Years of Endurance 1793–1802*, in which he suggested one might find 'many of the familiar phenomena of our own troubled time', and *Years of Victory 1802–1812*, works which were to establish his patriotic credentials beyond all peradventure.[7] But these publications were only part of a long and continuing British preoccupation with Napoleon. For more than a hundred years after his death, he enjoyed the honour of being the subject of more English-language studies than any other leader, British or European. Nor has this interest shown much sign of abating: there have been thousands of books in English – to say nothing of articles – published in the past thirty-five years, most recently Andrew Roberts's epic, and surprisingly positive, biography.[8]

The contest between Britain and Napoleon has been seen as a struggle between universal monarchy and the balance of power, between Carthage and Rome,[9] Parliament and Empire, Latin and Anglo-Saxon, between revolutionary upheaval and evolutionary change, hegemonic

European integration and national particularism and between empiricism and rationality, Behemoth and Leviathan, land and sea,[10] tiger and shark.[11] It was, as the London *Times* put it, 'a war of system against system'. Its start and end dates are disputed. Did it begin with the siege of Toulon in 1793, when the young Napoleon Bonaparte sustained a life-threatening wound in the thigh from a British soldier while commanding the besieging revolutionary forces? Or in 1797, when Napoleon was given command of the 'Army of England' but attacked Egypt instead. Or in 1799, when Napoleon became First Consul? Or even in 1803, when an isolated Britain faced the renewal of hostilities with France? Did it end with exile to St Helena in 1815? Or in 1821, when his death brought a long cold war with his jailor, Sir Hudson Lowe, to a close?

The United Kingdom was not the first power to take on Revolutionary France – the Austrians and Prussians beat her to it by about nine months – but she was engaged in a more or less continuous struggle against French domination for about twenty years. The second half of this period, the contest against Napoleon, saw Britain emerge as the leading coalition power and sometimes the only power fighting France. She was at peace for only two brief periods, in 1802–3 and again in 1814–15. For much of this time, Napoleon was advancing relentlessly, starting with his triumphal procession through Italy in the 1790s and continuing with victories in Germany in the early 1800s during the War of the Second Coalition. In the War of the Third Coalition, he forced Austria to submit, drove off the Russians and, shortly after, crushed Prussia. Another Austrian attempt to escape his domination was beaten down in 1809. By then, Napoleon had crowned himself 'emperor', and Britain noted with anxiety that he named two of his battleships *Charlemagne* and *Louis XIV*, after two iconic continental hegemons. His ambition to appropriate the legacy of the Holy Roman Empire was also underlined by his insistence in taking an Austrian princess as his second wife. 'I wished to found a European system,' Napoleon famously said, which would include 'a European code of laws, a European judiciary: there would be but one people in Europe.'[12] At the height of his power, Bonaparte controlled most of the continent, from the Atlantic to the Russian border, from the Baltic to the heel of the Italian boot. The 'universal monarchy' Britons had feared for so long appeared to have arrived.

Napoleon was obsessed by Britain and her part in his downfall.[13] Already as a schoolboy he had studied and made copious notes upon large sections of English history before William III;[14] this selection, it will be noted, skipped the salutary lesson of Louis XIV's contest with Britain. Napoleon was later to regret his failure to invade England – perhaps via Ireland – in 1797–8. On St Helena, he claimed that he would have captured London within four days of a landing and arrived as 'a liberator, a second William III, but more disinterested and generous than he'.[15] Yet such benevolent fantasies were generally crowded out by much harsher sentiments. In 1799, Napoleon described the 'English' – for a Corsican, his sense of the nuances of British identity was deplorably weak – as 'spirited, intriguing and active'. 'Our government,' he continued, 'must destroy the English monarchy or must expect to be destroyed by the corruption and intrigues of these active Islanders'; here Napoleon was echoing a widespread continental European stereotype of Britain. During the Third Coalition of 1805, he attacked the 'league which the hatred and gold of England has woven', and spoke of '[t]his Russian army which English gold has transported from the extremities of the universe'. The Russians – who boasted a much more formidable and proximate army than anything Britain ever fielded on land – were simply the 'hired servants of England'.[16] Throughout the contest his state-controlled propaganda machine, including his servile, clerical *Journal des Curés*, poured fire and brimstone on Britain, an early example perhaps of the *Gott strafe England* theme.[17] By 1808, he was calling the United Kingdom 'the enemy of the world'.[18] On St Helena, Napoleon claimed that '[w]ith my France, England should naturally have finished by being nothing more than an appendix. Nature had made her one of our islands as much as those of Oleron or of Corsica.'[19] Some island, some appendix!

British politicians – unsurprisingly – were a particular target. William Pitt the Younger, prime minister until 1801 and again from 1804 to 1806, was characterized as a 'real scourge, an evil genius', who 'set fire to the universe, and whose name will go down in history much as that of Erostratus has done amid flames, lamentations and tears'. Lord Castlereagh, minister for war and foreign secretary in a number of wartime administrations, was a man who 'raised all kinds of turpitudes and immoralities to their highest pitch'.[20] Retrospectively, Napoleon was to describe 'England' as 'the agent of victory, the linch-pin around which all the intrigues of the continent had formed'.[21] The catchphrase 'perfidious Albion' was first used – in its compound form – in a Napoleonic propaganda ditty in 1809. In 1813, after the defection of the Prussian General Yorck von Wartenburg, Napoleon's Proclamation of Alost interpreted his treason as 'an action which only the intrigues and the corrupting gold of perfidious Albion could have woven'.[22] Yet he had never been to Britain and spoke no English.

The British were equally fascinated. Pitt, his great adversary during the first half of the contest, famously saw 'various and opposite qualities – all the great and all the little passions unfavourable to public tranquillity – united in the breast of one man, unhappily, whose personal caprice can scarce fluctuate for an hour without affecting the destiny of Europe'.[23] Nor was this an elite preoccupation. Popular ballads and broadsides showered Napoleon with abuse and vied with each other in demonstrative patriotism. In the caricatures of Gillray, Cruickshank and many lesser talents, the emperor was mercilessly lampooned, as if the existential threat he represented could be somehow diluted by ridicule. More mundanely still, mothers and nannies the length and breadth of Britain would cajole recalcitrant children to eat or sleep with threats of 'Boney'.

A small but vocal minority – mainly the literary avant-garde and Whig radicals – sympathized with Napoleon.[24] This was part of the long affair between British radicals and foreign tyrants, preferably remote ones. For many long-standing critics of the Crown, and Pitt's administration, the Napoleonic threat was a useful device to batter George III and his ministers. As Charles James Fox observed to his political ally Charles Grey in 1801, 'The triumph of the French government over the English does in fact afford me a degree of pleasure which it is very difficult for me to disguise'.[25] In 1802, he famously acclaimed Napoleon the victor of the Peace of Amiens, and suggested darkly that the English had already disposed of one king and elected another. For most 'Napoleonists', perhaps, it was a matter of striking poses, some of them contradictory. A whig radical like Lord Holland, for example, managed to be an enthusiast both for Napoleon and the popular Spanish crusade against him.

The notion that the clash between Britain and France was a quintessential struggle between the sea and the dry land, between the imperial metropolis and a nest of corsairs, went back to the Revolutionary 1790s, and indeed to the *ancien régime*. Well before the advent of Napoleon, Britain was seen as the chief impediment to the imperial project of Jacobin rationalist expansionism. The first president of the French Committee for Public Safety, Georges Danton, urged the capture of the Netherlands with the words 'Take Holland and Carthage [Britain] is ours.' The Prussian Jacobin Anarcharsis Clootz, visiting Paris, claimed that '[t]he mouth of the Rhine is essential to our well-being. It is in Holland that we shall destroy Carthage.'[26] But it was under Napoleon that the clash between French predominance on land and British control of the seas took on its distinctive character. After the news of the total destruction of his navy by Admiral Nelson at Aboukir off the Egyptian coast in 1798, Napoleon observed that '[o]n this occasion, as so often in the past, the fates seem to have decided to prove to us that, if they have granted us hegemony on land, they have made our rivals rulers of the seas.'[27]

This frustration – even resignation – in the face of British naval superiority was reflected in Napoleon's recourse to an old Bourbon gambit, which had been abandoned after 1763. This was to attack the Electorate of Hanover, the German patrimony of the English monarch George III.[28] Whereas the revolutionary regimes had generally ignored the link – once a staple of eighteenth-century international constellations – Napoleon struck at least three times at what he believed to be Britain's weakest spot: in 1801, when he forced the Prussians to occupy the electorate as part of their obligations under the Armed Neutrality; in 1803, as a direct reprisal for the resumptions of hostility with Britain; and in 1806, when he made Hanover an object of the peace negotiations that year. As he observed wistfully in 1803, when he reigned supreme over much of the continent, 'The English dominate the seas, are at this moment the premier power of Europe . . . Before the fate of Europe is decided by the success or failure of an invasion of England, all I am left with is the territory of

Hanover.'[29] Possession of this territory brought him no more joy than it had his Bourbon predecessors.

Napoleon's resigned acceptance of British naval predominance might have been mistaken. After all, the combined tonnage of the French, Russian, Dutch, Danish and Spanish navies just about matched that of Britain in 1800; and it is not the case that the victory at Trafalgar in 1805 established British superiority beyond peradventure and banished the threat of invasion for good.[30] In fact, a substantial French fleet was maintained to the very end, and the last years of the war saw a sustained attempt to build a new naval base at Antwerp, right on the Royal Navy's doorstep. Lord Melville, the First Lord of the Admiralty, later admitted that, in time, Napoleon could have 'sent forth such powerful fleets that our navy must eventually have been destroyed, since we could never have kept pace with him in building ships nor equipped numbers sufficient to cope with the tremendous power he could have brought against us'.[31] Nevertheless, it is true that by 1810, when French control over the continent was at its height, British naval power was never stronger. In that year, the total British tonnage in large ships was a good one third greater than that of all her potential European adversaries put together.[32] After 1806, in fact, the British lost more ships to inclement weather than enemy action.[33]

The only way that Napoleon could hope to break Britain was through commercial warfare, partly on the high seas but particularly through the Continental System. The Berlin Decrees of November 1806 – issued after the Prussian defeats at Jena and Auerstedt – sought to exclude all British trade and thus starve her manufacturers of outlets. Napoleon's plan was to destroy Britain's export and re-export trade, reduce her revenue and thus undermine both her war-fighting capacity and her ability to fund continental coalitions. His aim, as he put it, was to 'conquer the sea by mastery of the land'.[34] It did not work: British trade with the Americas flourished, while smuggling and corruption kept avenues to the continent open. As Louis Napoleon, Bonaparte's long-suffering brother and king of Holland observed, one might as well try to prevent the skin from sweating as to try to stop continental trade with Britain.[35] The British response, on the other hand, was devastating. The Orders in Council of 1806 drastically reduced neutral trade with France and French-occupied Europe.

Indeed, throughout the war the British stuck to their punitive maritime code, even at the risk of alienating European allies and undermining peace efforts. So vital was this question that Britain even fought a war with the United States over it in 1812–14 at a time when she had her hands full elsewhere. As the foreign secretary Lord Castlereagh remarked to a colleague in December 1813, 'You know how acutely we feel upon all political subjects when our feelings have been long excited by animating events, but that, at all times, a maritime question touches us to the quick.'[36]

This British concern with naval security and predominance brought with it its own neuroses, ambitions and enmities. One by one, the colonies not merely of France but her (semi-voluntary) allies fell into British hands; by 1811, the French had lost, for the first time ever throughout the second Hundred Years War with Britain, all of her overseas possessions to the Royal Navy. Indeed, the clash between French pretensions to universal monarchy in Europe and British hegemony overseas explains the ambivalence with which other European states regarded the whole contest. They tended to equate the two – at least rhetorically – and at times they formed a common front with Napoleon against Britain. The Armed Neutrality of 1800–1801, which united Denmark, Sweden, Russia and Prussia in defiance of the British maritime code was the most extreme example of this. But some such combination, in various permutations, was a latent threat throughout the period. It underlay a series of pre-emptive attacks on European powers in order to prevent the feared imminent capture of their navies by France. The Danes were subjected to this indignity twice, in 1801 and 1807; on the second occasion more than two thousand innocent civilians were killed in Copenhagen. The Spaniards had to put up with the pre-emptive seizure of their treasure fleet in 1804. Indeed, it is a curious fact that during the Napoleonic period Britain – supposedly fighting for the defence of European liberties against French hegemony – actually found herself at war with almost all the major and many middling powers of Europe at some point before 1815. War was declared, and in many cases waged, against Russia, Prussia, Spain, Sweden, Denmark and Holland; the big exception was Austria.

The resulting sense of British isolation was summed up by one

Commander Inglis, who received news of the Armed Neutrality and the first attack on Copenhagen on his way to Egypt in 1801. 'I think we must have peace now,' he observed. 'We cannot fight the world.'[37] The idea that it was Britain, rather than Napoleon, which stood against the world had a wide currency and was encouraged by Napoleonic propaganda.[38] But even Friedrich von Gentz, a committed political Anglophile and critic of French power, wrote in 1800 that '[t]he dominant principle of all the political theorists and writers at the present moment is jealousy of British power.' Similarly, in 1807, after the second British attack on Copenhagen, William Augustus Miles, a former British diplomat, claimed that '[o]ur court must have been very badly informed of the tempers and feelings of the continent towards us if it has yet to learn that we are everywhere detested.'[39] Even amongst the Spaniards after 1808, and the French royalist émigrés, traditional suspicions of England persisted.

Much of this hostility stemmed from British colonial ambitions, her arrogant application of the maritime code and her high-handed destruction of potentially rival navies. But that was not all. European opinion and Cabinets were also deeply suspicious of the British aim of maintaining a balance of power on the continent, to which end they were believed to be willing to sacrifice the last Austrian, Prussian and Russian, while the Royal Navy swept up French colonies – and those of everyone else. By 1800, it is true, British colonial gains were and looked impressive: Tobago, St Pierre and Miquelon and Pondicherry in 1793; Martinique, St Lucia and Guadeloupe in 1794; Ceylon and the Cape of Good Hope in 1795; Trinidad in 1797; Minorca in 1798; Surinam in 1800; with more to come. After the prolonged haggling over subsidies in the 1790s and early 1800s, European powers were receptive to French propaganda about 'English gold'.[40] On three successive occasions, it appeared, Britain had inveigled the powers into precarious coalitions, risking very few of her own resources on the mainland, only to abandon her allies for colonial gains when the going got rough: in the First Coalition of the 1790s, in the Second Coalition of 1798–1800, and in the Third Coalition of 1804–5.

At first sight, this reserve seems justified. There was indeed a view within the British Cabinet, and particularly the political nation at large, that the war against Napoleonic France should be waged by maritime means for imperial ends. The classic exponent of this 'blue water' strategy, which had its roots in the great debates of colonialists versus continentalists in the eighteenth century, was Pitt's long-standing secretary for war Henry Dundas (later Viscount Melville). He formally set out his strategy in a famous series of memoranda penned in March and July 1800. Instead of fighting the enemy in Europe itself, a policy 'calculated beyond our means', Dundas demanded a new focus on expansion overseas, particularly the commercial penetration of South America, now only tenuously controlled by weak French-dominated Spain.[41] Instead of being hurled against the continent in futile sorties, the Royal Navy and the land-striking forces should be deployed against the enemy's commerce and colonial possessions. After 1806, with the collapse of the Third Coalition, the defeat of Prussia and the Franco-Russian rapprochement, the 'blue water' strategy appeared to gain wider currency as a cheap, profitable alternative to ruinous subsidies and land warfare.

Despite appearances, however, the continentalist orthodoxy with which Britain had entered the war was never displaced. In 1794, William Pitt had stated that '[t]his country had never so successfully combated [France] as when its maritime strength had been aided by the judicious application of a land force on the continent.'[42] Just over ten years later, Pitt still refused to be distracted by maritime chimeras when he expressed his 'resolve at this stage to husband all available strength for a potential contribution to a decisive result in Europe'.[43] Whenever Pitt pursued a 'blue water' strategy, it was out of necessity, not choice; and, with the disastrous exception of the Ministry of All the Talents in 1806–7, it was no different with his successors.[44] British strategists could see that for every continental fiasco – such as the expedition to Holland, the expedition to northern Germany in 1805–6 and the Walcheren catastrophe of 1809 – there was a matching quagmire overseas, be it the pestilential Spice Islands, which did for more British troops in the 1790s than the French, or the spectacular failure in South America in 1806–7.

There was, however, a discernible change of emphasis in British strategy after 1806–7. This was most – and untypically – evident during the Ministry of All the Talents, perhaps the only time throughout the Napoleonic period when a genuinely 'blue water' strategy was followed. The populist commitment to overseas expansion at the expense of continental expeditions and subsidies reflected not merely bitter recent experience but also financial parsimony and a deep-seated suspicion of the other European powers. As the Cabinet somewhat primly told the Austrians in 1807, 'If the great powers now at war, or threatened by France, cannot find in themselves the means of such exertion, it is vain to expect that this country, by any supplies which we could afford, would be able effectually to support them.'[45] Indeed, the secretary of state for war William Windham asked mournfully whether 'we [were] to be merely the great bank of Europe, on which the different nations of Europe should be empowered to draw on in defence of their own existence? Was not the result likely to be that they would make no spontaneous exertions?' This blend of resignation and strategic providentialism was summed up by the *Morning Chronicle* in October 1806, when it wrote that the continent must be left in Napoleon's hands 'till his domination, aided by more favourable circumstances, shall excite a general effort of resistance, and work its own deliverance'.[46]

The unhappy interlude of the Ministry of All the Talents gave way to a return to the Pittite orthodoxy, albeit with a more cautious approach to continental commitments. The traditional rhetoric of European powers was now turned back on them: instead of taking the initiative in building coalitions against Napoleon, London sought to avoid giving the French pretexts for further expansion, insisting that the Austrians, Russians and others go to war for their own ends and not at the pretended behest of Britain. Nevertheless, the underlying aim of defeating Napoleon through direct or subsidised action on the continent remained unchanged. This was summed up by George Canning – one of Pitt's most forthright heirs in foreign policy. Far from accepting a new order in which British maritime supremacy matched that of France on dry land, Canning announced in October 1807 that until 'there can be a final settlement that shall last, every thing should remain as unsettled as possible'. No usurper should assume that his spoils were safe and no oppressed peoples should accept their new masters. All bets, on other words, should be off until the final round. Nothing would be settled until everything was settled – to Britain's satisfaction.[47] Indeed, Canning explained a year later, 'We shall proceed from the principle, that any nation of Europe that starts up with a determination to oppose . . . the common enemy of all nations . . . becomes instantly our essential ally.'[48] Nearly fifteen years into a bloody and expensive war, and with no end in sight, Britain was signalling its determination to fight on until the European balance had been restored.

The primacy of Europe in British strategy throughout most of the Napoleonic period was to be demonstrated again and again. Whenever the opportunity presented itself, Britain engaged the French on land: in 1799 in Holland; in north Germany in 1805–6; in Walcheren in 1809; in the Peninsula after 1808; and, of course, in the Low Countries in 1815. The largest British expedition ever mounted thus far – forty thousand men and six hundred vessels – was sent to Walcheren and not on some imperial venture.[49] Only two major operations were mounted against colonial targets, those to the Cape of Good Hope in 1805 and South America in 1806–7; the latter, it should be added, was simply an opportunist exploitation of an unauthorized initiative by Sir Home Popham which ended in tears. It was no doubt to avoid such perils that Richard Wellesley in India was given strict instructions to undertake no further expansion and incur no new expenditures. Similarly, the powerful British presence in the Mediterranean, which had been confined to Gibraltar at the beginning of the period, did not correspond to any masterplan but resulted from cumulative strategic ad hocery: Malta was secured to keep the French out, Sicily was occupied to protect and feed Malta, and much the same reasoning lay behind the presence in the Ionian Islands. Moreover, the great wave of colonial successes between 1808 and 1811 was not the result of a new strategy or fresh resources sent from London. Rather, these gains were effected by local garrisons in response to immediate threats and opportunities. Insofar as these were endorsed or prompted by London, the aim was to release ships to confront Napoleon in Europe, particularly his nascent fleet at Antwerp. For the most part, in fact, London saw colonial possessions as pawns with which to re-establish the European balance of power. For example, the Cape of Good Hope was, temporarily, restored to the Dutch in 1802, much in the same way as Britain had returned colonial gains in earlier conflicts in order to uphold the European balance.

This great contest was not simply a *Weltanschauungskrieg*, a clash of irreconcilable ideologies and political systems, though it sometimes had that character. Even in the 1790s, when French Revolutionary fervour had been at its height and the threat of domestic subversion the greatest, Britain had been more preoccupied with the fate of Flanders than with the internal government of France. Pitt, for one, denied any 'intention to wage war against opinion'.[50] The advent of Napoleon somewhat eased the ideological tension, at least initially. Some, such as Dundas, thought – in effect – that the resulting domestic stability would enable Paris to 'cut a deal' on the basis of British maritime and French continental supremacy.[51] Those like William Wickham and William Windham, who saw the conflict as an ideological crusade, were a minority. The British government never officially recognized the Comte de Provence as king of France after the execution of Louis XVI, and the restoration of the Bourbon *status quo ante* was never a war aim. At first, there was no hesitation in using royalist and other subversives to sap French power, but even this gambit was little used after 1803, largely because each rising proved more disastrous than the last, a fruitless drain on British resources which tended simply to strengthen Napoleon's domestic position. Castlereagh, then minister for war, told the agent of Louis XVIII in 1807 that it was not consistent either with British or royalist interests 'to give any encouragement whatever to insurrectional movement'.[52] If Britain was unable to reach lasting agreement with Napoleon, this had nothing to do with any social distaste for the 'usurper' and everything to do with his general unreliability and the lack of any obvious limits to his ambition.

Britain's aims were simple and did not change throughout the contest: to restore the broader European balance, in particular to prevent the Low Countries from falling under French domination. She had entered the war in 1793 not to destroy the Revolution but to keep the French out of Flanders. Even during the Second and Third coalitions, restoring the Bourbons was not a declared aim of Pitt's, whereas the independence of the Low Countries and the creation of a credible barrier to French ambitions certainly was. As late as 1813, the British negotiator Lord Harrowby averred that 'Antwerp and Flushing out of the hands of France are worth twenty Martiniques in our own hands.'[53]

To this end, Britain was prepared time and again to re-enter the lists against Napoleon and to forgo maritime gains, if necessary. Napoleon's aims with regard to England, on the other hand, were less clear cut, more modest and at the same time more grandiose. For Britain – despite the contemporary fears and subsequent fond imaginings of the British themselves and the dictator's own later remarks – was rarely Napoleon's first priority. He had inherited the struggle with Britain from the revolutionary governments, and his medium- to short-term focus rested firmly on his relations with the European great powers. Unlike Vergennes after 1763, Napoleon never committed the bulk of French resources to winning the naval and colonial struggle with Britain overseas.[54] The not inconsiderable navy he assembled in 1805, and again from 1809, was in addition to, not in place of, the Grande Armée and Grande Empire, with which it always had to compete for resources.

At one level, of course, Napoleon had global ambitions which clashed with those of Britain. These were manifested in his famous attack on Egypt in 1798, the projected joint Russo-French attack on India via Persia in 1801, and the less well-known plans for a Persian gambit in 1807, when Napoleon's negotiations with a delegation from the Shah in a remote Pomeranian hunting lodge of Finkenstein was followed by the dispatch of an advance party under General Gardane to Tehran.[55] In fact, in the first fifteen years of the war the largest amphibious operations were launched by France: Hoche unsuccessfully to Ireland with fifteen thousand men in 1796 and the expedition to Egypt in 1798, with three hundred vessels and forty thousand men, a veritable Corps d'Afrique. Even as late as 1809, a French officer was captured as far afield as Sumatra in the Dutch East Indies – now Indonesia – and spoke of a planned descent of French frigates on the area.[56] Yet all this was less part of some imperial grand design than an attempt to carry the struggle to Britain in a more effective manner. The attack on Egypt was supposed to presage an assault on India and thus a hammer-blow against British power. So far as we know from his statements, Napoleon's territorial ambitions did not in practice stretch much beyond the Levant,[57] but, of course, had he been successful in Egypt and executed his design on Persia, his appetite might have grown with the eating.

The clash between Britain and Napoleon, therefore, may have taken on global characteristics but its essence and virulence derived from Napoleon's limitless ambitions within Europe. This explains the breakdown of the Peace of Amiens, concluded in 1802 on the basis of French continental and British maritime restraint. The immediate apparent cause of the breach was Britain's refusal to withdraw as agreed from Malta: Napoleon threatened the British envoy, Lord Whitworth, with 'a war of extermination' and 'Malta or war'. The British were indeed in violation of their treaty commitments in the narrow sense, and there has since been reasonable doubt – not just among French historians – about the blame for the resumption of hostilities in 1803. But Malta was not the real object of the quarrel. British hesitations derived not from any reluctance to surrender a maritime gain but from real doubts about Napoleon's European intentions. As far as London was concerned, the Treaty of Amiens was to be read together with the Treaty of Lunéville (1801), between the French and Austrians, by which Napoleon had agreed to withdraw from Holland and restore the independence of Switzerland. By late 1802, he had shown no sign of doing so, nor were British suspicions allayed by the capture of French spies checking out England's coasts and ports.

Napoleon transformed mainland Europe, and he also fundamentally changed Britain. To be sure, the United Kingdom did not experience the same profound domestic transformations as Prussia, the Rheinbund states, Holland, the Italian and other European states did between 1792 and 1815. Napoleon was defeated without any profound reform of Britain's political, social or even military system, though such changes were much discussed at the time.[58] The British fiscal-military simply did what it had done for a long time, only did more of it, in a bigger way. The pulsating economic development of Britain, which was already in full swing, not only continued unabated but was greatly stimulated by the war. The emerging 'workshop of the world' produced military and naval material of all kind, as well as consumer goods, many of them for export to the continent, despite all Napoleon's attempts to stop trade. That said, there were few aspects of British political and social life left untouched by the long European struggle to break French hegemony during the Revolutionary and Napoleonic wars. It formed the backdrop to daily life for two decades. 'Mrs Forster came an hour in the evening,' Norfolk brewer's wife Mary Hardy noted in her diary. 'The British troops and allies defeated in Flanders.' On another occasion, she wrote, 'Mrs Lebor and Miss Braithwaite drank tea here. A Great Battle fought in Germany.'[59]

At the level of high politics, the impact of Napoleon was mixed. As we have seen, Britain had been divided since the 1790s about how to deal with Revolutionary France. The advent of Napoleon did not bring any sense of national unity or political restraint but exacerbated these tensions. It is true that the decision to resume hostilities in May 1803 was overwhelmingly endorsed by about five sixths of the House of Commons, but the conduct of the war remained a furiously partisan issue throughout. The only remotely 'national' coalition – the Ministry of All the Talents, a colourful blend of Whig sybarites, colonial opportunists, fiscal rectitudinarians, Bourbon restorationists and the occasional orphaned Pittite – was in fact neither inclusive nor particularly talented. Military-political failures such as Walcheren were dissected in the full glare of a public inquiry. Unusually, however, no government ever fell directly over a war-related crisis: Pitt and the Talents went in 1801 and 1807 over Catholic emancipation, Addington was brought down over his financial policies in 1804, Pitt's second administration ended with his death in 1806, Portland resigned due to ill health in 1809, and Spencer Perceval's ministry was terminated by his assassination in 1812.

Despite all this, the impact of Napoleon on British society was considerable. For a start, the war required the most extensive mobilization of British manpower yet seen.[60] True, the available striking force was always small, particularly when large forces were committed to the Peninsula. But by the late Napoleonic period about one sixth of the population was available for military service in the army, navy, militia, volunteers and other formations, probably a higher proportion than in metropolitan France at that time.[61] In 1809, for example, the British could field some 240,000 regulars plus 100,000 seamen out of a population of 11 million; the French 310,000 front line troops out of a population more than twice that. The basis for this astonishing level of mobilization was the British 'fiscal-military' state, as it had developed throughout the eighteenth century and been refined and enlarged by the challenge of Revolutionary and Napoleonic France.[62] This implicit contract between the executive, the political nation and the financial elites for war, commerce and colonial expansion enabled Britain not merely to increase but also to access the national wealth for the great struggle.

Likewise, when Pitt and the Ministry of all the Talents unsuccessfully demanded the introduction of Catholic emancipation, they were not simply promoting religious toleration and reforming the British constitution. Rather, they had two war aims in mind. The first and more narrowly strategic was the desire to pacify Ireland and to prevent the French from opening up a new front there, as they had attempted to do in 1796 and 1798. The second and broader concern was to tap into the vast reservoir of untapped manpower and energies of disadvantaged British Catholics. Across Europe, the French challenge led to the questioning of traditional hierarchies, beliefs and inequalities. It was no different in Britain, and if the impact on societal structures and attitudes was ultimately less profound, this reflected not only the tenacious rearguard action of the Crown and other reactionary forces but was a consequence of the relative remoteness of the threat. As it turned out, the British army was able to employ large numbers of Irish Catholic recruits even without the incentive of Catholic emancipation, which had to wait until 1829.

The Napoleonic challenge also sparked a much broader debate about reforming state and society in Britain. The Earl of Selkirk wrote in a pamphlet of 1808 that there had been 'so vast a change in all the surround[ing] countries' of Great Britain, that 'our arrangements, internal as well as external, must be adapted to our new circumstances'. With the loss of her European allies, the only way in which the nation could hope to survive against the vastly superior population of France was 'by exertions unprecedented in the improvement of our internal resources'.[63] Increased taxation and recruitment was only part of the answer: the hidden energies of British society would have to be set free. 'In order to save this land from foreign subjugation,' the radical Whig MP Sir Francis Burdett argued, 'we must get rid of domestic oppression; we must have arms and reform.' A petition of the freeholders of Middlesex thus called for the restoration of both the 'civil branch' of the constitution, 'our parliamentary representation, which ought to be the perfect and impenetrable buckler of our defence', and the 'military branch', that 'power of the collective counties' which mustered all able-bodied men in the militia. Britain thus had, as the veteran electoral reformer John Cartwright argued in 1809, 'naught... but this alternative either parliamentary reformation under George the Third, or national subjugation under Napoleon the First'.[64]

For the moment, the British government resisted demands for franchise reform. The Whig Ministry of All the Talents made a fresh attempt to push through Catholic emancipation but was defeated in Parliament in 1807. Britain was more successful in promoting radical change in Europe and the wider world, as part of the war effort. In occupied Sicily, British administrators under Lord Bentinck embarked on a sustained programme of social and political modernization. This was designed not as a laboratory for radical Whig ideas but as a strategy to make the island a more effective ally against Napoleon and to serve as an inspiration to liberal Italian patriots who hated Napoleon but could not bear the thought of returning under the *ancien régime* yoke.[65] Britain also strongly supported greater political participation in Spain, where a national rebellion against Napoleon broke out in 1808, for similar reasons. Here the French subversion of the monarchy had prompted the Cortes to 'retrieve' the sovereignty previously vested in the Crown. Its first revolutionary act was the declaration of war against Napoleon.[66] A Spanish constitution, drawn up with British encouragement, soon followed. In this way, Britain articulated an alternative vision for Europe which went beyond simply opposing French Revolutionary ideas and supporting the conservative powers by default. Throughout the length and breadth of the continent, especially in Germany, British agents pursued covert action against Napoleon, subsidizing propaganda and supplying arms to guerrilla groups.[67] Britain also led the way in the abolition of the international slave trade, which the London parliament passed into law in 1807. The United States followed suit that same year, in accordance with the constitutional agreement of 1787 to end the trade after twenty years, and banned the carriage of slaves under its own flag. This marked the beginning of a subversive new humanitarian geopolitics, based on the coercive power of the Royal Navy, which made full use of its belligerent right to search and harass slavers on the high seas. It was of a piece with Britain's European mission to 'liberate' the continent from the slavery to which it had been reduced by Napoleon.[68]

Just as the threat of Louis XIV drove the English and Scots to enter into the Act of Union, so did the Napoleonic challenge cause London to look again at the constitutional relationship with Ireland. The 1798 Irish rising and the accompanying French expedition had demonstrated once again the dangers of an open flank to the west. William Pitt the Younger therefore introduced the Act of Union between Great Britain and Ireland in 1800, which merged the parliaments of both countries. This was supposed to be accompanied by Catholic emancipation, in order to reconcile the majority population to the British link, and to facilitate their recruitment in large numbers into the armed forces. The Union, as the liberal British Viceroy General Cornwallis hoped, was thus to be 'union with the Irish nation' not just 'with a party in Ireland', that is, the Protestant Ascendancy. In this, the under-secretary for Ireland Edward Cooke remarked, Britain was merely imitating her adversary. 'France well knows the principle and the force of incorporations,' he wrote 'Every state which she unites to herself, she makes part of her empire, *one and indivisible*.'[69] 'Supposing there were no other reasons which rendered the union of the sister kingdoms desirable,' Cooke concluded, 'the state of Europe, and especially of France, seems to dictate it.' Just as the Union with Scotland in 1707 was primarily motivated by the desire to forestall a Bourbon-backed Jacobite rebellion there and to mobilize resources more effectively for the struggle against Louis XIV, so the Union with Ireland was driven by the imperative to close the 'back door' to England, to mobilize Irish Catholics for the war effort against France and thus, as one advocate, John Bruce, put it to 'preserve the balance of power in Europe'.[70] Like the Union with Scotland, that with Ireland was in effect an enlargement of England through full and equal parliamentary union. The creation of the United Kingdom of Great Britain and Ireland, now complete, was thus primarily a response to the challenges of the European system.

The relationship between the contest with Napoleon and Britain's domestic structure was nearly tested by a strange little episode immediately after his defeat. Napoleon made a public request for asylum in an appeal to the Prince Regent in July 1815. 'I come,' Napoleon declaimed, 'like Themistocles to throw myself upon the hospitality of the British people. I put myself under the protection of their laws, which I claim from your Royal Highness as the most powerful, the most constant, and the most generous of my enemies.'[71] This was not the last such plea to be made by a defeated enemy – a very similar wish was expressed by the last emperor, Wilhelm II, who dearly wanted to live out his retirement as a private gentleman in England. It would be tempting, therefore, to interpret Napoleon's gambit as a typical instance of an abject affection-loving foreigner seeking acceptance by the British, or the English, even. But there is another explanation. For a start, the English option was always second best: Napoleon had originally wanted to go into exile in the United States but dithered until cut off by the Royal Navy.[72] Moreover, when giving himself up to HMS *Bellerophon*, Napoleon was well aware of the small but vocal and well-connected constituency he enjoyed in Britain. His final chance of avoiding banishment from Europe, or worse, lay in recruiting this group's not inconsiderable wealth and legal expertise to his cause. Once in England – and away from vengeful Prussians, Austrians and Russians – he could hope to turn the very constitutionality of Britain he had once despised to his advantage. This was also the hope of some Whig radicals, who busied themselves with plans to secure Napoleon's release on various technicalities. It may have been only the presence of mind of the captain of the *Bellerophon*, who prevented all attempts to serve Napoleon a subpoena to attend a court case in London, that prevented Napoleon from having the last laugh.

The United Kingdom played a crucial part in Napoleon's downfall. British naval supremacy and various British expeditionary forces, particularly in Spain, sapped French power. Of course, such peripheral strategies could, by themselves, be only peripheral to the eventual outcome. The Grande Armée was not bled to death by a thousand cuts, worn down by British-sponsored guerrillas or starved into submission by the Royal Navy: it was totally destroyed at great cost – in Russia 1812–13 – and its successor was defeated by the Russians,

Prussians and Austrians in 1813–14. It is clear that, had the Russian campaign been successful in 1812, the following year would have seen a reinforced French army cross the Pyrenees to scotch Wellington's skilfully won gains. His victory at Waterloo in 1815 owed much to the Prussians, the Hanoverians and the other Germans, Dutch and Belgians in the army with which the Duke began his iconic battle.[73] That, however, is the point: Britain's unique ability to secure and work with continental allies won the day for the common cause in Europe. It was an achievement in the grand tradition of Marlborough and the British commanders during the War of the Austrian Succession and the Seven Years War.

In political terms, moreover, the role of Britain was crucial. It is not quite true that Britain 'stood alone' against Napoleon: for much of the period she had the dubious honour of being supported by the unhinged king of Sweden Gustavus IV. But it is certainly fair to say that, with the exception of the year of uneasy peace in 1802–3, and perhaps the blue-water interlude of 1806–7, Britain remained the focal point of Europe-wide resistance to Napoleon. She articulated an all-embracing continental vision to which other powers could subscribe. For example, Pitt's 1805 plan for a general 'Public Law in Europe' sought to commit coalition partners not merely to the restoration of the European balance of power but also the maintenance of collective security in peacetime. This scheme anticipated the Vienna settlement and the Congress System. Britain was also thinking carefully about the future geopolitical order of Europe. The long tradition of strengthening Germany as a bulwark against France, and of securing the Low Countries, was given a new dimension by the foreign secretary Lord Mulgrave. In order to provide 'an effectual check on France', he wrote, in the same year as Pitt unveiled his plan, it was 'desirable to assign to Prussia a military line of frontier from Antwerp to Luxemburg with such a proportion of territory as may be found sufficient to induce Prussia to occupy that line'.[74] The traditional winning formula of British gold and European coalitions eluded Pitt and his successors until 1813, but it was eventually found not only because of changes within Europe itself but also because the British kept trying. In 1813–14, it was not least Castlereagh's clever diplomacy and a more sensitive and generous use of subsidies that prevented the final coalition from going the way of its three or four predecessors.[75] Eventually, Britain's efforts inspired others to follow, because they wanted the Europe she wanted, or at least preferred it to the alternative.

Moreover, the Duke of Wellington's coalition victory at Waterloo in 1815 was not only militarily but politically decisive. Had Napoleon won, it is likely that he would have eventually been crushed by the Austro-Russian juggernaut massing in central Europe. It is also perfectly possible, however, that he would have defeated some more of his enemies in detail and then driven a political wedge between them. At all events, his occupation of Brussels and pell-mell retreat would have created a completely different strategic situation. Even if Napoleon had been defeated at a later stage, the result would have been a renewed occupation of France by the eastern powers, a much harsher peace settlement and a much smaller role for Great Britain. As it was, the defeat of Napoleon was, and was perceived to be, a British victory more than that of any other state. Alone of all the great powers, she had stayed the course almost from the beginning to the triumphal end. In consequence, the Europe that emerged after 1815, a loose, non-hegemonic association of states, was much more 'British' in its international character than it would otherwise have been.

6

'Where the weather comes from'. Britain and Europe in the Age of Nationalism

We have gained then a rank and authority in Europe, such as must place this country upon an eminence which no probable reverses can shake. We have gained, or rather we have recovered, a splendour of military glory, which places us by the side of the greatest military nations of the world.

– George Canning, 1814[1]

The Germanic Confederation is not a Union formed solely by the voluntary association of the states that compose it, and which therefore can be altered and modified at the absolute will of these states without reference to a consultation with any other parties. The German Confederation is a Union of a different character and kind. It is the result and creation of a European treaty concluded at Vienna in 1815, and it forms part of the general settlement of Europe which that Treaty established and regulated.

– Lord Palmerston, 1850[2]

[German demands for a British declaration of neutrality in Europe would be a] derogation from the honourable role which Great Britain has played in Europe for more than three hundred years and which has greatly contributed to the peace of the world . . . No political agreement . . . would be acceptable on these lines . . . which are so far-reaching as to be likely to disturb the political equilibrium of Europe.

– Sir Charles Hardinge, permanent under-secretary at the Foreign Office, 1909[3]

The United Kingdom emerged from the Revolutionary and Napoleonic wars as the dominant European power.[4] Her global and commercial reach was unparalleled. The new European order was to a substantial degree her order, at least to begin with. Its maintenance absorbed a large amount of Britain's attention throughout the nineteenth century. The 'public law' of Europe which Pitt had defended against Napoleon was still being upheld by Sir Edward Grey against the violation of Belgian neutrality a hundred years later. Increasingly, moreover, Britons felt that ideology could not be separated from geopolitics. The defence of liberalism in the United Kingdom, they believed, could not be separated from the defence of liberalism in Europe: in the Iberian Peninsula, the Balkans and especially in central Europe. At the same time, Britain looked well beyond the confines of the continent, acquiring huge colonial territories. Towards the middle of the century, many Britons felt that they had outgrown the old continent, that they lived in an ecosystem and climate all their own, insulated from tempests blowing on the far side of the Channel, but they were soon disabused. The unification of Germany, in particular, created a completely new situation on the continent. By the end of the 'long nineteenth century', it was clear that for all the 'global' scope of the British Empire, the 'weather' still came from where it had always come: Europe.

Britain had won the war, she had secured what George Canning called 'the lawful commonwealth of European states',[5] now could she win the peace? Her main concern at the Congress of Vienna, which brought to an end the Revolutionary and Napoleonic wars, was the security of Europe and its central issue, namely the 'German Question'.[6] In February 1814, the allies had committed themselves to a central European framework 'composed of sovereign princes united by a federal bond which will assure and guarantee the independence of Germany'.[7] Eight months later, Castlereagh elaborated that Germany should constitute 'an intermediary system between Russia and France',[8] which contained both states without threatening them. Britain was determined to prevent Russia from filling the vacuum in central Europe. A resurrected Poland which was 'really Russian', Castlereagh's diplomat-brother Charles Stewart warned, 'would 'advanc[e] the Russian frontier . . . almost into the heart of Germany'.[9]

The resulting territorial settlement in Europe was largely to Britain's satisfaction. France was boxed in through the establishment of a Kingdom of the United Netherlands made up of Belgium and the former Dutch Republic, the enlargement of Savoy, the re-establishment of the independence of Spain and, especially, the Prussian annexation of the Rhineland on its eastern border. The stability of central Europe was ensured by the creation of the German Confederation, the successor to the Holy Roman Empire. This had its federal diet at Frankfurt, maintained fortresses and forces to keep out the French and (though less overtly) the Russians, all under the presidency of Austria, the dominant power in the Confederation. Russia was forced to relax its grip on Poland somewhat. The Personal Union with Hanover, and thus a direct dynastic link with the continent, was maintained. A British army of occupation was to remain in France until it had paid the large financial indemnity imposed upon it. In effect, Britain had resurrected the old barrier system on the continent and arranged its security architecture so as to ensure the continued maintenance of the balance of power and the safety of the south coast of England.

Unlike all the other victor powers, the United Kingdom made no territorial gains in Europe, though she did retain her colonial booty (including Ceylon and the Cape Colony) and a number of bases, including Malta. In North America, Britain effectively began to acknowledge the hemispheric supremacy of the United States at the Treaty of Ghent, which ended the war between the two powers in 1815, and later confirmed it through acceptance of the Monroe Doctrine, continued tensions over the border with Oregon and Maine notwithstanding. She supported Washington's demand that European powers should not establish new colonies in the Americas and generally accepted the US's claim to exercise an international police power in the western hemisphere. George Canning, who saw the United States as an ideological ally against European conservatism, celebrated all this as 'calling a new world into being in order to redress the balance of the old'. Anglo-American rivalry was by no means over, but the time of armed confrontation had passed for good, and the outlines of a new relationship based on the assumption that the United States would generally want what London wanted, at least with respect to Europe, were now visible.

The coalition victory at Waterloo was thus followed by a coalition peace. Thanks to her victory at Waterloo, Britain's role was much larger than it would otherwise have been, resulting in a more liberal settlement. For example, Castlereagh was unable to push through an outright ban against the international slave trade, but he did manage to secure a united declaration of 'repugnance' against it, which gave moral cover to the Royal Navy's illegal campaign against slave ships on the high seas. Of course, this provoked the fury of British abolitionists, because the treaty did not stipulate an immediate and complete end to the international slave trade, or – failing that – permit Britain to annex the French colonies with which it was carried out. 'We were masters of the negotiation,' the Whig Lord Grenville lamented. 'In this cause the example of Great Britain was all-powerful . . . her determination final.'[10] British restraint here was the result of Castlereagh's determination to collaborate with, rather than dictate to, the European powers. One way or the other, Britain's prestige was high, and this was reflected in the unparalleled European stature of the Duke of Wellington, who was lionized not merely in Britain but across the continent. Today, his residence at Apsley House is still stuffed with paintings, silver services, statues and other objects given in appreciation by the crowned heads of Europe and other admirers.

Britain's restraint in 1815 was deliberate. 'Our reputation on the continent as a feature of our strength, power and confidence,' Castlereagh argued in mid-April 1814, 'is of more real moment than any acquisition.'[11] He parlayed this standing into the Quadruple Alliance of 1815 between Russia, Prussia, Austria and Britain. This was designed to coordinate allied response to any future threat to the state system, especially from a resurgent France. Article 6 of this agreement pledged the parties to 'renew their meetings at fixed periods, either under the immediate auspices of the sovereigns themselves, or by their respective ministers, for the purpose of consulting upon their common interest, and for consideration of the measures which at each of those periods shall be considered the most salutary for the repose and prosperity of nations and the maintenance of the peace of Europe'. This arrangement became known as the 'Congress System' and was designed to manage the problems of the continent on a multilateral basis.

Peace in Europe had huge implications for government and society in Britain. The prime minister Lord Liverpool had a keen sense of Britain's role in Europe, but he also wanted to reduce expenditure and get the national debt under control.[12] As a result, the traditional 'fiscal-military' state gave way to the 'laissez-faire state'.[13] An army of 685,000 was cut to just 100,000, half of them serving overseas. This was in part driven by financial considerations, but it also reflected a politico-cultural shift. The army was increasingly despised as expensive and ruffianly, and became in consequence heavily dominated by indigent Irish recruits (or vice versa). In 1816, the young Whig Lord John Russell spoke against expenditure on the army on the grounds that it would transform Britain from 'a naval into a military nation, and, instead of continuing a mighty island, into a petty continental state'.[14] The fiscal-military state which had developed over the 'long' eighteenth century from about 1690 was largely dismantled. It was a decision which eased Britain's budget deficit after a long period of expensive warfare, probably helping to stimulate economic growth, but it left the nation exposed when it was next called upon to engage in major land warfare in Europe.

The main challenges to the stability of the continent after 1815, at least at first, came not from the great powers but new political forces at work across Europe.[15] Liberal and nationalist ideas, inspired by or in reaction to the French Revolution and Napoleon, subverted the domestic order in ways which often had profound international ramifications. The Austrian chancellor, Prince Metternich, was not a complete reactionary: he often sought to pressurize the more egregiously backward princes into reforms to pre-empt revolution, but his general concern was to suppress domestic dissent through interstate cooperation, either through what we would today call intelligence sharing or by outright military intervention. By and large, Prussia and Russia supported this arrangement, which became known as the 'Metternich system' within the European 'Concert' of great powers. The 'eastern powers', as they became known, united behind the Karlsbad Decrees, which Metternich rushed through in 1819 to suppress liberal nationalism in Germany. They also supported his demands, voiced at a series of congresses in the early 1820s, for military intervention against revolutions in Spain, Piedmont and Naples. Russia even went along, at least for the time being, with Metternich's insistence that no help should be sent to Greek rebels against Ottoman rule in the Balkans.

Britain viewed all this with suspicion. To be sure, she was as keen as the rest of the Concert of Europe to avoid revolutionary disturbances which might destabilize the balance of power. For this reason, Britain long remained a staunch supporter of Habsburg power against Italian revolutionary nationalism, principally in order to keep the French out of the peninsula. There was considerable unease, however, about the propriety and efficacy of constant intervention in the internal affairs of other states. The British statesman George Canning cautioned in October 1818 that regular European Congresses would involve the country 'deeply in all the politics of the continent, whereas our true policy has always been not to interfere except in great emergencies and then with a commanding force'.[16] Even such a staunch interventionist as Castlereagh agreed that the Quadruple Alliance was devised to contain France and 'never intended as union for the government of the world or for the superintendence of the internal affairs of other states'.

The difference between Britain and the other European powers lay in the realm of politics and ideology rather than abstract principles of international law. Castlereagh was anxious to prevent interference based on purely reactionary grounds. He observed that many European states were 'now employed in the difficult task of casting anew their Governments upon the representative principle', and that 'the notion of revising, limiting or regulating the course of such experiments, either by foreign Council or by foreign foe, would be as dangerous to avow as it w[ould] be impossible to execute.'[17] He did not object to intervention as such. London had, after all, intervened in the affairs of the continent since the foundation of the United Kingdom. It is therefore no surprise to find Castlereagh proclaiming in January 1821 that 'no government can be more prepared than the British government is to uphold the right of any state or states to interfere, where their own immediate security or essential interests are seriously endangered by the internal transactions of another state.'[18]

In geopolitical terms, Castlereagh agreed with Metternich that intervention should not be to the detriment of the balance of power, for example by providing a pretext for French or Russian expansionism. The British foreign minister also accepted that '[t]he general security of Germany' was 'inseparable' from that of 'Europe' as a whole. He was adamant, however, that the threat from revolution had to be 'direct and imminent' as well as 'military in character actual and existent'; otherwise, it would give Russia an excuse to move into Germany.[19] Castlereagh therefore did not approve, as he put it in his famous 'State Paper' of May 1820, of going to war simply 'upon abstract and speculative principles of precaution'.[20] There was in fact growing unease in Britain that the principle of intervention was being applied one-sidedly to promote an exclusively repressive agenda which clashed with the liberal and emancipatory principles which London was beginning to embrace. Castlereagh, in short, was opposed to accepting a principle which protected established governments from intervention, no matter how badly they were ruled. The absence of constitutional liberties, he believed, could be as dangerous to European stability as their proliferation. Besides, Britain saw the Spanish Revolution – and the continuing collapse of her empire – as an opportunity to move into the vacuum in Latin America, before any other European power did so, especially France.[21] Britain therefore sided with liberals against conservatives in the Iberian Peninsula. She even intervened militarily in Portugal with naval forces to defend the constitutionalist government against reactionary rebels. Britain also sent ships to Greece, not so much to back the rebels there as to contain Russia, which was resuming its march south towards Constantinople.

The revolutions of 1830–32 in France, Belgium and various German states, however, struck at the very core of Britain's European interests. A union between France and Belgium, where the rebels made the son of the French king their monarch, would destroy the barrier erected in 1815, expose the southern coast of England to attack and rip open the western border of the German Confederation. Unlike recent Russian advances at the expense of the Ottoman empire, it would also be a unilateral French territorial gain large enough to unhinge the European balance. 'Whether Russia possesses a degree or two of latitude more or less in the Caucasus,' the British foreign secretary Lord Palmerston remarked in May 1831, 'cannot be of the same importance to England, Prussia, Austria or Spain as any smaller variations in the territory and resources of France, because the former adds but little to the means of Russia to attack the rest of Europe, while the latter might materially increase the offensive faculties of France.'[22] The threat was neutralized by insistence on a neutral candidate for the Belgian throne and an international agreement on the neutrality of the new state, which was finally reached in 1839, allaying British anxieties about the security of the Low Countries, at least for the time being.

British statesmen were disturbed by the emergence of German nationalism as a major force. Any internal or external threat to Germany was a mortal threat to international stability and thus British security.[23] 'It is our interest,' a senior British diplomat remarked, 'that the Confederation should be strong and efficient. It is a decidedly defensive body, incapable of being used for the purpose of attack, while if it is united for defence it renders war upon a great scale in Europe almost impossible.' The political unification demanded by the German national movement would destroy the balance of power. For this reason, the British ambassador to the Confederation warned against the '[t]he extravagant doctrine of the Unity of Germany'.[24] Here the concern was not so much that the resulting colossus would develop hegemonic pretensions of its own, but rather that a liberal order in Germany might be less effective than the established regimes in resisting French or Russian encroachments.

In the Iberian Peninsula, by contrast, the interests of Britain and the new liberal French 'July Monarchy' were ideologically aligned. The eastern powers combined in 1833 at Münchengrätz to support conservatism across Europe, and especially in Spain and Portugal. A year later, Britain, France and the two liberal governments in Madrid and Lisbon united to oppose them in the Quadruple Alliance. To Palmerston, the first task of his 'western confederacy' was the protection of constitutionalism in the Iberian Peninsula, which he saw as the first line of defence for freedom closer to home.[25] 'It is there,' he told Parliament in mid-April 1837, 'and upon that contracted scene, that is to be decided by issue of battle that great contest between opposing and conflicting principles of government – arbitrary government on the one hand and constitutional government on the other – which is going on all over Europe'.[26] This reflected a strong sense that European peace and Britain's own security depended, as Palmerston put it, on the 'maint[enance] of the liberties and independence of all other nations'. Palmerston believed that constitutional states were 'less likely to go to war than despotic governments because money will not be voted lightly' by their representative assemblies.[27] This was an early example of what has subsequently been termed the 'Democratic Peace' theory.

The international politics of the 1830s had a profound impact on British domestic politics. Party rivalries in Westminster were exacerbated by differences over Europe, with Whigs and Tories trading increasingly bitter insults over Spain. Foreign policy was also a polarizing factor within the Whig party: Russell accused moderates of abandoning the cause of freedom; Palmerston sneered at the cautious 'broadbrims' – so-called because of their allegedly Quaker pacifist tendencies – who wanted to save money on the army.[28] The liberal camp was split between Palmerstonian interventionists and the orthodox economic liberal followers of Richard Cobden. The latter had developed his domestic politics through the study of international relations in his first published works: *England, Ireland and America* (1835) and *Russia* (1836). Cobden was strongly opposed to intervention and became associated with the cry 'No foreign politics!' Not only did he play down the tsarist threat but Cobden also believed that an activist foreign policy necessitated a backward domestic policy complete with a large standing army, spiralling national debt, colonies and Corn Laws designed to entrench aristocratic supremacy in state, society and the armed forces. It was the nineteenth-century equivalent of Jonathan Swift's critique of the British fiscal-military state during the closing years of the War of the Spanish Succession. For Cobden, the repeal of the Corn Laws and the promotion of international free trade were instruments to secure liberalism at home and thus peace abroad – and vice versa.[29] This was an early example of what has become known as 'interdependence', a belief tenaciously held by many British liberals up to 1914 and again after the end of the Cold War.

In 1848–9, Britain was once again forced to grapple with the European balance. Revolutions broke out in France, Austria, Prussia, Hungary, Italy and many other places, toppling established governments. The main concern, as ever, was the challenge to the German Confederation and the role of the Habsburgs in it.[30] Austria, Palmerston warned Parliament, was 'a most important element in the balance of power in Europe. Austria stands in the centre of Europe, a barrier against encroachment on the one side [by Russia], and against invasion on the other [by France]. The political independence and liberties of Europe are bound up . . . with the maintenance and integrity of Austria.'[31] They were also worried about Italy because it destroyed the southern bulwark against the expansion of French power. The region was, as Palmerston put it in June 1848, no longer 'the shield of Ajax', but 'the heel of Achilles'.[32] Recognizing that the Habsburgs had had their day in the peninsula, he and Russell now began to search for a new solution to the barrier problem, and he also began to contemplate the unity of Germany, providing this could be achieved under liberal auspices. It seemed that realpolitik and ideology could be reinforcing rather than contradictory dictates in Britain's European policy.

The relationship between the two was summed up by Palmerston in a famous speech to the House of Commons in March 1848, often misunderstood as the enunciation of a narrow British 'realism'. He announced that 'the real policy of England – apart from questions which involve her own particular interest, political or commercial – is to be the champion of justice and right.' This course, Palmerston continued, should be 'purs[ued] with moderation and prudence, not becoming the Quixote of the world, but giving the weight of her moral; sanction and support wherever she thinks that justice is, and wherever she thinks that wrong has been done'. He then went on to stress that Britain had 'no eternal allies, and . . . no perpetual enemies', so that policy should be guided 'by the interest of England'.[33] Palmerston, in other words, saw no necessary contradiction between the defence of British interests and that of justice; indeed, the two motivations were closely linked in his mind.

London's anxieties were not allayed by the defeat of the French revolutionaries. The new French president, soon to be Emperor Napoleon III, was in many respects an even greater menace. His very name was a programme for change. 'I think it very likely,' Malmesbury remarked to the prime minister Lord Derby after his *coup d'état* in 1851, 'that the President will, when once settled, try to have a European Congress to remodel the treaties of 1815. That *was* always his hobby and a rather dangerous one.' Derby was not a man disposed to worry too much about the internal complexion of European states. 'We have no right,' he famously remarked, 'to entertain particular prejudices, or particular sympathies, for this or that course of government that other countries may think fit to adopt, be these courses or forms of government the most absolute despotism, limited monarchy, constitutional republic, or, if such a thing could endure, absolute red republicanism'. This, Derby insisted, was 'the choice of a nation, so far as it affects its individual and internal concerns alone, it is the duty of a British government to recognize'. The trouble was that the internal structure of a European state could never, as experience showed and the future would show, be usefully separated. One way or the other, even at the height of Britain's industrial glory during the Great Exhibition of 1851, Derby and his Conservatives were profoundly concerned with events in Europe; the notion of isolating themselves from the continent simply did not feature on their 'mental map', as we would say today.[34]

Over the next decade, Britain's interests shifted eastwards to the Balkans and the Levant, where Russia was expanding relentlessly. She fought the Crimean War in alliance with France in order to preserve the integrity of the Ottoman empire. Yet the main focus remained central Europe. In the great parliamentary debate in February 1854 on the eve of the declaration of war, Russell argued that Britain should confront Russia in order to 'maintain the independence, not only of Turkey, but of Germany and of all European nations'.[35] In July 1855, the foreign secretary Lord Clarendon emphasized that 'Germany by its geographical position must be the principal bulwark against Russian aggression.'[36] Many British liberals saw the struggle with the tsar as a pan-European confrontation between constitutionalism and conservatism. 'Were Russia crippled and overthrown,' one of them wrote, 'the difference would be felt in every village in Germany, in every dungeon in Italy, at every hearth-stone and in every heart from the Baltic to the Mediterranean.'[37] William Ewart Gladstone, the former chancellor of the exchequer, told Parliament that the Franco-British alliance represented 'a principle ... that which I may almost call a sort of European law which has prevailed ... since the peace of 1815 ... to vindicate and enforce against [Russia] the public law of Europe'.[38] The conflict went badly at first, the war effort becoming a byword for incompetence. Eventually, however, the Russians were decisively beaten, on their very doorstep, in the Crimea. The superiority of the British parliamentary system over tsarist despotism could not have been more resoundingly demonstrated, and the outcome sparked a reform drive in Russia which culminated in the abolition of serfdom.

The Crimean War had a profound impact on British domestic politics.[39] News of the military and organizational fiascos provoked widespread consternation in Parliament and the public sphere. Lord Aberdeen's government fell in January 1855 over his defeat in a vote to establish a parliamentary select committee to look into the conduct of military operations; Palmerston replaced him as the man who could win the war. There was disagreement, however, over how best to bring British society into line with the needs of the European state system. Some, such as Samuel Morley, a Nottingham hosiery manufacturer and later MP, argued that the early disasters in the Crimea reflected a lack of popular legitimacy and that 'the people themselves' should take more responsibility for their own security through the militia and franchise reform.[40] Others pointed to the conservatism and unprofessionalism of the army, where officers bought their commissions rather than acquiring them through merit. To liberal and radical critics, all this was evidence of the continuing 'aristocratic' dominance of British institutions which enfeebled the nation in its struggle with external enemies. In order to prepare for the challenges ahead, Britain embarked on a round of internal and imperial reforms. A Royal Commission into the defences of the United Kingdom was set up, the Foreign Office was reformed and military expenditure substantially increased. A large proportion of this went not into the navy but into what we would today call 'target hardening', the most extensive programme of fortifications along the south coast since the time of Henry VIII.

Towards the end of the 1850s, the geographical focus of British policy moved again, back to the Italian peninsula. There Piedmont, France and the Italian national movement under Garibaldi expelled the Austrians in a series of dramatic events, culminating in the French annexation of Savoy and the establishment of a united Italy in 1861. Britain regarded these developments with ambivalence. On the one hand, the resurgence of France, which was now sloughing off the fetters erected in 1815, produced an invasion scare in southern England, and a 'volunteering' movement.[41] On the other hand, the Italian victory promoted a sense of liberal triumphalism: the conviction that the tide of events in Europe was heading inexorably towards nationalist and constitutionalist modernity along English lines. Gladstone, when asked what had turned him from a Conservative into a Liberal, replied succinctly: 'Italy.'[42] The hope, as the senior British diplomat Robert Morier explained, was to work with the grain of European nationalism in the British geopolitical interest. 'I believe it is in the interest of England,' he wrote, to achieve peace 'by the great national groups getting into their respective countries, instead of the present artificial treaty-born balance of power.'[43] There were also widespread hopes that the British example would inspire other European states to embrace constitutionalism.[44] This profound sense of engagement with events in Europe coexisted with deep opposition to state expenditure on armaments, on the grounds that these were not merely redundant but counter-productive. Thus the Anglo-French commercial treaty of 1860 was seen as an alternative to war or an arms race with Napoleon III. Free trade, not military force – so the argument ran – would keep the peace in Europe.

This confidence in the direction of European politics was sorely tested by the process of German unification, which dominated the state system during the 1860s. In 1864, the Prussian chief minister Otto von Bismarck shrugged aside Denmark and wrested Schleswig-Holstein from it, ignoring British objections. He called Palmerston's bluff, knowing that there was little the Royal Navy could do to help the Danes and trusting that no land army would be sent to the continent. Two years later, Bismarck defeated the Austrians and established a new North German Confederation without them under Prussian leadership. Then, in 1870–71, he dealt with Napoleon III. France was forced to surrender Alsace-Lorraine, to pay a punishing financial indemnity and to accept the creation of a United Germany stretching from the Rhine to East Prussia. This was the first time since Napoleon that this entire space was controlled by one power, and the first time ever that it was politically united in its own right. The territorial, demographic, military and economic map of Europe had been fundamentally transformed, and it was only a matter of time before this fact would force London to respond.

Unlike in previous situations, Britain did not lead a balancing coalition against Bismarck.[45] This was partly due to a sense that her destiny lay overseas. Disraeli famously announced in 1866 that Britain was no longer a European but a global power, echoing the 'blue water' rhetoric of an earlier age. Yet this sentiment should not be exaggerated. Even at the summit of Britain's Victorian imperial glory, Europe remained the chief preoccupation of her statesmen and diplomats.[46] The main reason for Britain's restraint was that London's strategic paradigm remained unchanged. British strategists were ambivalent about France. On the one hand, they saw it as a liberal bulwark against a conservative and expansionist Russia. On the other hand, they still saw France as a threat in central and western Europe, and they therefore welcomed the process of German unification. Palmerston reiterated just before his death in 1865 that a strong 'Germany' – led by Berlin – was necessary to deter Russia. Looking back, the British ambassador to Prussia, Lord Loftus, remarked that 'I could not view with any dissatisfaction or fear of danger to England an increase of power to Prussia. She will gradually advance in a constitutional system of government, and she will play the part of moderator in Europe.'[47] Britain's principal worry throughout the 1860s was that France would use the opportunity to reopen the territorial settlement in western Europe, especially Belgium. It was for this reason that London guaranteed the security of Luxemburg in May 1867, demonstrating not only a determination to keep France out of the Low Countries but a continued commitment to maintaining the European balance of power.[48]

The unification of Germany and the manner in which it was achieved sparked a lively debate in Britain. Some believed that the annexation of Alsace-Lorraine had revealed the new Germany to be a potential threat to the European balance.[49] 'I do not believe that the unification of Germany as a military despotism can be for the good of Europe,' one MP warned Parliament in February 1871.[50] Two years later, the British ambassador to Berlin, Odo Russell, cautioned that Bismarck aimed not only to hold down France in perpetuity but to achieve '[t]he supremacy of Germany in Europe and of the German race in the world'.[51] Most Britons, however, held that German unification was a good thing and posed no real threat to British security; indeed, Napoleon's defeat actually reduced the danger to the south coast.[52] Many diplomats and commentators were highly enthusiastic about the emergence of a Protestant, powerful and potentially liberal state in the centre of Europe, capable of containing both France and Russia.[53] Besides, most sceptics – including Russell – gradually accepted Bismarck's assurances that Germany was a 'satiated' power. The real reason the events of 1870–71 mattered, however, was not because they led to the unification of Germany but because they marked the collapse of French power, which would render the country less able to contain Russia. Disraeli described this development – in a much misunderstood speech – as the principal result of the 'German Revolution'.[54]

The Wars of German Unification had a profound effect on British domestic politics. They convinced many that Britain needed to mobilize fresh resources to defend her position in the state system. The radical John Morley argued in his 1866 article on 'England and the European Crises' that greater popular political participation was necessary to remedy the 'deep want of harmony at home and want of moral power abroad'.[55] In 1867, the franchise was duly extended in the Reform Act, a measure which had deep domestic roots, to be sure, but one which was enacted with a strong sense of its importance for Britain's international position.[56] Moreover, Britain was shaken in her liberal illusion. First, the unmistakably brutal process of German unification shattered the liberal belief in the ameliorative power of trade and the inexorable advance of international law.[57] The idea that liberal values would prevail without war, or did not need to be defended militarily, was no longer credible. As the former Conservative prime minister Lord Derby crushingly remarked in July 1870, 'Gladstone really believed in Cobden's theory that men were growing too civilized for war.' This was why the conflict 'found them [the Liberals] astonished and perplexed'.[58] A war scare gripped the country. Futurist tracts predicting the invasion and conquest of Britain sold in their hundreds of thousands. One famous example, *The Battle of Dorking*, penned by the army officer and subsequent MP G. T. Chesney in May 1871, posited a Prussian attack bulldozing aside ill-trained local militias while British regulars gnashed their teeth impotently overseas. 'Europe' suddenly seemed very near.

Some Britons now felt that more, not less, government was needed to deal with the new instability in Europe. Army reform, long a preoccupation of liberals and radicals critical of the 'unmanly' aristocrats, became imperative. The Franco-Prussian War convinced enough conservatives that aristocratic privileges and traditional practices in the army could no longer be justified, and sufficient liberals that their own freedoms depended on an effective army to defend them. In 1871, Gladstone's minister for war, Cardwell, finally pushed a military bill through Parliament in the teeth of intense opposition. His reforms put an end to the worst abuses, such as the purchase of commissions, and began to haul the British army into the late nineteenth century. It was now not possible for Gladstone to cut military expenditure, as planned, and thus abolish income tax. In April 1871, Chancellor Lowe presented a budget in which greater costs for the army were to be covered by an additional 1 per cent on income tax, a tax on matches and twice the previous succession tax on landed estates. This was intended as a pan-social contribution to national defence, but the ensuing outcry forced Gladstone to increase income tax instead. Over the next two years, the prime minister failed to solve the issue and, when the army and navy refused to agree to the reductions Gladstone wanted, he called a general election in January 1874.[59] His defeat, and replacement by the Conservative leader Disraeli, was thus to a very large degree a result of the Franco-Prussian War.

At the same time, Britain sought to make up in global and domestic weight for what she lacked in European military power.[60] The supporters of 'Imperial Federation', who demanded closer political bonds, perhaps including a common parliamentary assembly, between the white settler colonies and the mother country, met in London in July 1871, in the shadow of German unification.[61] One of its principal advocates, the Australian Edward Morris, wrote that the white population of the British colonies was not only about a third of that in the motherland itself but increasing at a much greater rate. It should find a common purpose in a hostile world, or risk 'complete effacement'. 'The whole set of history,' Morris wrote, 'has been in the direction of unification . . . The future belongs to the big states.' Moreover, he argued, 'Germany at least has not reached its full size,' and would 'continue to expand'. His prognosis was for 'three great empires, the United States and Russia, with Germany not far behind them'. If Britain was not to risk 'complete effacement', she would have to integrate her empire more effectively into imperial defence.[62] Disraeli made Victoria 'Empress of India', a move designed to keep pace with the old empire of Russia and the new German empire.[63] The European purpose of the overseas colonies could not have been more clearly demonstrated.

Strategic considerations also profoundly influenced thinking about constitutional arrangements within the British Isles themselves, especially with regard to the Home Rule movement in Ireland during the 1870s and 1880s. To Gladstone, the rift with Catholic Ireland was not only a moral stain on England's conscience but prevented the pursuit of a truly united British effort on the world stage. He envisaged a grand bargain with Irish nationalists, starting with land acts and ending with a Home Rule Bill, which would atone for past sins, bring Ireland into the imperial fold, reduce its susceptibility to popery and US-style republicanism, discourage outside powers from intervening there and generally make Britain a more plausible defender of liberal values across the world. The opponents of Home Rule, on the other hand, saw it as the thin end of a separatist wedge which would not only lead to the local dominance of the Roman Catholic Church but destroy the cohesion of the empire and weaken its western defences. They were particularly prominent among Ulster Protestants, part of whose enthusiasm for the Union lay in the sense of belonging to a powerful larger whole.[64] These anxieties were shared by government. Ireland, the Liberal Unionist and sometime chancellor of the exchequer George Goschen feared, would become 'a separate nation planted on our flanks'.[65] Here the debate had not moved on much since the sixteenth century, and the strategic arguments for Union advanced in 1800–1801 remained cogent. Europe had made the United Kingdom, and Europe helped to keep it together, at least for now.

The tension between realpolitik and ideology in British policy erupted anew in the mid-1870s, when rebellions against Ottoman rule broke out in Bosnia-Herzegovina and Bulgaria. The Turkish response involved much brutality, which outraged a vocal and orchestrated section of British opinion but left the Conservative government of Disraeli, who wished to maintain the Ottoman empire against Russia, completely unmoved. For Gladstone, now in opposition, the issue was a welcome stick with which to beat his rival. In September 1876, Gladstone published a passionate pamphlet on 'The Bulgarian Horrors and the Question of the East', which sold two hundred thousand copies within a month of publication. He called on the Turks to desist from their atrocities and leave the Balkans, 'bag and baggage'. Appealing to 'our common humanity',[66] Gladstone called upon the government to 'apply all its vigour to concur with other states of Europe in obtaining the extinction of the Turkish executive power in Bulgaria'.[67] The immorality of Conservative foreign policy was the centrepiece of Gladstone's famous Midlothian campaign, which emphasized the 'common humanity' and the 'brotherhood of man', a major milestone in the development of a British doctrine of humanitarian intervention.

Underlying Britain's attitude towards Europe was a deep sense of confidence in her own political system and its economy. She lacked, in peacetime, some of the classic instruments of land power, but her naval strength and her economic potential was massive. England had always been one of Europe's richest countries. In the late seventeenth and early eighteenth centuries, she became the leading commercial power, not only generating her own wealth but attracting that of others through its financial system. In the late eighteenth and early nineteenth centuries, Britain grew into the industrial 'workshop' of the world. Towards the end of the nineteenth century, her manufacturing power, in the relative sense, was beginning to wane with the rise of Germany and the United States. As a locus of political and financial power, however, London remained unrivalled until well into the next century. She could mobilize and concentrate much of the world's resources and turn them into hard military power, spewing out death and destruction into Europe, as she had demonstrated during the Crimean War. British statesmen knew it and, more importantly, the rest of Europe knew it, too.

This was essentially a maritime and commercial vision of Britain, descended from the 'blue water' tradition. It assumed that the defence of the realm could be left to the 'wooden walls' or, as they were now, 'steel hulks' of the Royal Navy. Thanks to the global span of the empire and its far-flung coaling stations, London could project power not just across the world but across the European continent. The Crimean War, in which Britain had been able to assemble a larger force more quickly by sea than the tsarist army could reinforce by land on terrible Russian roads, had proved the point very recently. This strategic advantage was soon to be celebrated by the American writer Alfred Thayer Mahan in his *The Influence of Sea-power upon History*, a work read widely not only in the Anglo-Saxon world but by its continental rivals as well. The resulting perceived ability of Britain to stay aloof from Europe and to enforce her will through what would today be called the 'stand-off' weapon of naval power was summed up approvingly by the term 'splendid isolation', often erroneously attributed to the long-serving prime minister the Marquess of Salisbury. He was in fact deeply critical of the 'sterile' and 'dangerous' policy of isolation.[68] Salisbury was entirely clear that Britain's destiny lay on the continent. 'We are part of the community of Europe,' Salisbury remarked, 'and we must do our duty as such.'[69]

The European scene took a sharp turn for the worse for Britain, however, from the late 1880s, as a rapprochement between France and Russia loomed. British statesmen and public opinion regarded the connection as directed at least as much against their own empire as against the German Reich. It was in this context that the Royal Navy proclaimed the 'two-power standard' in 1889, which laid down that Britain should build 'to a standard of strength equivalent to that of the combined forces of the next two biggest navies in the world'. Tensions with Russia in Central Asia, and with France in Africa, rose. Existing anxieties about Britain's failure to convert its economic potential into military and diplomatic muscle grew. Despite this, Britain rebuffed Bismarck's overtures for an alliance in 1889, and further attempts in the early 1890s by his successors made little progress. Britain was still largely focussed on her overseas empire and sought to avoid specific continental entanglements. When Britain cancelled a trade treaty with Germany, the German kaiser Wilhelm II remarked bitterly that '[i]f we had had a strong, respect-inducing fleet, then this abrogation would never have happened.'[70] Wilhelm became convinced that Britain would only take Germany seriously as a European partner if the Reich possessed naval and 'global' clout of its own. Germany would have to be either a useful ally or a formidable enemy. More generally, German strategists and important sections of the public began to subscribe to the Weltreichlehre, according to which the geo-economic power of the British and Russian empires and the United States would crush the weaker central European bloc. 'Three enormous empires of conquest,' the prominent academic Gustav von Schmoller warned, 'who with their greed for territory, their sea and land power, their trade, their export, [and] their expansionist power threaten to grind down, indeed to destroy all other smaller states, to box them in economically, and to starve them of light they need to live'.[71]

Thus was spawned 'Weltpolitik', Germany's aspiration to a global power rivalling Britain's. In mid-January 1896, Wilhelm announced that 'the German empire has become a world empire.'[72] He now began to seek Britain's attention. Wilhelm ostentatiously sent the Boer president, Kruger, a telegram congratulating him on defeating the 'Jameson raid', a semi-official British incursion. The Germans also began to take a keen interest in the affairs of South Africa more generally.[73] In November 1897, Germany moved into the Chinese port of Kiautschou. A year later, the kaiser made a highly publicised visit to the Ottoman empire, stopping off in Palestine; shortly afterwards, a German company was given the task of building a railway to Baghdad and down to the Gulf, the start of the 'Berlin–Baghdad railway'. At around the same time, Germany took possession of the Carolinas, Palau Islands and the Marianas in the Pacific, as well as showing renewed interest in Samoa. As if all this was not bad enough, Admiral Alfred Tirpitz, secretary of state of the German naval office, first announced a large-scale naval programme in 1897, primarily for deployment in the North Sea, that is, in British home waters.[74] The first naval law followed in 1898. The real point of all this global posturing, however, was not to challenge the British empire's world position but to frighten London into an alliance against Paris and St Petersburg.

Instead, German actions simply served to turn the British against them. The empire was already under threat from the tsar in Central Asia and the Far East; from the French in the Sudan; the Boers in South Africa; and the United States across the Americas. Now British official and public opinion was outraged at the 'Kruger Telegram': one British diplomat spoke of 'a determination on the part of the German government to make their influence felt in South-east Africa'.[75] The announcement of Tirpitz's naval programme in 1897 further heightened tensions. In a secret Anglo-German agreement in August 1898, Berlin left the Boers to their fate in return for an option on Portugal's African colonies, but the damage had been done. Henceforth, a strain of Germanophobia was distinctly audible, among the many other antagonisms. The two-power standard, scarcely a decade old, was no longer enough. Britain would need allies to survive the challenges ahead, and she would have to find them either in the New World or in the traditional European system on which it had turned its back for so long. Isolation from the rest of the continent was no longer an option.

The renewed primacy of Europe in British strategy was strikingly illustrated by events in South Africa. In October 1899, the Boers launched a lightning attack into the Cape Province. It took the combined might of the metropolis and the rest of the empire to defeat them. Throughout the contest London was haunted by the prospect that the great powers would intervene on behalf of the Boers and cut the British empire down to size, just as France and Spain had done during the American War of Independence. 'We have not a friend in Europe,' one Cabinet minister fretted at the beginning of the war in November 1899, 'and . . . the main cause of the dislike is . . . that we are like an octopus with gigantic feelers stretching out over the habitable world, constantly interrupting and preventing foreign nations from doing that which in the past we have done ourselves.'[76] Pro-Boer feeling ran high throughout Europe, especially in France, Germany and Ireland,[77] and there was joint military planning between Paris and St Petersburg in 1900 about a possible French descent on Britain and a Russian invasion of Afghanistan. There was even talk of a partition of the British empire, with Spain taking Gibraltar, France making gains in Africa and Russia in Central Asia. But the 'Saratoga' moment came and went and, by May 1902, the Boers had capitulated.

The experience of diplomatic isolation during the Boer War triggered a searching debate on grand strategy. At the height of the struggle, not a single full-strength infantry battalion had been left for home defence. 'The weary Titan,' Joseph Chamberlain remarked to an imperial conference in 1902, 'staggers under the too vast orb of its fate.' It was clear that the empire would have to do more for the common defence, in particular by helping to pay for the upkeep of the Royal Navy.[78] More important still was re-engagement in Europe. Britain needed allies, that was clear, and although there was still a lot of suspicion about French and Russian intentions the argument was moving inexorably against Germany.[79] One way or the other, Britain would once again need a large army for service on the continent. The Army Reform Bill of 1901 was introduced with this in mind. The young Winston Churchill was one of the few MPs to oppose it, on the Mahanian grounds that the navy rather than the army was the key to British security. Writing in the *Daily Mail*, Churchill argued that 'history' and 'geography' showed that the British empire was 'essentially commercial and marine', and had been defended by armies of 'foreigners'.[80] Churchill was in the minority, however, because it was not obvious, in the absence of alliances, where these foreigners were supposed to come from. The main deployment of the Royal Navy, in fact, would have to be in home waters to guard against sudden invasion. The Committee of Imperial Defence established in 1902 was, despite its name, largely designed to deal with the new threats coming from continental Europe.[81]

Exacerbating these anxieties was a growing sense that the high point of naval power had passed and that the future now belonged to the great continental powers. The spread of railways across the Eurasian land mass, such as those connecting the extremes of the Russian empire, or the projected line between Berlin and Baghdad, seemed to presage the end of the era when the Royal Navy could strike at will. Mahanianism, only recently elevated to orthodoxy, was now under attack, nowhere more than in Britain itself, where the eminent geographer Sir Halford Mackinder's much-discussed article

'The Geographical Pivot of History' appeared in 1904. The new century, the logic of his argument went, belonged to the land powers, especially those who could control Eurasia. If Mackinder was right, this meant that the next challenge to British security would come from central or eastern Europe, that is, either the German or the Russian empires, and perhaps from both.

On the positive side, Britain's relations with the United States improved markedly around the turn of the century. This was partly due to continued British restraint in the western hemisphere, in particular her support for Washington during the Spanish–American War of 1898.[82] It also reflected a sense of a common 'Anglo-Saxon' destiny in the world. This chiefly expressed itself in antagonism to continental European powers: to a certain extent, 'Latin' France and Spain, to a much greater degree the autocratic Slav tsarist Empire, and increasingly the 'Teuton' German empire. US suspicions of the kaiser, which were heartily reciprocated, grew in the decade after 1900. All this helped, but not even the most optimistic British statesman could have foreseen just how much London would rely on the New World redressing the balance of the old in the new century.

In 1904, Britain concluded an *entente cordiale* with France. It was an informal 'understanding' rather than an alliance and was partly driven by a concern to settle colonial differences, but the implication of a common purpose in Europe was clear. German attempts to divide the *entente* by attacking France's position in Morocco over a six-year period from 1905 simply drove Paris and London closer together. 'If Germany saw the slightest weakening on our part,' the British diplomat Harold Nicolson remarked, 'her pressure on France would become intolerable so that eventually she would have to fight or surrender. In the latter case, German hegemony would be solidly established.'[83] That same month, Lloyd George made a strong speech in the London Mansion House supporting France. The security of France and the Low Countries, which had not been an issue for decades, moved back into focus. The new director of military operations, Sir Henry Wilson, began to plan openly – and with considerable political encouragement – for a continental military commitment; it helped that he was a strong Francophile and Germanophobe.[84]

In January 1906, the British foreign secretary Sir Edward Grey authorized the first Anglo-French staff talks. The naval race with Germany, now focussing on a new, more advanced class of battleship called the *Dreadnought*, escalated.[85]

The emerging British view of Berlin was summarized by the senior diplomat Eyre Crowe in his famous 'memorandum on the present state of British relations with France and Germany' of January 1907. Far from being invulnerable behind its maritime moat, he argued, Britain was actually 'in the literal sense of the word, the neighbour of every country accessible by sea'. It therefore followed that the overriding interest of the British state, greater still than her concern for 'free intercourse and trade' was to make sure that there was no 'general combination of the world' against her, which would very quickly result in the loss of naval superiority. This in turn meant that it was 'almost a law of nature' that London should intervene to maintain the European balance of power, now endangered by Germany. After a long listing of Berlin's crimes in South Africa, China and in the naval race, Crowe pointed out that 'the edifice of Pan-Germanism, with its outlying bastions in the Netherlands, in the Scandinavian countries, in Switzerland, in the German provinces of Austria, and on the Adriatic, could never be built up on any other foundation than the wreckage of the liberties of Europe.' If that was what Berlin was aiming for, he concluded, this 'general political hegemony and maritime ascendancy' threatened the 'independence of her neighbours and ultimately the existence of England' and had to be stopped.[86]

Britain's new vulnerability and the difficulties she had had in dealing with the Boers sparked a fresh round of national performance anxiety. There were severe doubts as to whether the population was fit for a long struggle: the poor physical condition of many urban recruits suggested that the national stock had 'degenerated'. These fears spawned the 'national efficiency' movement, designed to make Britain a healthier, more productive, rational and thus robust society.[87] From February 1902, the National Service League, to which one in four MPs belonged, campaigned for the introduction of conscription, thus 'distributing the burdens of national defence equally among all classes, instead of allowing them to weigh crushingly upon the proletariat'.[88] A year later, Joe Chamberlain's 'Tariff Reform

League' sought to bind the empire more closely to Britain through 'imperial preference' against 'unfair' foreign imports, even if this resulted in reduced competition and thus in higher prices for consumers, especially with regard to agricultural produce.[89] Its aim was the transformation of the British empire into a consolidated trading bloc which could compete on equal terms with Germany and the United States. The money from high import duties, so the argument ran, could be used to fund the social reforms necessary to rally the population for the great tasks that lay ahead. Another central plank in the project of national regeneration was the land question. In 1904, the Liberal MP Herbert Samuel warned against the evils of 'tenements' and praised the virtues of land reform with reference to national security. 'Waterloo was won,' he reminded his readers, 'not on the playing fields of Eton alone but on the village greens of England as well; and if there are no more village greens, our Waterloos of the future, in spite of all that England can do, may have a different ending.'[90]

Foreign policy – and that meant, principally, Europe and the German threat – also shaped British electoral politics. 'Tariff Reform' was fiercely resisted by Liberals and many Conservatives on the grounds that it violated the principle of free trade and drove up the price of basic foodstuffs. In December 1905, the Conservative government of Arthur Balfour finally collapsed under the strains of this issue. The resulting January 1906 election resulted in a large Liberal majority under Campbell-Bannerman. Tariff reform was shelved, for the moment. Instead, the new government resorted to classic liberal methods to strengthen Britain. In 1907, the secretary for war, Lord Haldane, introduced the Territorial and Reserve Forces Act, with its provision for military training in schools and universities. This was seen as an alternative to conscription and 'militarism', and was intended to stiffen the moral and physical sinews of the nation against Germany.[91]

At the same time, the Liberal government sought to reconcile the working classes to the state through a programme of social and welfare reform, for instance through the introduction of health insurance and pensions. The trouble was that, while the policy of strength abroad and justice at home was complementary in conceptual terms, it was contradictory from the fiscal point of view. Budget hawks demanded to know what it would be: 'Dreadnoughts or old-age pensions',[92] guns or butter? Matters came to a head in 1909, when intelligence reports suggesting that the Germans were pulling ahead in naval construction were made public; these were aggravated by wild rumours that German spies were staking out East Anglia and the south coast.[93] In response, the government set up the Secret Service Bureau (which later divided into MI5 and MI6) specifically to deal with German penetration.[94] Two elections in 1910 showed Liberals and Conservatives to be neck and neck. The Liberals, who were very slightly ahead, eventually formed a government, supported by the Irish nationalists, and provided both pensions and more ships.

The security of the United Kingdom was also threatened by the invention of the aeroplane. Observing the experimental flights of the French aviation pioneer Santos-Dumont in November 1906, the press baron Lord Northcliffe remarked, 'England is no longer an island. It means the aerial chariots of a foe descending on British soil if war comes.' His organ, the *Daily Mail*, wrote of 'the military problem caused by the virtual annihilation of frontiers and the acquisition of the power to pass readily through the air above the sea'. This meant, the newspaper predicted, that '[t]he isolation of the United Kingdom may disappear.'[95] Not long after, the British government began to support the development of military aviation, which soon became a major arm of industry. The effect of all this was not so much to render the old strategic paradigms redundant as to reinforce them, because the principal bases for any aerial attack on England would likely be in the traditional areas of concern: northern France and the Low Countries. Moreover, time was to show that the aeroplane, far from just being a danger to the country could also serve for its defence and indeed as a sally port into continental Europe.

Britain was now firmly committed to her European partners – 'allies' would be perhaps too strong a term for the ever-closer *entente* with France – and the defence of the continental balance against Germany. If the 'equilibrium in Europe' were not protected, the permanent under-secretary for foreign affairs Arthur Nicolson warned in February 1911, and 'the Triple Entente were to be broken up', then 'we should be isolated and compelled to do the bidding of the power which assumed the hegemony in Europe [Germany].'[96]

Britain gave firm backing to the French in Morocco when Germany made another attempt to undermine her position there that same year. Grey ruminated that a general struggle for 'the supremacy of Europe' as in 'the old Napoleonic days' would inevitably draw in Britain, as she could not risk a continental 'combination that would deprive us of the command of the sea'.[97] This was the old Whig orthodoxy that the overall European balance was essential to the maintenance of maritime supremacy. In June 1912, a naval agreement gave France the lead role in the Mediterranean, allowing Britain to focus on the North Sea; the bulk of the fleet was now concentrated in home waters.[98] Europe, First Lord of the Admiralty Winston Churchill told the Australians and New Zealanders in April 1913, was 'where the weather came from'.[99]

It was against this background that the London government responded to the assassination of the Austrian Archduke Ferdinand in Sarajevo in June 1914. There was initially no appetite to interfere in a Balkan wrangle.[100] But when Russia backed Serbia against Austria-Hungary, and when France in turn backed Russia and Germany in turn supported her Austrian ally, it was clear that Britain would soon be called to state her position. Whether or not she was formally committed to support the French – which she was not – Britain could not afford France to go down to defeat again without risking the complete destruction of the European balance of power as London understood it. Even before the Germans attacked Belgium, dismissing Britain's guarantee as 'a scrap of paper', opinion was shifting in favour of intervention, but the threat to the Low Countries, the old 'counter-scarp of England', could not be ignored. Parliament, press and people went to war noisily, to be sure, but not ignorantly. They were upholding the 'liberties of Europe', the continental order upon which their own freedoms depended. They were not 'slithering' or 'sleepwalking' into conflict, though others were. In August 1914, after Berlin had ignored an ultimatum to withdraw from Belgium, Britain declared war on the German empire. The weather front had rolled in from Europe, just as Winston Churchill had predicted it would. Now one would see whether the home islands and the empire were equipped to master the storms which lay ahead.

7

'Under a single sway'. Britain and Europe in the Age of Total War

[I]f we would take the long view, must we not still reckon with the possibility that a large part of the Great [Eurasian] continent might some day be united under a single sway, and that invincible sea power might be based upon it? . . . Ought we not to recognize that that is the great ultimate threat to the world liberty so far as strategy is concerned and to provide against it in our new political system.

– Sir Halford Mackinder, 1919[1]

When you think of the defence of England, you no longer think of the chalk cliffs of Dover; you think of the Rhine. That is where our frontier lies.

– Stanley Baldwin, 1934[2]

When Europe, like a prison door,
Clangs; and the swift, enfranchised sea
Runs narrower than a village brook;
And men who love us not, yet look
To us for liberty;

– Dorothy Sayers, 'The English War', 1940

The first half of Britain's twentieth-century relationship with Europe was dominated by the German Question and, for ten terrible years, by the German wars. Britain was the only allied country which fought in both world conflagrations from the start (give or take a few days) to the finish. In both cases, she declared war on Germany, not vice versa, a tactically offensive move in support of a strategically defensive concern to prevent the enemy from dominating the continent and thus overturning the European equilibrium. In both cases, the British empire was not strong enough to win on her own, but she proved skilled at mobilizing a global coalition against the central powers during the First World War and the Axis powers during the Second. In both cases, Britain was defending the 'public law of Europe' and delivering common goods to the entire continent, linking her own self-interest to that of most Europeans. That said, Germany was not the only or – at times – the main enemy. There were periods when the threat of Soviet communism loomed larger, partly because of the threat it posed to the empire but mainly because of its stated aim of taking over central Europe, uniting Germany and Russia in one great ideologically hostile power. One way or the other, Britain was determined to prevent any one hostile power from controlling the vast land mass on the far side of the Channel.

Great Britain went to war in 1914 with her eyes open. She did so for the same reasons she had always had: to uphold the European balance of power. More specifically, Britain sought to prevent the Low Countries from falling into German hands, exposing the home island itself to attack. She was defending international law, in particular the neutrality of Belgium, which had been solemnly agreed to by all the European great powers, against German aggression.[3] There was also a strong ideological sense that 'kaiserism' – which many Britons regarded as simply the latest form of continental despotic affliction – represented a direct threat to their own political liberties. This was primarily a local and limited sentiment rather than a universal one. Britons were perfectly aware of the evils of tsarism – which they had decried and defeated in the Crimea only a few decades before – but vicinity made a big difference, as it always had. A 'Hun' in Belgium was a much greater threat than a Cossack in the Pale of Settlement, or so they believed. There was nothing inconsistent or hypocritical about that. Edmund Burke would have understood.

The First World War was, as its name suggests, a global conflict. It was fought in Africa, the Middle East and even East Asia. The main battle fronts, however, lay in Europe and, of these, none was more important than the Western Front in France and Flanders. In this relatively small place, familiar to English and British forces from centuries past, the empire's armies and their French allies grappled with Germany. On the five hundredth anniversary of the Battle of Agincourt, one newspaper recalled that England 'has yet greater wars today, and her sons again stand embattled in the very fields where noble Plantagenet with his "band of brothers" snatched overwhelming victory from the very jaws of disaster'.[4] Despite hopes that the conflict would be over by Christmas, both sides were quickly bogged down in trench warfare. Attrition, not manoeuvre, would decide the outcome of a contest of wills, demography and economic potential. It was an unequal struggle. To be sure, the Germans could mobilize all the resources of central Europe. Britain, however, was able to fall back on her deep fiscal-military state, which had been partially dismantled in 1815 and briefly cranked up again during the Crimean and Boer wars. The Royal Navy kept the sea lanes open, fed the home islands and enabled Britain, through her control of the global commons, to exclude Germany from them and to channel the resources of the world into London – raw materials, finished goods and men – where they would be converted into armies and ordnance to be thrown at the European mainland.

Over four years, the British empire pummelled Germany on the Western Front. In 1915, there were major offensives at Loos and Neuve Chapelle; an attempt to split the enemy and open a path to southern Russia by capturing Constantinople became bogged down in the Dardanelles. A year later, a greatly enlarged British army made a stupendous effort at the Battle of the Somme, which, though very costly, began the process of wearing down the Germans. A rising by German-backed Irish nationalists seeking to exploit 'England's difficulty' was seen off. Further offensives were launched in 1917, at Arras, Vimy Ridge, Cambrai and elsewhere, and though none achieved the desired breakthrough they all contributed to a growing German sense of physical and moral exhaustion. As in past contests, Britain began slowly. There were shortages of everything, especially shells, at the start and the army, in particular, suffered from a lack of professionalism. As in previous times, however, Britain got better as the struggle continued, with a government and a nation determined to see the contest through to the end with a restoration of the European balance. She took comfort in the idea of a historical pattern in her continental strategy. It had taken twenty years for 'England' [*sic*] to defeat Napoleon, the Welshman Lloyd George, then secretary for war, recalled some years into the conflict. 'It will not take twenty years to win this war,' he stated categorically, 'but whatever time is required, it will be done.'[5]

The conflict dominated every aspect of British politics and society. Irish Home Rulers and Unionists alike went off to fight the Germans rather than each other. The Conservatives rallied to support the Liberal government's war effort, not so much in order to protect Belgium as to prevent France from being crushed by Germany, thus destroying the whole European balance.[6] On the left, the Independent Labour party reconciled support for the war, opposition to capitalism and suspicion of Germany through hatred of 'Kruppism'.[7] Once battle was joined, the issue became the conduct of the war itself: the appointment of military commanders, the extraction of resources and the question of whether some innovative peripheral strategy could shorten the war, or whether, as the generals insisted and most politicians reluctantly agreed, the key to victory was a crushing blow against Germany on the Western Front.

In May 1915, the 'shell crisis' so damaged Asquith that he was forced to bring in senior Conservatives to form a coalition government dedicated to prosecuting the war more effectively. And in December 1916 Asquith's continued failure to win the war brought in the Liberal radical Lloyd George as the man who could deliver the 'knock-out blow' to end the war.[8] Britain proved able to combine an intense war effort with openness and parliamentary supremacy. For example, the failure at Gallipoli effectively destroyed Churchill's career for the time being, and led Parliament to set up a committee of inquiry in mid-1916.[9] Yet even for him parliament was the core of the war effort. In March 1917 he observed to a Scottish Liberal MP that 'This little place [Westminster] is what makes the difference between us and Germany. It is in virtue of this that we shall muddle through to success, and for lack of this Germany's brilliant efficiency leads her to final disaster.'[10] Even at the height of a global conflict, therefore, British politics maintained its capacity for public strategic critique. In fact, it was a precondition for her effectiveness in war.

The pressures of war increased popular political paranoia, government censorship and police surveillance.[11] In Britain, mobs smashed the windows of shops with Germanic names; nearly thirty thousand 'aliens' were interned. The long-standing German background of the monarchy, which went back to the Hanoverian Succession in the early eighteenth century and had been strengthened by Victoria's marriage to Prince Albert of Saxe-Coburg-Gotha in the nineteenth, came under attack. Bowing to pressure, the royal family renamed itself 'the House of Windsor'. On hearing the news, the Kaiser remarked that the British should now really retitle Shakespeare's play 'The Merry Wives of Saxe-Coburg Gotha'. An attempt to introduce identity cards, however, failed, due to widespread opposition.[12] The demands of war also had an emancipatory effect. Working-class women soon found paid work in the burgeoning munitions factories, while middle-class and aristocratic women threw themselves into various voluntary activities or nursing. The British feminist Vera Brittain, who worked in a hospital under the Voluntary Aid Detachment, told her father that 'I do not agree that my place is at home doing nothing, for I consider that the place now of anyone who is young and capable is where the work that is needed is to be done.' British women felt empowered by the fact that their country now needed them.[13] They accepted that the citizenship they sought also brought with it patriotic duties.

Britain fought the opening stages of the conflict with an all-volunteer army.[14] This unsustainable state of affairs was condemned by Liberals – many of them social radicals – as well as Conservatives. In the summer of 1915, the Manifesto for National Service demanded that 'every fit man, whatever his position in life, must be made available, as and when his country calls for him'; in the same vein, the *Manchester Guardian* proclaimed in August 1915 that 'the defence of the country is an obligation that should fall equally upon all citizens according to their capacity to render service.'[15] In 1916, conscription was finally introduced in Britain; politically sensitive Ireland was exempted, for the time being at least. Lloyd George supported the bill on the basis that 'every great democracy which has been challenged, which has had its liberties menaced, has defended itself by resort to compulsion.' Moreover, as the Liberal MP and former under-secretary of state for the home department Ellis Griffith argued, it was right to extend conscription to service abroad 'when in substance we are defending the realm as truly on the fields of France as if the invader were on British soil'.[16] It was a statement which would have resonated with Englishmen in centuries past. The front line of the United Kingdom, in other words, lay on the continent, not at the English Channel.

The empire, especially the white settler colonies, made a huge contribution to Britain's war effort in Europe. About four hundred thousand men served in the Canadian Expeditionary Force, mainly on the Western Front. Hundreds of thousands also came from Australia and New Zealand; the Australian prime minister undertook to support the mother country 'to the last man and the last shilling'.[17] There were more Australians killed fighting the Germans on the Western Front than battling the Turks at Gallipoli.[18] More than seventy thousand white South Africans, the vast majority English-speaking, and about forty thousand black Africans, were deployed in Europe. Approximately a million Indians served beyond the subcontinent, many on the main European battlefronts. In total, the dominions contributed more than 1 million men, most of them for service in Europe. The economic value of the imperial contribution was also enormous. By the end of 1916, Canada alone was producing about a quarter of Britain's total munitions needs and, with the partial exception of South Africa, the entire imperial war effort was paid from local revenue or loans.[19] The empire, in short, was fulfilling its original primary function, which was to enhance British power in Europe.

More important still, ultimately, was American support. The New World helped to redress the balance of the Old from the start of the conflict. US opinion was divided at first, but most of the East Coast white Anglo-Saxon Protestant establishment supported Britain. American money flowed to the *entente*; American ships carried war material to the allies. Many Americans volunteered for active service in Europe. In April 1917, President Wilson declared war on the German Reich, committing the second great Whig parliamentary union to defence of the European balance of power. Before the war was over, millions of Americans were deployed to France and, as the British diplomat had predicted shortly after the establishment of the United States in 1783, they spoke English, every single one of them.

Britain was the only major European power not to crack. The French suffered a series of mutinies in 1917. Russia erupted in revolution that same year. Germany was unplugged from the global system by the Royal Navy's blockade and withered on the vine, her population increasingly unable and unwilling to continue the struggle. Britain, by contrast, may have buckled under the German onslaught in March 1918, but the line held. In her most stupendous national effort to date, at great cost, she outperformed the Reich in every aspect of warfare. When the Americans, who had entered the war in 1917, finally arrived in France in substantial numbers in the summer and autumn of 1918, Germany was forced to admit defeat. The British empire, and her allies, had enforced its will on the continent in what had become a very familiar pattern.

Germany was crushed, but only after a terrific struggle. 'Germany could not have been beaten in the field, as she was beaten,' Sir Frederick Maurice, former director of military operations at the War Office, remarked shortly after the end of the war, 'without the intimate cooperation of all the allied armies on the Western Front directed by a great leader, nor without the co-ordination for a common purpose of all the resources of the Allies, naval, military, industrial and economic.'[20] The need to contain Germany was therefore at the heart of the Versailles settlement in 1919. The resulting treaty stripped Germany of much of her territory, her fleet and all her colonies. She was effectively disarmed by being reduced to an army of a hundred thousand men, without tanks or aircraft, in what was meant to be the start of a general process of European disarmament. The Rhineland was demilitarized altogether and a large allied army of occupation, including a 'British Army of the Rhine', installed there. British troops were back in Germany again, albeit this time as 'Watchers on the Rhine' to protect France and contain Germany rather than the other way around. The barrier system had been restored under new auspices.

The long-term answer to the German problem, many Britons believed, required more than just containment. Britain was suspicious of traditional French ambitions in central Europe and convinced that the best way of dealing with Germany was by changing her behaviour rather than her capabilities. There was agreement in London and Washington that the aggressiveness of the Wilhelmine empire abroad had been a product of her illiberalism at home. The obvious solution, therefore, was the destruction of 'Kaiserism' and the introduction of liberal democracy. Austen Chamberlain, the chancellor of the exchequer, argued shortly after the war that 'if Germany remains or becomes democratic, [it] cannot repeat the folly of Frederick the Great and Bismarck and his later followers.' 'No democracy can or will make aggressive war its year-long study and business, though it may flare up in sudden passion,' he argued in another instance of the tenacious 'democratic peace' thesis.[21] The liberalization of Germany, Chamberlain argued, should be achieved by local actors, if possible, and by outside pressure if necessary. 'The tragic fact remains,' the British historian and political advisor William Harbutt Dawson argued, 'that the German nation cannot by its own will shake off its political fetters.' He spoke for many in Britain and the United States when he added that it would require external intervention to remove 'that system, which for fifty years has proved a plague centre in the life of Europe'.[22]

Moreover, Britain feared that, if Germany did not dominate Europe, there was a danger that Bolshevism would. The best way of preventing this, London argued, was by recruiting Germany to the struggle against revolution, or at least denying her to the Bolsheviks. For this reason, Churchill called for 'the building up of a strong yet peaceful Germany which will not attack our French allies, but will at the same time act as a moral bulwark against Bolshevism', and thus 'build a dyke of peaceful, lawful, patient strength and virtue against the flood of Red barbarism flowing from the east'.[23] All this inclined the British and Americans towards a much more conciliatory treatment of their defeated enemy. Germany would have to be sufficiently weakened so that she could not menace the European balance, and yet not so completely enfeebled that she would succumb to the blandishments of the Bolsheviks. These were the same tensions that had underlain British relations with the continent over the past four hundred years, namely how to contain one hegemon without promoting another.

British domestic politics after 1918 remained deeply in Europe's shadow. Women over thirty were given the vote in recognition of their contribution to the war effort; the age restriction was intended, given the many male fatalities, to guard against a female preponderance, but it had the effect of depriving many women who had actually served of the franchise while granting it to many who had not. Millions of demobilized men flooded back into the workforce and an uncertain future. Sickened by the cost of the war and repelled by what they saw as French vindictiveness, many Britons now felt that the conflict had been a tragic mistake; this sentiment increasingly permeated political, popular and cultural discourse. So when John Maynard Keynes published *The Economic Consequences of the Peace* in 1919, he was pushing at an open door. Keynes, who had been a member of the British delegation at the Versailles conference, argued that the punitive reparation clauses were economically completely self-defeating. He pointed out that the general European recovery, on which the world and particularly the British economy depended, could begin only on the Rhine. Forcing the Germans to export their way to paying reparations would undercut British products. 'The treaty includes no provision for the economic rehabilitation of Europe,' he warned, 'nothing to make the defeated Central empires into good neighbours, nothing to stabilize the new States of Europe, nothing to reclaim Russia.'[24]

The end of the war brought little respite to the British empire globally. She was under attack in India, where Afghanistan launched an attack on the North-west Frontier in 1919, and from nationalist insurgencies in Iraq, Egypt, Ireland and many other places. London gave way in Ireland, permitting the establishment of the Irish Free State, largely because she wanted to appease American opinion, and because she was able to hold on to the strategically vital 'treaty ports' along the south coast, at least for the time being. Britain's principal concern remained Europe, which remained in turmoil for many years after 1918. The continent, especially its central, eastern and south-eastern parts, was convulsed by coups, wars and revolutions. Democracy gave way to dictatorship, in Italy after Mussolini's 'march on Rome' in 1922, in Poland and elsewhere. The eye of the storm, however, was Germany, where the new 'Weimar Republic' staggered under the challenge of left- and right-wing extremism. Here the problem was that the policy of containment, particularly reparations and the humiliating disarmament clauses of the Versailles Treaty, caused such economic misery and ill feeling in Germany as to subvert all hopes of the long-term shift in political mentality which might deliver security by other means. Moreover, the hoped for American commitment to the European settlement failed to materialize. The New World was no longer concerning itself with the balance of the Old, at least for now.

Matters came to a head in the Ruhr Crisis of 1923, when France and Belgium reacted to Germany's failure to keep up reparation payments by occupying the Ruhr and encouraging separatist movements in the Rhineland. Prime Minister Ramsay MacDonald condemned the move as evidence of a 'historical craving' to dominate central Europe. Likewise, the foreign secretary Lord Curzon accused France in early October 1923 of seeking 'the domination of the European continent'. A memorandum drawn up by the Foreign Office at his request in February 1924, which reflected the view of its *éminence grise* Eyre Crowe, erstwhile hammer of the Reich, argued that the French had to be prevented from making their presence in the Ruhr permanent and overturning the European balance on which British security depended. For this reason, London refused to recognize the 'so-called autonomous governments of the Palatinate',[25] which it regarded as mere French puppets. Simply balancing France by maintaining the integrity of Germany, however, would not be enough. 'Unless we want to return to the old system of the balance of power with all its attendant dangers of competition in armaments and inevitable wars,' the British ambassador to Washington Sir Esme Howard remarked, 'we must find something to take its place.'[26] Ramsay MacDonald therefore argued in June 1924 that a general European conference on security was required, which 'Germany should be invited to attend, not in order to be confronted with a document definitely settled', but 'to meet the allies in . . . negotiation'.[27]

The result was the Locarno Treaty of October 1925. This was a non-aggression treaty between France, Germany and Belgium, guaranteed by Britain and Italy. The Germans, under foreign minister Gustav Stresemann, surrendered all their territorial claims in the west, especially the demand for the return of Alsace-Lorraine, and were themselves admitted to the League of Nations. Britain promised to support France militarily not only if Germany attacked it but also if Germany was clearly preparing to do so by mobilizing in the demilitarized zone. Yet even if all the commitments entered into in that October of 1925 were honoured, the settlement held only in the west. Germany pointedly declined to guarantee its borders with Poland and Czechoslovakia, signalling its intention to seek revision at some stage in the near future. Moreover, Stresemann made no secret of his intention to use Germany's immense geo-economic power to restore its international position. Britain refused to extend her commitment to France and Belgium to cover eastern and central Europe. 'No British government,' Austen Chamberlain announced in a tone redolent of Bismarck, 'would even risk the bones of a single British grenadier' to defend Poland.[28] This forced the French to reaffirm their treaty commitments to the states of the cordon sanitaire in a series of treaties accompanying Locarno. Britain apparently believed that the security of Europe was divisible, and that the resulting territorial revisionism in the east could be contained.

The new European settlement profoundly shaped British strategic debates and domestic politics. There was general agreement that Britain should defend the integrity of Belgium and Luxembourg, and thus of southern England, but anything beyond that was highly contentious. Moreover, the new chancellor of the exchequer from 1925, Winston Churchill, was strongly opposed to the additional defence spending which upholding the guarantee advanced at Locarno required. Besides, when the question of a European security pact was discussed at the Committee of Imperial Defence (CID) in 1925, it soon became clear that it could not be concluded without consulting the empire. The trouble was, Chamberlain pointed out, that 'nowhere in that Empire has anyone the right to speak or act on its [collective] behalf';[29] there was therefore a strong risk that British defence policy would be 'paralysed'. In January 1926, the secretary to the CID, Maurice Hankey, penned an influential memorandum arguing that a new form of 'Pan-Britannic' imperial organization was required to cope with the revival of German power, the 'Balkanization of Europe' and the rise of Japan in the east.[30] This was achieved at the Imperial Conference at Westminster in October to November 1926, which recognized the equality of the dominions, and indeed their implicit right of secession from the empire. In return, all of the prime ministers present, except W. T. Cosgrave of the Irish Free State, promised to help Britain in time of war. This ensured that London would avoid the fate of her first empire in North America – traumatic confrontation – and would be able to rely on the settler colonies in the next European struggle.

Britain progressively withdrew her troops from Germany; they were all redeployed by the end of the 1920s. The 'watcher on the Rhine' was gone, the British barrier on the continent had been taken down. This put a particular premium on European disarmament, which would render German demands for military parity redundant. All now depended on whether the disarmament conference at Geneva could reach a settlement which would satisfy both Berlin and Paris.[31] This would embed Germany within European structures. Otherwise, the British Foreign Office warned, the Americans would recoil in disgust, the authority of the League would collapse, France would be left 'with no possible alternative to her military preponderance and her system of alliances and Germany [would be driven] to the edge of the abyss of despair'.[32]

One way of solving these problems was through European political unity. This concept had been present in British and continental European discourse for hundreds of years, its first modern iteration being the Quaker William Penn's late-seventeenth-century proposal for a European parliament. It was given a new urgency by the horrors of the World War and advanced most eloquently by Count Richard Coudenhove-Kalergi in his much-discussed book *Paneuropa* (1923). In May 1930, the president of the Pan-Europa Union, Aristide Briand, made a formal proposal for a 'European Federal Union' based on a 'European Conference' with an executive to coordinate economic and military cooperation. Britain rejected the surrender of sovereignty involved, but many were sympathetic to the idea of continental European union under liberal auspices. The arch-imperialist Leo Amery was a strong admirer of Coudenhove-Kalergi and his projects, which he regarded as the extension of Anglo-Saxon principles to the continent. Likewise, Winston Churchill, then chancellor of the exchequer, told Parliament in June 1925 that he hoped that one could 'weave Gaul and Teuton together so closely economically, socially and morally as to prevent the occasion of new quarrels and make old antagonisms die in the realization of mutual prosperity and interdependence'. Then, he continued, 'Europe could rise again.' Churchill did not believe, however, that Britain should be part of any continental political union. 'We are with Europe, but not of it,' he wrote in 1930. 'We are linked but not compromised. We are interested and associated but not absorbed.' Churchill went on to say that 'we [*sic*] must build a kind of United States of Europe' but with Britain on the outside, together with 'the British Commonwealth of Nations [and] mighty America [as] friends and sponsors of the new Europe'.[33]

Time, however, was running out for this positive British vision for Europe. The world economic crisis which began with the Wall Street Crash of 1929 spread throughout Europe, especially Germany, from the early 1930s. Banks failed and unemployment surged, undermining democratic governance. Political extremism and associated territorial revanchism grew across Europe. 'The present world "confidence crisis"', a Foreign Office memorandum of December 1931 argued, was caused by 'a series of interlocking problems, ranging from the purely financial and monetary problem at the one end to the purely territorial problem created by the Peace Settlements at the other end'.[34] This led to a relentless 'chain' linking 'monetary crisis inevitably back to the economic chaos in Europe', which in turn resulted from 'political questions of reparations and war debts'. These then had their roots in French concerns with the 'problem of security' and, ultimately, with the question of the 'territorial status quo in Europe'. At the bottom of everything, including economics, was geopolitics, in particular the question of how German power was to be contained and Europe to be ordered, issues which were two sides of the same coin.

Not long after the last British forces withdrew from Germany, and well before Hitler took power, Whitehall began thinking about a new continental commitment. The integrity of Belgium and the Netherlands was to be guaranteed at all costs. 'It was to secure the independence of the Low Countries,' Austen Chamberlain wrote in 1931, 'that we fought Spain in the sixteenth century, that we fought Napoleon in the nineteenth, and that we fought Germany in the twentieth.'[35] At the same time, the Cabinet announced in mid-December

1931 that it was 'not prepared to enter into some form of guarantee over and above Locarno under which, in conceivable circumstances, British forces might be engaged in a war on the continent of Europe'.[36] London justified this stance by arguing that the continued instability was the fault of the French, who were 'heavily over-insured' in Europe, and by insisting on German disarmament according to the provisions of Versailles, while refusing to move substantially to the general disarmament which that treaty had also envisaged. 'A high level of armaments,' one senior British diplomat argued, 'is no substitute for security. At best it creates the illusion of security in one quarter while at the same time aggravating the sense of insecurity in the other.'[37] London was wrestling with a problem which had plagued policy-makers since 1918, which was how to enable the Germans to become subjects of the European state system again, without automatically turning all the weaker actors into objects.

When Hitler became chancellor in January 1933 and began to rearm, all bets in Europe were off. He was instantly recognized as a major challenge to the European balance upon which British security depended. The 'Defence Requirements Sub-committee' was tasked by the Committee for Imperial Defence with assessing Britain's global position in November 1933 after Hitler's withdrawal from the League and the Geneva Disarmament Conference. It pronounced unmistakably that, while both Japan and, to a lesser extent, Italy were serious threats, the 'ultimate potential enemy was' Germany.[38] For the moment, the report argued towards the end of February 1934, 'her permanent system, with its full complement of armaments and trained reserves, has not yet taken shape'; within a 'few years', however, Germany would 'present a serious menace to this country'. The defence of the wider empire was a much lower priority. The permanent under-secretary for foreign affairs Robert Vansittart argued that 'Japan would [only] attack us after we had got into difficulties elsewhere ... and elsewhere could only mean Europe, and Europe could only mean Germany.'[39] For this reason, Britain decided in July 1934 to establish a substantial 'Field Force' for deployment to the continent in time of war. At the top of its tasks was the traditional mission of deterring an attack on the Low Countries. Those, such as the Conservative politician Leo Amery, who believed that Britain should place her imperial commitments first, remained in the minority, albeit a vocal and important one, and even Amery saw the empire primarily as an instrument to maintain Britain's position in Europe.[40] This was summed up by his slogan 'For Empire and Europe.'[41]

Neville Chamberlain, then chancellor of the exchequer, was profoundly conscious of the range of threats facing the empire, not only from Hitler but also in the Mediterranean, from Italy, and in the Far East, from Japan. 'The *fons et origo* of all our European troubles and anxieties,' he wrote in his diary in 1934, 'is Germany.' That said, Chamberlain feared imperial and fiscal overstretch. He preferred to deter Hitler through the creation of a large 'stand-off' fleet of bombing aircraft, rather than prepare the dispatch of a large expeditionary force to France, as interventionist orthodoxy demanded.

The perceived strength of the German Luftwaffe greatly increased the anxiety about Hitler. Stanley Baldwin, then Lord President of the Council and later prime minister, had already warned Parliament in 1932 that '[t]he bomber will always get through.'[42] Yet this did not lead to any fundamental change in the strategic concern which had preoccupied London since the Middle Ages: the security of the south coast of England. The Low Countries were, the chiefs of staff argued in late July 1934:

> if anything, even more important in the defence of this country than in the past. They are as vital as ever to our sea power. In addition, if the Germans were to succeed in over-running the Low Countries and in establishing air bases near the Belgian and Dutch coasts, not only London, but the whole of the industrial centres in the Midlands and the North, as well as our shipping approaching the coasts, would be within effective and even decisive range of air attacks, which owing to the short range, could be heavy, continuous and sustained.

For this reason, Baldwin warned Parliament in July 1934, during a debate on the expansion of the RAF, that 'since the days of the air, the old frontiers are gone.' 'When you think of the defence of England,' he continued, 'you no longer think of the chalk cliffs of Dover; you think of the Rhine. That is where our frontier lies.'[43] It was a statement which could, in fact, have been made two hundred years earlier. The emergence of air power, in other words, had not so much transformed traditional British geopolitical vulnerabilities as confirmed them.

For the moment, however, there was no enthusiasm for actually confronting Hitler. Suspicion of France, widespread since its perceived bullying of Germany in the 1920s, persisted. Cooperation with the United States was complicated by continuing tension over First World War debts.[44] Moreover, many within government felt that the status quo was untenable, that Germany had a right to rearm, within limits, and that the wrongs of Versailles should be redressed. The general sense was that Hitler should be 'appeased' by leaving him a free hand in central Europe while standing firm against demands for the return of colonies and any threat to France or the Low Countries.[45] There was a widespread hope in the first years after 1933 that Nazism could be contained, that it was 'not for export', and that peaceful coexistence between the west and the totalitarian powers was possible. 'We shall never get far,' in the work of mediation, the British prime minister Neville Chamberlain told Parliament, 'unless we can accustom ourselves to the idea that the democracies and the totalitarian states are not to be ranged against one another in two opposing blocs'. Much better, he argued, for Britain to 'work together' with its rivals and thereby 'facilitate the international exchange of goods and the regulation of international relations in various ways for the good of all'.[46]

The challenge of Hitler had a considerable impact on British domestic politics in the 1930s. A bitterly contested by-election at Fulham in October 1933 was dominated by the question of rearmament and won by the candidate opposed to greater military expenditure.[47] In the 1935 general election, both major parties were opposed – Labour strongly so – to large-scale rearmament, and the victorious Conservative prime minister Stanley Baldwin later notoriously admitted that any other position would have led to his defeat. At the heart of this hesitation was widespread fear of bombing, which was generally believed to cause hundreds of thousands, if not millions, of civilian casualties. The subject dominated Commons debates on foreign policy and rearmament in 1933–4, with the result that press, parliamentary and public interest in national security largely exhausted itself in demanding increased provision for air defence; it was expected that Hitler would be contained and in the end defeated by naval blockade. Basil Liddell Hart, the renowned military historian and commentator, spoke of a traditional British 'indirect approach'. It had the merit of combining restraint with economy. There was hardly any concern at all for the state of the European balance and the huge continental commitment which would be required to uphold it. In mid-1930s popular opinion, the 'blue water' policy of an earlier generation of British isolationists had become a 'blue skies' strategy designed to minimize British involvement in Europe as much as possible.

Few agreed with Winston Churchill that the Germans – 'this mighty people, the most powerful and most dangerous in the western world' – had voluntarily subjected themselves to Hitler and should be resisted without delay.[48] He and Sir Robert Vansittart were among the few who saw an epic struggle ahead between the democracies and the dictatorships. 'Germany will attract friends to her camp,' he warned in February 1934, 'if she is allowed to grow, while we remain weak. Were that to happen, there would eventually be a landslide in Europe and the democratic principle would vanish.'[49] Only a tiny number of Westminster politicians, such as Austen Chamberlain, Edward Spears, Harold Nicolson, Robert Boothby and Winston Churchill, made a direct link between the nature of the Nazi dictatorship and the strategic threat it presented to European peace.[50] Moreover, even ardent resisters such as Vansittart baulked at taking on Hitler openly, and this weakened their hand against the dominant 'appeasers'. 'It is easy to be brave in speech,' the permanent under-secretary in the Foreign Office Alexander Cadogan asked him at the time of Hitler's ultimatum over Austria, '[but] will you fight?' Vansittart replied: 'No.' 'Then what is it all about?' Cadogan rejoined, 'To me it seems a most cowardly thing to do to urge a small man to fight a big [man] if you won't help the former.'[51]

Emboldened by 'appeasement' and the apparent decline of the western democracies, the dictators ran riot across Europe. In 1935, Hitler introduced conscription and publicly announced the existence of the Luftwaffe; a year later, he remilitarized the Rhineland. Both measures were flagrant violations of the Locarno Treaty, but Britain did not react. Germany intervened on behalf of Franco in the Spanish

Civil War, beginning to build up an informal economic empire there and in the Balkans. In the Mediterranean, Mussolini flexed his muscles; in the Far East, Japan was on the move. Britain felt her 'imperial overstretch' keenly, yet she refused to enter into a common diplomatic and military front with Stalin's Soviet Union. In early 1938, Hitler annexed Austria, and towards the end of the year he seized the Sudetenland, the German-populated parts of Czechoslovakia, after Chamberlain and the French caved in at the notorious Munich Agreement. Six months later, in March 1939, Hitler grabbed what was left of Bohemia, extinguishing Czech statehood. The Versailles settlement, and thus the whole of British security in Europe, was in tatters.

The Nazi surge caused Britons to question appeasement. More and more members of the Labour party abjured pacifism and embraced the view that Hitler had to be stopped; the left-wing press, led by the *Daily Mirror*, now relentlessly battered appeasement.[52] The Conservatives remained a 'class divided' between those such as Churchill, Harold Macmillan and Anthony Eden, who believed that concessions simply encouraged further demands, and the Chamberlainite majority, which held that another war against Germany would destroy civilization as they knew it and open the door to a communist takeover of the whole of Europe. Some, such as the foreign secretary Lord Halifax, even saw Hitler as a 'bulwark of the west against Bolshevism'. Matters came to a head at the bitter by-elections in late October and early November 1938, when Liberals, Labour and Conservative dissidents rallied to support anti-appeasement candidates opposed to 'Munich'. In Oxford, their campaign literature announced that a vote for the official Conservative candidate Quintin Hogg was 'a vote for Hitler'; Hogg squeaked in with a greatly reduced majority. Three weeks later, however, a Conservative majority at Bridgwater was overturned in a result that was widely regarded as a popular rejection of appeasement. The message was clear: Chamberlain would have to stop Hitler, if only to halt his relentless slide in the polls.[53]

In the face of European threats, Britain looked, as she had for so long, to her empire for support. That of the self-governing British Dominions could no longer be taken entirely for granted. The isolationist Member of the Canadian Parliament who claimed that '[w]e live in a fire-proof house far from inflammable materials' spoke only for a minority, but there was still considerable doubt among the Canadians, Australians, New Zealanders and, especially, South Africans, where Boer sympathy for Germany ran high, that confronting Germany militarily was necessary or wise, not least because anxiety about Italian and especially Japanese power often loomed larger overseas. It was worth making the additional effort to persuade the Dominions, as the combined defence budget of the British empire was higher than that of the Third Reich once rearmament got under way. In short, the overseas possessions and dominions were primarily conceived not as ends in themselves but as assets to be deployed in defence of the European balance of power. Whatever imperial difficulties there might be, the priority, as the British permanent under-secretary Warren Fisher remarked in the mid-1930s, was to contain the 'Teutonic tribes, who century after century have been inspired by the philosophy of brute force'.[54]

British opinion tilted sharply against appeasement after Hitler's occupation of Prague effectively destroyed popular and press confidence in government strategy towards Germany; the parliamentary rumblings grew greater. *The Times* condemned the 'expansion of political tyranny', and most other British newspapers followed suit.[55] Chamberlain was relentlessly attacked from the opposition benches and was confronted with calls from Conservative resisters for an all-party government. The British government was forced to recognize that Hitler not only totally dominated central Europe – something they tolerated with severe misgivings – but intended to overturn the whole European balance on the strength of it. In the west, London feared a German descent on the Low Countries. The chiefs of staff recommended in January 1939 that this should be resisted. In late February, the Cabinet endorsed this view, agreeing to go to war in the event of a German attack on Holland, Belgium or Switzerland and issuing a public guarantee of French security. With this in mind, the continental 'Field Force' was mobilized in the first months of 1939; the first really intensive Anglo-French staff talks followed soon after. The *entente cordiale* had been revived. At the same time, the 'rape of Prague' stunned the Dominions, just as the fate of the Palatinate and Bohemia had outraged the English Protestant diaspora in the 1620s and 1630s. In March 1939, the Canadian prime minister Mackenzie King told Parliament in Ottawa that Canada would follow Britain into war with the Axis powers. What was being defended in Europe had global ramifications.

It was not enough, however, just to draw the line in the west. Substantial further German gains in eastern Europe – and rumours of a descent on Poland or Romania were already circulating – must also be prevented. Hitler, as under-secretary Cadogan, himself a strong supporter of appeasement, said in May 1939, must not gain 'a free hand to expand into the east and take control of the resources of central and eastern Europe', which would make her 'powerful enough to attack the western countries with overwhelming force'.[56] 'If Germany obtains access to the economic resources of Romania,' the service chiefs warned in mid-March 1939, 'she will have gone a long way to rendering herself immune from the effects of economic warfare.'[57] Moreover, Hitler could be defeated – or better still deterred – only if he was forced to fight on two fronts; keeping the Poles in play was therefore vital. For this reason, Britain joined France in guaranteeing Polish and Romanian independence in March 1939, though not necessarily their territorial integrity.[58] This was designed to allow some room for a Polish–German territorial settlement but to deter Hitler from outright annexation of another swathe of Europe, thus denying him the resources to wage a successful war against them. It was the same strategy that had informed British foreign policy towards the continent for hundreds of years.

For London, the main issue was the threat which Hitler posed to the entire European balance of power, and that the ideological complexion of Nazi Germany rendered her an inherent danger to world peace. In late August 1939, the formerly pro-appeasement *Times* had warned that the Nazi–Soviet partition plans against Poland showed that brutal cynicism can credibly be attributed to states in which all vestiges of individual liberty have disappeared, and that 'such disregard of international morality and of human rights . . . cannot be localized.'[59] By November 1939, even Lord Halifax was arguing that while:

> [i]n general it is no business of one nation to interfere with the internal administration of another, and history has plenty of examples of the

> futility of such attempts . . . when the challenge in the sphere of international relations is sharpened, as today in Germany, by the denial to men and women of elementary human rights, that challenge is at once extended to something instinctive and profound in the universal conscience of mankind.[60]

Hitler, however, was not deterred. In September 1939, he attacked and crushed Poland; the Russians helped him to partition the country. Britain declared war on Germany: the only one of the major allied belligerents who lasted the course to fight from start to finish and to enter the war by choice without waiting to be attacked. She sent the British Expeditionary Force to France, expecting a repeat of the First World War, with a battle of attrition to be decided by the slow economic strangulation of the Reich. Instead, Britain suffered catastrophic early defeats and long periods of isolation before new allies appeared on the scene. After a short respite, the Germans seized Norway and Denmark. The Low Countries and France were overrun in a lightning campaign. The British garrison at Calais put up a ferocious fight in order to enable the withdrawal of the bulk of the BEF through Dunkirk. Russia occupied the Baltic states, forced Romania to surrender Bessarabia and grabbed a chunk of Finland. Britain seriously considered action against Stalin, but thought better of it.[61] The USSR was expelled from the League of Nations in November 1939, yet no declaration of war followed. Virtually the entire continent was now in hostile hands. A Nazi–Soviet totalitarian bloc stood in self-conscious opposition to the western plutocratic democracies,[62] of which Britain was the last man standing on the near side of the Atlantic. It was the darkest prospect she had faced since the Napoleonic Wars, perhaps even bleaker.

The outbreak of war fundamentally changed British politics and society. It nearly destroyed Chamberlain's government, which was widely believed to have failed to contain Hitler, right away. When the prime minister addressed Parliament a day after the invasion of Poland, he recommended further negotiations, not war. When an opposition leader rose to respond, another MP memorably called: 'Speak for England.' The Cabinet began to revolt. In the end, Chamberlain was pushed into taking action by a popular, press and parliamentary determination to confront Germany. As a result, Britain entered the war unenthusiastically but united. The Territorial soldier Private G. E. Tapp summed up the mood when he remarked that Britain was fighting for 'the settlement of the European problem – to be brought about only by the complete destruction of Hitler's regime'.[63] Moreover, Australia, Canada, New Zealand and South Africa all rallied to the cause, in the latter case only after a very bitter parliamentary debate; Ireland remained neutral. The war economy worked efficiently from the start of hostilities, thanks not least to government-sponsored cooperation between industry and trade unions in order to boost arms production.[64]

The war also hastened the emergence of the welfare state. The credibility of the old elites was irreparably damaged by their perceived strategic incompetence between 1936 and 1940. In 1941, the coalition government – at the instigation of the Labour party – commissioned a report designed to map out a full-scale transformation of British society. The resulting document – which has gone down in history as the Beveridge Report – was published in late 1942. It contained proposals for a National Health Service, improved public housing and a comprehensive system of social welfare. The main aim here was to promote the social cohesion and demographic strength necessary to support Britain's great power position, not only during the war but also in times to come. This came across very clearly in the report's attitude to the family and to women's health, where the emphasis was on increasing the birth rate through maternity benefits. 'In the next thirty years,' Beveridge wrote, 'housewives as mothers have vital work to do in ensuring the adequate continuance of the British race and of the British ideal in the world.'[65] More generally, the report was designed to hold out to the soldiers and the home front a tangible reward for their exertions against Hitler. Welfare and warfare were inextricably intertwined. The logic was inescapable: if Britons were to be mobilized in defence of hearth and home, it made sense to give those who had neither hearths and homes to defend.

Defeat in the west precipitated a parliamentary revolt against Chamberlain in May 1940. The new government under Winston Churchill was determined to fight on and to make whatever military, economic, social and constitutional sacrifices were necessary to achieve victory. 'I believe I can save this country,' the new prime minister announced, echoing William Pitt the Elder's words of 1756, 'and no-one else can.'[66] In mid-June 1940, Churchill made an unsuccessful offer of Union with France – involving joint citizenship and a common government – designed to lock the French into the war effort against Germany, or failing that to secure their fleet.[67] The Nazi threat was so existential, in other words, that it justified the surrender, or at least the pooling, of British sovereignty. Not long after, once the French had capitulated, Britain rejected Hitler's peace overtures. That summer, the Royal Air Force repulsed the Luftwaffe's attempt to gain control of the skies over England and, even with air superiority, Germany's ability to get past the Royal Navy would have been highly doubtful.[68] Hitler called off Operation Sealion, the projected invasion of the south coast. The threat of invasion had thus passed. Britain had saved herself by her efforts. Now she could set about saving Europe.[69] In October 1940, Churchill penned an introduction to some of Pitt the Younger's speeches during the struggle against Napoleon. He expressed Britain's 'determination to fight on, as Pitt and his successors fought on, till we in our turn achieve our Waterloo'.[70]

Britain began to bring its immense economic strength, and that of the empire, to bear on Europe.[71] Hundreds of invaluable 'imperial' pilots flew in the Battle of Britain, and millions of empire men and women served on all fronts in the course of the war.[72] New Zealand battle casualties were the highest among all belligerents as a proportion of the population, with the single exception of the Soviet Union.[73] The combined industrial output of the British empire soon exceeded that of German-occupied Europe in every category, with the exception of rifles.[74] Slowly but surely, this superiority was felt on the mainland. A Royal Air Force bombing offensive directed largely against German civilian targets started slowly, and was conducted at great cost, but delivered considerable psychological effect from late 1940 onwards.[75] London supported various continental resistance movements with the aim of 'setting Europe' ablaze against the Axis.[76] The Royal Navy maintained a close blockade of Hitler's Europe, unplugging the Reich from the global economic system while ensuring that Britain could continue to profit from it. American war equipment, provided by President Roosevelt on favourable terms, poured across the Atlantic. Cut off from the markets and raw materials of the world, the productive power of the European economies under Hitler's New Order, though considerable, was a pale shadow of their pre-war performances. The contest continued to go badly for Britain, at first, with a string of defeats in the Balkans and North Africa, and from June 1941 German armies surged into the Soviet Union, threatening to bring the entire Eurasian land mass under the control of a single hostile power – Mackinder's nightmare vision. In December 1941, however, the strategic picture shifted decisively in Britain's favour. Hitler became bogged down before Moscow, and around the same time he declared war on the United States.

From late 1941, two great coalitions, the 'Grand Alliance' – to use a phrase which Churchill borrowed from his ancestor Marlborough – of Britain, the Soviet Union and the United States and the 'Axis' of Germany, Italy and Japan, together with their various satellites and allies, locked horns across the globe. That same year, the British prime minister pointedly brought out an extract from the fourth volume of his biography of Marlborough, dealing with his coalition triumph at Blenheim. Its very first line, reproduced from the pre-war original, ran: 'In a war involving nearly the whole world it was natural that each campaign should offer to both sides a wide choice of plans.'[77] In January 1942, the Allied powers issued their 'Declaration by the United Nations', pledging to employ their 'full resources' to 'the struggle for victory over Hitlerism'.[78] Here the two Anglo-Saxons were picking up a theme from Robert Byron's celebrated epic poem *Childe Harold's Pilgrimage*, which had described Waterloo as a 'place of skulls' where the 'United Nations' had prevailed over the tyrant, Napoleon; yet another example of how history served to spur the Grand Alliance on. Now Anglo-America could bring the full weight of its power to bear on the Axis.[79]

Determined to win the war before the United States could intervene in strength, or at least acquire the critical mass to force a stalemate, the Axis surged forward. The Japanese occupied much of South-east Asia, including Hong Kong and Singapore, and menaced India. In North Africa, Rommel advanced as far as El Alamein, just inside Egypt, threatening the Suez Canal. On the Russian front,

German armies penetrated deep into the Caucasus and nearly captured Stalingrad, on the Volga. At sea, U-boat wolf-packs came close to cutting Britain off from the global supply of food and war materials. By the beginning of 1943, however, it was clear that continental supremacy would be beyond Hitler's grasp. Rommel had been decisively beaten by Montgomery. German armies were encircled at Stalingrad, and a subsequent offensive at Kursk failed miserably. The U-boats were beaten off in the Atlantic. Allied aircraft were well on their way to controlling the skies above Europe, opening a 'second front' which tied down immense German resources long before they landed in Normandy.[80] It was now only a matter of time before Britain and her allies returned to the continent, on the ground, in force.

Britain began to think about the future shape of Europe well before the final defeat of the Axis. Her two principal preoccupations had not changed much since 1919. On the one hand, there was the question of what to do about Germany. The problem seemed to be not just the form the state should take, but the Germans themselves. Sir Con O'Neill, a senior British diplomat, opined that because 'National Socialism has been no more than a special form of organization of the instincts and capacities of the German people,' the best solution would be to turn the country into a 'super-Sweden', prosperous and inoffensive. Churchill instinctively inclined towards more extreme measures: he periodically spoke of the need to 'castrate' German men to prevent future aggression, or hoped that Germans would become 'fat and impotent'. On the other hand, echoing the post-Versailles concerns, the prime minister worried that communism might fill the resulting vacuum. He warned the Cabinet not to 'weaken Germany too much – we may need her against Russia'.[81] Most British planners, however, supported partition schemes of one sort and another, even at the cost of Soviet hegemony in central Europe. 'It is better,' Sir William Strang, the British envoy to the European Advisory Commission, the inter-allied commission tasked with proposing a new order for the continent, argued in late May 1943, 'that Russia should dominate Eastern Europe than that Germany should dominate Western Europe,' because 'however strong Russia may become, she is unlikely ever to be so grim a menace to us as Germany could again be within a few years.'[82]

The only way of squaring these circles was continental European integration, which would embed Germany in a wider union and mobilize its resources for the common defence against Stalin. In October 1942, Churchill, not for the first or last time, 'look[ed] forward to a United States of Europe in which barriers between the nations will be greatly minimized'. He 'hope[d] to see the economy of Europe studied as a whole', and the establishment of a Council of 'ten units, including the former Great powers [and thus, presumably, Britain], with several confederations – Scandinavian, Danubian, Balkan, etc. which would possess an international police and be charged with keeping Prussia disarmed'.[83] The Americans, too, were highly sympathetic to closer European integration, which would relieve them of the obligation of protecting the continent ad infinitum and encourage transatlantic trade.[84]

First, however, Hitler had to be defeated. Britain persuaded Washington, which was half convinced anyway, that it should be 'Germany First'. The British differed radically from the Americans, however, about the timing of the cross-Channel assault which would be necessary to defeat Hitler. They preferred to 'wear down' Hitler through operations in the Mediterranean and other marginal fronts first, while US commanders favoured delivering an early 'knock out' blow in northern France.[85] In many ways, the Americans were the heirs to the old British tradition of Whig continental engagement, impatient to operate in Marlborough country, while Britain – partly out of a healthy respect for German military capabilities even after Stalingrad – cleaved to the old Tory 'blue water' and 'peripheral' approach. These disagreements climaxed at the Casablanca Conference of 1943, when the British succeeded in beating back US demands for an early invasion of France, agreeing a Mediterranean strategy instead.[86] By late 1943, however, Anglo-American strategic differences were resolved at the Tehran Conference, where the three allies agreed that a cross-Channel invasion should be launched in the early summer of the following year.[87] They also agreed to establish a United Nations Organisation to manage the post-war world.

In early June 1944 – on D-Day – the British, Americans and Canadians hurled themselves into northern France as their fathers and forefathers had done since the late Middle Ages. At least one British officer tried to inspire his men that morning as the landing craft approached the strongly defended beaches by reading out Henry V's famous speech before Harfleur, when Shakespeare has him exhort the men 'unto the breach' once more. The film version of the play was released that same year, dedicated to the 'Commando and airborne troops of Great Britain'. In the popular mind, these Englishmen and their North American descendants were part of the continuity of a European story which went back to the medieval English empire in France. Over the course of the next eleven months, they fought their way across the traditional battlefields of northern France and the Low Countries, including the Walcheren swamps in which their ancestors had been mired in Napoleonic times, and through western Germany into the centre of the Reich. They were to stay there, at the heart of Europe, for some sixty years.

The Second World War was the culmination and the vindication of British history. 'This is your victory,' Churchill told the London crowd in May 1945, acclaiming 'the unbending resolve of the British nation'. It was not Hitler's 'Thousand-year Reich' but the thousand-year kingdom of England that had prevailed. For eighteen months in 1940–41, the British empire had stood alone, with some brief assistance from the Greeks and Yugoslavs, for the maintenance of the European balance of power. They were strong enough to deter Hitler from invasion and would almost certainly have repelled any attempt, had it been made. With the help of their allies, they restored the equilibrium of the mainland, more or less. Britain had once again mobilized impressively, without permanently forfeiting her constitutional freedoms. Above all, the United Kingdom had persuaded much of the rest of the world to 'want what it wanted'. It was the same tried and trusted European strategy which had stood the test during the First World War, the Napoleonic Wars and on many other occasions. Whether it would serve as well in the face of new and in some respects very different challenges from the continent remained to be seen.

8

'Our destiny has been to help shape Europe'. Britain and the Continent in the Age of European Integration

Germany is no longer the dominating power in Europe – Russia is. She cannot fail to become the main threat in fifteen years from now. Therefore, foster Germany, gradually build her up and bring her into a Federation of Western Europe.

– Chief of the Imperial General Staff,
Lord Alanbrooke, 1944[1]

Western Europe dominated in fact by Germany and used as an instrument for the revival of power through economic means . . . is really giving them on a plate what we fought two wars to prevent.

– Harold Macmillan, 1958[2]

How did one talk of events in Europe nowadays? The Common Market. Well, that was fair enough, that dealt with trade, with economics, with the inter-relationship of countries.

– Agatha Christie, *Passenger to Frankfurt*, 1970

Over the past seventy years or so, Britain has found herself facing a new European question which differs in one crucial respect from all earlier challenges. For the first time ever, she has been confronted not with a hostile takeover but by the offer of a negotiated merger. In contrast to the earlier acts of Union with Scotland and Ireland, this would entail an enlargement of England so great as to dilute and negate its distinct political identity and the supremacy of the Westminster parliament. Rejecting the threat to the sovereignty of the United

Kingdom has been the easy part, however. Recognizing it has been far more contentious. London governments have been confronted with the question of whether they should join the European project in some attenuated form or 'let' the rest of Europe proceed. They have also had to deal with criticism from their continental European partners for whom the claim of British exceptionalism has been as irritating as it has been historically well-founded.

In 1945, Britain once again became a guarantor power of the European settlement agreed at the conferences at Yalta and Potsdam. The independent states of western and southern Europe were reconstituted. Democracy did not return of its own accord. It was restored to France, Italy, Denmark, Norway and the Low Countries as an Allied war aim. 'We have one principle about the liberated countries or the repentant satellite countries,' Churchill announced, echoing Abraham Lincoln, as the war was drawing to a close. 'Government of the people, by the people, for the people, set up on the basis of election by free and universal suffrage.'[3] Eastern Europe, by contrast, came under Soviet domination. One-party communist rule was eventually established in Poland, Czechoslovakia, Bulgaria, Romania, Hungary and Russian-controlled Germany. Germany was partitioned by the victor powers and divided into zones of occupation. Millions of Germans were expelled from eastern territories annexed or reclaimed by Poland, the Soviet Union and Czechoslovakia. A substantial British force was left in Germany: a second British Army of the Rhine (BAOR). The 'watcher on the Rhine' was back.

Britain still faced the same problem in Europe, however, as she had after the First World War, namely 'dual containment'. On the one hand, London was determined to guard against German revanchism. She saw 'Prussian militarism' as the primary threat to European stability.[4] 'Don't break up Germany,' the chief diplomatic advisor to the government Sir Robert Vansittart argued early in the war. 'Break up Prussia, and do it good and proper.' It was also considered vital to destroy Germany's capacity to wage war, even if this caused economic damage to Britain in terms of trade and markets. She should be left only with the peacetime industries compatible with that aim. 'Our policy ought to be to draw the fangs while leaving some of the teeth,' the chancellor of the exchequer Sir John Anderson remarked in the summer of 1944.[5] It was in this spirit that Britain entered into a fifty-year mutual defence pact with France against Germany, together with a somewhat shaky security guarantee to the continent, at the Treaty of Dunkirk (1947).

On the other hand, Britain needed to maintain Germany, and perhaps also some German military potential, as a bulwark against the Soviet Union. Churchill repeatedly warned of the danger of 'inflicting severities upon Germany, which is ruined and prostrate . . . open[ing] to the Russians in a very short time to advance if they chose to the waters of the North Sea and the Atlantic'. The best way of doing so, figures such as the chief of the imperial general staff Lord Alanbrooke were arguing well before the war ended, was to create a strong Germany and to bring her into some sort of powerful federal union with other European states capable of resisting Stalin. For this reason, Churchill floated the idea of a Danubian Confederation, which would fulfil some of the same functions as the old Austro-Hungarian empire.[6]

The war's end brought fundamental change to British domestic politics following the end of the coalition that had existed since 1940. Churchill suffered a surprise defeat in the July 1945 election, a reflection not so much on him personally, or of any irresistible tide of popular radicalism, as a withering judgement on the Conservative policy of appeasement and the fall of France. 'It was not Churchill who lost the 1945 election,' Harold Macmillan later remarked, 'it was the ghost of Neville Chamberlain.' This theme was hammered home relentlessly in Labour election propaganda.[7] The British Labour party saw itself as socio-economically equidistant between Washington and Moscow; it spoke of itself as a 'Third Force'. Geopolitically, it was strongly committed to the European balance of power, the containment of Germany and the deterrence of any Soviet aggression, through British leadership of western Europe as the 'third force' in the world, 'in the middle of the planet', as the foreign secretary Ernest Bevin put it.

Peace led to the immediate termination of the American Lend-Lease programme, precipitating a financial crisis in Britain.[8] It was far from clear where the new Labour government would find the resources to fund the domestic 'New Jerusalem' it had promised the people as a reward for 'their' victory, and in order to prepare the nation for future struggles. There was also the question of Britain's enormous strategic ambitions and obligations, which still spanned the globe.[9] Labour agreed that the retention of overseas possessions and the reassertion of imperial control over territories occupied by the Axis was essential not only to make up for resources missing back home but also in order to increase her weight on the European and world stage. So in the autumn of 1945 Britain sent substantial forces to finish off Japan in the Far East, partly to assert her imperial interests but mainly to build up goodwill in Washington which could be traded for American engagement with European post-war security.[10] In the same spirit, the new Labour foreign minister Ernest Bevin spoke of the need to 'mobilize the resources of Africa in support of a western European Union . . . [to] form a bloc which, both in populations and productive capacity, could stand on an equality with the western hemisphere and the Soviet blocs'.[11] It was for this reason that Britain held on so long in India, Africa and Asia after 1945. The empire had primarily been acquired for purposes to do with the European balance, and these considerations still prevailed.

So, while the Labour election victory began the construction of a 'welfare state', Britain did not yet stop being a 'warfare state'. Expenditure on the military and empire still exceeded that on hospitals and social services. Indeed, Britain was a 'welfare' state the better to be a 'warfare' state, because social justice was essential to enable the nation to stand together on the world, and especially the European, stage. Vast sums went into the navy and the air force. Peacetime conscription for one year of service was introduced on a permanent basis in 1947. Moreover, the British chiefs of staff were adamant that they needed to have 'every club in the bag', and began to adapt the bomber force for the delivery of the atomic bomb even before they had the technology itself. 'We've got to have this thing over here whatever it costs,' the British foreign secretary Ernest Bevin memorably demanded, 'We've got to have the bloody Union Jack on top of it.'[12] By 1952, at great expense, Britain had developed its own nuclear deterrent.

Meanwhile, Stalin progressively consolidated his hold on eastern Europe. In March 1946, Winston Churchill, now out of office, summed up the new anti-Soviet mood at Fulton, Missouri, in a famous speech entitled 'Sinews of Peace'. He began by announcing that the right to 'free and unfettered elections' and all the other liberties enjoyed by Britons and Americans had universal applicability and 'should lie in every cottage home'. The reality, however, was that 'from Stettin in the Baltic to Trieste in the Adriatic, an iron curtain has descended across the Continent.' 'Behind that line,' Churchill continued, 'lie all the capitals of the ancient states of central and eastern Europe: Warsaw, Berlin, Prague, Vienna, Budapest, Belgrade, Bucharest and Sofia.' The Russians, moreover, were pressing forward on every front, aiming for 'the indefinite expansion of their power and doctrines'. This was 'certainly not the liberated Europe we fought to build up', Churchill continued, but it was also one which did not 'contain the essentials of permanent peace'. Britain was therefore embarking on both a strategic and an ideological mission. 'If the Soviet Union disappeared, or if Russia were under a different ideology,' a British Foreign Office memorandum argued in similar terms in January 1947, 'the world could soon settle down to peace.'[13] The defence of liberty in Europe, in other words, was synonymous in British minds with the prevention of another European war.

London now fundamentally reassessed its German policy. 'Until recent months,' Bevin remarked in early May 1946, 'we have thought of the German problem in terms of Germany itself, our purpose having been to devise the best means of preventing the revival of a strong aggressive Germany.' But now, he continued, 'it can no longer be regarded as our sole purpose, or, indeed, perhaps as our primary one. For the danger of Russia has certainly become as great as, and possibly greater than, that of a revived Germany.'[14] This was, again, an ideological as much as a geopolitical struggle. 'It is not overstating the matter,' the deputy under-secretary of state at the Foreign Office Sir Orme Sargent argued, 'to say that if Germany is won this may well decide the fate of liberalism throughout the world'.[15] In June 1946, the Anglo-American occupation authorities held elections for regional assemblies. They also laid particular emphasis on the 're-education' of Germans away from Nazism towards western values: this was about changing German behaviour rather than just limiting their capabilities. The Americans and British then set up a 'bi-zonal' German government and, at the London accords in April to June 1948, the

French reluctantly agreed to the creation of an independent, albeit federal, western Germany, which came into being as the Federal Republic of Germany in 1949. The aspiration to become part of a future European political union was written into its constitution – the 'Basic Law'.

By then it had become clear that Britain's global role was no longer sustainable. In the late 1940s, she was constantly engaged in some sort of military action or occupation duties across the Middle East, the eastern Mediterranean and the Indian subcontinent, not to mention the 'Cold War' with the Soviet Union. Priorities would have to be reset. The shedding of responsibilities began in February 1947, when Britain announced that it wished to transfer the costly task of defending Greece from communist subversion to the Americans. Shortly after, Britain withdrew from India and, a little later again, she quit Palestine. These were the first of many retrenchments over the next twenty years. They were all done with a view to concentrating British attention as much as possible on Europe, from whence the main challenge to her security came.

The onset of open confrontation with the Soviet Union inspired British statesmen to promote greater western European unity. They conceived this as an intergovernmental and not primarily as a supranational exercise, at least as far as London was concerned. It was 'not enough to reinforce the physical barriers which still guard our western civilization', Bevin told the Cabinet in early January 1948, '[w]e must organize and consolidate the ethical and spiritual forces inherent in this western civilization of which we are the chief protagonists.' This could only be done, he argued, 'by creating some form of union in western Europe, whether of a formal or informal character, backed by the Americas and the Dominions'.[16] London now briefly became the leader of the European political project, taking the initiative to create the Brussels Pact in March 1948. This brought together Britain, France, Belgium, Holland and Luxembourg in a Western European Union partly to hedge against the revival of German power but primarily to contain the Soviet Union. The signatories committed themselves to mutual defence in the event of external aggression and soon began military planning on how to repel the Red Army.[17] This arrangement provided a solution to Britain's security interests in Europe which did not compromise her national sovereignty.

To some Britons, a new system of alliances, however close, was not enough, at least not for continental Europe. They had come out of the war convinced that some form of federalism or shared sovereignty would be essential to prevent a relapse into barbarism, and the threat from Stalin only reinforced this view. In a speech at Zürich University in September 1946, Winston Churchill once again urged Europe to 'unite', with Britain supporting the project from the outside.[18] Once again, including the Germans was central to his conception. Washington, wanting to contain Germany and mobilize the continent against the Soviet Union, strongly encouraged the Europeans to integrate economically and politically.[19] In early May 1948, hundreds of European politicians, trade unionists, intellectuals and other representatives of civil society, including the future prime minister Harold Macmillan, met at The Hague under the chairmanship of Churchill and at the invitation of the International Committee of the Movements for European Unity. The British government was sympathetic to closer European cooperation, which it hoped would give the continent sufficient weight to act on the world stage on terms of equality with the United States and the Soviet Union.[20] London resisted, however, any attempt to merge its own sovereignty into a larger whole, partly because of its Commonwealth links. The principal reason for the reticence, however, was that, Britain not having experienced defeat and occupation, British opinion regarded European political unification as an attempt to repair something that was not broken in the first place.[21] Ernest Bevin agreed: cooperation and even 'spiritual confederation' – yes; complete political union – no.[22]

There were no such reservations about joining the North Atlantic Treaty Organisation (NATO), consisting of the United States, Britain, Canada, France and the Low Countries in 1949. The contractants committed themselves to mutual defence in the later legendary Article 5 of the Treaty. Its military implications were somewhat limited at first, as no serious planning or preparations followed, but the political symbolism of a US commitment to the European balance was enormous. There would be no repeat of the period after Versailles, when Washington had refused to commit to the security of Europe. This time, the United States would be there from the start. In due course, NATO acquired a sophisticated command structure and a

'Supreme Allied Commander Europe', by convention always an American. The first of them was General Eisenhower, who had led the western allies to victory over Hitler in the Second World War. In return, London accepted that Germany would have to rearm, within some broader European framework, as the foreign secretary Herbert Morison, the French foreign minister Robert Schuman and US secretary of state Dean Acheson demanded in a joint statement in September 1951 supporting 'the inclusion of a democratic Germany . . . in a Continental European Community, which will itself form part of a constantly developing Atlantic Community'.[23] One way or the other, as the British first general secretary of NATO, General Hastings 'Pug' Ismay, memorably put it, a security architecture for Europe had been created which 'kept the Americans in, the Russians out and the Germans down'.

Britain remained aloof, however, from the European Coal and Steel Community (ECSC) in 1950. This was the brainchild of Robert Schuman and was announced on the fifth anniversary of the end of war in Europe. It was designed to ensure both long-term Franco-German economic cooperation and Germany's structural inability to engage in independent warfare by putting the coal and steel industries of both countries under the supervision of a supranational 'High Authority'. The scheme caught British diplomats, who were convinced that the Germans and French would never agree, unawares, but in any case there was never any chance of Britain joining it. Membership would have jeopardized relations with the Commonwealth, which still took about half of British exports, more than double the share then going to western Europe. This was not just a question of past services: Canada had a whole infantry brigade with NATO in Germany. Besides, the British coal industry was then dominant in Europe, and its nationalized workforce highly sceptical. 'It is no good', the new Labour foreign secretary Herbert Morrison famously remarked, 'We can't do it, the Durham miners won't wear it.'[24] The main reason for refusing to join the ECSC, however, was that, unlike France, Britain was not prepared to countenance the loss of essential national sovereignty necessary to contain Germany. 'It would seem to us that, even if desirable,' the chancellor of the exchequer Stafford Cripps told Parliament, 'such a scheme could hardly prove to be workable . . . unless it were preceded by complete political federation.'[25] Nor did she want to embark on any process whose end goal was a form of supranational federation incompatible with the independence of the United Kingdom.

Britain's refusal to commit to European political integration distressed the Americans, for whom it would have been the tidiest solution to all their problems. First, because British involvement would give 'Europe' some much-needed substance and a psychological lift after the depredations of war. Second, because it would have ensured a 'steady' voice in European counsels against that of the potentially more wayward continental Europeans, especially the French. Third, because it would have obviated the awkwardness of dealing with Britain on the basis of a 'special relationship', thus relegating the rest to some kind of second-class status. The United States never really gave up on its ambition to push Britain into Europe, or to keep her there, not realizing that full political integration would either happen without Britain or not at all. This was a failure of imagination on Washington's part, because although the United States had been primarily created by Englishmen, on Anglo-Scottish lines, it began as a largely symmetrical union of newly independent states, unlike the United Kingdom, which was an asymmetric union based on an enlarged England.

The question of European integration returned to the top of the agenda in the early 1950s with the plan for a European Defence Community (EDC). This was designed partly to mobilize western Europe against Soviet communism and partly to serve as a vehicle for full political union. It was strongly supported by the United States, which hoped that London would join. Harold Macmillan was in favour, telling the Strasbourg assembly that 'Britain's frontier is not on the Channel; it is not even on the Rhine; it is at least on the Elbe.'[26] Britain resolutely refused to participate in supranational integration herself. 'This is something which we know in our bones we cannot do,' the foreign secretary Anthony Eden told a New York audience in January 1952.[27] London was, however, deeply sympathetic to other European states participating in the EDC, because – as Eden put it – there was no other way of 'anchoring Germany to the west' and preventing her from 'drift[ing] in the centre of Europe with the certainty that she would be sucked into the Soviet system sooner or later'. Once again, London was recommending to continental Europeans a measure which compromised – indeed, subverted – national sovereignty, which she did not wish to participate in herself. This weakened the proposal in the eyes of many other Europeans, and it was ultimately defeated in the French parliament. The episode epitomized the cross-Channel divide on European integration.

The Schuman plan did not register much at home, and where it did it was largely rejected. The near-simultaneous Labour party pamphlet 'European Unity' stated bluntly that 'in every respect except distance, we in Britain are closer to our kinsmen in Australia and New Zealand on the far side of the world, than we are to Europe.'[28] These sentiments, which were widely shared by Conservatives, resonated over the next two decades during the long debate on 'Europe'. Labour supporters were also deeply suspicious of the European project as a 'cartel' of industrialists, which suggested that it was a 'capitalist plot'. For now, however, there was relatively little popular controversy about Britain's role on the continent, a subject which had already gripped elite imaginations but which seemed of little relevance to them in their daily lives.

By contrast, British domestic politics were profoundly shaped by the early Cold War in Europe. In 1950, the intensification of the Cold War led to an increase of national service to two years.[29] Troops were sent to contain communist aggression in Korea. Britain's army was now actually bigger than it had been at her imperial zenith in 1920, its main purpose not to defend the overseas possessions but to deter the Russians in Europe. The spiralling costs of defence (about 12 per cent of GNP) associated with the maintenance of an overseas empire, the prosecution of war in Korea, the development of the atom bomb (achieved by 1950) and defensive measures against a possible Soviet invasion of Europe forced the government into painful cuts to domestic spending.[30] When in the spring of the following year, the chancellor of the exchequer Hugh Gaitskell proposed to introduce charges on dental and eye treatment in order to pay for increased armaments, the minister for health Aneurin Bevan resigned in protest. He was supported by left-wingers such as Michael Foot and Harold Wilson. Gaitskell's cuts were to no avail, in any case, because in September 1951 Britain suffered a balance of payments crisis largely caused by massive defence expenditure, especially the huge cost of the British Army of the Rhine.[31] At around the same time, Britain began to observe the recovery of the German economy – the *Wirtschaftswunder* – with awe.[32] In October 1951, the Labour party went down to a narrow defeat in a general election in which foreign policy – the unpopular Korean War, the cost of rearmament and the shaky British position in the Middle East – were central issues.[33]

Thereafter, British domestic politics continued to polarize around Europe. The dividing lines ran not so much between the parties as within them.[34] A full-scale battle erupted within Labour over Germany.[35] The dominant anti-communists, such as Denis Healey and Hugh Gaitskell, strongly supported NATO and were prepared to tolerate German rearmament within a system of multilateral constraints. They pointed out that the European Defence Community corresponded to the old socialist principle of transcending narrow national boundaries and preoccupations. A significant minority in the Labour party, however, was deeply opposed to the creation of a new German army under the auspices of the EDC or any other umbrella organization. The question of what to do about Germany transcended the left–right split, though. Two of the most strident opponents of German rearmament were the left-winger Bevan and Hugh Dalton, who was firmly on the right of the party.[36] In 1954, the Labour Party Conference narrowly endorsed German rearmament, but only by using the trade union 'block vote' to overrule the rank-and-file sceptics. There were also serious splits over Europe among the Conservatives. The 'Strasbourgers', a group of Tories more sympathetic to 'Europe' than the rest of the party, contained many prominent figures, such as the anti-appeaser Robert Boothby and the sometime appeaser Duncan Sandys, as well as the rising star Harold Macmillan.

The collapse of the European Defence Community enabled Britain to move into the resulting political vacuum and once again briefly seize control of the European project.[37] In September 1954, Anthony Eden agreed to 'continue to maintain on the mainland of Europe, including Germany, the effective strength of the United Kingdom forces now assigned to SACEUR [Supreme Allied Commander Europe]'. The British Army of the Rhine was reinforced. In late October

1954, Britain, France, Germany, Greece, Italy, Luxembourg, the Netherlands, Portugal and Spain came together to agree to 'promote the unity and to encourage the progressive integration of Europe'. Seven months later, this pact was formally christened the 'Western European Union' (WEU). Unlike the supranational European Defence Community, however, this was an intergovernmental organization acceptable to London.

Supporters of European integration, appalled by the failure of the Defence Community, now changed tactics. Open moves towards full political union were largely abandoned in favour of a more gradual and stealthy approach based on economic cooperation, in the first instance. In 1955, Jean Monnet founded the Action Committee for a United States of Europe, which was made up of leading Christian Democrat, socialist, liberal and labour leaders. That same year, the European Coal and Steel Community countries met in the Sicilian city of Messina to deepen their supranational economic ties. The foreign ministers of France, Germany, Italy and the Benelux countries agreed to form a customs union – known as a 'common market' – and to integrate the transport and civil atomic energy sectors. Britain, which was not a member of the Coal and Steel Community, wanted a much looser free-trade association. She argued that further economic union would divide western Europe and, far from containing Bonn, would actually – in the words of one official – provide 'a means of re-establishing the hegemony of Germany'.[38] Nevertheless, an intergovernmental committee under the Belgian Paul-Henri Spaak began to investigate how a European 'common market' might be achieved. This made London uneasy. 'I do not like the prospect,' Harold Macmillan remarked in February 1956, 'of a world divided into the Russian sphere, the American sphere and a united Europe of which we are not a member.'[39] 'The Common Market is the Continental system all over again,' he warned de Gaulle. 'Britain cannot accept it. I beg you to give it up. Otherwise, we shall be embarking on a war which will doubtless be economic at first but which runs the risk of gradually spreading into other fields.'[40]

The new European solidarity was about to be sorely tested. In the face of intense US scepticism about her 'imperial' ambitions, Britain decided to stand her ground against Egyptian president Nasser's ambition to nationalize the Suez Canal. What was at stake, London believed, was not just Egypt, or even the wider Middle East, but Europe itself. Nasser's challenge, as prime minister Anthony Eden put it, was a direct threat to 'Western Europe's economic security'. Moreover, dealing with Egypt was seen as vital to the success of the 'Eurafrican' project of collectively mobilizing the continent in support of European power.[41] France was totally supportive. Some other European states – like Italy, which expected to move into the vacuum left by Britain and France – were opposed to action against Nasser. Most, including the German chancellor Konrad Adenauer, strongly supported military intervention on the grounds of '*European raison d'état*'.[42]

In July 1956, Nasser announced the nationalization of the Suez Canal. London and Paris were outraged. In early September, the French prime minister Guy Mollet secretly proposed a Franco-British Union of states – a revival of the Churchill scheme of 1940 – in order to present a united front to the world. London rejected these overtures as a dilution of national sovereignty, but she did agree to joint action against Nasser in (covert) conjunction with the Israelis. In November 1956, the British and French launched Operation Musketeer against Nasser and occupied the Canal Zone.[43] Egyptian resistance collapsed quickly. In the UN, US and at the bar of world opinion, however, London and Paris were mercilessly pilloried for their 'colonialist' adventure. President Eisenhower was furious. Using massive economic pressure – through the IMF and the crash sale of sterling bonds – the United States sought to compel the two European powers to back down. London – confronted by a run on the pound – soon buckled.[44] She had completely withdrawn from the Canal Area by the end of the year.

London was determined never to find herself on the wrong side of an argument with the Americans again. Moreover, there was now a widespread realization that the empire, once a major bulwark of the British position in Europe, was now a liability which complicated attempts to rally the world against communism.[45] Britain could no longer stand for the defence of democracy in Europe and imperialism overseas, even if the former plausibly required the latter.[46] She came to an arrangement with Greek nationalists in Cyprus and soon abandoned most of her African and Asian empire, which had become a distraction from her European destiny and a cause of suspicion to friendly capitals on both sides of the Atlantic. Britain had built up her colonial empire largely for strategic purposes, and it was for the same sorts of reason that she relinquished it: in deference to US wishes, to strengthen the argument against Soviet human rights abuses and in order to ease Britain's path back into 'Europe'.

Paris, resolved never to trust Washington again, clung grimly to her overseas possessions, especially North Africa. She also pushed ahead with European integration: 'Europe,' Adenauer comforted them, 'will be your revenge.' In 1957, the six Messina countries concluded the Treaties of Rome, which brought about the establishment of the EEC, a European Common Market, a year later. Britain, once again, refused to join. Partly, this was for fear of alienating the Commonwealth, which still took well over 40 per cent of British exports. The main reason, however, was that London did not share the Belgian Spaak's view that the containment of Germany required supranational integration in Europe. Britain, moreover, was confident that she could survive outside, a view bolstered by the fact that she still held nearly a quarter of world trade. So, in 1960, she set up a looser European Free Trade Association (EFTA) instead, together with Sweden, Norway, Denmark, Austria, Portugal and Switzerland. Western Europe was now, economically, divided into two separate camps, and Britain was leading the weaker one.

Towards the end of the decade, the realities of geo-economics began to assert themselves. As the British chancellor of the exchequer Peter Thorneycroft remarked in early January 1957, the Achilles heel of Britain at Suez had been the 'weakness of [its] post-war economy'.[47] That summer, London was rocked by a sterling crisis: wages were growing, inflation was on the increase and speculation against the pound resumed. Public expenditure soared. Manufacturing output was about to drop behind that of West Germany. 'With relatively few assets and large debts,' Thorneycroft warned prime minister Macmillan at the end of the year, 'we continue to live upon the scale of a great power. We have the most expensive defence forces in Europe. We have joined the nuclear "club". We claim at the same time a very high standard of life. We seek to lead the world in the social services we provide.'[48] It would have to be either guns or butter. Britain chose butter. The population was appeased with throwaway budgets: Macmillan told them in 1957 that they had 'never had it so good'. The United Kingdom had become primarily a 'welfare' rather than a 'warfare' state, though she still maintained considerable military capabilities.

The price was paid in terms of Britain's European standing. In the late 1950s, financial pressures became so great that, after the Sandys Defence Report of 1957, she was forced to cut the RAF and the British Army of the Rhine. National service was phased out for cost reasons; ever greater reliance was placed on the independent nuclear deterrent. For now, however, the British still refused to compromise their sovereignty and antagonize the Commonwealth by participating in an economic union in Europe. Moreover, the British feared that Germany would use the resulting agreement as a vehicle for the return to great power status. Macmillan warned that the EEC would lead to 'western Europe dominated in fact by Germany and used as an instrument for the revival of power through economic means. It is really giving them on a plate what we fought two wars to prevent.'[49] Paris shared these concerns but believed that political and economic – though not military – integration with Bonn was the best way to guard against them. This Anglo-French divergence on Europe and Germany persisted, and it re-emerged with a vengeance in the late 1980s and early 1990s.

Britain was by no means the only European state wary of joining the Franco-German project: the Irish, Norwegians, Swedes and Swiss also refused, for now. The taoiseach of the Republic of Ireland, Eamon de Valera, spoke for many when he warned Dáil Éireann, the Irish parliament, that a political federation 'would mean that you had a European parliament deciding the economic circumstances . . . of our life here'. Rather than cooperation, he complained, the European process seemed to be 'an attempt to provide a full-blooded Political Constitution'. 'A small nation,' de Valera went on, 'has to be extremely cautious when it enters into alliances which bring it willy-nilly into . . . wars . . . we would not be consulted in how such a war would be started – the great powers would do that – and when it ended, no matter who won . . . we would not be consulted as to the terms on which it would end.'[50] Why, he wondered, would Ireland submit to this, having spent so long trying to throw off the British yoke? It was no coincidence, of course, that the nations declining (for now) to enter into closer political union were mostly – though not exclusively – those who had escaped the rigours of occupation in the Second World War, either through their own efforts – as in the case of Britain – or by free-riding, as in the case of the Irish Free State (now a Republic).

In the early 1960s, Britain's military commitment to Europe, always strong, deepened further. The emerging NATO doctrine of 'flexible response' and increased West German unwillingness to surrender whole swathes of the country to the invading Soviet forces at the start of a war put a greater emphasis on conventional forces over nuclear deterrence. The British Army of the Rhine was now deployed ever further forward, east of the Weser in northern Germany. It was eventually given authority to use tactical nuclear weapons. One British corps was instructed to hold the line there 'for a maximum of thirty days. No fall-back position is envisaged.'[51] The implication was clear. If the Soviet Union attacked, British forces would fight and die deep inside Germany. As in days gone by, they were manning the outworks of a defensive system designed to hold, or at least delay, the enemy well before he was within striking distance of the south coast of England. Much had changed over the years, but much had also stayed the same.

Meanwhile, the terms of trade with Europe were shifting. Throughout the late 1950s and early 1960s, the extent to which Britain was falling behind continental Europe financially and technologically became painfully clear. Trade with the Common Market countries grew larger than with the Free Trade Area and even outstripped that with the Commonwealth. British industry was now increasingly convinced that its future lay with the Common Market. Only by joining the European Economic Community, Macmillan felt, could the nation hope to regain the weight she had lost on the international stage. It was also the best hope of containing Germany. 'Shall we be caught between a hostile (or at least less and less friendly) America,' he remarked in July 1960, 'and a boastful, powerful "Empire of Charlemagne" – now under French but later bound to come under German control'.[52] Besides, ever since the collapse of the European

Defence Community and the ascendancy of President de Gaulle in France, the European project had changed from a threateningly supranational concept to a much more congenial intergovernmental arrangement,[53] or so it seemed. 'Believe that we rather tend to exaggerate the horror of actually joining the Common Market,' the erstwhile sceptic and Foreign Office mandarin Sir Gladwyn Jebb wrote to Macmillan in May 1960, adding that 'if we ever did, we should be no more committed to the prospect of an actual federation than the government of General de Gaulle, that celebrated nationalist.'[54]

In July 1961, Britain made a formal application to be admitted to the EEC, to the fury of Australia and New Zealand, whose agricultural produce would suffer.[55] The Dominions, so long a support of Britain's position in Europe, were to be sacrificed to the same end; there was a sad and brutal logic to the move. Supporters of the EEC, such as the Labour party stalwart Roy Jenkins, condemned the 'ghastly complacency and insularity' of the opponents. He criticized their 'grossly exaggerated and completely outmoded view of Britain's importance in the world and her capacity for independent action'.[56] Here Jenkins struck a note which has been audible among British supporters of European membership ever since: that one should join because there was something wrong with Britain. It echoed the principal reason why the continental powers had begun to pool their in any case rather flimsy sovereignty and suggested that, when all was said and done, the United Kingdom was just another European state. The opponents of membership, by contrast, believed that they lived in what was still an exceptional country. Membership of the EEC, the Labour party leader Hugh Gaitskell announced in a dramatic speech at the annual congress in 1962, should not lead Britain to become 'a Texas or California in the United States of Europe'. That, he warned, would spell 'the end of Britain as an independent nation state . . . the end of a thousand years of history'.

Britain's bid to join the EEC was strongly supported by Washington, as part of its last-ditch attempt to sponsor thoroughgoing European political and military integration. President Kennedy's 'Grand Atlantic Design' was an ambitious attempt to renew NATO, bind Germany even more closely to the west and mobilize more European energies for the common struggle against the Soviet Union.[57]

Part of this plan was a scheme for a Multi-Lateral (nuclear) Force (MLF), involving a shared European shipborne atomic deterrent, under NATO rather than national US command. Full West German participation was envisaged. Kennedy hoped that all this would be accompanied by a new wave of political integration, preferably supranational rather than intergovernmental. Britain was expected to play an important role in driving this process forward. Kennedy, in turn, promised to supply Britain with Polaris nuclear missiles on the understanding that these would eventually be deployed under the MLF umbrella, a move London feared would give the Germans nuclear parity with them.[58]

In mid-January 1963, however, de Gaulle unilaterally vetoed Britain's admission to the EEC. 'If Britain were admitted,' he told the press conference, 'Europe would eventually be absorbed into a colossal Atlantic community dependent on America and under American control, and this France could not permit.' It was clear that Britain had been comprehensively outfoxed. There was in fact no immediate danger of a 'United States of Europe'. France had transformed the European project from an all-encompassing political union incompatible with her national sovereignty into an intergovernmental force-multiplier in which German power was not only contained but mobilized to balance that of the dreaded 'Anglo-Saxons'. De Gaulle played both ends against each other. He leveraged his morally and physically shattered nation from the depths of 1940–44 back to a position of near-equality on the United Nations Security Council, of military superiority over Germany and an affectation of equidistance between the two superpowers. The establishment of the French nuclear *force de frappe* in the early 1960s completed the picture. The problem was not that Britain had 'missed the European bus' ten years earlier, because the bus was then headed in a supranational direction that she had no intention of taking, but rather that, once it changed course towards a more acceptable destination, the French were taking their time about letting them on.

Rejection by Europe was a considerable psychological shock to the British government and political class. Edward Heath, the chief British negotiator, dubbed 'Mr Europe' by the press, responded with a heartfelt reaffirmation of the continentalist creed. 'We in Britain,' he said, 'are not going to turn our backs on the mainland of Europe or on the countries of the community. We are a part of Europe: by geography, tradition, history, culture and civilization.'[59] In April 1963, he was consoled with the award of the prestigious Charlemagne Prize. The new Labour government geared up to make a second attempt, this time meeting Gaitskell's charge of the loss of sovereignty head on. 'Nations are not free at the moment to take their own decisions,' the chancellor of the exchequer Jim Callaghan claimed. 'The argument about sovereignty is rapidly becoming outdated.'[60] Prime Minister Harold Wilson warned de Gaulle that if he did not admit Britain to the Common Market London would review its commitment to the Army of the Rhine, and perhaps even to NATO. The trade-off that Wilson was suggesting here was reasonable enough; what was implausible was that Britain could carry through on the threat without cutting off her nose to spite her face.

Meanwhile, the slide in Britain's geo-economic potential continued relentlessly, deeply affecting her position in and over Europe. By the 1960s, the country was in the midst of one of her periodic bouts of national performance anxiety. This expressed itself in concern over her relative economic decline compared to western Europe, especially the Federal Republic of Germany. There was also a pervasive sense of malaise about the 'British disease' or 'sickness' which went well beyond the economic health of the country. Critics were gripped by a veritable moral panic which linked the collapse in international standing with varying degrees of plausibility to foreign subversion, the decline in scientific innovation, growing immigration, the spread of pornography, rampant homosexuality and prostitution. All these themes came together in the Profumo scandal of June 1963, when it was alleged that the secretary of state for war had shared the favours of a prostitute with a naval attaché at the Soviet embassy in London.

Europe was now more important than ever to Britain's future.[61] The costs of maintaining an 'imperial' presence in Asia and the Middle East, however, threatened Britain's ability to fulfil her obligations in Germany, the main battleground. In 1966, she announced her withdrawal 'east of Suez'. Henceforth, the deterrence of Soviet aggression in Germany would not merely be the most important but the only large mission for the British Army; from the end of the decade, there was also a substantial commitment to keep the peace in Northern Ireland. So, in 1967, London made a fresh application to join the EEC, and was again rejected by de Gaulle. In 1969, however, de Gaulle resigned, and London seized the chance to launch a third campaign to join the EEC. At a closely fought general election in 1970 – in which Europe played an important though not decisive part – Britain chose a strongly pro-EEC Conservative prime minister, Edward Heath, whose first priority was to 'take Britain into Europe'.[62]

This decision was partly driven by concern over Britain's low economic growth rates. The main purpose of the bid, however, was political and strategic: to regain the nation's historic pivotal role in Europe by concentrating her main political and military attention there. Locking in Germany was also an important part of Heath's thinking on Europe. More broadly, he argued that membership of the Common Market would open up a whole new vista for the country. 'For twenty-five years we've been looking for something to get us going again,' Heath said in a TV broadcast in 1971. 'Now here it is. We have the chance of new greatness. Now we must take it.'[63] Failure to join the EEC, the 1971 White Paper argued, would mean that '[i]n a single generation we should have renounced an imperial past and rejected a European future'.[64] 'Either we choose to enter the community,' the authors argued, 'and join in building a strong Europe on the foundations the six have laid; or we choose to stand aside from this great enterprise and seek to maintain our interests from the narrow – and narrowing – base we have known in recent years.'[65] In 1971, after a dramatic debate, the government won a parliamentary vote on membership. Once the result was known, former prime minister Harold Macmillan lit a bonfire at Dover, which was met with a matching one at Calais. The Narrow Sea once again connected rather than separated England from the far shores.

On the very first day of 1973, Britain was duly admitted to the EEC, an occasion celebrated by a musical 'fanfare for Europe'. That, however, was not the end of the matter. Heath lost the 1974 election. In early June 1975, the new Labour government under Harold Wilson put membership of the EEC to a national referendum. The resulting debate divided the country, the parties and even families. At the outset, opinion polls suggested that about 70 per cent of the population were opposed to membership, with fewer than a fifth actively in favour. Some were concerned about the loss of imperial trade preference and the exorbitant cost of the Common Agricultural Policy. Others felt deep concern at what a White Paper of the time described as the loss of 'essential national sovereignty' to Brussels. Wilson acknowledged these fears when he told the German chancellor Helmut Schmidt that the 'sovereignty of parliament' was a key issue in the referendum.[66] He himself recommended a yes vote, though without much enthusiasm. However, thanks to the efforts of the European movement, the Information Research Department of the Foreign Office, various MPs, elements of the BBC and the force of the argument itself, most Britons were persuaded to change their minds.[67] In the end, just over two thirds of the electorate voted to stay in the EEC; support in England was higher than in any other part of the United Kingdom, substantially so in the cases of Scotland and Northern Ireland. The dire state of the economy and the grave international situation – the poll took place in the shadow of the apparently irresistible advance of world communism – substantially contributed to the outcome. The vote, as Roy Jenkins noted piquantly, had taken place on 6 June, the anniversary of D-Day, 'when Britain had ended a previous period of exclusion from Europe'.[68]

The Common Market was generally good for British business, but it could not compensate for serious structural economic deficiencies which had accumulated since the end of the Second World War and were greatly aggravated by the oil shock: the surge in fuel prices caused by political instability in the Middle East. Throughout 1976, the country was convulsed by economic problems, which culminated in a sterling crisis and a bail-out by the International Monetary Fund (IMF). The implications for Britain's strategic position were dire: there were plans to repair the public finances by reducing the troop presence in Germany and withdrawing from Cyprus altogether.[69] As the United Kingdom retreated globally, Scottish nationalism reappeared in the form of the Scottish National Party. Britain was also on the defensive against IRA terrorism in Northern Ireland, which appeared the more sinister in the light of its partial sponsorship by Moscow.[70] In the course of the resulting struggle, elements of the

British security forces and justice system were involved in illegal beatings, some shootings and secured convictions based on flimsy and at times fabricated evidence. In September 1976, the British government was subjected to a humiliating verdict from the European Court of Human Rights which held that interrogation techniques used since the early 1970s had amounted to torture.[71] Irrespective of the merits of this judgement, the episode was one of many object lessons in the way in which 'Europe' could embarrass and limit the power of the democratically accountable London government. More generally, Britain was beginning to experience what Lord Denning had predicted a few years earlier, which was that the mass of legal implications of membership was 'like an incoming tide. It flows into the estuaries and up the rivers. It cannot be held back.'[72]

In 1979, Margaret Thatcher was elected prime minister. She had a reputation for toughness, soon demonstrated over the economy, in Northern Ireland, during the escalating tensions with a more activist Kremlin and, most spectacularly, during the Falklands Crisis, when Argentina invaded the remote island group in the South Atlantic. There was initially little sign of this combativeness over Europe, however. Thatcher had been a pro-Marketeer in the 1970s. The Conservatives were the more pro-European of the two parties in the 1979 election, though the issue made little difference to the outcome. To be sure, Thatcher's first term saw a robust discussion with the continental Europeans over the 'rebate', that is, a repayment of part of the large sum which the UK, one of the greatest contributors, paid into the common coffers to support the Common Agricultural Policy and other projects. 'I cannot play Sister Bountiful to the Community,'[73] Thatcher announced. This was essentially a redistributionist struggle in the national interest, however, rather than an indication of the kind of fundamental hostility to 'Europe' prevalent at the time on the British left. In general, the prime minister was pro-EEC, because she saw the Community as a vehicle to rally the continent more effectively against communism. 'Who is there in the EEC to speak up for defence?' she pointedly asked in Brussels. 'I feel no assurance that all these connected matters are being looked at together.' Labour was then committed to unilateral nuclear disarmament and withdrawal from the EEC, causing much of the pro-European wing of the party to break off and form the Social Democratic party in 1981. When Thatcher won re-election two years later, in any case, the Conservatives were even more the 'party of Europe'.[74]

During her second term, Thatcher supported substantial further integration on the continent in the shape of the Single European Act of 1985, with its provisions for greater political cooperation, especially in the field of foreign policy. Conceived at the height of the Second Cold War, this was primarily intended by her to ensure a common front against the rampant Soviet Union. It was also designed to promote another British objective: the Single Market. Significantly, the task of ending customs, currency and capital controls across Europe was entrusted to a UK commissioner, Lord Cockfield. These were, of course, all intergovernmental rather than supranational initiatives, and thus did not compromise the sovereignty of the member states.

Soon after her third election victory, Thatcher's view of Europe changed for two reasons,[75] both of which reflected a new surge in integration, not a change of heart on her side. First, Jacques Delors, the activist President of the European Commission appointed in 1985, revised the left-wing view of the Community as a 'capitalist club' by suggesting that it could soften the rigours of conservative market economics through a pan-European programme of social rights. In early September 1988, this culminated in a much-discussed speech by Delors at the Trades Union Congress (TUC) in Bournemouth which marked the 'conversion' of the British left to Europe. Not long afterwards, Thatcher retaliated in a famous speech in the Flemish town of Bruges. She recommended that 'willing and active co-operation between independent sovereign states is the best way to build a successful European community'. Germany, France and the Brussels bureaucracy, she argued, were not sticking to the letter and spirit of the financial and economic deregulation which had underpinned her support for integration in the mid-1980s. Early the following year, the announcement of a European 'Social Chapter', which guaranteed workers rights of consultation and parental leave in ways not compatible with the 'Thatcherite' economic model, rubbed salt in the wound. By the late 1980s, ministers began to refer to Britain's 'island status' and the Shakespearean 'moat' of the Channel in ways not heard for decades.[76] It was clear that the new socio-economic weather would come from Brussels, and Thatcher was resolved that it should go no further than the water's edge.

Secondly, there was the revival of the German question, based on the growing economy of the Federal Republic and the mighty Deutschmark. This profoundly concerned Thatcher. Having grown up in the shadow of the Second World War, she shared the concerns of many of her compatriots about Germany in general, and the growth of the Federal Republic in particular. The French felt the same way, but they were convinced that the best way of dealing with Germany was to embed her ever more firmly in new, all-embracing European structures. In June 1988, a European Council meeting at Hanover backed the creation of the single currency. Nine months later, within the context of rising German power, Delors reported on the establishment of monetary union with the express purpose of containing Germany. Thatcher, by contrast, believed that deeper European integration would tend to increase rather than curb German power. In short, while economics mattered deeply to Thatcher, the core of her anxiety about Europe was political. She feared the loss of British sovereignty and the prospect of German domination either directly or by European proxy. For this reason, Thatcher signalled that she not merely did not wish to participate in further integration herself but that she opposed it for the rest of the Community as well.

The fall of the Berlin Wall in November 1989, the collapse of communism across Europe and the prospect of German unification brought matters to a head. First, there was the German Question, now back on the agenda in the most dramatic possible way. With reunification on the cards, Margaret Thatcher feared that Germany 'would, once again, dominate the whole of Europe'.[77] She summoned a special conference of experts to the prime minister's country residence of Chequers to brief her on whether a united Germany could be 'trusted'. Washington, however, supported German unity and its view ultimately prevailed. Eventually, Thatcher acquiesced: 'I shall be sweet to the Germans,' she announced through gritted teeth.[78]

This was not the end but the start of her real troubles over Europe. France and other European states, worried about the increase in German power through unification, now pressed ahead with deeper integration. Chancellor Kohl himself strongly believed that the process should be accompanied by the political and monetary unification of the entire continent. In December 1989, at the Strasburg European Council, France agreed to German unification in return for a treaty on monetary union and further integration in the near-future. Britain was still formally keeping her options open: she had been 'shadowing' the Deutschmark since the late 1980s and, in early October 1990, a few days after German unification, Britain entered the European Exchange Rate Mechanism, an arrangement designed to allow currencies to converge in advance of monetary union. There was no chance, however, of Britain entering any matching political union. So Thatcher continued to resist deeper European integration, partly because she did not fear Germany enough to compromise her own sovereignty, and partly because she did not think that the French strategy would work in any case. A showdown between Britain and the rest of the Community now seemed inevitable.

Throughout the last four years of the Thatcher administration, British domestic politics were increasingly dominated by her feud with Europe. In January 1986, the Conservative government in Britain was convulsed by the Westland Affair, when the defence secretary Michael Heseltine clashed with the prime minister over whether the British military helicopter company Westland should be taken over by a European consortium – which he favoured – or an American one, which she preferred. Thatcher briefly considered resigning, but in the end it was Heseltine who took his leave, beginning a deep split in the party over the issue of Europe. The trade and industry minister Nicholas Ridley was forced to resign in early 1990 over provocative comments about Chancellor Kohl and German unification. By then, the prime minister was already under fire for her unpopular domestic policies – especially the 'poll tax' – but what turned the Conservative party establishment against her was Europe. The deputy prime minister Geoffrey Howe, a strong supporter of the Community, resigned amid great controversy in early November 1990, and Thatcher herself was gone a few weeks later. Europe had claimed two more British political scalps.

If Thatcher's last years had been preoccupied by Europe, then the entire administration of her successor, John Major, was dominated by it almost from start to finish. Once the Gulf Crisis occasioned by Saddam Hussein's invasion of Kuwait in August 1990 had been mastered, most of Major's attention was absorbed by the new continental order. Yugoslavia descended into civil war, generating a huge humanitarian crisis and, in due course, a security threat which severely tested the transatlantic alliance. Britain also wrestled with the shape of the new post-Cold War security architecture for Europe, in particular whether NATO should be enlarged eastwards. Above all, the new government was completely absorbed by Britain's position in the European Community, or the European Union as it became in 1992. Wherever Major looked at home or abroad, therefore, Europe was never far from the agenda. His undertaking, symbolically proclaimed on his visit to Germany in March 1991, to put Britain 'where we belong [a]t the very heart of Europe'[79] would now be tested.

Europe was divided between those who wanted to respond to the collapse of communism and the unification of Germany by 'widening' the Community by admitting new members, and those who wanted to 'deepen' it by strengthening the bonds between the existing members. The British, who feared being dominated by Germany through Europe and were determined to safeguard their national sovereignty, were ardent 'wideners' in the hope of slowing down further integration.[80] The French, no less anxious to contain the growing power of a united Germany, were staunch 'deepeners', in particular with respect to political and military matters. The Germans themselves favoured both widening and deepening, partly in the spirit of compromise but also because their security and prosperity was better guaranteed by a larger and more cohesive 'Europe', which would also give them a buffer to the east. The result, ultimately, was an 'enlargement' process which began in the 1990s and had encompassed nearly all of continental Europe west of Russia within twenty years.

Europe would not just be wider, it would also be deeper. In late 1991, the European Community summit at Maastricht established the 'European Union' and reaffirmed the commitment to 'ever closer union'. Members agreed 'to support the Union's external and security policy actively and unreservedly in a spirit of loyalty and mutual solidarity, and 'to inform and consult one another within the Council on any matter of foreign and security policy . . . in order to ensure that their combined influence is exerted as effectively as possible by means of concerted and convergent action'. A date was set for the introduction of the euro. There was, however, no complementary political and defence union to match the Single Market and the planned common currency. The French had secured a European solution for Germany, by which the euro replaced the Deutschmark, and a French solution for France, by which it maintained its sovereignty and armed forces. Further integration was expected, however. Chancellor Kohl predicted that the treaty would soon lead to 'the creation of what the founding fathers of modern Europe dreamed of after the last war: the United States of Europe'.[81] After considerable wrangling, John Major secured an 'opt out' from the Social Chapter and the common currency. Returning home, he declared he had won 'game, set and match' for Britain, but it was clear that, wherever the United Kingdom was in this process, it was not at the heart of Europe. The integration of the continent, however partial and half baked, would go ahead without her.

The reunification of Germany and European attempts to mitigate against it soon made themselves felt across the Channel. The costs of German unification had a profound impact on the European Exchange Rate Mechanism,[82] by which most currencies in the Community were supposed to fluctuate only within pre-determined 'bands', in order to achieve the harmonization necessary for subsequent Monetary Union. The problem was that German interest rates were high in order to balance the huge inflationary threat from the massive costs of reunification. This put pressure on other European economies, especially the British one, which was forced to intervene to support the pound against the German mark, at huge cost to the Treasury at a time when a lower rate was desperately necessary for exports as the country slipped into recession. Within two years, in fact, the British had been forced to withdraw from the ERM in a humiliating manner after a brutal run on the pound during 'Black Wednesday' in September 1992. Anglo-German relations plummeted as the two capitals engaged in a 'blame game'; London felt that strong hints from the Bundesbank's powerful president Helmut Schlesinger that the pound was overvalued had unleashed the speculators.[83] To some, it was an omen of how the European framework designed to dilute and constrain German power actually increased it.

On NATO, Britain was determined to prevent any change to the tried-and-tested model. France, in particular, sought to replace the existing US-dominated hierarchy with a 'two-tier' NATO in which all but the gravest threats to western Europe would in future be dealt with by the Europeans working through the Conference on Security and Cooperation in Europe or a reactivated Western European Union.[84] This would have effectively relegated the security of the old Soviet empire to the second tier. The British resisted the Europeanization of continental security, not least because they had been underwhelmed by the performance of her allies, especially Germany, during the Gulf Crisis. British forces remained in Europe, though they were reduced. In 1994, the British Army of the Rhine was renamed 'British Forces Germany'.

London rejected the extension of the NATO alliance, however, because the defence secretary Malcolm Rifkind believed that it could not deliver the security promised under Article 5 of the treaty to countries such as Poland or wherever the new eastern border of NATO was to be. The Americans and the Germans, by contrast, were determined to ensure that the security vacuum opened up by the collapse of Soviet power was rapidly filled, and their views prevailed. Over the next decade or so, the alliance was progressively enlarged eastwards to include Poland, the Czech Republic, Slovakia, Hungary, Romania, Bulgaria and the Baltic states. Thanks to the NATO clause committing members to the collective defence, the United Kingdom's eastern defence perimeter now effectively ran and runs along the eastern flank of the European Union.

The most immediate foreign policy challenge to the United Kingdom, however, was posed by the disintegration of Yugoslavia. Radical Serb nationalists sponsored by the government in Belgrade occupied large swathes of Croatia and Bosnia, murdered tens of thousands of mainly Muslim and Croat civilians and expelled many hundreds of thousands more in their quest to create an ethnically pure 'Greater Serbia'. Britain led the campaign to deliver humanitarian aid on the ground but was also the most determined of all the powers to prevent any outside military intervention in favour of the embattled Bosnian government in Sarajevo. She saw no national interest in doing so and feared being sucked 1914-style into a wider European conflagration. The United States disagreed strongly with this policy, partly on moral grounds but mainly because it feared that the failure to deal with war and ethnic cleansing in Europe undermined the credibility of NATO and the idea of continental collective security. Transatlantic relations were plunged into their greatest crisis since Suez.[85] In the autumn of 1995, Washington finally railroaded London into a full-scale NATO aerial intervention which contained the Serbs and led to a negotiated peace.

It was not obvious at the time, but the impact of the war in Europe on British domestic politics was profound. The intervention debate raged for three years, reprising many of the issues discussed at the time of the 'Bulgarian agitation' of the 1870s.[86] Muslim opinion in Britain was outraged. 'Bosnia Today – Brick Lane Tomorrow' warned the banners held in one East London demonstration.[87] Extremist organizations such as Hizb ut-Tahrir went from strength to strength. Dozens of Islamic charities funnelled food, medicines and even arms to the Bosnian government. Hundreds of British Muslims went to join the mujahideen there. Some of the most prominent subsequent British jihadists – such as Ahmed Saeed Sheikh, who masterminded the kidnapping and murder of the journalist Daniel Pearl, and the Guantanamo detainee Moazzam Begg – were radicalized by the situation in Bosnia.[88] Activists from across the Muslim world converged on the British capital and mingled with local Islamists. Algerian radicals, probably operating from London, planted bombs on the Paris metro in 1995. Britain, however, refused to act against the extremists in its midst. Much to the despair of the French and Middle Eastern intelligence services, the government was anxious not to upset the fragile domestic multicultural consensus. Whitehall also believed that it enjoyed an informal understanding with Islamist groups that Britain would not be targeted so long as they were permitted to associate. Commentators began to speak of 'Londonistan'.[89]

It was his European policy, however, that really did for John Major. His entire tenure was dominated by attacks from Eurosceptics within his own Conservative party, and from the press, determined to defend British sovereignty against 'Brussels'. The integration project – especially the common currency – was condemned as a cloak for German domination. 'To hand [Germany] the key to the legal structure of Europe with European Monetary Union (including the Central

Bank)' and 'European Political Cooperation with a majority voting system gravitating around alliances dependent upon Germany,' the Conservative MP Bill Cash warned, 'simply hands her legitimate power on a plate.' This former supporter of the Common Market also cautioned that the single currency would destroy the competitiveness of the smaller economies, leading to 'economic decline and rising unemployment on the periphery of the EC financing the German stranglehold'.[90] Whatever the public made of these questions, the humiliation of Black Wednesday destroyed the government's, and the Conservative Party's, reputation for economic competence. The constant Tory divisions over Europe wearied the country. It was mainly for this reason that the electorate, despite the prosperity of the country, voted John Major out of office in May 1997. Once again, Europe had proved decisive in British domestic politics.

The new Labour leader, Tony Blair, articulated a very different vision for Britain in Europe. He attacked the Major government's failure in Yugoslavia during the 1997 election campaign, stressed the close link between morality and foreign policy and reaffirmed the idea of British exceptionalism and global leadership. This leadership was to be exercised in and through Europe. 'The drift towards isolation in Europe must stop and be replaced by a policy of constructive engagement,' Blair argued, even before his election. 'The fact is that Europe is today the only route through which Britain can exercise power and influence.' He added that '[i]f it is to maintain its historic role as a global player, Britain has to be a central part of the politics of Europe.' 'For four centuries,' Blair later reiterated, 'our destiny has been to help to shape Europe. Let it be so again.'

The Labour election victory therefore marked a distinct shift in Britain's relationship with the continent. Robin Cook, the new foreign secretary, vowed 'to make Britain a leading player in Europe'. The Blair government announced that because Britain was 'a major European state and a leading member of the European Union ... [her] security [was] indivisible from that of European partners and allies. We therefore have a fundamental interest in the security and stability of the continent as a whole and in the effectiveness of NATO as a collective political and military instrument to underpin these interests.' The first concrete step was joining the Social Chapter. Next on the agenda was the question of whether Britain would change course on John Major's other 'opt out' at Maastricht: the forthcoming common currency. In October 1997, London announced that any decision to join the euro was dependent on the outcome of five economic 'tests' – mainly concerning business cycles, the flexibility of the euro in responding to crises and the likely impact on investment – set by the chancellor of the exchequer Gordon Brown to determine the long-term compatibility between the British economy and those of the projected eurozone. It rapidly became clear that these tests were not likely to be met any time soon. If Britain was to lead Europe, another approach would be necessary.

This put a particular premium on military integration as the principal vehicle of British influence in Europe. In December 1998, the British and French prime ministers met at Saint-Malo, where Tony Blair declared that the Union 'should develop the capacity for autonomous action, backed up by credible military force'. This paved the way for participation in a European Security and Defence Policy which was – at least conceptually – compatible with a vibrant Atlantic Alliance. The prime minister was attempting to straddle the transatlantic and the EU–NATO divide. 'We are the bridge between the US and Europe,' he proclaimed at the Lord Mayor's Banquet in 1997. Alluding to the cult film *The Blair Witch Project*, the analyst and writer Timothy Garton Ash dubbed this policy 'the Blair Bridge Project'. With Britain on board, there were hopes that the EU might now become more effective in defence matters. This notion was soon put to the test during the Kosovo crisis of 1999, when Europe was once again faced with ethnic cleansing, this time of the Kosovar Albanians by the Serbian government of Slobodan Milošević. The resulting air campaign, in which the United States dominated, was no advertisement for European defence cooperation, but it greatly strengthened the position of Tony Blair, whose robust stance won him plaudits across the continent and indeed the Atlantic.

The optimistic new consensus was summed up by Tony Blair in his much-discussed 'Chicago Speech' of April 1999. In it, he proclaimed a doctrine of 'international community', in which global interdependence and the increasing reach of communication technologies made every state a neighbour of every other. Breaking with what he understood as the 'Westphalian' insistence on sovereignty, Blair argued that the abuse of human rights was not merely a moral outrage but threatened the security of the developed world through the spread of instability. In this regard, he specifically singled out by name only 'two dangerous and ruthless men', the Serbian and Iraqi leaders, whose policies had sucked the west into conflict on more than one occasion during the past decade. The prime minister announced that it was up to Europe and the United States working in partnership to eliminate these and other threats. 'In the end,' Blair argued, 'values and interests merge. If we can establish and spread the values of liberty, the rule of law, human rights and an open society then that is in our national interests too. The spread of our values makes us safer.' As we have seen, if one substitutes 'Protestantism', 'liberty', 'liberalism' or 'humanity' for 'values', this sentiment was part of a long tradition in British foreign policy.

There was no inherent contradiction, then, between the interests of Washington, London and Brussels. On the contrary, all clocks seemed to be set to the same time. The Clinton administration was content that Europe should share the burdens of common security.[91] Tony Blair was on a mission to put Britain back at the head of the European project and mediate between the United States and Europe. Germany saw the cooperation of the Anglo-Saxon powers as central to its policy of securing its eastern border and embedding its growing power in the broader European project. The German foreign minister Joschka Fischer summed up these developments in late March 1999, on the eve of the Kosovo War. 'Today Britain has, when it comes to Europe, the most open government it has yet had,' he rejoiced, 'seeking its future not just *with*, but *in* Europe. No one's happier about that than the Germans.'[92]

Britain became ever more enmeshed with the continent as the European Union waxed. In 1994, the Channel Tunnel was opened, greatly facilitating communication between the United Kingdom and the continent. Britain's economy grew, sucking in migration from across the union, with EU citizens eventually securing a pan-continental right of residence. Despite Britain's non-membership of the euro, the City of London boomed as a commercial and financial centre for the entire continent. Nor did Britain's refusal to join the Schengen Area of passportless travel within Europe cause much difficulty, at least at first. The French authorities checked documents in London, while the British did so in Calais. It seemed as if the Narrow Sea had become a European lake.

The end of the Cold War and the progress of European integration also enabled new relationships within the United Kingdom. Moscow ended its support for the Irish Republican Army, which lost a global sponsor with the collapse of communism. In the Downing Street declaration of December 1993, the British government proclaimed it had 'no selfish strategic or economic interest' in Northern Ireland. After two ceasefires, a power-sharing arrangement was concluded in the Anglo-Irish Agreement, which largely ended the military conflict. Devolution for Wales and Scotland followed, which was partly in response to local demands but also a reflection of the new-found confidence in the wider continental order. As the threat level across the Channel dropped, so the bonds of union in the British Isles loosened. Significantly, support for the Union with England went up when there was war in Europe, for example during the Kosovo campaign of 1999, during which the standing of Alex Salmond's Nationalists dropped.

British prestige and that of Tony Blair ran high in Europe around the Millennium. The British economy was widely regarded as the dynamic model of the future. Britain was by a comfortable margin the greatest European military power and was recognized as such by the ultimate arbiter, the United States. Moreover, Mr Blair was far and away the most robust and realistic of the leaders who faced down Milošević over Kosovo, and secured peace in Northern Ireland. He had engaged in a genuinely post-imperial humanitarian intervention in Sierra Leone. Everybody in Europe had heard of him, from the bureaucrats in Brussels to the chanting refugees who welcomed him like John the Baptist to the camps of Kosovo. He had the aura and ambivalence of power. If popular elections for a European president had been held then, Blair would surely have come out well ahead of any alternative candidate. The vision the prime minister articulated was one in which Britain immerses itself in Europe and in so doing transforms the Union decisively. Europe was to become an extension of Britain and a force-multiplier for British grand strategy, which in turn was intended to evolve in symbiosis with Europe. Blair seemed poised for destiny in Europe.

The best analogy for Britain's potential role then was that of nineteenth-century Prussia.[93] At the turn of the Millennium, the project of European Unity was roughly at the same stage as that of German Unification by 1865. Ever since the Customs Union – the Zollverein – of 1834, economic integration had proceeded apace, but political unification had continued to founder on the determination of the smaller German states not to surrender their hard-won sovereignty. It was also hamstrung by the Austrian pretension to hegemony in Germany and its bitter opposition to Prussian leadership. What finally persuaded the fiercely independent states of Baden, Württemberg and Bavaria to accept political unity – which was little more than a Confederation of Princes in 1871 – was the manifest failure of the German Confederation, a loose, amiable and ineffectual political commonwealth, to provide security against French aggression. So it could have been with the European Union. There, too, the project of economic integration via the Single Market and single currency was well advanced. There, too, political and military integration had repeatedly stalled, despite numerous opportunities. The challenge of Bosnia in the early 1990s was comprehensively fluffed. The European defence identity was exposed as the very model of a modern chocolate soldier: swathed in a gaudy multilateralist wrapper, saccharine sweet on the principles of consensus but flaky when put to the test. What was needed to deal with these and other challenges, it seemed to some, was not a meddling European 'superstate' but an intergovernmentally based European superpower, perhaps with stronger confederal links, under British leadership. Britain could have become the Prussia of European unification and Mr Blair could have been its Bismarck.

This sentiment emboldened the Labour government to back the Bush government in its war in Iraq in 2003. Tony Blair came out in strong support, not least because Saddam Hussein had featured in the Chicago Speech of 1999, delivered while George Bush was still a mere candidate for the Republican nomination. In the intervening period he had seen the US president move decisively in his direction on the questions of nation-building, democratization and humanitarian intervention. More generally, Blair saw the shock of 11 September 2001 as an opportunity to create a more just and secure world. 'The kaleidoscope has been shaken,' he announced, 'the pieces are in flux . . . let us reorder this world around us.'

Whatever one thinks of the decision to remove Saddam Hussein by force and attempt the democratization of Iraq,[94] there is no doubt that the war did not achieve its objectives. Saddam was duly toppled, but no weapons of mass destruction were found, and in the subsequent chaotic power vacuum all hopes of a thoroughgoing democratic transformation of the region, starting with Iraq, proved to be illusory. The war was also highly controversial at home, especially among British Muslims,[95] and divided Britain from the two principal European powers, France and Germany. Tony Blair's standing on the continent plummeted, and he proved unable to regain the initiative. It was a tragedy for the man, and perhaps for Britain's role on the continent. He could have been a contender in Europe.

Ironically, for someone so committed to the continent, Tony Blair accelerated the reduction of British land forces in Europe which had begun after the end of the Cold War. The December 2003 Defence White Paper announced that 'we no longer need to maintain a capability against the re-emergence of a direct conventional strategic threat to the United Kingdom or our allies.' Instead, it argued that 'priority must be given to meeting a wider range of expeditionary tasks' globally, and with the capacity to react quickly to emerging threats.[96] Just as in the late nineteenth century, the assumption was that the armed forces would primarily be required to engage in humanitarian intervention, 'complex emergencies' and the 'war on terror' – the early twenty-first-century military equivalent to the imperial policing and 'small wars' of yesteryear. Few reckoned with the return of large-scale conventional threats which would require the deployment of 'heavy metal' and advanced weapons systems on the European mainland.

At the same time, British popular and parliamentary enthusiasm for 'Europe' waned. A large proportion of the new Conservative MPs at the 2005 election were Eurosceptics. So, in many ways, was Gordon Brown, who succeeded as prime minister in 2007 and who continued his long-standing opposition to joining the euro. These reservations were shared by the new coalition government under David Cameron after 2010, not least because of the manifest failure of the eurozone to deal with the escalating sovereign debt crisis and the suffering this imposed on peripheral countries such as Greece. This seemed to vindicate Eurosceptic claims about the euro and the lack of democracy in the European Union, or at least the impossibility of establishing an economic and currency union without the political integration to match it. Over recent years, this dim view of the European Union was further confirmed by its failure to get to grips with any of the challenges facing the continent, from the revival of Russian power in the east and the migration crisis to Islamist terror and state breakdown in the Middle East and, of course, the escalating euro sovereign debt crisis. Britain, for her part, weathered the storm more easily, thanks to the Treasury's ability to print its own money, and her critical economic mass. She continued to retreat from the continent, however. In 2010, London announced the withdrawal of all British forces from Germany within ten years, the end of a large continuous presence on the continent. She was largely absent from attempts to contain Russia after the annexation of the Crimea in 2014. One way or the other, the 'British moment' in Europe, the chance for a close intergovernmental union under the leadership of London, had well and truly passed.

9
Britain: The Last European Great Power[1]

Under the Conservatives, Britain has regained her rightful influence in the world. We have stood up for the values our country has always represented. We play a central part in world affairs. Britain is at the heart of Europe; a strong and respected partner. We have played a decisive part in the development of the Community over the past decade.

– Conservative Election manifesto, 1992[2]

Century upon century, it has been the destiny of Britain to lead other nations. This should not be a destiny that is part of our history. It should be a part of our future; we are a leader of nations, or nothing.

– Tony Blair, Bridgewater Hall speech, 1997

Until recently, it was generally regarded as axiomatic in our 'post-post Cold War' world that the new global power centres lie, or will soon lie, to the east and to the south. For more than a decade now, analysts have traced the rise of the BRICS – Brazil, Russia, India and China – noting their surging GDPs, increasing confidence in International Organizations and mounting military expenditures.[3] A fearsome array of statistics boosts these claims and predictions.[4] Some foresaw a 'new Asian hemisphere'.[5] The west, by contrast, was held to be in precipitate decline.[6] In the United States, the skies seemed to darken with chickens coming home to roost: there was imperial overstretch abroad, lack of investment and innovation at home. Manufacturing was crumbling. Educational standards were plummeting. The debt overhang crippled government, the banks and the private sector. In 2008, one analyst spoke of *The Post-American World*.[7] Another suggested that, by 2020, China will even have overtaken the United States in the number of citations in international scientific papers.[8] President Obama's decisions to withdraw from Iraq and Afghanistan and his stated intention to concentrate on East Asia and the containment of China are seen as a belated realization of these facts.[9]

More abject still has been the alleged European decline. This began, of course, after the catastrophes of 1914–18 and 1939–45, and continued with the retreat from empire and the rise of the superpowers after the Second World War. The hope and expectation that the continent would increase its global presence through the European Union has been cruelly dashed by the euro debt crisis which erupted in 2010 and has yet to run its course. To add insult to injury, so the argument runs, the states of the old continent have struggled to make their voices heard either individually or collectively on the key global issues of international terrorism, the Middle East and nuclear proliferation.

The last prize, however, in this narrative downward spiral usually falls to Great Britain, which did not even enjoy the temporary resurgence of the 'core' EU powers at the height of the integration project but has supposedly declined steadily since 1945, suffering the indignity of being overtaken by France and West Germany.[10] After the Second World War, as Dean Acheson said in a phrase that has now become something of a cliché, Britain lost an empire without finding a role.[11] The historian A. L. Rowse wrote sadly in his diary that the period when '[i]t was an unquestioned assumption, the air one breathed, that England [*sic!*] and the Empire were the greatest thing in the world', had passed.[12] Britain failed to find a niche in the new Europe, being twice rejected for membership of the European Economic Community and remaining a semi-detached member even after she joined in the early 1970s. Reflecting the consensus view of British decline, synoptic overviews of the past two decades by political scientists have tended to pay very little attention to British power.[13]

More recently, the critique runs, Britain risks isolation in the European Union and perhaps even pariah status if she leaves. Prime Minister David Cameron was left in an embarrassing minority of one on the issue of the stability pact, abandoned even by non-euro members, being subsequently joined only by the Czech Republic. In Iraq and Afghanistan, the army left with its tail between its legs and, more recently, swingeing cuts to the defence budget have reduced the lion's growl to a whimper.[14] The proud southern coastal towns declined from Cinque Ports into sink estates. And if all this were not bad enough in September 2014, on the anniversary of the Battle of Bannockburn, more than two fifths of all Scots voted to leave the United Kingdom. Against this background, the former prime minister Gordon Brown cautioned in March 2015 that a British departure from the European Union would be 'the North Korea option, out in the cold with few friends, no influence, little new trade and even less new investment'.[15] At the start of 2016, the former ambassador to the United Nations remarked sadly that '[w]e are not so much a power any more, our relative power has faded, put us into the shade,' so much so that the country would be hard put to justify its seat on the UN Security Council.[16]

There is something to this view, but not much. The Strategic Defence Review of 2010 imposed drastic cuts on the British armed forces. British military spending was substantially reduced. The number of active-duty personnel was cut. The Royal Navy suffered particularly, fielding fewer and fewer ships. The sight of HMS *Ark Royal* being towed past the scene of the fighting in Libya in 2011 towards a scrapyard in Turkey seemed to epitomize what had gone wrong. Britain, it seemed, could not even scrap its own ships. Moreover, the Libyan intervention could not have taken place without extensive US logistical support. The army largely failed to get to grips with the insurgency in Iraq and Afghanistan.[17] The anarchy which Britain left behind in Basra province contrasted badly with the rally of US fortunes in the Sunni triangle during the military 'Surge' and 'Awakening' from mid-2007. Britain's unique military selling point of high-quality, low-intensity warfare is no more, at least for the time being, even if the appetite for deployment within the forces remains high. Her support of President George W. Bush's war in Iraq was widely derided as the behaviour of a 'poodle' rather than a 'bulldog'.[18] The British economy was scrambling to keep up with the growth of the BRICS.[19] India even contemptuously rejected London's development aid, in a gesture of new-found confidence. All in all, there are plenty of plausible arguments for British decline, all of which are regularly rehearsed by the local cottage industry on the subject.

In fact, reports of British decline are far from new, are premature and unlikely to be vindicated in the foreseeable future. As we have seen throughout this book, Britain has always been 'in crisis'. Fear of decline has animated English and, later, British debate at least since the fall of France in the mid-fifteenth century. Then, Englishmen fretted that they had lost their French empire on account of effeminacy, division at home and weak monarchy. In the early modern period, the inexorable advance of the Habsburgs in central Europe sparked widespread concern. It was one of the main causes of the English Civil War, as parliamentary outrage at royal abandonment of the 'Protestant cause' in Germany mounted.[20] In the eighteenth century, French victories at sea and on land regularly sparked new rounds of national performance anxiety. There was also widespread fear that power was shifting eastwards. As Britain struggled with a global coalition against her during the American War of Independence, her statesmen fretted that the future lay not in parliamentary systems, which were going down to defeat in Poland, Sweden and the Dutch Republic, but with the 'military' eastern monarchies of Prussia, Austria and Russia. 'The great military powers in the interior parts of Europe,' the British under-secretary for war wrote in March 1778, 'who have amassed together their great treasures, and have modelled their subjects into great armies, will in the next and succeeding period of time, become the predominant powers.'[21]

Britain's relative economic decline was evident from the early 1870s, after the reunification of the United States and the unification of Germany. It was around the turn of the last century, however, that the decline debate really erupted – at the peak of the British empire – when London made heavy weather of the Boers in South Africa.[22] At that time, observers feared that a global coalition would pile in against them, just as they had during the American War of Independence. The quest to survive in the new era of large states drove demands for a 'Greater Britain' which would harness the energies of the empire against her competitors.[23] The 'National Efficiency' movement examined at length the question of whether industrialization had so stunted the growth of the urban proletariat that they had been rendered unfit for military service. Some observers even predicted the rise of China at Britain's expense. Sir Robert Hart, the long-serving inspector-general of her customs service suggested in 1900 that she could become 'the most powerful empire on earth' within a century. In the 1960s and 1970s, 'decline' became an even greater preoccupation, leading to the retreat from 'East of Suez' in the 1960s and culminating in a humiliating appeal to the IMF in 1976.[24] It became customary to suggest that Britain was now a mere regional power.[25] 'Today,' the British ambassador to Paris Sir Nico Henderson wrote in 1979, 'we are not only no longer a world power, but we are not in the first rank even as a European one.'[26] In the 1970s and 1980s, critics argued that Britain's imperial ambitions had diverted resources from the vital European theatre and prevented investment in industry and education at home, causing her to fall behind the German *Wirtschaftswunder*.[27] In *Tinker, Tailor, Soldier, Spy*, Le Carré's traitor Bob Haydon tells his nemesis, George Smiley, that he thought Britain was 'without relevance or moral viability in world affairs'.[28] The historian Paul Kennedy's assessment in his classic *Rise and Fall of the Great Powers* was much less bleak, but even he described the country as a 'mid-sized power' with defence pretensions out of keeping with her shrinking economic base.[29] The mood found its way into standard texts.[30]

In reality, though, predictions of British decline proved to be greatly exaggerated. After losing her French empire, English power revived under Henry VIII and Elizabeth I. In the seventeenth and eighteenth centuries, Cromwell, William of Orange and Pitt the Elder held the European balance of power. Far from being overwhelmed by the eastern empires, Britain played a pivotal role in the Revolutionary and Napoleonic wars. During the nineteenth century, she was widely described as enjoying a 'hegemonic' role. In the twentieth century, as is well known, Britain played a major role in both world wars, and – for good or for ill – was central to the two post-conflict orders. She was at the top table at Versailles in 1919 and centrally involved in the establishment of the United Nations and the Bretton Woods economic system. Subsequently, Britain was a key player in the Cold

War. In the early 1950s, British troops were in action against the troops of a major power, Mao's China, along the Imjin River in Korea. Britain was the most important European power in NATO and played a major role in deterring the Soviet Union. In the 1980s, Britain experienced an economic, psychological and military revival under Margaret Thatcher. 'We have ceased to be a nation in retreat,' she claimed in 1982. 'We have instead a new-found confidence – born in the economic battles at home and tested and found true eight thousand miles away,' where the Argentinians had just been ejected from the Falkland Islands.[31] Even at the height of her supposed decline in the past thirty years, Britain went to war more than thirty times, in two dozen countries in almost every part of the world.[32]

If anything, British influence in Europe grew after the end of the Cold War, when Russian power collapsed. In the 1990s, Britain played a pivotal role in Bosnia, where London – with French help – was instrumental in delaying intervention against the Serbs and keeping US demands for air strikes at arm's length for nearly three years. Large sections of western opinion, ranging from the president of the European Commission Jacques Delors to Bob Dole, the leader of the US Republican party, came to identify Britain as the greatest obstacle to collective action. 'Any time there was a likelihood of effective action,' Tadeusz Mazowiecki, the first democratically elected prime minister of Poland and UN rapporteur on human rights, observed in May 1993, 'a particular western statesman [the British foreign secretary Lord Hurd] intervened to prevent it.'[33]

After 1997, Prime Minister Tony Blair increasingly set the global agenda with his advocacy of 'humanitarian intervention', culminating in the Kosovo War and the controversial invasion of Iraq. It was the British prime minister who pressed most strongly for the deployment of ground troops into Kosovo, and it was probably fears that this would happen which drove Milošević to compromise in the end.[34] Blair's remarkable Chicago Speech, which enunciated the doctrine of international community, paved the way for the adoption of the 'Responsibility to Protect' principle at the United Nations. In late September and early October 2008, Britain's Gordon Brown played a central role in coordinating the western response to the global credit crunch.[35] More recently, it was David Cameron who joined the French president Nicolas Sarkozy in putting intervention in Libya on the international agenda, and it was his advocacy especially which brought the Americans onside in NATO. Whatever one makes of the results in Libya itself, the event was a showcase for the value of cooperation between London and Paris, which is central to French thinking on defence. This was obvious again in November 2015, when President Hollande instinctively turned to Britain rather than his other EU partners for help in Europe after the Islamic State attacks on Paris. Moreover, if it is true that a declining United States will rely increasingly on ad hoc coalitions rather than organizations, then the power to which it will turn first in matters of security is surely Great Britain. America's concentration on the rise of China in East Asia makes her more dependent on British help in Europe and the Middle East. If NATO and the European Union lose cohesion, the 'special relationship' between London and Washington may regain its importance.

In order to assess Britain's true place in the world historically and today, we need to recognize two things. First of all, power is relative.[36] We must therefore measure British capabilities today not against the reach of the Royal Navy in the past but against the country's competitors today. In terms of GDP, Britain is number five; in per capita terms among the largest countries she ranks behind only the United States. Her population is growing, thanks partly to fertility and large net inward migration, much of it skilled and hard-working. Predictions are often to be taken with a large pinch of salt, but the most recent ones suggest that the United Kingdom will overtake both Germany and Japan as the third-largest world economy within twenty years or so, and Germany also in terms of population. The report by the Centre for Economics, Business and Research adds, however, that this would depend on navigating 'a number of political risks such as the break-up of the UK or an exit from the European Union'.[37]

Britain also has the third-highest military spending in the world, behind the USA and China, and it is rising after a large increase in the 2015 budget. Moreover, when comparing Britain with her economic rivals, one should bear in mind that, whatever their current and potential military capacity, both Germany and Japan remain constrained in the exercise of force for historical and constitutional reasons. Neither possesses London's nuclear deterrent. The quality of the newer British equipment is very high: the new Type 45 Destroyer HMS *Dauntless* enjoys an anti-aircraft capability second to none; it is reckoned to have more than five times the firepower of the old Type 42 Destroyers. The planned new 65,000-tonne pocket supercarriers (with their restored F35B aircraft) and remotely piloted stealth aircraft are more sophisticated than anything any other power bar the United States can field.

Above all, Great Britain is still a sovereign state, unlike France and Germany, who are now increasingly locked into a single framework, along with the rest of the eurozone. Despite various mutterings about 'Security Council reform', she commands a seat on the United Nations Security Council, not just by tradition but by dint of her current strength. In fact, it is hard to imagine a five-member body in which global power – as opposed to regional strength – is the main criterion which would *not* include the United Kingdom.[38] Not only could Britain recapture the Falklands from Argentina again today, but her naval and air presence there is now so strong as to make any second attempt at invasion far riskier than it was thirty years ago. By contrast, Argentina has invested so little in defence since 1982 that it would not be able to launch one. In short, if one measures British power relatively, there is no doubt that it not merely remains substantial but that it has recovered in recent decades.

This picture is confirmed if we look at the second aspect of power, which is that capabilities and assets have no value in and of themselves but only in relation to the vital interests of the state. In this sense, the decline in Britain's defence spending tells us relatively little about her actual military potential. England disarmed extensively after the Napoleonic Wars but mobilized again quickly to defeat Russia in the Crimea. In 1914, she sent a paltry hundred thousand men to France. The Kaiser dismissively referred to the British Expeditionary Force as 'that contemptible little army'; despite the creation of the Territorials, her trained reserves were low. Within eighteen months, however, she had fielded a huge volunteer force, made larger still by the introduction of conscription. By the end of the First World War, in fact, Britain was the only continental European major power which was not 'broken' by the contest, as France was in 1917 – at least temporarily – by the mutinies, as the Russians were by the revolutions that same year, and the Germans by their own upheaval in

1918. In the same way, and in ways not true of most other states, with the exception of the US, France and a few others, were Britain ever to be seriously threatened her armed forces would grow to a multiple of what they are now. London, in short, enjoys huge 'latent' as well as actual capabilities.

This is also the context in which Britain's reduced global role should be understood. Her strategic aims are easily summarized. First of all, she always sought to prevent invasion by securing the Low Countries – the 'counter-scarp of England'. Second, in the longer term, Britain tried to prevent the emergence of a continental European hegemon capable of mounting a cross-Channel assault. One of the ways in which British strategists sought to achieve this in the past was by building up an overseas empire in order to increase her weight on the old continent, or deny these territories to her rivals. Conversely, once these territories became strategic and ideological liabilities in the second half of the twentieth century, they were abandoned as soon as Britain had found alternative security guarantees in Europe through the transatlantic alliance. *Pace* Acheson and the 'declinists', therefore, the empire was never an end in itself, but only a means. It was given up rather than 'lost' because the metropolis found more effective ways of defending its vital interests closer to home. The same principle applies to Scottish devolution and the SNP's hopes for independence. The absence of threat encourages disintegration. Just as the Act of Union was originally passed in the early eighteenth century in order to unite England and Scotland against the common French foe, and was later strengthened by the battles against Napoleon, imperial and Nazi Germany and Soviet Russia, so the more relaxed international situation in the late twentieth and early twenty-first centuries has led to the loosening of the bonds of union between the two parts of the United Kingdom. This reflects not British weakness but her sense of security.

Today, the threat facing Britain is both different and similar to that mastered in the past. Beyond the Channel, the escalating sovereign debt crisis has the potential to wreck the economic and political progress of the continent during the past decades and to reverse the British economic recovery after the crash of 2008. Calls from the prime minister Mr Cameron and the chancellor of the exchequer Mr

Osborne for eurozone political unity to stave off a complete collapse of the common currency demonstrate that, while Britain is relaxed about the integration of the continent under what promises to be a (mainly) friendly regime, she remains profoundly concerned about the emergence of an unstable, disordered space on her doorstep. Moreover, the revival of Russian power in the east, as evidenced by the annexation of the Crimea, the invasion of eastern Ukraine and threats to the Baltic states, has profound implications for Britain, which is committed to the security of the continent through NATO's Article 5 clause on collective defence. One way or the other, Europe remains the place 'where the weather comes from'.

The extraordinary resilience of British power is attributable to three factors. First of all, there is the intrinsic strength of England. As we have seen, the realm of England has been a great power since the Middle Ages: she has historically always been among the strongest, richest and most populous European states, long before the era of transatlantic expansion and industrialization. The acquisition of Ireland, Scotland and Wales added to England's power, certainly, but essentially reflected it. The same is true of the overseas empire. For this reason, British power has survived the loss of Ireland in 1921–2, that of the empire after the Second World War, and, for the very same reason, it would have survived the loss of Scotland in 2014, though with a considerable diminution of power. This partly reflects the population of England, which began to grow exponentially in the eighteenth century and now tops 50 million. As well as being among the most populous of European nations, over the past three hundred years she has certainly also been the most cohesive. Unlike most of the rest of Europe, the United Kingdom has not experienced civil war (if one excepts Ireland), foreign occupation or revolution since the seventeenth century. She probably has the strongest sense of national identity on the continent today and is the only larger member of the European Union where there is no chance at all of a vote in support of pooling sovereignty within a single state.[39]

Second, there is the strength of Anglo-British 'soft power': her ability to get others to want what she wants.[40] England, and later Britain, has always been able to identify herself with a cause or broad principle in international politics, for a long time as sheriff and lately as deputy. In the sixteenth century, this was the fear of Philip II; in the seventeenth century, the threat of Louis XIV; in the late eighteenth and early nineteenth centuries, it was Revolutionary and Napoleonic France; in the twentieth century, it was Imperial and Nazi Germany, and then the Soviet Union. In each case, Britain provided what would now be called 'public goods': the maintenance of the balance of power and, later, an open economy and liberal international system. As the British diplomat Eyre Crowe wrote in 1907:

> Second only to the ideal of independence, nations have always cherished the right of free intercourse and trade in the world's markets, and in proportion as England champions the principle of the largest measure of general freedom of commerce, she undoubtedly strengthens her hold on the interested friendship of other nations, at least to the extent of making them less apprehensive of naval supremacy in the hands of a free trade England than they would in the face of a predominant protectionist power.'[41]

It was 'empire by invitation'.[42]

Third, there is the resilience of the British constitutional model, which has not been seriously challenged from within for hundreds of years. Thanks to Parliament and the 'public sphere', Britain's grand strategy rested on a broad political base: it was 'owned' by the political nation.[43] This enabled the system to break with a failed policy without at the same time destroying the political system. For example, Britain recovered quickly after the loss of America in the late 1780s, after the ministry of Lord North was ejected and William Pitt the Younger put the nation's finances back on an even keel. Contrast this with the brutal settling of accounts with the French *ancien régime* after its defeat in the Seven Years War, which led ultimately to the Revolution of 1789. Moreover, this same ownership facilitated the extraction of Britain's domestic resources for international competition through the 'fiscal-military' state. No European polity was as intensively taxed and bureaucratic as the United Kingdom.[44]

Finally, the parliamentary structure of Britain brought her the confidence of the international money markets, enabling her to borrow much more cheaply abroad than other powers. It was this resilience that enabled England and then Britain to sustain so many conflicts over the hundreds of years covered by this book, especially the second Hundred Years War against France and the two world wars. Today, this continued strength is reflected in the existence of the pound sterling, which remains one of the world's premier currencies.

The strength of the British model is also shown by its exports over the past two hundred or so years.[45] In the early twentieth century, the white parliamentary settler colonies – Canada, Australia, New Zealand and South Africa – were major contributors to British power: industrially and militarily.[46] Not only did they bring their own natural resources to the table, and the energies of the emigrants from the British Isles, but also those of immigrants from other countries.[47] The German chancellor Leo von Caprivi expressed this anxiety about German emigration when he remarked in the 1890s that the Reich would have either to export goods or people, who would then enrich her rivals. This process was epitomized by the experience of Hitler's regiment during the First World War, which was astonished to find itself fighting German-speaking immigrants to Australia on the battlefields of Flanders;[48] there were not many English-speakers on the German side in either war (some Irishmen and the odd traitor excepted). Today, with the possible exception of South Africa, all of the old settler colonies are major contributors to the liberal international order upon which Britain depends.

More importantly still, the United States originated as an improved version of Great Britain. The patriots were, after all, 'vexed and troubled Englishmen'.[49] The colonists rebelled not because they opposed the British empire but because it was not British enough – by taxing them without representation – and insufficiently imperial, because it refused to expand further west into French and Indian lands. The determination of the patriots to build on the British tradition emerges very clearly from the debates around the Constitutional Convention, where the Anglo-Scottish Union was touted as a model for the future United States.[50] It is true that Anglo-American relations since then have not always run smoothly, and the two powers went to war against each other once two hundred years ago, but, in general, the rise of the United States has been a huge boon to Britain: informal cooperation against Revolutionary and Napoleonic France, cooperation against

Germany in the first half of the twentieth century, against the Soviet Union during the Cold War, and so on.[51] As the radical journalist W. T. Stead remarked around the turn of the century, 'there is no reason to resent the part the Americans are playing in fashioning the world in their image, which, after all, is substantially the image of ourselves.'[52] The US succeeded rather than supplanted Great Britain.[53] Even though the United States has long ceased to be just the ethnic or 'racial' kin of the old country – a fact lamented by the political scientist Samuel Huntington and celebrated by others – she remains a descendant of the British project in *political* terms. The concept of the 'Anglo-sphere' has outlasted the 'Anglo-Saxon' solidarity of the first half of the twentieth century.[54]

In short, British decline – like that of the United States – has been much heralded but slow to arrive. The United Kingdom remains one of the world's greatest powers, thanks to its military strength, it economic size, its demographic vibrancy, its societal and political resilience and, above all, the global attraction of its constitutional 'model'. The examples of the Falklands, Bosnia, Iraq and Libya, and her continuing deterrent role within NATO, show that Britain is still able to project power within and beyond Europe, both unilaterally and as part of a coalition. She is still the most credible European bulwark against Russian expansionism, and is likely to be the first port of call on this side of the Atlantic for front-line states such as Poland in the event of a military emergency.[55] These instances, however, are but a pale indication of Britain's real strength, which is manifested only when the vital interests of the nation are threatened. All this makes the United Kingdom the last European great power.

10

A European Britain or a British Europe? The United Kingdom and Continental Union[1]

If Europe is to be saved from infinite misery, and indeed from final doom, there must be an act of faith in the European family and an act of oblivion against all the crimes and follies of the past.

The structure of the United States of Europe, if well and truly built, will be such as to make the material strength of a single state less important. Small nations will count as much as large ones and gain their honour by their contribution to the common cause.

But I must give you warning. Time may be short . . .

If we are to form the United States of Europe, or whatever name or form it may take, we must begin now.

– Winston Churchill, speaking at Zurich, 19 September 1946

The storm fronts are rolling in again from Europe. Our continent faces a series of interlocking challenges which are individually and cumulatively bringing Europe to its knees. It has experienced the unchecked resurgence of an authoritarian and expansionist Russia since 2007. Mr Putin has annexed the Crimea in violation of all solemn commitments, the first such breach of international law in Europe since 1945. He has invaded eastern Ukraine and menaces the Baltic states. His aircraft regularly threaten British airspace. Europe has also been wracked by a financial and economic crisis since 2008. It has seen the return of the 'German problem' with the imposition of EU-wide austerity policies at Berlin's behest from 2010. The

Schengen Area of passportless travel has buckled under a refugee crisis produced by the unchecked civil war in Syria and state failure more generally. Some of these unfortunates have found their way to the French channel ports. 'Algiers', to borrow Edmund's phrase, has indeed come to 'Calais'. The sea once again runs narrower than a village brook. Islamist extremism threatens the European way of life. There are secessionist movements in Scotland, Catalonia and elsewhere, and we have seen the rise of Eurosceptic feeling across the Union in places as diverse as the United Kingdom, Germany, France, Hungary and Greece. Finally, there is the crippling uncertainty sparked by the forthcoming referendum on UK membership of the European Union in June 2016. All of these challenges pose a mortal threat to the European Union and some of its member states. The United Kingdom may be much less exposed to some of these challenges than the rest of the continent, but she will nonetheless be deeply affected by their outcomes.

Over the past few years, the long-running 'British Question' in Europe has re-emerged with a vengeance.[2] This goes back to the original ambivalence at the time of the United Kingdom's accession in 1973 as to whether she was merely joining a free-trading association or signing up to a programme of ever closer political and economic union. When the Currency Crisis prompted a fresh surge of fiscal and political integration, the British Question was posed anew.[3] What implications would the new measures have for the sovereignty of the United Kingdom, and by what right did she participate in decisions designed to rescue the eurozone of which she was not a member? Alternatively, why should she pay for mistakes made in Brussels? Matters came to a head at the 2011 summit, when Prime Minister David Cameron vetoed the EU treaty designed to save the euro in order to protect the interests of the City of London and immediately found himself not merely isolated but circumvented by the rest of Europe.[4] Since then, the EU's principle of free movement has reignited the immigration issue in the UK, as the relative dynamism of her economy there sucks in labour from across the Union. The European Arrest Warrant, which the senior Conservative MP and former shadow home secretary David Davis condemned as 'leaving Britain in handcuffs', provokes resistance.[5] Old grievances about Brussels 'red tape' continue to fester, as exemplified by a letter to the conservative *Sunday Telegraph* signed by more than five hundred business leaders.[6] The relationship has also been soured by an argument over the size of the increase of Britain's contribution to the budget in order to reflect her greater economic weight since the last calculation was made in 1995.[7]

Above all, the prime minister is facing a serious domestic challenge over Europe. The Conservative right, after a long period of relative quiescence, has been cranking up the pressure for a withdrawal from the European Union. To make matters worse, the formerly fringe United Kingdom Independence Party (UKIP) is growing stronger, even if this is not yet reflected in the number of parliamentary seats it has. In the autumn of 2014 two Conservative MPs resigned their seats and won them again as UKIP candidates in the resulting by-elections. The first of these contests, when the Tories lost against the defector Douglas Carswell in the long-Eurosceptic Clacton-on-Sea, was no surprise, but the victory of Mark Reckless in the demographically more diverse constituency of Rochester and Strood was ominous for Mr Cameron. The prime minister staved off this threat and won the 2015 general election convincingly, recapturing Rochester and Strood, but only at the price of a prior commitment to hold a referendum on British membership of the European Union by the end of 2017 at the latest.

Mr Cameron's stated hope is that he will be able to renegotiate Britain's position in the EU, or even 'reform' the EU as a whole, in such a way that he can recommend a 'yes' vote. In order to make this strategy work, the prime minister needs the prospect of withdrawal to be credible, and, judging by his rhetoric, the mood of his party[8] and the general drift of British public opinion, he is not bluffing.[9] Moreover, the election of Jeremy Corbyn as Labour leader has put somebody at the helm of the main opposition party whose recorded views on the European Union are more negative than any of his predecessors before the 1950s. A 'Brexit' in 2016 is therefore perfectly possible.[10]

At the same time, the British Question is being posed in a different way by the campaign for Scottish independence.[11] The long period of Tory government under Margaret Thatcher during the 1980s opened a divide between the more conservative English and the supposedly more socialist Scots (much magnified by the first-past-the-post electoral system). It was papered over but never closed by the Blair government's devolution of powers to the Scottish Assembly in the late 1990s. In October 2012 the ruling Scottish National Party in Edinburgh under Alex Salmond secured a highly advantageous deal for a referendum on independence two years later. Scottish independence would have encouraged separatism in Wales and Northern Ireland. It would certainly have damaged the Good Friday Agreement of 1998 in Ulster and the institutions deriving from it, which have placed relations between nations on both sides of the Irish Sea on a more amicable footing. It would have weakened the United Kingdom on the world stage by reducing its economic, demographic and military weight. It would have exposed a coastline which had been secure for hundreds of years and generally constituted a serious psychological blow to 'brand Britain', right down to the issue of whether the country was still entitled to fly the Union flag with the cross of St Andrew in it. It would have had substantial implications for Britain's role in Europe and the world.

Scottish independence would also have created a major headache for the European Union. It was far from clear whether an independent Scotland would automatically become a member of the European Union. This raised the bizarre prospect of a largely pro-EU Scotland being extruded while the much more sceptical England remained. Even if London made no difficulties, furious Spanish objections, fearing the precedent for Catalonia, seemed likely. If Scotland was (re-) admitted to the EU, it was not obvious whether it would be required, like other new members, to adopt the euro. The departure of Scotland would also have increased 'Little Englanderism' south of the border and greatly reduced the chances that the United Kingdom would remain within the EU. Above all, the dissolution of the Anglo-Scottish Union would have been a terrible blow to the whole concept of supranational political integration upon which the concept of ever closer union in Europe rests. I shall return to this theme later.

Even though Scotland eventually voted 'no' by a clear margin, Mr Cameron is by no means out of the constitutional woods.[12] All else being equal, the SNP cannot bring forward another referendum for the next twenty years or so. That said, the 2015 general election produced another Tory government with tiny Conservative representation in Scotland, damaging the legitimacy of the Union, or at least of the administration. Moreover, the Edinburgh authorities are holding Mr Cameron's feet to the fire over a last-minute promise of far-reaching additional powers for Scotland – 'devo[lution] max'. They have recently criticized a far-reaching package as insufficient, signalling that they will continue partisan warfare until they can reopen conventional hostilities through a fresh referendum. Worse still, immediately after the vote, Mr Cameron promised a balancing arrangement for England, the nature of which is fiercely contested. Granting to England a similar self-government on Scottish lines would unbalance the entire union, as the English chief minister would be more powerful than the prime minister of the United Kingdom. There is no popular demand at all for the tidiest solution, which would be to divide England into German-style *Länder*; a proposal to grant greater powers to the north-east was roundly defeated in a referendum ten years ago. Breaking up England would in some ways turn the clock back to the Dark Ages, before the kingdoms of Northumbria, Mercia, Wessex, Kent and the East Angles were united. The suggestion that English MPs meet at Westminster on separate days to decide purely 'English' issues – 'English votes for English laws' (EVEL) – would create a two-tier parliament and completely negate the principle of collective responsibility. Besides, a Conservative majority in England could then vote down the (non-Scottish) budget devised by a UK government whose own majority rested on Scottish votes.[13] The profound partisan political implications of any arrangement greatly complicates matters,[14] because, while the Conservatives want to reduce the power of Scottish MPs, most of whom were, until recently, Labour, it is in the current opposition's interest to prevent that from happening.

Above all, the Scottish Question is being revived by the forthcoming referendum on Europe. This has given the SNP an opportunity to reopen the issue of independence much earlier than otherwise, as they argue plausibly that the terms of the recently renewed union with England are in danger of changing. It seems likely that, as matters stand, England will vote to exit the European Union, whereas Scotland would vote to remain. If Britain were to leave the EU on the basis of English votes alone, then Scottish nationalists would certainly demand a fresh ballot on independence. Wales and Northern

Ireland would probably not follow suit, for various reasons, but there would be considerable unhappiness, not least among Ulster Catholics who felt themselves being driven further apart from their brethren in the Irish Republic. Conversely, if Britain voted to remain with Scottish votes making the difference, then that could boost English nationalism and support for UKIP, and even demands to dump Scotland so as to preserve the sovereignty of the United Kingdom. In these circumstances, a 'central secession' through a 'Unilateral English Declaration of Independence from Europe', and even the UK, would become a real possibility.

Even if the English Question could be solved through a symmetrical arrangement, it would risk provoking an English backlash against the dilution of their identity. As we have seen, England has been a remarkably cohesive and centralized state for about a thousand years. Over the past three hundred years, she has enlarged that state in the British Isles through conquest and then full parliamentary union.[15] This is not England's weakness but her strength, the basis – through a remarkable synthesis between taxation, representation and mobilization – of her unique standing in Europe. England's bitter late-medieval and early modern quarrels were not really regional in origin but contests for control of the metropolis. Breaking up England would not serve the interest of any well-intentioned elements in Europe. From the European, or eurozone, perspective, if one cannot have a strong United Kingdom, one should settle for a strong England as second best.

Beyond its implications for the Anglo-Scottish relationship, a hostile and uncoordinated exit from the European Union would have profound consequences for Great Britain. It is true that Britain would regain control over her borders. She would be in a better position to ensure that tax credits for the lower-paid benefit native British workers rather than incomers from the EU. The 'national compact', which has become frayed through globalization and immigration, could be renewed. But there would also be considerable costs to bailing precipitately out of the current European Union, which have been documented by numerous studies.[16] Britain would lose access to the European Court of Justice to protect her position in the Single Market. She could continue to trade with Europe as before, but she might be compelled, like Norway and Switzerland, to abide by rules which she no longer participated in setting. This would have particularly serious consequences for the City of London, which would be exposed to French or German attempts to shift the financial capital of Europe to Paris or Frankfurt, or to deny London the right to trade in euro-dominated financial products. If Britain exercised her right to restrict immigration, she would be in danger of depriving her economy of much-needed skilled and willing labour, which is why most business opinion opposes withdrawal from the European Union. There is also the danger of retaliation against British citizens living in southern Europe, who cost the countries there more than they bring in.

Britain, of course, would survive. The United Kingdom is still one of the world's most important powers, probably in third place after the United States and China, and certainly among the top four or five actors in the global system. Britain has a permanent seat on the United Nations Security Council and a formidable diplomatic service. Her armed services are highly respected, and on their way to being properly funded again, and her military potential is huge. Unlike the labile eurozone, Britain has a stable currency, the pound sterling, whose strength varies but whose existence is not in doubt. While the debt-to-GDP ratio is high, all these factors have historically guaranteed that the creditworthiness of the state is good. Above all, the resilience of British society is considerable, and the country's capacity to wage conflicts of varying intensity for longer periods, once fully mobilized, is second only to that of the United States.

What is beyond question, though, is that a shambolic and uncoordinated 'Brexit' would have a catastrophic effect on the rest of the continent. A legislative Dunkirk, in which Britain repatriated her sovereignty as the eurozone slipped further and further into crisis, would have a shattering psychological impact on her European partners. It might well accentuate the break-up of the currency union, as the Germans and other states likewise wished to regain their national freedom of action. If Germany stayed, it would dominate the rump even more than it already does, without wishing to.[17] The result would most likely be a fragmented, fearful and vulnerable Europe, less likely to be sure to caucus against Britain but also much less capable of delivering the economic and political stability of the continent on which not only Britain's prosperity but also her security has always depended. Even more benign scenarios stress the negative impact that a British withdrawal would have on the rest of the Union. It would weaken the free-market constituency in the union and, while it would not precipitate a scramble for the door, it would certainly unsettle the other member states. At the very least, 'Brexit', as matters stand, will deprive Europe of its most effective armed forces and render the common foreign and security policy largely toothless. It will be 'an unprecedented event, with unclear and potentially transformative implications for the whole of Europe'.[18]

At this point we must take a step back and remind ourselves how both the United Kingdom and the European Union came to exist in the first place, because therein will lie the key to solving their present predicament. For hundreds of years, England and Scotland were rivals. From 1603, they were linked through a 'Union of Crowns', but this was a temporary dynastic, not a permanent political arrangement, similar to the later 'Personal Union' between Britain and Hanover, which was broken after more than one hundred and twenty years of a shared ruling house.[19] The Anglo-Scottish union of 1707, which ended hundreds of years of open or latent warfare between the two neighbours, was a much more fundamental measure, which was driven partly by Scottish bankruptcy but mainly by shared geopolitical anxieties.[20] Elites on both sides of the border contemplated the strategic and ideological threat of Louis XIV's Catholic, absolutist and territorially expansionist France with dread. Scotland had bankrupted itself in an attempt to pursue a separate imperial policy in Central America (the infamous Darien project). England sought to deny France the opportunity to pressurize her northern flank, encircling her through the 'Auld Alliance' with Scotland. To this end, England and Scotland embarked on a parliamentary, debt and foreign policy merger which enabled both countries not only to end their long hostility but to 'punch above their weight' on the European stage. This was an event, not a process. The United Kingdom, which was later enlarged by the Union with Ireland, created a new common British identity but no new nation. It was and remained a *union* of four nations – the English, the Scots, the Irish and the Welsh – whose creation cannot be understood outside of the European balance which gave birth to it.

The Anglo-Scottish union was so successful that it served as the model for the American patriots after the thirteen colonies broke away from Britain in the late eighteenth century.[21] They were acutely conscious that the existing loose 'Articles of Confederation' under which they had conducted their struggle with George III were not fit for purpose. Contemplating their precarious geopolitical situation with predatory great powers on all sides, conscious of the danger of falling out among themselves and concerned to settle the divisive question of how the debts incurred during the revolutionary war were to be repaid, the Americans studied the various European historical precedents carefully. They explicitly rejected the divided Italy of Machiavelli, the chaos of the Polish–Lithuanian Commonwealth and the sclerotic Holy Roman Empire of the German nation as polities unable to keep external predators at bay. The solution agreed at the Philadelphia Constitutional Convention in 1787–8 bore some distinctive features, including a directly elected presidency and a Senate to represent state interests, but it was in its essence, and was understood by contemporaries to be, an improved variant of the Anglo-Scottish Union. Americans soon pooled their debts, created a treasury bond, a national bank and, in due course, a strong military. Once again, union was an *event*, not a *process*. The rest is well-known: the United States eventually became the most powerful actor in the world system. Its creation, however, cannot be understood outside of the international balance of power from which it emerged.

Likewise, the project of European integration is a product of the strategic rivalries which culminated in the Second World War. As we have seen, its aim was to make war between western and central European countries impossible, and in particular to solve the German problem, by embedding the country in broader European institutions. The integration project also sought to mobilize the energies of democratic Europe, especially the Federal Republic of Germany, against the threat of Soviet communism. This endeavour had the potential to develop into something akin to the United Kingdom or the United States. Instead, economic and cultural integration was pursued by the European Economic Community (later, the EU), which eventually established the euro in order to decommission the mighty German Deutschmark. The idea of relatively rapid political union, completed against the background of a traumatic war, was superseded by the notion of gradual unity through many small steps. Rather than presenting an open plan for political integration in tandem with an underpinning economic unity, elites hoped that it would result from pressures and loyalties generated by the common currency. Defence integration, and German rearmament, by contrast, was devolved to the North Atlantic Treaty Organisation (NATO). As a result, 'Europe', unlike the UK or the USA, never became a matter of life or death, fatally reducing the external pressure without which no polity will take the final steps towards full political union. What should have been an *event* became an interminable *process*.

Thus, the future of the European project, and Britain's role in it, cannot be addressed in isolation from the continental and global balance of power, or in defiance of the lessons of history. At the moment, the eurozone is a currency without a state and a joint political project without joint military instruments or a common sense of its mission on its own continent, let alone in the world. Due to the lack of a common parliamentary representation transcending the sovereignty of the national assemblies, Europe is unable to issue the eurobonds which would stabilize the markets and the currency. The EU established a passportless travel area without also creating a Union-policed external border, which was often left to overstretched and corrupt local police forces to guard. This eventually led to the migration crisis of 2015–16 which threatens to blow the Schengen Area apart. Due to the absence of a common army and a truly common foreign and security policy, Europe can mount only a feeble response to the massive ideological and military challenge of Vladimir Putin's Russia on her eastern borders, or to any of the other threats, such as Islamist terrorism or state failure on its southern periphery. Southern Europe – for example, Italy and Spain – does not feel the pain of Russian ambitions in the same way as Poland, Finland and the Baltic states, as their opposition to sanctions has shown. The states of northern and eastern Europe, for their part, are unworried about the Mediterranean, as Polish hostility to the Libyan intervention demonstrated.

All this results from mounting a *confederal* response to a European problem which requires a *federal* solution.

Against this background, neither the proposed German nor the British government solutions to the European problem makes any sense. Berlin and Brussels believe that 'Europe' will cohere through a series of fiscal and economic measures. They have pushed through European rescue funds for the common currency, and they want a European commissioner with the power to veto member-state budgets which violate the commonly agreed guidelines;[22] they privilege rules rather than democratic participation. Political union, they say, will not accompany currency and fiscal union but complete it. It is to be the crowning moment, not the point of departure, the process seemingly a goal in itself rather than a means to an end. In other words, European federal union is to be a process crowned by an event, rather than – like the Anglo-American cases – an event followed by a process. This vision is doomed to failure. The resulting austerity policies will have crushed the countries on the periphery before they see real economic benefits, or the return of their suspended participatory rights through the establishment of full political union. The planned Europe-wide border defence force with the power to impose on member states will, in the absence of political union, constitute a grievous violation of Greek and Hungarian territorial sovereignty. Moreover, the *confederal* nature of Europe's democratic legitimation and the *federal* nature of its fiscal-economic governance mean that control of the whole has devolved largely to its largest and most powerful part, namely, Germany. This is the very outcome that the European project – admittedly under rather different circumstances – was originally designed to prevent.

Above all, the current strategy rests on the 'gradualist' fallacy on which European integration has long been based, which is that a European political union will be built *peu à peu* in a series of small steps. Eurozone leaders do not seem to have grasped that, contrary to EU lore and culture, successful unions have resulted not from gradual processes of convergence in relatively benign circumstances but through sharp ruptures in periods of extreme crisis. As we have seen from the Anglo-American examples, they come about not through evolution but with a 'big bang'. They are *events* rather than *processes*. Even in Germany, the customs union (Zollverein) of 1833–4 did not lead automatically to unity over the next sixty years or so: that was forged by Bismarck in a series of intense wars with neighbouring powers. The current political integration strategy, therefore, is a long-term, permanent engagement which will end not in marriage but in tears.

Mr Cameron's two-part solution is equally unviable. The idea of growing out of the crisis through structural reform is attractive but insufficient. Mr Cameron's appeal for the completion of the Single Market, particularly in services, is perfectly legitimate and resonates among many. His plan to keep out 'benefit cheats' who come to the UK to abuse her generous welfare provision can be achieved without new legislation and certainly without treaty change;[23] this is, in fact, a common concern among the wealthier member states. The rest of his demands, however, are much more problematic. The justice 'opt out' has proven fraught in practice, so that Britain has recently had to opt back in. Blocking benefits for migrants in employment, or who have lost work, cannot be done without discrimination and thus violates existing legislation and treaties. Indeed, some of what the prime minister requests, such as jettisoning the Human Rights Charter,[24] actually requires Britain to leave the Union altogether, at least as it is currently constituted. One way or the other, the issue is not one of economics but of politics.

Nor is Mr Cameron's constitutional vision for a looser Union much help. In his much-discussed Bloomberg speech of January 2013, the prime minister set out a more 'British' and 'flexible' Europe, which would restore its global competitiveness by allowing powers to 'flow back' from the centre.[25] He called for 'a structure that can accommodate the diversity of its members', some of whom, 'including Britain', could 'never embrace' closer economic and political integration. This would require 'a new Treaty . . . for the entire EU, not just for Britain'. The prime minister's presuppositions have already been invalidated by events, however. He was assuming that the 'twin marauders of war and tyranny have almost entirely been banished from our continent'. As the recent Russian annexation of Crimea, its state of undeclared war with Ukraine in Donetsk and Luhansk, and Mr Putin's steady reduction in domestic liberties suggest, however, the 'twin marauders' have returned. No design for a future Europe can ignore this fact. The 'looser' the bonds, the weaker its response to outside threats will be.

Besides, the prime minister's vista risks opening the clichéd 'Pandora's Box' of demands for national exemptions among other member states. This would make the whole Union unworkable. There are therefore increasing signs within the 'core', especially in Berlin, of a resigned acceptance that Britain cannot be accommodated. Moreover, the story has moved on since the 1990s and early 2000s, when London posed as the champion of the 'new' Europe against the centralizing tendencies of Brussels on the economic front. Berlin, not London, is now their primary focus, as these countries try to ride out the currency and economic storms.[26] For the members of the eurozone, and the aspirant states, Europe has become a community of fate they cannot, and do not want to, escape. 'New' and Old Europe would almost certainly accept some reforms to accommodate Britain, but it cannot countenance the large-scale changes that would be required to satisfy London. Once negotiated, treaty changes will have to be laboriously ratified in national parliaments or through referenda.[27]

The main problem with the current British government solution for Europe, in any case, is that it is based on the exact opposite of the principles on which the United Kingdom was created. It was established as a strong state with clarity on debt, parliamentary sovereignty and the common defence; this is why the Scottish demands for greater devolution have, rightly, produced such consternation. To insist that Europe retreat from closer union in order to solve the crisis, and make it possible for Britain to remain, is to fly in the face of Britain's own historical experience, and that of her American cognate. Here the prime minister is not being hypocritical so much as uncomprehending. The loosening of federal bonds may be conceived by London as pores through which peoples can breathe but they will in practice prove to be cuts out of which the lifeblood of the Union will flow.

The political unity which the eurozone so desperately needs therefore requires a single collective act of will, by its governments and elites and, ultimately, by its citizens.[28] It demands a recognition that its predicaments – an interlocking series of political, fiscal and strategic challenges – closely resemble those that led the British and the Americans to take the plunge for union in 1707 and 1787–8. There is no need for continental Europe to 'reinvent the wheel' when a tried-and-tested model is available to us across the Channel and the Atlantic. This United States of Europe would take from the Anglo-Scottish Union the principle that national identities and histories can be transcended through political union without loss of cultural heritage. It would take from the United States the model of how to reconcile the needs of the centre and the region in a union of numerous states of vastly differing size, economic strength and strategic interests. It would take from both the lesson that only a consolidated debt for which common parliamentary representation takes responsibility can put the state on a sound financial footing and ultimately enable it to defend its position in the world. All this requires Europeans to abandon the cherished nostrum that the process will lead to the event and to embrace a strategy beginning with an event, with an open-ended process to follow.

The construction of a single eurozone state on Anglo-American constitutional principles must begin with the simultaneous consolidation of debt into a 'Union Bond' for which the parliamentary representation of the entire union would be responsible. This must consist of a House of Citizens elected by population, and a Senate which represents the regions on an equal basis. The executive should be headed by an American-style president, elected by popular vote from across the Union (without an electoral college, however). Foreign policy and border security must be the exclusive preserve of the Union. There would be a single army within NATO. The language of government would be English.

These arrangements would give the continent the capacity to deal with its most pressing problems. They will mobilize the entire resources of the eurozone, especially those of Germany, for common projects. The Union Bond will end the euro crisis by creating a sustainable aggregate debt backed by the productive power of the whole Union; the end of national sovereignty will remove, or at least seriously curtail, the capacity of the individual member states to incur fresh obligations. A single foreign policy and military force will contain Russia. The end of the national state will solve problems like Catalonia, and other places where there are demands to separate from the local metropolis but not for full independence outside the EU. By embedding Germany in a larger whole, and thus mobilizing it more effectively for the common good, eurozone political union on Anglo-American constitutional lines also provides the only answer to the prospect of German structural dominance, which Berlin wants as little as anyone else. It goes without saying that any such new constitution for the eurozone would need to be approved by a same-day referendum in all the participating countries. The union would come into being in those countries where it gained a simple majority; no existing EU member state would exercise a veto. Those voting against could negotiate accession in due course if they wished, subject to the consent of the Union government, Senate and House of Citizens (but not the veto of any individual member states, which would have ceased to exist for this purpose).

None of the conventional objections to such a federal union really stands up. Against those who invoke the national peculiarities of Europeans, there is the historical example of the United Kingdom, which joined two quite distinct, and in many ways hostile, nations into a political union. Most eurozone nations actually have a higher opinion of each other than do the Scots and the English. The alternative to supranational union, and thus rescuing the euro, is a return to the national state, which would make Germany by far the largest single actor on the mainland, whether it wanted to be or not. Full federal union would not increase the power of Germany – which is currently inflated by the confederal design of the EU – but rather embed its 80 million-odd citizens within a Union which would probably include upwards of 350 million people. As for language, English is already the lingua franca of the continent. Finally, those who object to the surrender of state sovereignty should know that this pass was already sold with the introduction of the common currency. It is striking that none of the populations most affected by the austerity measures designed to save the euro wishes to return to its old national currency, or its old style of national politics. The populations of the eurozone have already given up their national sovereignty, the rich as much as the poor, and only a Union parliament will give them democratic representation on an equal basis.

Nor let it be objected that 'social Europe' is incompatible with the 'Anglo-Saxon' model. The debate about the right design for Europe should not be a beauty contest about the best form of domestic organization per se, but about the right constitutional architecture for a continent with a history of tearing itself apart and failing to respond to external threats. This must be the Anglo-American Union model. It can coexist with many different forms of domestic organization. The United Kingdom, after all, produced both the welfare state and Thatcherism. The United States brought forth both the New Deal and Ronald Reagan. One should therefore make no general assumption about the domestic or ideological configuration of a future single eurozone state, save that it would be democratic, and that it would evolve and mutate, as democracies do and should. Its purpose would not be to promote any particular form of western democracy but rather to ensure that the eurozone has the means to protect itself against undemocratic challenges from within and, particularly, without.

A full federal union of the eurozone would be very much in Britain's interest. It would solve the euro crisis, rescuing the British from the danger of economic contagion after a blow-out of the common currency or interminable deflation through austerity. By stabilizing the continent militarily and containing Mr Putin, the new state would reduce the strain on the two countries bearing the largest burden of deterrence in the Baltic and elsewhere, the United States and the United Kingdom. This benefit should outweigh and transcend the old British balance-of-power thinking, which might otherwise tempt London to oppose the creation of a single and potentially dominant European state. If the establishment of the United States of America began as a British trauma, in the long run it not only relieved Britain of responsibility for the western hemisphere but also supplied a vital ally against the terrible challenges of the twentieth century. Likewise, the creation of a cognate eurozone union within NATO would secure the UK's eastern flank for generations, and free up British capacity for involvement in other parts of the world.

Winston Churchill pointed the way to such a solution seventy years ago, immediately after the Second World War.[29] In his famous Zurich speech of September 1946 the former British prime minister urged the full political union of the continent in a 'kind of United States of Europe' under the 'principles embodied in the Atlantic Charter'. He praised the work of Count Coudenhove-Kalergi's 'Pan-European Union', which had commanded widespread support in 1920s France, Germany and other parts of Europe. Churchill demanded an 'act of faith', beginning with 'a partnership between France and Germany', assembling around them the states of Europe 'who will and . . . can' join such a Union. Its purpose was clear, namely 'to make the material strength of a single state less important. Small nations will count as much as large ones and gain their honour by their contribution to the common cause.' Moreover, 'the ancient states and principalities of Germany, freely joined together for mutual convenience in a federal system, might each take their individual place among the United States of Europe.' In short, the new polity was designed to solve not merely the European Question but the German Problem, the two being one and the same. Strikingly, however, Churchill conceived of this United States of Europe alongside but not including the United Kingdom and the British 'Commonwealth of Nations', that is, the empire. Instead, he believed that Britain should be one of the 'sponsors of the new Europe'.

Even though the world has greatly changed since 1946, there is still little chance that the United Kingdom would vote to join such a United States of Europe today. To be sure, England entered into full parliamentary union with Scotland in 1707 and Ireland in 1801, but in both cases these were enlargements of the Westminster parliament, essentially enlargements of England, with a view to securing her position in Europe. They are not precedents for the surrender of the sovereignty of Westminster. Winston Churchill and others did seriously consider a full parliamentary union with France in 1940, which would effectively have diluted the sovereignty of Westminster, but that was in the context of an extreme external threat from Nazi Germany. A similar threat cannot be completely ruled out in the future, for example from Mr Putin's Russia or from Islamic State, but for now there is no sign of any threat so existential that it would warrant the end of the thousand years of English national independence and the three-hundred-year-old United Kingdom. There are, however, very good reasons why Britain should support closer continental European integration.

A full federal union of the eurozone should solve the Scottish problem, if it can be achieved before a fresh referendum. As matters stand, Scots will almost certainly vote to stay in the EU, or in a subsequent referendum on independence triggered by an English-led 'Brexit'. They will only do so, however, if Europe remains merely a loose confederation of notionally sovereign member states. Full federal union on the continent, by contrast, would present them with a much starker choice. They would have to choose between remaining in the United Kingdom, joining the new European state (replacing London with another even more remote capital) and full independence outside a eurozone Union and the UK. Previous role models, such as Ireland, would no longer be even notionally independent. There is no polling data on this scenario yet, but it seems likely that the status quo would prevail. If Scots disliked the old United Kingdom, with its strong state and many wars, they will recoil at the new United States of Europe. Even if Scotland decided to go for independence from both the UK and the eurozone, it would be corseted by two strong unions to the south and north, which would reserve the right to intervene in the event of undue Russian or other hostile interference. London could view the (unlikely) prospect of Scotland joining the eurozone state with equanimity, as it would secure England's northern flank for the foreseeable future, mobilize Scots to defend the security of the continent far more comprehensively than they are at the moment and thus fulfil the aims of the 1707 Anglo-Scottish union by other means. The old United Kingdom could then be safely wound up: her work would have been done.

At first sight, this final British 'opt-out' will perplex and irritate other Europeans and British 'Europhiles'. Won't the United Kingdom be isolated in Europe and dwarfed by the united economic power of the new state? If Britain is not part of the relaunched European Union, why should it benefit from the Common Market? Would it not be absurd to create an English-speaking eurozone union without

Britain? Why not choose another language? Some of these objections are more cogent than others, but none of them amounts to much.

There are, of course, many states outside the United Kingdom which speak English, including another member of the EU which would probably join a full federal union, namely, the Irish Republic. Most relevantly in this context, the United States uses English without any sense of absurdity, despite having broken away from the British empire. So there is no logical reason at all why a single European state without Britain should not use English as its language of government. A 'Brexit' might even make it psychologically easier to accept such a solution, certainly for France. Moreover, the option for English is also a choice against another language, such as German, French or (if one is a pessimist) Russian, Chinese or even Arabic. Several European political figures, including President Joachim Gauck of Germany, have already recommended the adoption of English as the language of the Union. Of course, there is no reason in principle why a new union should not choose any other language it wishes, perhaps Latin, Hebrew or Esperanto. English, however, does seem the most realistic option.

Most importantly of all, this book has shown that the United Kingdom is an *exceptional* power in Europe. The British peoples, or at least the English, are not prepared to sacrifice their sovereignty through membership of a full federal Europe, and are willing to pay a high economic price for that stance. Virtually all other peoples in Europe, by contrast, are ultimately either willing to sacrifice that sovereignty or have already lost it, for one reason or another, most notably by surrendering national control over their currencies. Moreover, almost uniquely among European states, Britain is strong enough to survive on her own. This partly reflects a constitutional tradition unbroken by dictatorship or defeat in the twentieth century, and partly her enduring economic and military potential. Nearly all the other European states, by contrast, are too weak to prosper as independent actors – with survival being the limit of their ambitions – while Germany is too large to be permitted to do so. In other words, Europe was designed to fix something that was never broken in Britain. Plainly, if the rest of the Europe had been or were like Britain, capable of defending its own sovereignty and contributing to the common good, and thus entitled to the same special status, then there would have been no need for the European Union in the first place. But it was not and is not.

The central point is that if the eurozone is not to collapse 'Europe' will have to become something quite different from the Community which Britain joined forty years ago and closer to the planned full political union she explicitly rejected in the 1940s and 1950s. It is therefore not a case of Britain leaving the EU but of the eurozone leaving the original European Union: a 'Euroexit', so to speak. To talk about a 'Brexit' without a 'Euroexit' makes no sense, for it is only the latter that really necessitates the former. What is needed is a political unification of the eurozone followed by a pan-EU referendum, in which the UK would be merely one of the participants, but most likely the most important, perhaps the only, state not to vote yes. This would then necessitate a revised European Confederation between the UK and the new eurozone state.

However, as the legendary strategist Carl von Clausewitz said, while things may be simple, the simplest things are often very difficult. How can 'Europe' be given the constitutional structure it needs, without marginalizing Britain, in the event of a eurozone union? The conventional Europhile line here is that London can probably still remain part of the Single Market but that if she is 'outside' she will simply have to accept EU Single Market regulation without having had a say in drafting it; this is currently the case with Norway and Switzerland. There is a serious flaw in this argument. Britain simply cannot be compared to the other non-euro members, or non-EU states. Her economic strength, her permanent seat in the Security Council, her credible currency, her independent nuclear deterrent and what the prime minister calls her general 'military prowess', combine to make her one of the top three or four powers in the world. Indeed, recent events have tended to strengthen Britain's position in Europe, as the common currency wobbles and the Obama administration 'pivots' towards Asia. (It is striking that, in military terms, Britain has remained the second port of call after the US for those states threatened by Mr Putin's ambitions.) All this not only makes Britain so resilient that she cannot simply be dictated to by the eurozone but also a massive net contributor to European security.

It therefore follows that a grand bargain between London and a putative eurozone state is necessary and possible. No less a figure than Jacques Delors remarked in December 2012 that '[t]he British are solely concerned about their economic interest, nothing else. They could be offered a different form of partnership . . . If the British cannot support the trend towards more integration in Europe, we can nevertheless remain friends, but on a different basis. I could imagine a form such as a European economic area or a free-trade agreement.'[30] Many senior eurozone politicians say the same thing in private conversation. They are fully aware that Britain is a special case.

Here is what such an arrangement might look like. Britain would continue to contribute to Europe over the odds militarily (through NATO) and take out over the odds economically (through the Single Market). Immigration and travel could be resolved amicably on the basis of reciprocity, whether in a restrictive or permissive sense. Justice and the budget would be repatriated. Most importantly of all, there would have to be a confederal management of the Single Market and the City of London, giving Britain a much bigger role than Norway and Switzerland, and indeed than she has today, as is her due. There might well be restrictions on the City (though probably no more than a UK government would be inclined to impose anyway), but they would be legitimate so long as they were driven by a genuine desire to curb risky behaviour rather than a discriminatory political project to shift Europe's financial capital to Frankfurt or Paris. There would have to be an understanding that, just as Britain would desist from obstructing closer eurozone political links, indeed would promote them, Brussels would not attempt to lure Scotland back into its fold, to offer British Europhiles anything more than verbal sympathy or in any other way subvert the integrity of its main European ally, the United Kingdom.

In order to achieve such a bargain, the United Kingdom will have to do a great deal more on defence. It will have to take a much closer interest in the east, where the containment of Russian aggression will require the dispatch of large-scale ground forces for permanent basing in Poland and the Baltic states. The Polish government's willingness in early 2016 to countenance reductions in benefits for their nationals in Britain in return for British support for permanent NATO bases in the east to deter Russia has showed that a deal is possible.[31] The United Kingdom will also have to coordinate her economic and environmental policies with the single eurozone state in order to avoid a competitive 'race to the bottom' in trade with dictatorships, particularly the 'People's Republic of China'.

All this needs to be embedded in a new grand settlement for Europe, achieved in one fell swoop over a relatively short and intense period, rather than through the current agony of perpetual referendum and renegotiation. At the heart of it must lie a new agreed single eurozone state which will be guaranteed by the principal external stakeholders; these do not include disruptive rent-seekers such as Mr Putin's Russia. The United States, the United Kingdom and Canada claim this role by virtue of the fact that they have three times rescued 'Europe' from itself, or from outsiders, during the First World War, the Second World War and the Cold War. All three powers continue, to varying degrees, to make good Europe's military deficit. It is their interest and their right, as much as it is in the interest of the eurozoners themselves, that they support the construction of a new and mighty Union on the mainland.

In short, a single European federal state including Britain is not compatible with British sovereignty. A fragmenting Europe with an unstable currency, a Heath-Robinson constitutional structure and without any serious capacity to deter threats, conventional or terrorist, is not in Britain's interests. A united eurozone constructed along Anglo-American constitutional lines in confederation with Great Britain, and in security partnership with Canada and the United States through NATO, is not only compatible with British sovereignty but very much in Britain's interests. What is urgently needed on both sides of the Channel, therefore, is not a European Britain but a 'British Europe'.

There is therefore no point in the British thinking about or deciding upon Britain's place in Europe without a clear sense of the kind of European Union they require. As matters stand, the very thing the prime minister, the Eurosceptics, and many soft Europhiles profess to *most* want the European Union to be – a more flexible 'British' arrangement reversing the trend towards 'ever closer union' – is *least* compatible with the outcomes Britain desires, which are the effective management of the common currency and a concerted response to the enormous security challenges we face, especially in the east. Mr Cameron's vision for Europe is also – given the fact that the United Kingdom was created as a tight parliamentary union to defend Britain's corner in the world – very *un*British. It is therefore in Britain's interests not to force other Europeans to try to adapt to a false halfway house that nobody wants but to encourage the eurozoners to go their separate way, confident in the belief that, where it matters, Britain and Europe will retain a key relationship.

Let it not be objected that a British Europe without Britain makes no sense. History suggests the opposite. The United States originated as a breakaway state from the United Kingdom, based on the principles of the Anglo-Scottish Union. By the same token, Europe can become more British only by separating from Britain. If it does so, and thereby realizes its potential, the resulting polity will eventually be more powerful than these two previous mighty unions put together. The Europeans would thus become more 'British' than the Americans, and indeed the British themselves.

Conclusion

Our links to the rest of Europe, the continent of Europe, have been the dominant factor in our history. We British have in a very special way contributed to Europe. Over the centuries we have fought to prevent Europe from falling under the dominance of a single power. We have fought and we have died for her freedom. And still, today, we stand together.

– Margaret Thatcher, Bruges, 1988

Europe made us. The emergence of England as a nation state was the product of European pressures. So was the formation of the United Kingdom. Relations between the English, Scots, Irish and Welsh have always been fundamentally determined by the continental context. Europe almost invariably posed the biggest threat to the security of the island, strategically and ideologically. The principal function of the Royal Navy and, in time, the Royal Air Force, was homeland defence and European deployment, not overseas power projection. These military priorities remained remarkably stable despite major technological change, ranging from new shipbuilding techniques, through the invention of aircraft to nuclear weaponry. Until the late eighteenth century, naval superiority was no guarantee against invasion, and in the twentieth century the power of the Royal Navy was challenged by land-based aircraft. Moreover, the maintenance of naval and later air superiority from Louis XIV to Hitler was always dependent on preventing the emergence of a continental hegemon who could out-build Britain at sea or in the air.

Europe has almost always been more important to us than the rest of the world. Edmund Burke spoke of a 'Commonwealth of Europe' long before the British Commonwealth of Nations was even thought of. The British empire was conquered largely for European reasons. Colonies gave Britain the demographic and financial weight she lacked on the continent; denying them to rival powers was equally important. At the same time, the overseas empire was acquired and maintained through the management of the European balance of power. This was a virtuous cycle, to be sure, but one which began and ended in Europe. When the empire became an embarrassment in Europe and the world after the Second World War, it was mostly wound down. In short: no Europe, no England, no United Kingdom, no British empire and no decolonization.

The nature of the European challenge varied greatly over time. It was always strategic. In the Middle Ages, the main enemy was France; in the sixteenth century and early seventeenth centuries, it was Spain; from the late seventeenth to the early nineteenth centuries, it was France again; in the mid- to late nineteenth century, it was Tsarist Russia; in the early and mid-twentieth century, it was first the Kaiser and then Hitler's Germany; and then Russia again – with a brief interruption after the fall of the Berlin Wall – from the end of the Second World War down to the present day. Very often, the danger was also ideological, from continental heresy in the Middle Ages, through Counter-Reformation Catholicism (which also became a synonym for absolutism and continental tyranny) in the sixteenth and seventeenth centuries, Jacobinism in the late eighteenth century, continental autocracy in the nineteenth century, right- and left-wing totalitarianism in the twentieth century, to Islamist terrorists arriving from Europe as migrants. The external threat was exacerbated by the fact that all of these ideologies had a domestic constituency of varying strength within the British Isles.

Furthermore, Europe profoundly shaped domestic politics. It was the subject of argument without end for hundreds of years. The debates began with the question of how to protect the realm against external attack, mainly from France and Scotland. They continued over whether and how to vindicate the king's claim to the French throne. In the sixteenth and seventeenth centuries, these discussions gave way to disputes about the best way of protecting Protestantism and parliamentary freedoms in a Europe in which both were under severe attack. From the eighteenth century onwards, Britons disagreed on the best strategy for maintaining the European balance of power. The prevailing Whig orthodoxy looked to alliances and armies on the continent; Tory and radical heresies called for greater restraint in Europe and more concentration on the naval and the colonial. The reality was often less clear cut, of course, and the Whigs were often ardent imperialists (albeit for European reasons), just as many Tories were far from crudely isolationist and were often well-informed about and concerned with Europe. Throughout these debates, some have argued for military intervention on the continent and interference in the internal politics of sovereign states there, while others have demanded equally passionately that one should stay out, for reasons of pragmatism as well as principle. Both views are well represented in both major political parties today.

The careers of many English, and later British, monarchs and statesmen were decided by events on the continent, from the impeachment of Michael de la Pole in the late fourteenth century, through that of his namesake after the fall of France a hundred years later, the decline of Mary's reputation following the loss of Calais, the failure of the Stuarts to defend the Protestant cause in Germany or to contain Louis XIV, the fall of Walpole due to his refusal to maintain the House of Austria against France, that of diverse other ministries throughout the eighteenth and nineteenth centuries, and the fall of Thatcher to the tribulations of John Major in the 1990s. Likewise, the forthcoming referendum on membership of the European Union will probably determine the fate of the current prime minister, Mr Cameron. Moreover, the internal structure of England was in many ways a product of European pressures, from the Danegeld levied to appease the Vikings, the seventeenth- and eighteenth-century 'fiscal-military' state, through the first income tax levied to pay for war with France, to the 'warfare state' and 'welfare state' of the twentieth century.

Britain has therefore always been part of Europe, 'a piece of the continent'. At the start of our story, the principal framework was the North Sea across which the Viking raids struck at England. For much of the Middle Ages, English kings held land in France and the French

Channel ports were regarded by many as part of the defensive perimeter of the realm. In the sixteenth and early seventeenth centuries, Englishmen developed a close and enduring interest in the Low Countries, which many regarded as part of England herself. Over time, these geographically bounded preoccupations developed into a concern for the overall European balance, revolving principally around Germany. More generally, the history of Britain unfolded within the European context, the shared experiences and conflicts of a continent. It formed part of the common core of Christendom for hundreds of years. Like most of the rest of Europe, it experienced the Reformation, the Enlightenment and the Industrial Revolution, albeit at different times and with varying intensity.

If Europe made Britain, then Britain also made Europe. The British shaped Europe in their interests and increasingly in their image. Their military presence and reputation on the continent was usually formidable, from the nobles who took their levies to the *chevauchées* of the thirteenth century, through the iconic victories for English arms at Agincourt, Dunkirk, Blenheim, Dettingen, Waterloo, in the Crimea and during the two world wars, to the deterrence in Europe under NATO. It was enhanced rather than reduced by the fact that many, even most, of these triumphs had been secured with the help of coalition partners. Britain played an important and often a decisive role in most of the major European settlements since the late seventeenth century. This is true from the Treaty of Utrecht, which enshrined the principle of the 'balance of power', through the Congress of Vienna, which remodelled Europe after the Revolutionary and Napoleonic wars, right down to the treaties on European Union in the present day. Moreover, England and, later, the United Kingdom, saw and realized her security in ideological terms, beginning with the defence of the Protestant interest in the sixteenth and seventeenth centuries, the protection of European 'liberties' in the eighteenth century, the promotion of liberalism in the nineteenth century, and the spread of democracy in the twentieth and twenty-first centuries. Britain reached her greatest territorial extent in Europe with the Acts of Union, but she has enlarged herself ideologically much more since then.

England, and then the United Kingdom, has been distinctive in Europe, and not just in the lazy sense that all histories are somehow 'special'. Our European story is not merely separate and equal to that of the continent but fundamentally different and more benign. This is a subjective judgement, to be sure, but not an arbitrary one. Britain's good fortune has been partly a matter of luck and location on the western edge of the continent. In this sense, the Poles have been born unlucky, between Germany and Russia, and in the twentieth century between Nazism and Stalinism. But the English and the British have also made their own luck. They pioneered two innovative forms of political organization: the nation state, as represented in Parliament, however selectively; and then the concept of multinational union based on a parliamentary merger. This model has been adopted by the great democracies of the Anglo-sphere, the United States, Canada, Australia and New Zealand, and it is the reason why all these happy polities are so fundamentally alike, despite important differences. They had and have their problems, no doubt, but these pale into insignificance with those of continental Europe, past and present. Over the past five hundred years, as we have seen, Europeans have explored political unhappiness in many different forms, from absolutism, through Jacobinism, Napoleonic tyranny, Nazism, Soviet communism, to the well-meaning but broken-backed European Union today.

Continental Europe, in short, had failed before 1945, and even now the European Union is only failing better. Unlike virtually every other Europe state which has at some point or other been occupied and dismembered, often repeatedly, England, and the United Kingdom, has largely – with very brief exceptions – been a subject of European politics, never merely an object. In this sense, too, she is exceptional. This should not be an occasion for British triumphalism; on the contrary. Whatever the outcome of the referendum on membership in June 2016, the European Union is not an enemy of the United Kingdom. It should best be understood as a modern version of the old Holy Roman Empire, hapless and officious, perhaps, but not malign. It needs help. The failure of the European project, and the collapse of the current continental order, would be not only a catastrophic blow to the populations on the far side of the Channel but also to the United Kingdom, which would be directly exposed to the resulting storms, as it always has been.

This will change only if the eurozone takes on board the lessons of history and imports the Anglo-American model of full parliamentary multinational political union. Only the creation of a new Whig state, free and financially stable at home and robust abroad, acting in concert with its cognates across the Channel and in other hemispheres, will enable the continent to master its numerous challenges today. If that happens, then the peoples of the United Kingdom will not only have saved themselves in Europe by their efforts but will have rescued the eurozone by their example.

Notes

INTRODUCTION: OUR EUROPEAN STORY

1. Republished in 2005 by the think-tank Civitas; Arthur Bryant, *Freedom's Own Island. The British Oceanic Expansion* (London, 1986); Raphael Samuel, *Island Stories. Unravelling Britain. Theatres of Memory, Volume II* (London and New York, 1998).
2. Christopher Lee, *This Sceptred Isle* (London, 1997). Another example of the insular theme would be Norman Longmate, *Island Fortress. The Defence of Great Britain 1603–1945* (London, 1991).
3. Jonathan Clark (ed.), *A World by Itself. A History of the British Isles* (London, 2010).
4. Quoted in Richard J. Evans, 'The Wonderfulness of Us (the Tory interpretation of History)', *London Review of Books*, vol. 33, no. 6, 17 March 2011, pp. 9–11 (p. 9).
5. In this respect I follow Norman Davies in his bracing *The Isles. A History* (London, 1999). See also his 'Not Forever England. A European History of Britain', in Norman Davies, *Europe between East and West* (London, 2007), pp. 83–105. For the rest, I generally agree with the emphasis on English exceptionalism in Robert Tombs, *The English and Their History* (London, 2014).
6. On this, see Peter Mandler, *The English National Character. The History of an Idea from Edmund Burke to Tony Blair* (New Haven and London, 2006).

1. THE BONDS OF 'CHRISTENDOM'. EUROPE AND THE CREATION OF ENGLAND

1. Quoted in J. J. N. Palmer, *England, France and Christendom, 1377–99* (North Carolina, 1972), p. 182.

2. Quoted in Juliet Barker, *Conquest. The English Kingdom of France, 1417–1450* (Cambridge, MA, 2012), p. 367.
3. P. H. Sawyer, *From Roman Britain to Norman England* (London, 1978), p. 2.
4. See James Campbell, 'Observations on the Conversion of England', in his *Essays in Anglo-Saxon History* (London and Roncerverte, 1986), pp. 69–84).
5. This is based generally on Robert Tombs, *The English and Their History* (London, 2014)
6. Thus Wilhelm Levison, *England and the Continent in the Eighth Century* (Oxford, 1946), pp. 94–107 *et passim*, and (with qualifications) Andreas Bihrer, *Begegnungen zwischen dem ostfränkisch-deutschen Reich und England (850–1100). Kontakte, Konstellationen, Funktionaliserungen, Wirkungen* (Ostildern, 2012), pp. 509–16. See also Veronica Ortenberg, *The English Church and the Continent in the Tenth and Eleventh Centuries. Cultural, Spiritual and Artistic Exchanges* (Oxford, 1992), and David Rollason, Conrad Leyser and Hannah Williams (eds.), *England and the Continent in the Tenth Century. Studies in Honour of Wilhelm Levison (1876–1947)* (Turnhout, 2010). For the prosperity of England see the opening chapters of Nicholas Vincent, *A Brief History of Britain, 1066–1485. The Birth of a Nation* (London, 2011).
7. Thus Pauline Stafford, *Unification and Conquest. A Political and Social History in the Tenth and Eleventh Centuries* (London, 1989).
8. Quoted in James Campbell, 'The United Kingdom of England. The Anglo-Saxon Achievement', in his *The Anglo-Saxon State* (London, 2000), p. 37.
9. Thus J. R. Maddicott, *The Origins of the English Parliament, 924–1327* (Oxford, 2010), p. 37 *et passim*.
10. See James Campbell, 'The Late Anglo-Saxon State: A Maximum View', in *The Anglo-Saxon State*, pp. 10–12 *et passim*. For a more 'minimal' view of England's distinctiveness in Europe see George Molyneaux, *The Formation of the English Kingdom in the Tenth Century* (Oxford, 2015), especially pp. 231–49.
11. For common patterns in political culture see Johanna Dale, 'Royal Inauguration and the Liturgical Calendar in England, France and the Empire, *c.* 1050–*c.* 1250', in Elisabeth van Houts (ed.), *Anglo-Norman Studies XXXVII. Proceedings of the Battle Conference, 2014* (Woodbridge, 2015), pp. 83–98, especially pp. 84–5.
12. Michael Swanton (trans. and ed.), *The Anglo-Saxon Chronicles* (London, 2000).

13. On the connections across the North Sea generally see David Bates and Robert Liddiard (eds.), *East Anglia and Its North Sea World in the Middle Ages* (Woodbridge, 2013).
14. Thus Donald Matthew, *Britain and the Continent, 1000–1300* (London, 2005), p. 9 *et passim.*
15. Thus Eljas Oksanen, *Flanders and the Anglo-Norman World, 1066–1216* (Cambridge, 2012), pp. 4–5 *et passim.*
16. Peter Unwin, *The Narrow Sea. Barrier, Bridge and Gateway to the World. The History of the English Channel* (London, 2003), pp. 56–7.
17. Thus N. A. M. Rodger, *The Safeguard of the Sea. A Naval History of Britain, 660–1649* (London, 1997), p. 99 *et passim.*
18. See M. A. Pollock, *Scotland, England and France after the Loss of Normandy, 1204–1296. 'Auld Amitie'* (Woodbridge, 2015).
19. See R. R. Davies, *The First English Empire. Power and Identities in the British Isles, 1093–1343* (Oxford, 2000), pp. 35–9.
20. Amanda Power, *Roger Bacon and the Defence of Christendom* (Cambridge, 2014) p. 232.
21. Power, *Roger Bacon and the Defence of Christendom*, p. 238.
22. Thus Christopher Tyerman, *England and the Crusades, 1095–1588* (Chicago and London, 1988), pp. 36–7 *et passim.*
23. See, generally, John France, *The Crusades and the Expansion of Catholic Christendom, 1000–1714* (London, 2005).
24. Quoted in Anthony Goodman, *John of Gaunt. The Exercise of Princely Power in Fourteenth-century Europe* (Harlow, 1992), p. 203.
25. Quoted in Nancy Bisaha, *Creating East and West. Renaissance Humanists and the Ottoman Turks* (Philadelphia, 2004) p. 105.
26. See David Carpenter, *The Penguin History of Britain. The Struggle for Mastery. Britain, 1066–1284* (London, 2004), pp. 24, 50 *et passim.*
27. See the description in Davies, *The First English Empire*, p. 32.
28. Quoted from a fourteenth-century translation in G. G. Coulton, *Medieval Panorama. The English Scene from Conquest to Reformation* (Cambridge, 1938), p. 65.
29. Quoted in G. L. Harriss, 'The King and His Subjects', in Rosemary Horrox (ed.), *Fifteenth-century Attitudes. Perceptions of Society in Late Medieval England* (Cambridge, 1994), p. 13.
30. Thus Maddicott, *The Origins of the English Parliament*, pp. 378, 386, *et passim*; and Michael Prestwich, *The Three Edwards. War and State in England, 1272–1377* (London, 1980), pp. 226–8, 299 *et passim.*
31. Maddicott, *The Origins of the English Parliament*, p. 392.

32. Thus Ralph V. Turner and Richard R. Heiser, *The Reign of Richard Lionheart. Ruler of the Angevin Empire, 1189–99* (Harlow, 2000), p. 3.
33. See Tombs, *The English and Their History*, p. 77.
34. 'Song against the King's Taxes', in Peter Coss (ed.), *Thomas Wright's Political Songs of England. From the Reign of John to that of Edward II* (Cambridge, 1996), p. 182
35. For the popularity of the war, see Prestwich, *The Three Edwards*, p. 27.
36. Quoted in Prestwich, *The Three Edwards*, p. 210.
37. E. B. Fryde, 'Parliament and the French War, 1336–40', in T. A. Sandquist and M. R. Powicke (eds.), *Essays in Medieval History presented to Bertie Wilkinson* (Toronto, 1969), pp. 242–61.
38. See Prestwich, *The Three Edwards*, p. 211, and p. 225 (quotation).
39. Quotations in Palmer, *England, France and Christendom*, p. 7.
40. Quoted in M. H. Keen, *England in the Later Middle Ages. A Political History* (London, 1973; 1988 edn), p. 142.
41. I owe this phrase to Lord Hurd, who has used it to describe late-twentieth-century Britain.
42. Quoted in Palmer, *England, France and Christendom*, p. 29.
43. John Gillingham, *Richard I* (New Haven and London, 1999), pp. 1, 3. For the pan-European celebration of Richard see also Turner and Heiser, *The Reign of Richard Lionheart*, p. 3.
44. Quoted in Keen, *England in the Later Middle Ages*, p. 142.
45. Anne Hudson, 'Lollardy: The English Heresy?' in her *Lollards and Their Books* (London and Ronceverte, 1985), pp. 141–63.
46. Quoted in Frank Welsh, *The Battle for Christendom. The Council of Constance, 1415, and the Struggle to Unite against Islam* (London, 2008), pp. 170–71.
47. Quoted in Jocelyne Gledhill Dickinson, *The Congress of Arras 1435. A Study in Medieval Diplomacy* (Oxford, 1955), p. 24 (the spelling has been modernized).
48. C. F. Richmond, 'The Keeping of the Seas during the Hundred Years War, 1422–1440', *History*, 49 (1964), 283–98; G. A. Holmes, 'The Libel of English Policy', *English Historical Review*, 76 (1961), 193–216.
49. Quoted in Keen, *England in the Late Middle Ages*, p. 404.

2. 'A PIECE OF THE CONTINENT'. EUROPE AND THE MAKING OF THE UNITED KINGDOM

1. David Nicolle, *The Fall of English France, 1449–53* (Oxford, 2012).
2. See Juliet Barker, *Conquest. The English Kingdom of France* (London, 2010).

3. Bale's Chronicle in Ralph Flenley (ed.), *Six Town Chronicles of England* (Oxford, 1911).
4. Cited in Helen Castor, *Blood and Roses. The Paston Family in the Fifteenth Century* (London, 2004), p. 61.
5. For an overview see Maurice Keen, 'The End of the Hundred Years War. Lancastrian France and Lancastrian England', in Michael Jones and Malcolm Vale (eds.), *England and Her Neighbours, 1066–1453* (London, 1989), pp. 297– 311, especially pp. 299–301.
6. See Castor, *Blood and Roses*, pp. 56–7.
7. Cited in Castor, *Blood and Roses*, p. 60
8. See G. L. Harriss, 'The Struggle for Calais. An Aspect of the Rivalry between Lancaster and York', *English Historical Review*, LXXV (1960), pp. 30–53, especially pp. 30–31.
9. For the parliamentary critique of grand strategy and the flashing of fiscal teeth see J. S. Roskell, *The History of Parliament. The House of Commons, 1386–1421* (Stroud, 1992), pp. 89, 101, 101–15, 126, 129, 137. See also Eleanor Searle and Robert Burghart, 'The Defense of England and the Peasants' Revolt', *Viator*, 3 (1972), pp. 370–75.
10. http://www.british-history.ac.uk/cal-papal-registers/brit-ie/vol10/pp 259-266
11. For the existence of a 'political sphere' before print and the centrality of the English wars see Clementine Oliver, *Parliament and Political Pamphleteering in Fourteenth-century England* (Woodbridge, 2010), p. 4 *et passim.*
12. On the English inquest into the fall of France see Catherine Nall, 'William Worcester Reads Alain Chartier: *Le Quadrilogue invectif* and Its English readers', and 'Perceptions of Financial Mismanagement and the English Diagnosis of Defeat', *The Fifteenth Century*, 7 (2007), pp. 119–35. I thank Dr Nall for allowing me to see her unpublished texts. Her work has since appeared as: Catherine Nall, 'Reading and War in the Aftermath of Defeat' in *Reading and War in Fifteenth-century England. From Lydgate to Malory* (Cambridge, 2012), pp. 48–74, 143–4. See also Christopher Allmand and Maurice Keen, 'History and the Literature of War: The *Boke of noblesse* of William of Worcester', in Christopher Allmand (ed.), *War, Government and Power in Late Medieval France* (Liverpool, 2000), pp. 92–105, especially pp. 98–9 re: *respublica.*
13. See Glenn Richardson (ed.), *The Contending Kingdoms. France and England, 1420–1700* (Aldershot, 2008).
14. Quotations in J. R. Maddicott, *The Origins of the English Parliament, 924–1327* (Oxford, 2010), p. 376.

15. For the continuing English preoccupation with France see David Grummitt (ed.), *The English Experience in France, c. 1450–1558. War, Diplomacy and Cultural Exchange* (Aldershot, 2002). For the maritime dimension see Beatrice Heuser, 'Regina Maris and the Command of the Sea. The Sixteenth-century Origins of Modern Maritime Strategy', in *Journal of Strategic Studies*, 2015, pp. 1–38, especially p. 6.
16. Quoted in Susan Doran, *England and Europe, 1485–1603* (London and New York, 1986), p. 89.
17. See C. S. L. Davies, ' "Roy de France et roy d'Angleterre": The English Claims to France, 1453–1558', *Publications du Centre Européen d'Études Bourguignonnes (XIVe–XVIe siècles)*, 35 (1995).
18. Steven J. Gunn, 'The French Wars of Henry VIII', in Jeremy Black, (ed.), *The Origins of War in Early Modern Europe* (Edinburgh, 1987), pp. 28–51.
19. J. J. Scarisbrick, *Henry VIII* (London, 1968), p. 135. The relevant chapter is entitled 'The Renewal of the Hundred Years' War', pp. 21–40.
20. Scarisbrick, *Henry VIII*, p. 58. Wolsey, p. 63.
21. Stella Fletcher, *Cardinal Wolsey. A Life in Renaissance Europe* (London and New York, 2009), pp. 61–2.
22. See John Guy, *Tudor England* (Oxford, 1985), p. 105 (Tunstall quotation).
23. See C. S. L. Davies, 'Tournai and the English Crown, 1513–1519', *Historical Journal*, 41 (1998), pp. 1–26, especially pp. 11–12.
24. Quoted in Scarisbrick, *Henry VIII*, p. 70.
25. Quoted in Scarisbrick, *Henry VIII*, pp. 142–3.
26. Quoted in Scarisbrick, *Henry VIII*, p. 48.
27. Thus Ralph Houlbrooke, *Britain and Europe, 1500–1780* (London, 2011), p. 56.
28. Thus Steven Gunn, David Grummitt and Hans Cools, *War, State and Society in England and the Netherlands, 1477–1559* (Oxford), pp. 329–34.
29. See Wallace MacCaffrey, 'Parliament and Foreign Policy', in D. M. Dean and N. L. Jones (eds.), *The Parliaments of Elizabethan England* (Oxford, 1990), pp. 65–90, especially pp. 65–7.
30. Lesley B. Cormack, 'The Fashioning of an Empire. Geography and the State in Elizabethan England', in Anne Godlewska and Neil Smith (eds.), *Georgraphy and Empire* (Oxford, 1994), p. 16.
31. See Guy, *Tudor England*, p. 135.
32. See Jeremy Goring, 'Social Change and Military Decline in Mid-Tudor England', *History*, 60 (1975), pp. 185–97 (Hales quotation p. 185).

33. 'The Lord Keeper Bacon's Speech on Opening Parliament', *Cobbett's Parliamentary History of England. From the Norman Conquest in 1066 to the year 1803*, vol. I (London, 1806), col. 640. This was the first parliament of Elizabeth's reign.
34. Quoted in Doran, *England and Europe*, p. 183.
35. Quoted in C. S. L. Davies, 'England and the French War, 1557–9', in Robert Tittler and Jennifer Loach (eds.), *The Mid-Tudor Polity, c. 1540–1560* (Totowa, NJ, 1980), pp. 159–85 (quotation p. 179).
36. On the sealing of England's northern border see Jane E. A. Dawson, 'William Cecil and the British Dimension of Early Elizabethan Foreign Policy', *History*, 74 (1989), pp. 196–216.
37. Quoted in Doran, *England and Europe*, p. 100.
38. Quoted in Doran, *England and Europe*, p. 99.
39. See Geoffrey Parker, *The Grand Strategy of Philip II* (New Haven and London, 1998), p. 4.
40. See David J. B. Trim, 'Seeking a Protestant Alliance and Liberty of Conscience on the Continent, 1558–85', in Susan Doran and Glenn Richardson, *Tudor England and Its Neighbours*, p. 151. Sir Walter Mildmay is quoted in Wallace McCaffrey, 'Parliament and Foreign Policy', in D. M. Dean and N. L. Jones (eds.), *The Parliaments of Elizabethan England* (Oxford, 1990), p. 79.
41. Cited in R. B. Wernham, *Before the Armada. The Growth of English Foreign Policy, 1485–1588* (London, 1966), p. 292. On the 'counterscarp' see D. J. B. Trim, 'The Continental Commitment: A Tudor–Stuart Perspective', at the conference 'The Continental Commitment', De Montfort University, July 1999, pp. 1–17, especially pp. 7–8.
42. See J. Raitt, 'The Elector John Casimir, Queen Elizabeth, and the Protestant League', in D. Visser (ed.), *Controversy and Conciliation. The Reformation and the Palatinate, 1559–1583* (Allison Park, PA, 1986), pp. 117–45.
43. Cecil on the German princes is cited in Trim, 'Seeking a Protestant Alliance', p. 157.
44. Quoted in Doran, *England and Europe*, p. 99.
45. Drake is cited in Carol Z. Wiener, 'The Beleaguered Isle. A Study of Elizabethan and Early Jacobean Anti-Catholicism', in *Past & Present*, 51 (1971), p. 62. For the *Vindiciae* see D. J. B. Trim, '"If a Prince Use Tyrannie Towards His People". Interventions on Behalf of Foreign Populations in Early Modern Europe', in Brendan Simms and D. J. B. Trim (eds.), *Humanitarian Intervention. A History* (Cambridge, 2011), pp. 29–66.

46. For Elizabeth's reservations about territorial expansion into the Low Countries see Simon Adams, 'Elizabeth I and the Sovereignty of the Netherlands, 1576–1585', in *Transactions of the Royal Historical Society*, 6th series, 14 (2004), pp. 309–19.
47. Cecil is cited in Wernham, *Before the Armada*, pp. 384, 386.
48. The impact of the expansion of Europe on the state system is discussed in J. H. Elliott, *The Old World and the New, 1492–1650* (Cambridge, 1970), pp. 79–10 (Hakluyt quotation pp. 90–91). On the importance of the New World to Spain's European position see, most recently, J. H. Elliott, *Empires of the Atlantic World. Britain and Spain in America, 1492–1830* (New Haven and London, 2006).
49. Thus Stephen Ellis, *Tudor Ireland. Crown, Community and the Conflict of Cultures, 1470–1603* (London and New York, 1985), p. 14.
50. See David Potter, 'French Intrigue in Ireland during the Reign of Henri II, 1547–1559', in *International History* Review, V (1983). For the close links between Ireland and Europe at the time, and Habsburgism among the Gaelic Irish, see Declan M. Downey, 'Irish-European Integration: The Legacy of Charles V', in Judith Devlin and Howard B. Clarke (eds.), *European Encounters. Essays in Memory of Albert Lovett* (Dublin, 2003), pp. 97–117.
51. William Palmer, *The Problem of Ireland in Tudor Foreign Policy, 1485–1603* (Woodbridge, 1995), p. 79 *et passim*. See also the 'geopolitical moments' described in 'Armada, Elizabethan Conquest and the Opening of the Atlantic', in G. R. Sloan, *The Geopolitics of Anglo-Irish Relations in the Twentieth Century* (London and Washington, 1997), pp. 75–88. For an example of the more local 'archipelagic' and 'three kingdoms' view see Brendan Bradshaw and John Morrill (eds.), *The British Problem, c. 1534–1707. State Formation in the Atlantic Archipelago* (Basingstoke, 1996).
52. Cecil is cited in Dawson, 'Cecil and Foreign Policy', p. 209. The limitations of the 1603 union of crowns are well explored in Bruce Galloway, *The Union of England and Scotland, 1603–1608* (Edinburgh, 1986).
53. W. B. Patterson, *King James VI and I and the Reunion of Christendom*, pp. Ix, 48–51, 294–5 (quotation p. 50).
54. Thus Franklin Le Van Baumer, 'The Conception of Christendom in Renaissance England', *Journal of the History of Ideas*, 6, 2 (1945) p. 133 *et passim* (the quotation by James as King of Scotland is on p. 140).
55. See Jonathan Israel, 'Garrisons and Empire: Spain's Strongholds in North-west Germany, 1589–1659', in Jonathan I. Israel, *Conflicts of Empires. Spain, the Low Countries and the Struggle for World*

Supremacy, 1585–1713 (London and Rio Grande, 1995), pp. 23–44, especially the map on Spanish garrisons in north Germany, p. 25. Cecil is cited in Hans Werner, 'The View from the Popular Stage', in R. Malcolm Smuts (ed.), *The Stuart Court and Europe. Essays in Politics and Political Culture* (Cambridge, 1996), p. 125.

56. See 'Debate on the Motion for a Supply', 12.4.1614, in cols. 1163–5 in *Cobbett's Parliamentary History*, vol. I.
57. Thus Jonathan Scott, *England's Troubles: Seventeenth-century English Political Instability in European Context* (Cambridge, 2000).
58. See Richard Cust, *Charles I. A Political Life* (Harlow, 2007), pp. 31–62.
59. Thus Jayne E. E. Boys, *London's News Press and the Thirty Years' War* (Woodbridge, 2011), pp. 272–4 and C. John Sommerville, *The News Revolution in England. Cultural Dynamics of Daily Information* (New York and Oxford, 1996), pp. 24–9.
60. Davies is cited in Cobbett's *Parliamentary History of England* (36 vols., London, 1806–20), vol. I, col. 1186. See also Noel Malcolm, *Reason of State, Propaganda and the Thirty Years' War. An Unknown Translation by Thomas Hobbes* (Oxford, 2007), ch. 5, 'Palatine Politics: Cavendish, Mansfield, and Hobbes', especially pp. 74–8, and Anthony Milton, 'The Church of England and the Palatinate, 1566–1642', in *Proceedings of the British Academy*, 164 (2010), 137–65.
61. On the link between styles of dress and strategic concerns see Anna Bayman, 'Cross-dressing and Pamphleteering in Early Seventeenth-century London', in David Lemmings and Claire Walker (eds.), *Moral Panics, the Media and the Law in Early Modern England* (Basingstoke, 2009), pp. 63–78, especially pp. 63–5.
62. Thus Malcolm Smuts, 'Religion, European Politics and Henrietta Maria's Circle, 1625–41', in Erin Griffey (ed.), *Henrietta Maria. Piety, Politics and Patronage* (Aldershot, 2008), pp. 13–38. On the rise of Calvinist internationalism in England see David Trim, 'Calvinist Internationalism and the Shaping of Jacobean Foreign Policy', in Timothy Wilks (ed.), *Prince Henry Revived: Image and Exemplarity in Early Modern England* (London, 2008), pp. 239–58.
63. 'Resolutions on Religion Drawn by a Sub-committee of the House of Commons, 24 February 1629', in S. R. Gardiner (ed.), *The Constitutional Documents of the Puritan Revolution, 1625–1660* (Oxford, 1889), p. 78.
64. See E. A. Wrigley, 'The Divergence of England: The Growth of the English Economy in the Seventeenth and Eighteenth Centuries', in E. A. Wigley, *Poverty, Progress and Population* (Cambridge, 2004), pp. 44–67.

65. See 'The Grand Remonstrance', 1.12.1641, in Gardiner (ed.), *Constitutional Documents*, pp. 208–9; Simon Adams, 'Spain or the Netherlands? The Dilemmas of Early Stuart Foreign Policy', in Howard Tomlinson (ed.), *Before the English Civil War. Essays on Early Stuart Politics and Government* (London, 1983), p. 101; Werner, 'The View from the Popular Stage', p. 116 Cogswell, *Blessed Revolution*, p. 76. See generally Scott, *England's Troubles*.
66. The English parliamentarians are cited in Cogswell, *Blessed Revolution*, pp. 72–3. Rudyerd is cited in Elliott, *The Old World and the New*, pp. 90–91.
67. For the importance of the contest with Spain to control the tobacco trade see Thomas Cogswell, '"In the Power of the State". Mr Anys's Project and the Tobacco Colonies, 1626–1628', *English Historical Review*, CXXII (2008), pp. 35–64.
68. On the two-way traffic across the Atlantic and the English identity of the colonists generally see: Susan Hardman Moore, *Pilgrims. New World Settlers and the Call of Home* (New Haven and London, 2007) and Malcolm Gaskill, *Between Two Worlds. How the English became Americans* (Oxford, 2014).
69. See Joachim Whaley, 'A Tolerant Society? Religious Toleration in the Holy Roman Empire, 1648–1806', in Ole Grell and Roy Porter (eds.), *Toleration in Enlightenment Europe* (Cambridge, 2000), pp. 175–95, especially pp. 176–7, 179.
70. On the 'humanitarian intervention' over Savoy see David Trim, 'Interventions in Early Modern Europe', in Simms and Trim (eds.), *Humanitarian Intervention. A History*, pp. 54–64.
71. Thomas Gage's remarks of about 1654 are cited in Charles P. Korr, *Cromwell and the New Model Foreign Policy. England's Policy toward France, 1649–1658* (Berkeley, Los Angeles, and London, 1975) p. 89.
72. See Michael Braddick, *State Formation in Early Modern England, c. 1550–1700* (Cambridge, 2000), pp. 213–21.
73. See Lucy Campbell, 'English Perspectives on the Holy Roman Empire, 1660–1688' (MPhil dissertation, University of Cambridge, 2015).
74. Paul Sonnino, *Louis XIV and the Origins of the Dutch War* (Cambridge, 1988).
75. Thus Klaus Malettke, *Universalmonarchie, kollektive Sicherheit und Gleichgewicht im 17 Jahrhundert*, in Michael Jonas, Ulrich Lappenkueper and Bernd Wegner (eds.), *Stabilität durch Gleichgewicht. Balance of power im internationalen System der Neuzeit* (Paderborn, 2015), p. 31. For the ambivalence of the Franco-British relationship see

Robert and Isabelle Tombs, *That Sweet Enemy. The French and the British from the Sun King to the Present* (London, 2006).

76. See Gabriel Glickman, 'Conflicting Visions: Foreign Affairs in Domestic Debate, 1660–1689', in William Mulligan and Brendan Simms (eds.), *The Primacy of Foreign Policy in British History, 1660–2000. How Strategic Concerns Shaped Modern Britain* (Basingstoke, 2010), pp. 15–31. See also Steven C. A. Pincus, 'From Butterboxes to Wooden Shoes: The Shift in English Popular Sentiment from Anti-Dutch to Anti-French in the 1670s', in *Historical Journal*, 38, 2 (1995), p. 360
77. Quoted in Brendan Simms, *Three Victories and a Defeat. The Rise and Fall of the First British Empire, 1714–1783* (London, 2007), p. 32. For the centrality of the strategic critique see Annabel Patterson, *The Long Parliament of Charles II* (New Haven and London, 2008), pp. 178–208, especially pp. 179–180
78. See Gabriel Glickman, 'Empire, "Popery", and the Fall of English Tangier, 1662–1684', *Journal of Modern History*, 87 (June 2015), pp. 247–80 (quotations p. 271).
79. Quotations from Tony Claydon, *Europe and the Making of England* (Cambridge, 2007), pp. 56 and 239.
80. William and Bentinck are quoted in David Onnekirk, 'Primacy Contested: Foreign and Domestic Policy in the Reign of William III', in Mulligan and Simms (eds.), *The Primacy of Foreign Policy in British History*, pp. 36–7.
81. See Tony Claydon, *William III and the Godly Revolution* (Cambridge, 1996), pp, 138–40 *et passim.*
82. Quoted in Simms, *Three Victories*, p. 44.
83. Quoted in Glickman, 'Conflicting Visions', in Mulligan and Simms (eds.), *The Primacy of Foreign Policy in British History*, p. 27.
84. The Admiralty instructions are quoted in Simms, *Three Victories*, p. 50.
85. Steve Pincus, *1688. The First Modern Revolution* (New Haven and London, 2009), pp. 475–7 *et passim.*
86. See E. S. de Beer, 'The English Newspapers from 1695 to 1702', in Ragnhild Hatton and J. S. Bromley (eds.), *William III and Louis XIV* (Liverpool, 1968), especially pp. 123–4, for the centrality of foreign news.
87. See Robert D. McJimsey, 'A Country Divided? English Politics and the Nine Years' War', *Albion*, 23/1 (1991), 61–74, and 'Shaping the Revolution in Foreign Policy: Parliament and the Press, 1689–1730', in *Parliamentary History*, 25 (2006), pp. 17–31; and K. A. J. McLay, 'Combined Operations and the European Theatre during the Nine Years' War, 1688–97', in *Historical Research*, 78 (2005), especially p. 539.

88. Quoted in Glickman, 'Conflicting Visions', in Mulligan and Simms (eds.), *The Primacy of Foreign Policy in British History*, p. 24.
89. Quoted in Miles Ogborn, 'The Capacities of the State: Charles Davenant and the Management of the Excise, 1683–1698', in *Journal of Historical Geography*, 24 (1998), 289–312.
90. Quoted in Simms, *Three Victories*, p. 48.
91. Brian Levack, *The Formation of the British State. Scotland and the Union, 1603–1707* (Oxford, 1987).
92. Quoted in Doohwan Ahn, 'From "Jealous Emulation" to "Cautious Politics": British Foreign Policy and Public Discourse in the Mirror of Ancient Athens, *c.* 1730–*c.* 1750', in David Onnekink and Gijs Rommelse (eds.), *Ideology and Foreign Policy in Early Modern Europe (1650–1750)*, (Farnham, 2011), p. 3.
93. See Christopher Storrs, 'The Union of 1707 and the War of the Spanish Succession', in Stewart J. Brown and Christopher A. Whatley (eds.), *The Union of 1707: New Dimensions* (Edinburgh, 2008), pp. 31–44, and Allan I. Macinnes, *Union and Empire. The Making of the United Kingdom in 1707* (Cambridge, 2007), pp. 243–76. On the connection between the Union and preserving the liberties of Europe see Colin Kidd, *Union and Unionism. Political Thought in Scotland, 1500–2000* (Cambridge, 2008), p. 79.
94. Swift is cited from Simms, *Three Victories*, p. 60.
95. St John is quoted in Simms, *Three Victories*, p. 65.
96. I. K. Steel, *Politics of Colonial Policy. The Board of Trade in Colonial Administration, 1696–1720* (Oxford, 1968), pp. 134–42; John Carswell, *The South Sea Bubble* (Stanford/California, 1960), pp. 40–59.
97. Thus Houlbrooke, *Britain and Europe*, pp. 149–66.

3. 'THE BULWARKS OF GREAT BRITAIN'. THE UNITED KINGDOM AND THE CONTINENT IN THE AGE OF ABSOLUTISM

1. This chapter uses material from Brendan Simms, '"Ministers of Europe". British Strategic Culture, 1714–1760', in Hamish Scott and Brendan Simms (eds.), *Cultures of Power in Europe during the Long Eighteenth Century* (Cambridge, 2007), pp. 110–32. For a narrative of British foreign policy and strategic debate during this period see Brendan Simms, *Three Victories and a Defeat. The Rise and Fall of the First British Empire, 1714–1783* (London, 2007).
2. *Cobbett's Parliamentary History of England. From the Norman Conquest in 1066 to the Year 1803* (London, 1806), XII, 13.4.1741, col. 178.

3. Quoted in Simms, *Three Victories*, p. 484.
4. A point made in Jeremy Black, *Natural and Necessary Enemies. Anglo-French Relations in the Eighteenth Century* (London, 1986), pp. 2–3.
5. See Jeremy Black, *The Grand Tour in the Eighteenth Century* (Stroud, 1992).
6. See Uta Richter-Uhlig, *Hof und Politik unter den Bedingungen der Personalunion zwischen Hannover und England* (Hanover, 1992), pp. 43–4.
7. See Jeremy Black, 'The Press and Europe', in *The English Press in the Eighteenth Century* (London and Sydney, 1987), pp. 197–244; Graham Gibbs, 'Newspapers, Parliament and Foreign Policy in the Age of Stanhope and Walpole', in *Mélanges offerts à G. Jacquemyns* (Brussels, 1968), pp. 293–315, especially p. 295.
8. For the traditional view of an 'ignorant' parliament see C. H. Firth, 'The Study of British Foreign Policy', *Quarterly Review*, 226 (1916), pp. 470–71; Jeremy Black, *Parliament and Foreign Policy in the Eighteenth Century* (Cambridge, 2004), p. 146, also 170 *et passim*. On the high quality of parliamentary speeches see also Schweizer, 'An unpublished parliamentary speech by the Elder Pitt, 9 December 1761', *Historical Research*, 64, 1991, pp. 98–105.
9. See Simms, 'British Strategic Culture', p. 115.
10. Basil Williams, *Carteret and Newcastle. A Contrast in Contemporaries* (Cambridge 1943), p. 9.
11. See Simms, 'British Strategic Culture', p. 115.
12. A point first made by Black, *Parliament and Foreign Policy*, p. 86. See also David Armitage, 'The British Conception of Empire in the Eighteenth Century', in Hermann Hiery and Christoph Kampmann (eds.), *Imperium/Empire/Reich. Ein Konzept politischer Herrschaft im deutsch-britischen Vergleich. [An Anglo-German Comparison of a Concept of Rule]* (Munich, 1999), p. 92. Some statistics are provided in Doohwan Ahn and Brendan Simms, 'European Great Power Politics in British Public Discourse, 1714–1763', in William Mulligan and Brendan Simms (eds.), *The Primacy of Foreign Policy in British History, 1660–2000. How Strategic Concerns Shaped Modern Britain* (Basingstoke, 2010), pp. 79–101.
13. Cited in A. W. Ward, *Great Britain and Hanover. Some Aspects of the Personal Union* (Oxford, 1899) p. 133.
14. See Simms, 'British Strategic Culture', p. 116.
15. Daniel Baugh deals with this debate in 'Great Britain's "Blue-water" Policy, 1689–1815', *International History Review*, 10, 1 (1988), 33–58.
16. See Philip Woodfine, *Britannia's Glories. The Walpole Ministry and the 1739 War with Spain* (Woodbridge, 1998), especially pp. 128–53.

17. Bolingbroke, *Letters on the Spirit of Patriotism and on the Idea of a Patriot King*, with an introduction by A. Hassall (Oxford, 1926), pp. 116, 122.
18. E.g. William Cobbett (ed.), *The Parliamentary History of England from the Earliest Period to the Year 1803*, 36 vols. (1806–1820) (hereafter *Cobbett*), XIII, 6.12.1742, col. 913. For examples of navalist and anti-European rhetoric in popular ballads see Jeremy Black, *America or Europe? British Foreign Policy, 1739–1763* (London, 1998), p. 60.
19. *Cobbett*, IX, 23.1.1734, col. 208; *Cobbett*, XIII, 27.1.1744, cols. 587–88.
20. See Brendan Simms, 'Pitt and Hanover', in Simms and Torsten Riotte (eds.), *The Hanoverian Dimension in British History, 1714–1837* (Cambridge, 2007), pp. 28–57.
21. Cited in Mitchell Dale Allen, 'The Anglo-Hanoverian Connection, 1727–1760' (Unpublished PhD dissertation, Boston University, 2000), p. 274.
22. For the primacy of foreign policy over economics in this period see Simms, *Three Victories*, pp. 74–5.
23. Cited in Basil Williams, *Stanhope. A Study in Eighteenth-century War and Diplomacy* (Oxford, 1932), p. 243.
24. Cited in Black, *America or Europe?*, p. 122.
25. Cited in Peters, *Pitt and Popularity. The Prime Minister and London Opinion during the Seven Years War*, Oxford, 1980. p. 69.
26. *Cobbett* XII, 10.12.1742, col. 1047; *Cobbett* XIII, 11.1.1744, col. 428.
27. Parliamentary speech of 27.1.1744, in J. H. Plumb and Joel H. Wiener (eds.), *Great Britain. Foreign Policy and the Span of Empire* (New York, 1972), vol. I, pp. 85–6.
28. N. A. M. Rodger, *The Safeguard of the Sea. A Naval History of Britain, 660–1649* (London, 1997), vol. 2.
29. *The Case of the Hanover Forces* (1742) cited in Nicholas Harding, 'Hanoverian Rulership and Dynastic Union with Britain, 1700–1760', in Rex Rexhauser (ed.), *Die Personalunionen von Sachen-Polen, 1697–1763 und Hannover-England, 1714–1837. Ein Vergleich* (Wiesbaden, 2005), p. 183.
30. That said, Britain and Hanover were always two distinct international realities, as is made clear in R. Hatton, *The Anglo-Hanoverian Connection, 1714–1760* (1982 Creighton lecture; London, 1982), p. 3.
31. Both Townshend quotations are in Simms, 'British Strategic Culture', p. 119.
32. Cited in Williams, *Carteret and Newcastle*, p. 127.
33. Hardwicke to Newcastle, 11.9.1757, in P. C. Yorke (ed.), *The Life and Correspondence of Philip Yorke, Earl of Hardwicke*, 3 vols. (Cambridge, 1913), (*Hardwicke*), III, p. 176.

34. See e.g. Carteret's remarks cited in Harding, 'Dynastic Union', p. 211; Williams, *Carteret and Newcastle*, p. 127.
35. Simms, 'British Strategic Culture', p. 119.
36. *A Letter to a Friend Concerning the Electorate of Hanover* (London, 1744), cited in Harding, 'Dynastic Union', p. 212.
37. See in general terms: Michael Sheehan, 'Balance of Power Intervention: Britain's Decisions for or against Aar, 1733–56', *Diplomacy and Statecraft*, 7/2 (1996), 271–89; 'The Sincerity of the British Commitment to the Maintenance of the Balance of Power, 1714–1763', *Diplomacy and Statecraft* 15, 3 (2004), 489–506.
38. *Cobbett*, XII, 9.4.1741, col. 149; *Cobbett*, XII, 29.4.1742, col. 614.
39. On 'universal monarchy' in contemporary rhetoric see (re: France) Carteret, in *Cobbett*, XIII, 1.12.1743, col. 129; *Cobbett* XII, 4.12.1741, col. 227; Cobbett XII, 10.12.1742, col. 942.
40. See the slightly two-edged account in Jeremy Black, 'An "Ignoramus" in European Affairs?', *British Journal for Eighteenth-century Studies*, 6 (1983), 55–65 and Nick Harding, 'Sir Robert Walpole and Hanover', *Historical Research*, 76/192 (May 2003), 165–86.
41. The quotations are taken from Simms, *Three Victories*, p. 289 (Motion for the removal of Sir Robert Walpole), p. 290 (Pitt).
42. Quoted in Matthew McCormack, 'The New Militia: War, Politics and Gender in 1750s Britain', *Gender & History*, 19 (2007), pp. 483–500 (quotation p. 484). See also Philip Carter, 'An "Effeminate" or "Efficient" Nation? Masculinity and Eighteenth-century Social Documentary', *Textual Practice*, 11 (1997), pp. 429–43.
43. Quoted in David Porter, 'A Peculiar but Uninteresting Nation: China and the Discourse of Commerce in Eighteenth-century England', *Eighteenth-century Studies*, 33/2 (2000), pp. 181–99. (quotation p. 83).
44. See David Nokes's review of James A. Harris (ed.), *Sketches of the History of Man*, *TLS*, 21.3.2008, p. 23.
45. Carter, 'An "effeminate" or "efficient" nation?' p. 429.
46. Quoted in McCormack, 'War, Politics and Gender in 1750s Britain', p. 497.
47. Thus Erica Charters, 'The Caring Fiscal-military State during the Seven Years War, 1756–1763', *Historical Journal*, 52 (2009), pp. 921–41, especially 937–40 (quotation p. 939).
48. On the subject of religion and English/British foreign policy see Steven C. A. Pincus, *Protestantism and Patriotism. Ideologies and the Making of English Foreign Policy, 1650–1668* (Cambridge, 1996), and Andrew C. Thompson, *Britain, Hanover and the Protestant Interest, 1688–1756* (Woodbridge, 2006).

49. Baruch Mevorach, 'Die Interventionsbestrebungen in Europa zur Verhinderung der Vertreibung der Juden aus Böhmen und Mähren, 1744–1745', *Jahrbuch des Instituts für deutsche Geschichte*, IX (1980), pp. 16–81 (quotations pp. 34 and 54). J. Krengel, 'Die englische Intervention zu Gunsten der böhmischen Juden', *MGWJ*, 44 (1900), pp. 269–81.
50. See Horn, *Great Britain and Europe in the Eighteenth Century*, (Oxford, 1967), p. 178.
51. See D. B. Horn (ed.), *British Diplomatic Representatives, 1689–1789*, RHS, Camden Third Series, vol. XLVI (London, 1932), pp. 40–69.
52. Pelham and Doddington quotations are in: *Cobbett*, XII, 13.4.1741, col. 178; *Cobbett*, XIII, 6.12.1743, col. 259.
53. See Horn, *Britain and Europe*, p. 198.
54. Newcastle to Chesterfield, 22.2.1745, Newcastle House, in Richard Lodge (ed.), *Private Correspondence of Chesterfield and Newcastle, 1744–46* (London, 1930), p. 16.
55. See the remarks of an anonymous parliamentarian in *Cobbett*, IX, 15.1.1736, cols. 981–2.
56. Quotations in Simms, 'British Strategic Culture', p. 122.
57. See Thomas Pitt to Pitt, 12.10.1756, in W. S. Taylor and J. H. Pringle (eds.), *The Correspondence of William Pitt, Earl of Chatham*, vol. I (London, 1838), pp. 176–7. Pitt to Thomas Pitt, 13.1.1756, Horse Guards, in Taylor and Pringle (eds.), *The Correspondence of Pitt*, I, p. 152.
58. See Cobbett XIV, cols. 965–7.
59. See Horn, *Britain and Europe*, p. 56.
60. Cited in Stephen Conway, 'Continental Connections. Britain and Europe in the Eighteenth Century', *History* (90), 3, pp. 253–374, p. 358.
61. Simms, 'British Strategic Culture', p. 123.
62. Thus Jeremy Black, *British Foreign Policy in the Age of Walpole* (Edinburgh, 1985). p. 119.
63. Cited in James Frederick Chance, *The Alliance of Hanover. A Study of British Foreign Policy in the Last Years of George I*, (1923) , p. 1.
64. Chance, *Alliance of Hanover*, p. 492.
65. Simms, 'British Strategic Culture', p. 124.
66. Cited in D. B. Horn, *Sir Charles Hanbury Williams and European Diplomacy, 1747–58* (London, 1930), p. 202.
67. See Veronica Baker-Smith, *A Life of Anne of Hanover. Princess Royal* (Leiden, New York, Cologne, 1995)
68. Simms, 'British Strategic Culture', p. 125.
69. Cited in Chance, *Alliance of Hanover*, p. 214.

70. Cited in Jeremy Black, 'Recovering Lost Years. British Foreign Policy after the War of the Polish Succession', *Diplomacy and Statescraft*, 15 (2004), pp. 465–87, p. 482.
71. Quotations are in: anon. parliamentarian, 28.3.1734, *Cobbett*, IX, col. 599; Cobbett, XIII, 11.1.1744, col. 425; *Cobbett*, XII, 6.12. 1742, col. 914.
72. Quoted in Jeremy Black, *Pitt the Elder* (Cambridge, 1992), p. 224.
73. On the 'practical problems of employing naval power to achieve diplomatic ends' see Black, *America or Europe?*, p. 60, and Black, 'British Naval Power and International Commitments: Political and Strategic Problems, 1688–1770', in Michael Duffy (ed.), *Parameters of British Naval Power, 1650–1850* (Exeter, 1992), especially pp. 39 and 43. See also Herbert Richmond, *The Navy as an Instrument of Policy, 1558–1727*, E. A. Hughes (ed.) (Cambridge, 1953), p. 380 *et passim*.
74. See John Childs, 'The Army and the State in Britain and Germany during the Eighteenth Century', in Brewer and Hellmuth (eds.), *Re-thinking Leviathan. The Eighteenth-century State in Britain and Germany* (Oxford, 1999), p. 56.
75. Quoted in Peters, *Pitt and Popularity*, p. 158.
76. See Jens Metzdorf, *Politik-Propaganda-Patronage. Francis Hare und die englische Publizistik im spanischen Erbfolgekrieg* (Mainz, 2000), pp. 353–416.
77. *Cobbett*, XI, 13.2.1741, col. 1047.
78. *Cobbett*, XIII, 11.1.1744, col. 392.
79. Cited in Peters, *Pitt and Popularity*, p. 133.
80. Bishop of Gloucester to Pitt, 17.10.1761, Prior Park, in Taylor and Pringle (eds.), *The Correspondence of Pitt*, II, p. 161.
81. Pitt to Keene, 23.8.1757, Whitehall, in Taylor and Pringle (eds.), *The Correspondence of Pitt*, I, p. 251.
82. Quoted in Reed Browning, *The Duke of Newcastle* (Newhaven and London, 1975), p. 268.
83. Bedford to Bute, 9.7.1761, in Lord John Russell (ed.), *Correspondence of John, Fourth Duke of Bedford*, vol. III (London, 1846), p. 26.
84. Hardwicke to Newcastle, 10.4.1760, Moor Park, in Earl of Hardwicke, *The Life and Correspondence of Philip Yorke, Earl of Hardwicke, Lord High Chancellor of Great Britain*, ed. P. C. Yorke (3 vols., Cambridge, 1913), p. 245.
85. For a contrary view see N. A. M. Rodger, 'The Continental Commitment in the Eighteenth Century', in Lawrence Freedman, Paul Hayes and Robert O'Neill (eds.), *War, Strategy and International Politics* (Oxford, 1992), pp. 39–55.

86. See Manfred Mimler, *Der Einfluss kolonialer Interessen in Nordamerika auf die Strategie und Diplomatie Grossbritanniens während des Österreichischen Erbfolgekrieges 1744–1748. Ein Beitrag zur Identitätsbestimmung des britischen Empire um die Mitte des 18. Jahrhundert* (Hildesheim, Zurich, New York, 1983), p. 135 *et passim.*
87. Thus Jack M. Sosin, 'Louisburg and the Peace of Aix-la-Chapelle 1748', *William and Mary Quarterly*, 14 (1957), p. 535.
88. For the figures see Middleton, *Bells of Victory*, p. 25.
89. See the figures in W. D. Bird, 'British land strategy', part 3, *Army Quarterly*, 21 (1930–31), p. 50.
90. Cited in Richard Middleton, *The Bells of Victory. The Pitt–Newcastle Ministry and Conduct of the Seven Years War, 1757–62* (Cambridge, 2002), p. 101.
91. Cited in Paul Langford, *The Eighteenth Century, 1688–1815* (London, 1976), p. 141.
92. Cited in Middleton, *Bells of* Victory, p. 148.
93. I have used the second edition (Israel Mauduit), *Considerations on the Present German War* (London, 1760).
94. See Kathleen Wilson, *The Sense of the People. Politics, Culture and Imperialism in England, 1715–1785* (Cambridge, 1995), pp. 215–16, and John Brewer, 'The Misfortunes of Lord Bute: A Case Study in Eighteenth-century Political Argument and Public Opinion', *Historical Journal*, XVI (1973), pp. 3–43, especially pp. 9, 113.
95. H. M. Scott, *British Foreign Policy in the Age of the American Revolution* (Oxford, 1990), *passim.*
96. Thus Black, *America or Europe?*, p. 102. See also Daniel A. Baugh, 'Withdrawing from Europe. Anglo-French Maritime Geopolitics, 1750–1800', *International History Review*, 20, 1 (1998), pp. 1–32.
97. See Michael Roberts, *Splendid Isolation, 1763–80* (1969 Stenton lecture, Reading).
98. H. V. Bowen, 'British Conceptions of Global Empire, 1756–1783', *Journal of Imperial and Commonwealth History*, 26 (1998), pp. 1–27, on the shift to a territorial empire. For the political and strategic implications see P. J. Marshall, 'Britain and the World in the Eighteenth Century: I, Reshaping the Empire', *Transactions of the Royal Historical Society*, Sixth Series, VIII (Cambridge), pp. 1–18, especially pp. 9–17.
99. See 'Royal Proclamation', 7.10.1763, in Frederick Madden and David Fieldhouse (eds.), *The Classical Period of the First British Empire, 1689–1783. The Foundations of a Colonial System of Government* (Westport, CT, 1985), pp. 520–23.

100. Quoted from Simms, *Three Victories*, p. 536. See also P. J. Marshall, *The Making and Unmaking of Empires. Britain, India and America, c. 1750–1783* (Oxford, 2005), pp. 1–3, 59–60, 273–310, *et passim*.

4. THERE GOES THE NEIGHBOURHOOD. BRITAIN AND EUROPE IN THE AGE OF REVOLUTION

1. This chapter uses material from Brendan Simms, '"A False Principle in the Law of Nations". Burke, State Sovereignty, [German] Liberty and Intervention in the Age of Westphalia', in Brendan Simms and D. J. B. Trim (eds.), *Humanitarian Intervention: A History* (Cambridge, 2011), pp. 89–110
2. Edmund Burke to Lord Grenville, Beaconsfield, 18.8.1792, in P. J. Marshall and John A. Woods (eds.), *The Correspondence of Edmund Burke. Volume VII, January–August* 1794 (Cambridge and Chicago, 1968), pp. 176–7
3. Europe looms large in the new biography by Richard Bourke, *Empire and Revolution. The Political Life of Edmund Burke* (Princeton and Oxford, 2015).
4. See R. J. Vincent, 'Edmund Burke and the Theory of International Relations', *Review of International Studies*, 10 (1984), p. 206.
5. Thus Jennifer M. Welsh, 'Edmund Burke and the Commonwealth of Europe: The Cultural Bases of International Order', in Ian Clark and Iver Neumann (eds.), *Classical Theories of International Relations* (Basingstoke, 1996), pp. 173–92. Jennifer M. Welsh, *Edmund Burke and International Relations* (Basingstoke, 1995), *passim* and especially pp. 70–88
6. Conor Cruise O'Brien, *The Great Melody. A Thematic Biography of Edmund Burke* (London, 1992).
7. See Geoffrey W. Rice, 'Deceit and Distraction: Britain, France and the Corsican Crisis of 1768', *International History Review*, 28 (2006), pp. 287–315, and Thadd E. Hall, *France and the Eighteenth-century Corsican Question* (New York, 1971), pp. 155–214.
8. See Frederick A. Pottle, *James Boswell. The Earlier Years, 1740–1769* (London, 1966), pp. 390–95. I thank Jennifer Pitts for letting me have sight of her unpublished paper 'The Stronger Ties of Humanity: Humanitarian Intervention in the Eighteenth Century', presented to the American Political Science Association annual meeting, Philadelphia, 28–31 August 2003.
9. 'Speech on Address, 8 November 1768', in Paul Langford (ed.), *The Writings and Speeches of Edmund Burke. Volume II. Party. Parliament and the American Crisis, 1766–1774* (Oxford, 1981), pp. 98–9.

10. 'Thoughts on the Present Discontents', in Paul Langford (ed.), *The Writings and Speeches of Edmund Burke. Volume II. Party. Parliament and the American crisis, 1766–1774* (Oxford, 1981), p. 283.
11. Quoted in F. P. Lock, *Edmund Burke. Volume I, 1730–1784* (Oxford, 1998), p. 341.
12. *The Annual Register for the Year 1772*, preface p. 1 and pp. 1–3, 6, authorship of which has been plausibly attributed to Burke. See also G. L. Vincitorio, 'Edmund Burke and the First Partition of Poland', in G. L. Vincitorio (ed.), *Crisis in the Great Republic. Essays Presented to Ross J. S. Hoffman* (New York, 1969), pp. 14–46, especially pp. 33, 37, and 42 for quotations.
13. *The Annual Register for the Year 1772*, pp. 3–5; *Annual Register for the Year 1773*, pp. 3–4; *Annual Register for the Year 1773*, pp. 8–9.
14. *The Annual Register for the Year 1772*, preface, p. 1; *The Annual Register for the Year 1772*, p. 3.
15. Quoted in Brendan Simms, *Three Victories and a Defeat. The Rise and Fall of the First British Empire, 1714–1783* (London, 2007), p. 567.
16. See Jennifer Pitts, 'The Stronger ties of Humanity'.
17. Quoted in Simms, *Three Victories*, p. 642.
18. Cited in Robert Rhodes Crout, 'In Search of a "Just and Lasting Peace": The Treaty of 1783, Louis XVI, Vergennes and the Regeneration of the Realm', *International History Review*, 5/3 (1983), p. 374.
19. Sandwich remarks to Cabinet 19.1.1781, Queens' House, in presence of King, in Barnes and Owen (eds.), *Sandwich Papers*, p. 24.
20. Quotations in: *Cobbett*, XIX, 30.5.1777, cols. 316–17; *Cobbett*, XIX, 11.12.1777, col. 601.
21. On Britain generally, see Stephen Conway, *The British Isles and the War of American Independence* (Oxford, 2002), pp. 16, 350, and 17 (for figures). On Ireland see Thomas Bartlett, ' "A Weapon of War Yet Untried": Irish Catholics and the Armed Forces of the Crown, 1760–1830', in T. G. Fraser and Keith Jeffery (eds.), *Men, Women and War* (Historical Studies, vol. XVIII, Dublin, 1993), and R. Kent Donovan, 'The Military Origins of the Roman Catholic Relief Programme of 1778', *Historical Journal*, 28 (1985), pp. 79–102.
22. Cited in Crout, 'A "Just and Lasting Peace"', p. 398; Cited in Stanley Weintraub, *Iron Tears. America's Battle for Freedom, Britain's Quagmire 1775–1783* (London, 2005), p. 87.
23. See David C. Hendrickson, *Peace Pact. The Lost World of the American Founding* (Lawrence, KS, 2003), p. 63.
24. *Federalist* no. 19, 8.12.1787, in J. Pole (ed.), *The Federalist Papers* (Indianapolis and Cambridge, 2005), pp. 99–102. For the impact of

the Polish partition on the constitutional convention see Frederick W. Marks, *Independence on Trial. Foreign Affairs and the Making of the Constitution* (Baton Rouge, 1773), pp. 3–51.

25. *Federalist* no. 5, 10.11.1787, in Pole (ed.), *Federalist Papers*, pp. 17–18.
26. Cited in Hamish Scott, *The Emergence of the Eastern Powers, 1756–1775* (Cambridge, 2001), p. 1.
27. See V. T. Harlow, *The Founding of the Second British Empire*, 2 vols (London, 1952–64) and Christopher A. Bayly, *Imperial Meridian. The British Empire and the World, 1780–1830* (London, 1989). On the loyalists as a demographic reserve for empire see: Maya Jasanoff, *Liberty's Exiles. American Loyalists in the Revolutionary World* (New York, 2011).
28. Quoted in Jeremy Black, 'Recovering Lost Years. British Foreign Policy after the War of the Polish Succession', *Diplomacy and Statescraft*, 15 (2004), p. 13.
29. Quoted in T. C. W. Blanning, *The Origins of the French Revolutionary Wars, 1787–1802* (London, 1996), p. 132,
30. The British quotations are taken from Alan Crawford, 'British Perceptions of a Russian Strategic Threat, 1790–1793' (MSc dissertation, London School of Economics and Political Science, 2007).
31. J. C. D. Clark describes him as a 'Whig in politics' in J. C. D. Clark (ed.), *Edmund Burke. Reflections on the Revolution* (Stanford, 2001), p. 23.
32. See Jennifer Pitts, *A Turn to Empire. The Rise of Imperial Liberalism in Britain and France* (Princeton, NJ, 2005), Chapter 3 'Edmund Burke's Peculiar Universalism', pp. 59–95.
33. Quoted in Pitts, *A Turn to Empire*, p. 78.
34. F. P. Lock, *Burke's Reflections on the Revolution in France* (London, 1985), p. 31.
35. Burke to Lord Grenville, 18.8.1792, in P. J. Marshall and John A. Woods (eds.), *The Correspondence of Edmund Burke. Volume VII, January 1792–August 1794* (Cambridge, 1968), p. 176n.
36. Introductory note to the speech on Fox's India Bill, in David Fidler and Jennifer Welsh (eds.), *Empire and Community. Edmund Burke's Writings and Speeches on International Relations* (Boulder, CO, and Oxford, 1999), p. 199.
37. Quoted in Welsh, *Edmund Burke and International Relations*, p. 100. See also David Boucher, 'The Character of the History of the Philosophy of International Relations and the Case of Edmund Burke', *Review of International Studies*, 17 (1991), pp. 127–48, especially, pp. 142–4; and Iain Hampsher-Monk, 'Edmund Burke's Changing Justification for Intervention', *Historical Journal*, 48 (2005), pp. 65–100.

38. On the ambivalence of Burke's initial response see Welsh, *Edmund Burke and International Relations*, p. 100.
39. Thus Conor Cruise O'Brien, 'Introduction' to *Edmund Burke. Reflections on the Revolution in France and on the Proceedings in Certain Societies in London Relative to that Event* (London, 1968), p. 9.
40. See L. G. Mitchell's 'Introduction' to Edmund Burke, *Reflections on the Revolution in France* (Oxford, 1993), pp. ix–xi; J. C. D. Clark's 'Introduction' to his edition of *Edmund Burke. Reflections on the Revolution in France* (Stanford, 2001), especially pp. 97–108; and F. P. Lock, *Reflections*, Chapter 5 'Contemporary Reception', pp. 132–65, especially p. 133.
41. Jonathan Swift, 'The Conduct of the Allies and of the Late Ministry, in Beginning and Carrying on the War (London, 1713), in Thomas Roscoe (ed.), *The Works of Jonathan Swift Containing Interesting and Valuable Papers Not Hitherto Published, in Two Volumes, with Memoir of the Author*, vol. I (London, 1841), pp. 410–28.; Israel Mauduit, *Considerations on the Present German* War (London, 1760). See also Heinz-Joachim Müllenbrock, *The Culture of Contention: A Rhetorical Analysis of the Public Controversy about the Ending of the War of the Spanish Succession, 1710–1713* (Munich, 1997), and K. W. Schweizer, 'Pamphleteering and Foreign Policy in the Age of the Elder Pitt', in Stephen Taylor, Richard Connors and Clyve Jones (eds.), *Hanoverian Britain and Empire: Essays in Memory of Philip Lawson* (Woodbridge, 1998), pp. 94–108.
42. 'Reflections on the Revolution in France', in Paul Langford (ed.), *The Writings and Speeches of Edmund Burke. Volume VIII. The French Revolution, 1790–1794* (Oxford, 1989), p. 131. Religion also played a key role in European resistance to France: see T. C. W. Blanning, 'The Role of Religion in European Counter-revolution, 1789–1815', in Derek Beales and Geoffrey Best (eds.), *History, Society and the Churches: Essays in Honour of Owen Chadwick* (Cambridge, 1985), pp. 195–214.
43. *'Reflections on the Revolution in France'*, pp. 60 and 127.
44. On Pitt and Burke see Jennifer Mori, *William Pitt and the French Revolution 1785–1795* (Edinburgh, 1997), pp. 81–2; and Jeremy Black, *British Foreign Policy in an Age of Revolutions, 1783–1793* (Cambridge, 1994).
45. The quotations are (in order) in Burke, 'Reflections on the Revolution in France', pp. 131, 165, 140.
46. 'Letter to a Member of the National Assembly', in Langford (ed.), *Writings and Speeches*, VIII, pp. 305–6. 'Compassion' is mentioned again on p. 308.

47. 'Remarks on the Policy of the Allies', in L. G. Mitchell (ed.), *The Writings and Speeches of Edmund Burke. Volume VIII, 1790–1794* (Oxford, 1989), p. 463.
48. Edmund Burke to Charles-Jean-François Depont, November 1789, in Cobban and Smith (eds.), *Correspondence of Burke*, VI, p. 41.
49. Burke to Comtesse d'Osmond, 8.12.1794, Beaconsfield, in R. B. McDowell (ed.), *Burke Correspondence*, vol. VIII, p. 93.
50. Burke to Mrs John Crewe, *c.* 11.8.1795 (summarizing the views of the Duke of Portland), in McDowell (ed.), *Burke Correspondence*, VIII, p. 300.
51. 'First Letter on a Regicide Peace', in R. B. McDowell (ed.), *The Writings and Speeches of Edmund Burke. Volume IX. I. The Revolutionary War, 1794–1797. II. Ireland* (Oxford, 1991), IX, p. 195.
52. Cited in Hampsher-Monk, 'Burke and Intervention', p. 70.
53. 'Thoughts on French Affairs', in Langford (ed.), *Writings and Speeches*, p. 368.
54. Quoted in Hampsher-Monk, 'Burke and Intervention', p. 71.
55. 'Heads for Consideration on the Present State of Affairs', in L. G. Mitchell (ed.), *The Writings and Speeches of Edmund Burke. Volume VIII. The French Revolution* (Oxford, 1989), pp. 392–3.
56. 'Letter to a Member of the National Assembly', VIII, pp. 305–6.
57. 15.12.1792, *Cobbett*, XXX, col. 115.
58. 'First Letter on a Regicide Peace', p. 199.
59. Burke to William Lushington, 26.10.1796, in R. B. McDowell and John A. Woods (eds.), *The Correspondence of Edmund Burke Volume IX, Part One. May 1796–July 1797. Part II. Additional and Undated Letters* (Chicago, 1970), p. 99.
60. Re: 'vicinity' see 'Thoughts on French Affairs' (published after Burke's death in 1797), p. 307.
61. 'Reflections on the Revolution in France', p. 185.
62. Quoted in Welsh, *Edmund Burke and International Relations*, p. 113. For other examples of 'vicinity' see for example Burke to Lushington, 26.10.1796, in R. B. McDowell and John A. Woods (eds.), *The Correspondence of Edmund Burke*, p. 99. See also the *Letters on a Regicide Peace, passim.*
63. Cited in Welsh, *Edmund Burke and International Relations*, p. 113; 'Second Letter on a Regicide Peace', in McDowell (ed.), *Writings and Speeches*, IX, p. 267.
64. 'First Letter on a Regicide Peace', pp. 250–52.
65. 15.12.1792, *Cobbett*, XXX, col. 112. In the same vein on the 'Commonwealth of Europe' and Britain's central role in it see 'Fourth Letter

on a Regicide Peace', pp. 56, 248; 'First Letter on a Regicide Peace', p. 195; 'Third Letter on a Regicide Peace'; 'Heads', pp. 399, 404.

66. 'Fourth Letter on a Regicide Peace' (1795), in McDowell, *Writings and Speeches*, vol. IX, p. 93.
67. 'Second Letter on a Regicide Peace' (1796), in McDowell, *Writings and Speeches*, vol. IX, p. 271.
68. R. B. McDowell and John A. Woods (eds.), *The Correspondence of Edmund Burke*, p. 300.
69. Edmund Burke to Charles-Jean-François Depont, November 1789, in Cobban and Smith (eds.), *Correspondence of Edmund Burke*, p. 48.
70. Burke to Lord Grenville, Beaconsfield, 18.8.1792, in Marshall and Woods (eds.), *Correspondence of Burke*, VII, pp. 176–7.
71. Thus Hampsher-Monk, 'Burke's Changing Justifications for Intervention', p. 77.
72. Quotations in 'First Letter on a Regicide Peace', pp. 251–2.
73. On this tension more generally, see Jennifer M. Welsh, 'Taking Consequences Seriously: Objections to Humanitarian Intervention', in Jennifer M. Welsh (ed.), *Humanitarian Intervention and International Relations* (Oxford, 2004), pp. 52–68.
74. 'Third Letter on a Regicide Peace', p. 307.
75. 'Observations on the Conduct of the Minority', in Mitchell (ed.), *Writings and Speeches,* VIII, p. 423. In the same vein see Edmund Burke to Richard Burke Jnr, in Marshall and Woods (eds.), *Corrrespondence of Edmund Burke*, VII, 29.7.1792, pp. 158–9.
76. 'First Letter on a Regicide Peace', p. 259.
77. See chapter and verse in Simms, 'Intervention in the Age of Westphalia', p. 107 *et passim.*
78. 'Thoughts on French Affairs', p. 352.
79. On this see T. C. W. Blanning, *The Origins of the French Revolutionary Wars*, especially pp. 99–104. On the clash between the 'new diplomacy' of the revolutionaries and the *ancien régime* see Felix Gilbert, 'The "New Diplomacy" of the Eighteenth Century', *World Politics,* IV (1951/52), pp. 15–17.
80. 'Thoughts on French Affairs', p. 350.
81. Ibid., p. 352.
82. Ibid., p. 353.
83. Ibid., p. 352. For further examples of Burke's preoccupation with the Holy Roman Empire and British security see 'Heads for Consideration on the Present State of Affairs', in Mitchell (ed.), *Writings and Speeches*, VIII, p. 398; P. J. Marshall and John A. Woods (eds.), *The Correspondence of Edmund Burke. Volume VII, January*

1792–August 1794 (Chicago, 1968), pp. 271ff, 277, 307, 316–17, 383, 387, 393, 430; and 'First Letter on a Regicide Peace', pp. 195–6.

84. 'Third Letter on a Regicide Peace', p. 358.
85. 'Observations on the Conduct of the Minority', Mitchell (ed.), *Writings and Speeches*, VIII, p. 426. See in same vein 'Third Letter on a Regicide Peace', p. 305.
86. *Cobbett*, XXIX, 29.3.1791, col. 77.
87. Burke to William Windham, 30.3.1797, *Correspondence*, IX, p.301. In 'Letter to a Noble Lord', in McDowell (ed.), *Writings and Speeches*, IX, p. 186 he refers to the barrier as 'the most precious part of England'.
88. For Burke's subsequent concern with the French presence in the Low Countries see for example: 15.12.1792, *Cobbett*, XXX, col. 114 (Burke to William Windham, c. 2.2.1795, *Correspondence*, VIII, p. 134; Burke to John Wilmot, 12.2.1795, ibid., pp. 148–9. For his anxieties about 'the new system of giving to modern France the limits of ancient Gaul' , see Burke to French Laurence, 1.3.1797, *Correspondence,* Volume IX, p. 265.
89. See Brendan Simms, *Three Victories.*

5. 'THE GREAT BANK OF EUROPE'. BRITAIN AND THE CONTINENT IN THE AGE OF NAPOLEON

1. This chapter is partly based on Brendan Simms, 'Britain and Napoleon', in Philip G. Dwyer (ed.), *Napoleon and Europe* (London, 2001), pp. 189–203.
2. Quoted in John Ehrman, *The Younger Pitt: The Consuming Struggle* (London, 1996), p. 688.
3. Cited in Rory Muir, *Britain and the Defeat of Napoleon, 1807–1815* (New Haven, 1996), p. 6.
4. Paul Frischauer, *England's Years of Danger. A New History of the World War, 1792–1815 Dramatized in Documents* (London, 1938).
5. Carola Oman, *Britain against Napoleon* (London, 1943).
6. Frank J. Klingberg and Sigurd B. Hustvedt, *The Warning Drum. The British Home Front Faces Napoleon. Broadsides of 1803* (Berkeley and Los Angeles, 1944), p. 4.
7. Arthur Bryant, *The Years of Endurance, 1793–1802* (London, 1942); *The Years of Victory, 1802–1812* (London, 1944).
8. Andrew Roberts, *Napoleon the Great* (London, 2014).

9. See Emmanuel Berl, '*Denn wie Karthago muß auch England zerstört werden!*', in Heinz-Otto Sieburg (ed.), *Napoleon und Europa* (Cologne and Berlin, 1971), pp. 161–70.
10. See Roman Schnur, '*Land und Meer – Napoleon gegen England. Ein Kapitel der Geschichte internationaler Politik*', in Roman Schnur, *Revolution und Weltbürgerkrieg. Studien zur Ouverture nach 1789* (Berlin, 1983), pp. 33–58.
11. See Brendan Simms, '*Fra Land e Meer. La Gran Bretagna, la Prussia e il problemo del decisionismo (1804–1806)*', *Ricerche di Storia Politica*, 6 (1991), pp. 5–34.
12. Quoted in Linda Colley, 'Facing Napoleon's Own EU', *New York Review of Books*, 5.11.2015, p. 51.
13. See now Stuart Semmel, *Napoleon and the British* (New Haven and London, 2004).
14. See Henry Foljambe Hall (ed.), *Napoleon's Notes on English History* (London, 1905).
15. Cited in E. Tangye Lean, *The Napoleonists. A Study in Political Disaffection 1760/1960* (Oxford, 1970), p. 7.
16. Cited in A. D. Harvey, 'European Attitudes to Britain during the French Revolutionary and Napoleonic Era', *History*, 63 (1978), p. 358.
17. Thus Geoffrey Ellis, *Napoleon* (London and New York, 1997), p. 170.
18. Cited in François Crouzet, 'Great Britain's Response to the French Revolution and to Napoleon', in François Crouzet, *Britain Ascendant: Comparative Studies in Franco-British Economic History* (Cambridge, 1990), p. 285.
19. Cited in Jean Tranié and J. C. Carmigiani, *Napoléon et l'Angleterre. Vingt-deux ans d'affrontements sur terre et sur mer, 1793–1815* with a preface by Jean Tulard (Paris, 1994), p. 11.
20. Cited in Crouzet, 'Great Britain's Response', p. 287.
21. Cited in Crouzet, 'Great Britain's Response', p. 285.
22. See H. D. Schmidt, 'The Idea and Slogan of "Perfidious Albion" ', *History*, 14 (1953), pp. 612–13.
23. Cited in Ehrman, *The Consuming Struggle*, p. 688.
24. See Lean, *The Napoleonists*, p. 209.
25. Cited in Herbert Butterfield, *Charles James Fox and Napoleon. The Peace Negotiations of 1806* (Creighton lecture in History, 1961), (London, 1962), p. 2.
26. Both cited in *Karl Goldmann, Die preussisch-britischen Beziehungen in den Jahren 1812–1815* (Würzburg, 1934), p. 34.
27. T. C. W. Blanning, *The French Revolutionary Wars, 1787–1802* (London, 1996), p. 196.

28. See Torsten Riotte, *Hannover in der britischen Politik (1792–1815). Dynastische Verbindung als Element aussenpolitischer Entscheidungsprozesse* (Münster, 2005).
29. Cited in Paul Bailleu (ed.), *Preußen und Frankreich von 1795 bis 1807. Diplomatische Correspondenzen* vol. II (Leipzig, 1887), pp. 215–16
30. Thus Richard Glover, *Britain at Bay. Defence against Bonaparte, 1803–1814* (London and New York, 1973), p. 13. See also N. A. M. Rodger, *The Command of the Ocean. A Naval History of Britain 1649–1815* (London, 2004), pp. 542–4, for a nuanced view.
31. Cited in Glover, *Britain at Bay*, p. 19.
32. See the table in Michael Duffy, 'World-wide war and British Expansion, 1793–1815', in P. J. Marshall (ed.) and Alaine Low (assistant editor), *The Oxford History of the British Empire. vol. III: The Eighteenth Century* (Oxford, 1998), p. 204.
33. Muir, *Britain and the Defeat of Napoleon*, p. 17.
34. Cited in Geoffrey Ellis, *The Napoleonic Empire* (Basingstoke, 1991), p. 97
35. See Herbert Butterfield, *Napoleon* (London, 1939), p. 91.
36. Cited in Goldmann, *Die preussisch-britischen Beziehungen*, p. 37.
37. Cited in Piers Mackesy, *British Victory in Egypt, 1801. The End of Napoleon's Conquest* (London and New York, 1995), p. 52.
38. See Therese Ebbinghaus, *Napoleon, England und die Presse, 1800–1803* (Munich and Berlin, 1914), pp. 123–43.
39. Both cited in Harvey, 'European Attitudes', p. 356.
40. See Robert Holtman, *Napoleonic Propaganda* (Louisiana, 1950; reprint New York, 1969), pp. 3–6.
41. See Ehrman, *The Consuming Struggle*, pp. 354–67.
42. Cited in Ehrman, *The Consuming Struggle*, p. 4.
43. Cited in Ehrman, *The Consuming Struggle*, p. 796.
44. Thus Piers Mackesy, 'Strategic Problems of the British War Effort', in H. T. Dickinson (ed.), *Britain and the French Revolution, 1789–1815* (London and Basingstoke, 1989), p. 159.
45. Cited in Christopher D. Hall, *British Strategy in the Napoleonic War, 1803–1815* (Manchester and New York, 1992), p. 137.
46. Cited in Hartmut Gembries, *Das Thema Preußen in der politischen Diskussion Englands zwischen 1792 und 1807* (unpublished PhD dissertation, University of Freiburg, 1988), p. 154
47. Cited in Muir, *Britain and the Defeat of Napoleon*, p. 6.
48. Cited in Muir, *Britain and the Defeat of Napoleon*, p. 39.
49. Muir, *Britain and the Defeat of Napoleon*, p. 101.
50. Cited in Ehrman, *The Consuming Struggle*, p. 228.

51. See Mackesy, 'Strategic problems', p. 161.
52. Cited in Michael Duffy, 'British diplomacy and the French Wars, 1789–1815'', in Dickinson (ed.), *Britain and the French Revolution*, p. 136.
53. Cited in Muir, *Britain and the Defeat of Napoleon*, p. 309.
54. A point made by Crouzet, 'Great Britain's Response', p. 287.
55. Iradji Amini, *Napoleon and Persia: Franco-Persian Relations under the First Empire* (London, 1999).
56. See Hall, *British Strategy in the Napoleonic War*, p. 189.
57. See Duffy, 'World-wide Empire', p. 196
58. Charles J. Esdaile, *The Wars of Napoleon* (London, 1995), p. 143. On the reform debate see Brendan Simms, 'Reform in Britain and Prussia, 1797–1815: (Confessional) Fiscal-military State and Military Agrarian Complex', *Proceedings of the British Academy*, 100 (1999), pp. 79–100.
59. Quoted in Jenny Uglow, *In These Times. Living in Britain through Napoleon's Wars, 1793–1815* (London, 2015).
60. J. E. Cookson, *The British Armed Nation, 1793–1815* (Oxford, 1997), and K. Linch, *Britain and Wellington's Army. Recruitment, Society and Tradition, 1807–1815* (Basingstoke, 2011).
61. So Esdaile, *The Wars of Napoleon*, p. 144
62. See Roger Knight, *Britain against Napoleon. The Organization of Victory, 1793–1815* (London, 2013).
63. Quoted in Simms, 'Reform in Britain and Prussia', pp. 83–4. See also Cookson, *British Armed Nation*.
64. Quotations in Simms, 'Reform in Britain and Prussia', p. 98.
65. On Sicily see Muir, *Britain and the Defeat of Napoleon*, p. 175.
66. Thus Isabel Burdieu, 'Myths of Failure, Myths of Success: New Perspectives on Nineteenth-century Spanish Liberalism', *Journal of Modern History*, 70 (1998), pp. 892–912, p. 899.
67. See for example Otto Johnston, 'British Espionage and Prussian Politics in the Age of Napoleon', *Intelligence and National Security*, 2 (1987), especially p. 238.
68. See generally Maeve Ryan, 'The Price of Legitimacy in Humanitarian Intervention: Britain, the Right of Search, and the Abolition of the West African Slave Trade, 1807–1867', in Brendan Simms and D. J. B. Trim (eds.), *Humanitarian Intervention: A History* (Cambridge, 2011), pp. 231–56.
69. For concerns about cooperation between local rebels and an outside power even before the rising see William O'Reilly, 'Charles Vallancey and the Military Itinerary of Ireland', in *Proceedings of the Royal Irish Academy*, vol. 106C, pp. 125–217, especially pp. 155 and 197. On the centrality of the strategic argument for Union see Thomas Bartlett, *Acts*

of Union. An Inaugural Lecture Delivered at University College Dublin on 24 February 2000, p. 3, and Peter Jupp, 'Britain and the Union, 1797–1801', in *Transactions of the Royal Historical Society*, pp. 202–5, 214–15. Cornwallis and Cooke are quoted in K. Theodore Hoppen, 'An Incorporating Union? British Politicians and Ireland, 1800–1830', *English Historical* Review, *CXXIII*, (2008), pp. 328–50, p. 330.

70. Cooke and Bruce are quoted in James Livesey, 'Acts of Union and Disunion: Ireland in Atlantic and European Contexts', in Daire Keogh and Kevin Whelan (eds.), *Acts of Union. The Causes, Contexts and Consequences of the Act of Union*, pp. 95–105 (quotations pp. 97 and 103).
71. Cited in Muir, *Britain and the Defeat of Napoleon*, pp. 367–8.
72. See Michael John Thornton, *Napoleon and the St Helena decision* (Stanford, CA, 1968), pp. 14–15.
73. See Peter Hofschröer, *1815. The Waterloo Campaign, Wellington, His German allies and the Battles of Ligny and Quatre Bras* (London, 1998) and *The Waterloo Campaign. The German Victory* (London, 1999). For the crucial Hanoverian contribution see Brendan Simms, *The Longest Afternoon. The 400 Men Who Decided the Battle of Waterloo* (London, 2014).
74. Quoted in Brendan Simms, *The Impact of Napoleon. Prussian High Politics, Foreign Policy and the Crisis of the Executive, 1797–1806* (Cambridge, 1997).
75. See J. H. Sherwig, *Guineas and Gunpowder. British Foreign Aid in the Wars with France* (Cambridge, MA, 1969).

6. 'WHERE THE WEATHER COMES FROM'. BRITAIN AND EUROPE IN THE AGE OF NATIONALISM

1. Quoted in Andrew Lambert, 'The Tory World View: Sea Power, Strategy and Party Politics, 1815–1914', in Jeremy Black (ed.), *The Tory World. Deep History and the Tory Theme in British Foreign Policy, 1679–2014* (Farnham, 2015), p. 128.
2. Quoted in Anselm Doering-Manteuffel, *Vom Wiener Kongress zur Pariser Konferenz. England, die deutsche Frage und das Mächtesystem, 1815–1856* (Göttingen and Zürich, 1991), pp. 137–8.
3. Quoted in T. G. Otte, *The Foreign Office Mind. The Making of British Foreign Policy, 1865–1914* (Cambridge, 2011), p. 349.
4. Keith Robbins, *Britain and Europe, 1789–2005* (London, 2005), adds the tsarist empire as a co-hegemon, p. 67 *et passim*.
5. Quoted in Lambert 'The Tory World View', p. 128.

6. See Anselm Doering-Manteuffel, *Vom Wiener Kongress zur Pariser Konferenz. England, die deutsche Frage und das europäische Mächtesystem* (Göttingen, 1991) .
7. Quoted in Ulrike Eich, *Russland und Europa. Studien zur russischen Deutschlandpolitik in der Zeit des Wiener Kongresses* (Cologne, 1986), p. 172.
8. Quoted in Hermann Wentker, '*Der Pitt-Plan von 1805 in Krieg und Frieden. Zum Kontinuitätsproblem der britischen Europapolitik in der Ära der napoleonischen Kriege*', in *Francia*, 29, 2 (2002), pp. 129–45', p. 141.
9. Quoted in John Bew, *Castlereagh. Enlightenment, War and Tyranny, 1769–1822* (London, 2011), p. 377.
10. See Paul Kielstra, *The Politics of the Slave Trade Suppression in Britain and France, 1814–48* (Basingstoke, 2000), pp. 26–9 (quotation p. 28), and Fabian Klose, 'Enforcing Abolition: The Entanglement of Civil Society Action, Humanitarian Norm-setting, and Military Intervention', in Fabian Klose (ed.), *The Emergence of Humanitarian Intervention. Ideas and Practice from the Nineteenth Century to the Present* (Cambridge, 2016), pp. 91–120.
11. Quoted in Henry A. Kissinger, *A World Restored* (Boston, MA, 1957; reprint 1977), p. 33.
12. See William Anthony Hay, 'Lord Liverpool: Alliances, Intervention and the National Interest', in Black (ed.), *The Tory World*, pp. 103–20.
13. See Philip Harling and Peter Mandler, 'From "Fscal-military State" to "Laissez-faire State", 1760–1850', *Journal of British Studies*, 33 (1993), pp. 44–70.
14. Quoted in Jonathan Parry, *The Politics of Patriotism. English Liberalism, National Identity and Europe, 1830–1886* (Cambridge, 2006), p. 46.
15. Adam Zamoyski, *Phantom Terror. The Threat of Revolution and the Repression of Liberty, 1789–1848* (London, 2014).
16. Quoted in Kissinger, *A World Restored*, p. 34.
17. This paragraph and the following is closely based on John Bew, ' "From an Umpire to a Competitor": Castlereagh, Canning and the Issue of International Intervention in the Wake of the Napoleonic Wars', in Brendan Simms and D. J. B. Trim (eds.), *Humanitarian Intervention: A History* (Cambridge, 2011), pp. 117–38 (quotations p. 122).
18. Quoted in D. L. Hafner, "Castlereagh, the Balance of Power, and "Non-intervention" ', *Australian Journal of Politics and History*, 26, 1 (1980), p. 75.

19. See Günther Heydemann, *Konstitution gegen Revolution. Die britische Deutschland und Italienpolitik, 1815–1848* (Göttingen and Zürich, 1995), pp. 47–9 (quotation p. 49).
20. Hafner, 'Castlereagh, the Balance of Power, and "Non-intervention"', pp. 78 and 80.
21. See Norihito Yamada, 'George Canning and the Spanish Question, September 1822 to March 1823', *Historical Journal*, 52, 2 (2009), p. 354.
22. Quoted in Roger Bullen, *Palmerston, Guizot and the Collapse of the Entente Cordiale* (London, 1974), p. 7.
23. See Frank Lorenz Müller, *Britain and the German Question. Perceptions of Nationalism and Political Reform, 1830–63* (Basingstoke, 2002), p. 29.
24. Quoted in Heydemann, *Konstitution gegen Revolution*, pp. 239–40 and p. 347.
25. See Roger Bullen, 'The Great Powers and the Iberian Peninsula, 1815–1848', in Sked (ed.), pp. 70–1 *et passim*.
26. Quoted in James Chambers, *Palmerston, the People's Darling* (London, 2004), pp. 174–5. See also P. Moseley, 'Intervention and Non-intervention in Spain, 1838–1839', *Journal of Modern History*, XIII (1941), pp. 195–217.
27. K. Bourne, *Palmerston: The Early Years, 1784–1841* (London, 1982), p. 626. I thank Jon Parry for this reference.
28. See Parry, *The Politics of Patriotism*, p. 147, on this.
29. On all this see Anthony Howe, 'Radicalism, Free Trade and Foreign Policy in Mid-nineteenth century Britain', in William Mulligan and Brendan Simms (eds.), *The Primacy of Foreign Policy in British History, 1660–2000. How Strategic Concerns Shaped Modern Britain* (Basingstoke, 2010), pp. 167–80
30. See Frank Lorenz Müller, *Britain and the German Question. Perceptions of Nationalism and Political Reform, 1830–63* (Basingstoke, 2002).
31. Quoted in Doering-Manteuffel, *Vom Wiener Kongress zur Pariser Konferenz*, pp. 87 and 117.
32. Quoted in Parry, *The Politics of Patriotism*, p. 196.
33. Quoted in Chambers, *Palmerston*, p. 263.
34. Thus Geoffrey Hicks, *Peace, War and Party Politics. The Conservatives and Europe, 1846–59* (Manchester and New York, 2007), pp. 247–8 *et passim* (quotations pp. 34 and p. 72).
35. Quoted in Doering-Manteuffel, *Vom Wiener Kongress zur Pariser Konferenz*, p. 215.
36. Quoted in Müller, *Britain and the German Question*, p. 162.

37. Quoted from Parry, *The Politics of Patriotism*, p. 212. The author, W. R. Greg, was writing once the conflict was already under way.
38. Quoted from a speech made in 1855 in Thomas Stamm-Kuhlmann, 'Gladstone: Morality in the Age of Popular Wars', in Brendan Simms and Karina Urbach (eds.), *Bringing Personality back in. Leadership and Aar. A British–German comparison, 1740–1945* (Berlin and New York, 2010), p. 76.
39. On the centrality of foreign policy to British domestic politics throughout the 1850s see Adrian Brettle, 'The Enduring Importance of Foreign Policy Dominance in Mid-nineteenth-century Politics', in Mulligan and Simms (eds.), *Primacy of Foreign Policy in British History*, pp. 154–66.
40. Quoted in Parry, *The Politics of Patriotism*, p. 71.
41. See Michael J. Salevouris, *Riflemen Form. The War Scare of 1859–1860 in England* (New York and London, 1982), pp. 152–95.
42. See D. M. Schreuder, 'Gladstone and Italian Unification, 1848–70: The Making of a Liberal', *English Historical Review*, LXXXV (1970), p. 475.
43. Quoted in Otte, *The Foreign Office Mind*, p. 36.
44. D. R. Watson, 'The British Parliamentary System and the Growth of Constitutional Government in Western Europe', in C. J. Bartlett (ed.), *Britain Pre-eminent: Studies in British World Influence in the Nineteenth Century* (London, 1969), pp. 101–27.
45. Thus Klaus Hildebrand, *No Intervention. Die Pax-Britannica und Preussen, 1865/6–1869/70. Eine Untersuchung zur englischen Weltpolitik im 19. Jahrhundert* (Munich, 1997).
46. Thus Otte, *The Foreign Office Mind*, pp. 398–9 *et passim.*
47. Augustus Loftus, *The Diplomatic Reminiscences of Lord Augustus Loftus, 1862–1879*, vol. I (London, 1894), p. 99.
48. Geoffrey Hicks, '"Appeasement" or Consistent Conservatism? British Foreign Policy, Party Politics and the Guarantees of 1867 and 1939', *Historical Research*, 84 (2011), pp. 520–1 and 525–6 (Stanley quotation pp. 526–7).
49. Deryck Schreuder, 'Gladstone as "Troublemaker": Liberal Foreign Policy and the German Annexation of Alsace-Lorraine, 1870–1871', *Journal of British Studies*, 17 (1978). I am grateful to Eddie Fishman for conversations on the subject.
50. Quoted in Hildebrand, *No Intervention*, p. 393.
51. Quoted in Karina Urbach, *Bismarck's Favourite Englishman. Lord Odo Russell's Mission to Berlin* (London, 1999), p. 208.
52. Thus Hildebrand, *No Intervention*, pp. 393–4 *et passim.*

53. See Scott W. Murray, *Liberal Diplomacy and German Unification. The Early Career of Robert Morier* (Westport, CN, 2000), pp. 91–138.
54. Thus William Mulligan, 'Britain, the "German Revolution", and the Fall of France, 1870–71', *Historical Research*, 84 (2011), pp. 310–27.
55. Quoted in Parry, *The Politics of Patriotism*, pp. 243 and 241.
56. For the link between foreign policy and electoral reform see William Mulligan, 'Gladstone and the Primacy of Foreign Policy', in Mulligan and Simms (eds.), *The Primacy of Foreign Policy in British History*, pp. 181–96, especially pp. 186–7.
57. See Michael Pratt, 'A Fallen Idol: The Impact of the Franco-Prussian War on the Perception of Germany by British Intellectuals', *International History Review*, 7 (1985), pp. 543–75.
58. Early of Derby, diary entry of 19.7.1870, in John Vincent (ed.), *A Selection from the Diaries of Edward Henry Stanley, 5th Earl of Derby (1826–1893) between September 1869 and March 1878*, p. 66.
59. See Parry, *The Politics of Patriotism*, p. 276, and pp. 292–3 on the connection between 1870–71 and the failure of Gladstone's Liberal administration, and W. H. Maehl, 'Gladstone, the Liberals and the Election of 1874', *Bulletin of the Institute of Historical Research*, 36 (1963), pp. 53–69.
60. On the importance of the empire to Britain's great power standing see Edward Ingram, *The British Empire as World Power* (London, 2001), especially pp. 25–45; James Belich, *Replenishing the Earth. The Settler Revolution and the Rise of the Anglo-World, 1783–1939* (Oxford, 2009); and Duncan Bell, *The Idea of Greater Britain. Empire and the Future of World Order, 1860–1900* (Princeton, NJ, 2006).
61. See Georgios Varouxakis, '"Great" versus "Small" Nations: Scale and National Greatness in Victorian Political Thought', in Duncan Bell (ed.), *Victorian Visions of Global Order: Empire and International Relations in Nineteenth-century Political Thought* (Cambridge, 2007), pp. 136–59.
62. Edward E. Morris, *Imperial Federation. A Lecture* (Melbourne, 1885), quotations pp. 8–9 See also Ged Martin, 'Empire Federalism and Imperial Parliamentary Union, 1820–1870', *Historical Journal*, 16 (1973), pp. 65–92.
63. Thus Max Beloff, *Imperial Sunset: Britain's Liberal Empire, 1897–1921* (London, 1969), p. 37.
64. Thus John Bew, 'Debating the Union on Foreign Fields. Ulster Unionism and the Importance of Britain's "Place in the World"', *c.* 1830–*c.* 1870', in Mulligan and Simms (eds.), *The Primacy of Foreign Policy in British History*, pp. 137–53.

65. Quoted in William Mulligan, 'Gladstone, the Liberal Party and the Primacy of Foreign Policy', p. 190.
66. Quoted in Parry, *The Politics of Patriotism*, p. 341.
67. Quoted in Matthias Schulz, 'The Guarantees of Humanity: The Concert of Europe and the Origins of the Russo-Ottoman War of 1877', in Simms and Trim (eds.), *Humanitarian Intervention*, p. 194.
68. Thus Andrew Roberts, *Salisbury. Victorian Titan* (London, 1999), pp. 629–30 (quotations p. 629).
69. See T. G. Otte, '"We are Part of the Community of Europe". The Tories, Empire and Foreign Policy, 1874–1914', in Jeremy Black (ed.), *The Tory World. Deep History and the Tory Theme in British Foreign Policy, 1679–2014* (Farnham, 2015), pp. 203–29.
70. Quoted 1897 from Klaus Hildebrand, *Das vergangene Reich. Deutsche Aussenpolitik von Bismarck bis Hitler* (Munich, 1995), p. 202.
71. Quoted in Sönke Neitzel, *Weltmacht oder Untergang. Die Weltreichslehre im Zeitalter des Imperialismus* (Paderborn, 2000), p. 89.
72. Quoted in Hildebrand, *Das vergangene Reich*, p. 187.
73. See Harald Rosenbach, *Das deutsche Reich, Grossbritannien und der Transvaal (1896–1902)* (Göttingen, 1993), pp. 309–14.
74. Quotation in Jonathan Steinberg, 'The Copenhagen Complex', in *Journal of Contemporary History* 1 (3) 1914 (July, 1966), pp. 23–46, p. 29.
75. Matthew S. Seligmann, *Rivalry in Southern Africa, 1893–99. The Transformation of German Colonial Policy* (Basingstoke, 1998), pp. 16–17, 58–61, 128–131 (quotation p. 16).
76. Quoted in John Darwin, *The Empire Project. The Rise and Fall of the British World-System, 1830–1970* (Cambridge, 2009) p. 66.
77. See Apollon Davidson and Irina Filatova, *The Russians and the Anglo-Boer War, 1899–1902* (Cape Town, Pretoria, Johannesburg, 1998), and Keith Wilson (ed.), *The International Impact of the Boer War* (Chesham, 2001).
78. Thus David Reynolds, *Britannia Overruled. British Policy and World Power in the Twentieth Century* (Harlow, 1991; 2nd edn, 2000), pp. 64–5.
79. See William Mulligan, 'From Case to Narrative: The Marquess of Lansdowne, Sir Edward Grey, and the Threat from Germany, 1900–1906', *International History Review*, XXX, 2 (2008), and Matthew Seligmann, 'Switching Horses: The Admiralty's Recognition of the Threat from Germany, 1900–1905', *International History Review*, 30 (2008), pp. 237–472. K. M. Wilson, 'The Question of Anti-Germanism at the Foreign Office before the First World War', in K. M. Wilson, *Empire*

and Continent. Studies in British Foreign Policy from the 1880s to the First World War (London and New York, 1987), pp. 50–72, sees British fears of Germany as imperially motivated rather than focussed on the threat of continental domination.

80. Quoted in Frank Johnson, 'How the Brown-Heseltine-Clarke-Patten Cause Would Have Lost us the Battle of Britain', *Spectator*, 17.7.1999, p. 10.
81. Matthew Seligmann, 'A Prelude to the Reforms of Admiral Sir John Fisher: The Creation of the Home Fleet, 1902–3', *Historical Research*, 83 (2010), pp. 506–19, especially pp. 517–18 on the German threat.
82. S. Anderson, *Race and Rapprochement. Anglo-Saxonism and Anglo-American relations, 1895–1904* (East Brunswick, NJ, 1981).
83. Quoted in Otte, '"Almost a Law of Nature". Sir Edward Grey, the Foreign Office and the Balance of Power in Europe, 1905–12', *Diplomacy and Statecraft*, 14, 2 (2003), p. 104.
84. See Keith Jeffery, *Field Marshal Sir Henry Wilson. A Political Soldier* (Oxford, 2006), pp. 99–100 *et passim*.
85. See Michael Epkenhans, *Die wilhelminische Flottenrüstung, 1908–1914. Weltmachtstreben, industrieller Fortschritt, soziale Integration* (Munich, 1991). For the capacity of the twentieth-century British state for massive military mobilization even in peacetime see G. C. Peden, *Arms, Economics and British Strategy. From Dreadnoughts to Hydrogen Bombs* (Cambridge, 2007), pp. 1–16.
86. The text of the memorandum is in J. S. Dunn, *The Crowe Memorandum. Sir Eyre Crowe and Foreign Office Perceptions of Germany, 1918–1925* (Newcastle, 2013), pp. 220–28.
87. See G. R. Searle, *The Quest for National Efficiency* (Berkeley, 1971), and T. E. Otte, '"Avenge England's Dishonour". By-elections, Parliament and the Politics of Foreign Policy in 1898', *English Historical Review*, CXXI (2006), pp. 385–428.
88. Quoted in Matthew Johnson, 'The Liberal War Committee and the Liberal Advocacy of Conscription in Britain, 1914–1916', *Historical Journal* 51 (2008), who cites the *National Service Journal* of November 1903. See also R. J. Q. Adams, *The Conscription Controversy in Great Britain, 1900–1918* (Basingstoke, 1987), especially pp. 5, 24–5.
89. For the centrality of foreign policy to Chamberlain's conception of tariff reform see Paul Readman, 'Patriotism and the Politics of Foreign Policy, *c.* 1870–*c.* 1914', in Mulligan and Simms (eds.), *The Primacy of Foreign Policy in British History*, especially pp. 264–5.

90. Quoted in Paul Readman, *Land and Nation in England. Patriotism, National Identity and the Politics of Land, 1880–1914* (London, 2008), p. 72.
91. See Zara Steiner, 'Views of War. Britain before the "Great War" and After', *International Relations*, 17 (1), pp. 15–16 *et passim.*
92. The phrase is taken from Steiner, 'Views of War', p. 18. On this issue see also T. G. Otte, '"No Large Conceptions or Great Schemes". High Politics, Finance and Foreign Policy, 1865–1914', in Mulligan and Simms (eds.), *The Primacy of Foreign Policy in British History.*
93. See Matthew Seligmann, 'Intelligence Information and the 1909 Naval Scare: The Secret Foundations of a Public Panic', *War in History*, 17, 1 (2010), pp. 37–59; G. J. Marcus, 'The Naval Crisis of 1909 and the Croydon By-election', *Journal of the Royal United Services Institute* (1958), pp. 500–514; O'Brien, 'The 1910 Elections and the Primacy of Foreign Policy', in Mulligan and Simms (eds.), *The Primacy of Foreign Policy in British History.*
94. Thus Christopher Andrew, *The Defence of the Realm. The Authorized History of MI5* (London, 2009), pp. 3–18.
95. Quotations in Alfred Gollin, *No Longer an Island. Britain and the Wright Brothers, 1902–1909* (London, 1984), pp. 193–4. See also Hugh Driver, *The Birth of Military Aviation. Britain, 1903–1914* (Woodbridge, 1997).
96. Quoted in Otte, *The Foreign Office Mind*, p. 353.
97. Quoted in Reynolds, *Britannia Overruled*, p. 86.
98. See Philipps Payson O'Brien, 'The Titan Refreshed: Imperial Overstretch and the British Navy before the First World War', *Past and Present*, 172 (2001), pp. 145–69, especially pp. 154–5, p. 167.
99. Quoted in Darwin, *The Empire Project*, p. 306.
100. The hesitations are described in Christopher Clark, *The Sleepwalkers. How Europe Went to War in 1914* (London, 2012), p. 542 *et passim.*

7. 'UNDER A SINGLE SWAY'. BRITAIN AND EUROPE IN THE AGE OF TOTAL WAR

1. Halford Mackinder, *Democratic Ideals and Reality. A Study in the Politics of Reconstruction (1919)*, p. 92.
2. Quoted in Bret Holman, 'The Air Panic of 1935: British Press Opinion between Disarmament and Rearmament', *Journal of Contemporary History*, 46 (2011), pp. 288–307 (quotation p. 295).

3. Thus Isabel V. Hull, *A Scrap of Paper. Breaking and Making International Law during the Great War* (Ithaca and London, 2014), pp. 38–9, 42 *et passim.*
4. Quoted in Stephen Cooper, 'The Legacy of Agincourt', *History Today*, October 2015, p. 29.
5. Quoted in Keith Jeffery, *1916. A Global History* (London, 2015), p. 366. (Lloyd George was speaking in 1916.)
6. Thus Frank McDonough, *The Conservative Party and Anglo-German Relations, 1905–1914* (Basingstoke, 2007), p. 143.
7. Thus Paul Bridgen, *The Labour Party and the Politics of War and Peace, 1900–1924* (Woodbridge, 2009), p. 51.
8. Thus Keith Robbins, 'The Welsh Wizard Who Won the War: David Lloyd George as War Leader', in Brendan Simms and Karina Urbach (eds.), *Die Rückkehr der "Grossen Männer". Staatsmänner im Krieg. Ein deutsche-britischer Vergleich* (Berlin and New York, 2010), pp. 96–107, especially p. 105.
9. See Tim Coates, *Lord Kitchener and Winston Churchill: The Dardanelles Commission Part I, 1914–15* (London, 2000), and *Defeat at Gallipolli: The Dardanelles Commission* Part II, 1915–1916 (London, 2000).
10. Quoted in Boris Johnson, *The Churchill Factor. How One Man Made History* (London, 2014), p. 309.
11. See Brock Millman, *Managing Domestic Dissent in First World War Britain* (London, 2001). See also Jo Vellacott, *Pacifists, Patriots and the Vote. The Erosion of Democratic Suffragism in Britain during the First World War* (Basingstoke, 2007).
12. Rosemary Elliot, 'An Early Experiment in National Identity Cards: The Battle over Registration in the First World War', *Twentieth Century British History*, 17 (2006), 145–76.
13. Quotations in Sheila Rowbotham, *A Century of Women. The History of Women in Britain and the United States* (London, 1997), p. 65.
14. On the balance between conscription and volunteering see Alexander Watson, 'Voluntary Enlistment in the Great War: A European Phenomenon?', in Krueger and Levsen, *War Volunteering in Modern Times, From the French Revolution to the Second World War* (London, 2011), pp. 163–88.
15. Quoted in Matthew Johnson, 'The Liberal War Committee and the Liberal Advocacy of Conscription in Britain, 1914–1916', *Historical Journal*, 51, 2 (2008), pp. 402, 416.
16. Quotations in Johnson, 'The Liberal War Committee', pp. 414–15.

17. Quoted in John Darwin, *The Empire Project. The Rise and Fall of the British World-System, 1830–1970* (Cambridge, 2009), p. 333.
18. Thus Keith Jeffery, *1916. A Global History* (London, 2015), p. 266.
19. I base this paragraph on Darwin, *The Empire Project*, pp. 324–5.
20. Quoted in Elizabeth Greenhalgh, *Victory through Coalition. Britain and France during the First World War* (Cambridge, 2005), p. 281.
21. Quoted in Patrick O. Cohrs, *The Unfinished Peace after World War I. America, Britain and the Stabilization of Europe, 1919–1932* (Cambridge, 2006), p. 213.
22. Quoted in Stefan Berger, 'The Career and Politics of an Historian of Germany', *English Historical Review*, 116 (2001), p. 91.
23. John Ramsden, 'Churchill and the Germans', *Contemporary British History*, 25 (2011), pp. 125–39 (quotations pp 129–130).
24. John Maynard Keynes, *The Economic Consequences of the Peace* in *Collected Writings of John Maynard Keynes, vol.* 2 (London, 1971), p. 226.
25. Quoted in Cohrs, *The Unfinished Peace*, pp. 105, 135.
26. Quoted in M. L. Roi and B. J. C. McKercher, '"Ideal" and "Punch-Bag". Conflicting Views of the Balance of Power and Their Influence on Interwar British Foreign Policy', *Diplomacy and Statecraft*, 12 (2001), p. 57 (in December 1924).
27. Quoted in Cohrs, *The Unfinished Peace*, p. 147.
28. Quoted in Cohrs, *The Unfinished Peace*, p. 215.
29. Quoted in Richard S. Grayson, 'The Historiography of Inter-war Politics. Competing Conservative World Views in High Politics, 1924–1929', in William Mulligan and Brendan Simms (eds.), *The Primacy of Foreign Policy in British History, 1660–2000* (Basingstoke, 2010), p. 287. See also Richard S. Grayson, 'Imperialism in Conservative Defence and Foreign Policy: Leo Amery and the Chamberlains, 1903–1939', *Journal of Imperial and Commonwealth History*, 34 (2006).
30. Benedikt Stuchtey, '"Not by Law but by Sentiment". Great Britain and Imperial Defense, 1918–1939', in Roger Chickering and Stig Förster (eds.), *The Shadows of Total War. Europe, East Asia, and the United States, 1919–1939* (Cambridge, 2003), pp. 255–70, 260.
31. See Andrew Webster, 'An Argument without End: Britain, France and the Disarmament Process, 1925–34', in Martin S. Alexander and William J. Philpott (eds.), *Anglo-French Defence Relations between the Wars*, pp. 49–71, especially pp. 58–61.
32. Quoted in Zara Steiner, 'The League of Nations and the Quest for Security', in Rolf Ahmann et al. (eds.), *The Quest for Stability, Problems of West European Security, 1918–1957* (London, 1993), p. 68.

33. Quoted in Christopher Booker and Richard North, *The Great Deception. The Secret History of the European Union* (London, 2003), pp. 10–11.
34. Quoted in Cohrs, *The Unfinished Peace*, pp. 587–8.
35. Austen Chamberlain, 'The Permanent Bases of British Foreign Policy', *Foreign Affairs*, July 1971 (online version p. 6).
36. Both quotations are from Webster, 'An Argument without End', pp. 57–8.
37. Quoted in Roi and McKercher, '"Ideal" and "Punch-Bag"', p. 132.
38. Thus Wesley K. Wark, *The Ultimate Enemy. British Intelligence and Nazi Germany, 1933–1939* (Ithaca, NY, 1985). The tension between imperial and European concerns in the interwar period is discussed in Michael Howard's classic *The Continental Commitment* (London, 1972).
39. Quoted in B. J. C. McKercher, 'Deterrence and the European Balance of Power: The Field Force and British Grand Strategy', *English Historical* Review, 123 (2006), pp. 108–9. For the importance of keeping Hitler out of central Europe see Keith Neilson, 'Orme Sargent, Appeasement and British Policy in Europe, 1933–39', *Twentieth Century British History*, 21 (2010), pp. 1–28, especially pp. 21–3.
40. See Richard S. Grayson, 'Leo Amery's Imperialist Alternative to Appeasement in the 1930s' in *Twentieth Century British History* 17 (4), pp. 499–515, especially pp. 494–6.
41. Quoted in Richard Bassett, *Last Imperialist. A Portrait of Julian Amery* (Settrington, 2015), p. 145.
42. Quoted in Uri Bialer, 'Elite Opinion and Defence Policy: Air Power Advocacy and British Rearmament during the 1930s', *British Journal of International Studies*, 6 (1980), p. 336.
43. See Bret Holman, 'The Air Panic of 1935: British Press Opinion between Disarmament and Rearmament', *Journal of Contemporary History*, 46 (2011), pp. 288–307 (quotation p. 295).
44. Thus Greg Kennedy, 'Neville Chamberlain and Strategic Relations with the US during His Chancellorship', *Diplomacy and Statecraft*, 13 (2002), pp. 95–120, especially pp. 111–14.
45. See Grayson, 'Leo Amery's Imperialist Alternative to Appeasement in the 1930s', especially pp. 494–6.
46. Quoted in Roi and McKercher, '"Ideal" and "Punchbag"', p. 53.
47. R. Heller, 'East Fulham Revisited', *Journal of Contemporary History*, IV (1971), 172–96; M. Ceadel, 'Interpreting East Fulham', in C. Cook and J. Ramsden (eds.), *By-elections in British Politics* (London, 1973), pp. 118–40.
48. Quoted in Ramsden, 'Churchill and the Germans', p. 131.

49. Quoted in Roi and McKercher, '"Ideal" and "Punchbag"', p. 67.
50. Thus Philip Towle, 'Taming or Demonizing an Aggressor: The British Debate on the End of the Locarno System', in Gaynor Johnson (ed.), *Locarno Revisited: European Diplomacy, 1920–1929* (London and New York, 2004), pp. 178–198, especially pp. 190–1.
51. Quoted in David Dilks, '"We Must Hope for the Best and Prepare for the Worst." The Prime Minister, the Cabinet and Hitler's Germany, 1937–1939', *Proceedings of the British Academy,* LXXIII (1987), p. 325. For the healthy respect for German power see especially pp. 311–12.
52. James McMillan, *Twentieth-century France. Politics and Society in France, 1898–1991* (London, 1992), p. 119 and Daniel Hucker, 'French Public Attitudes towards the Prospect of War in 1938–1939', *French History*, 21 (2007), pp. 431–4; Jerry H. Brookshire, 'Speak for England, Act for England: Labour's Leadership and British National Security under the Threat of War in the Late 1930s', *European History Quarterly*, 29 (1999), pp. 251–87.
53. Thus Maurice Cowling, *The Impact of Hitler. British Politics and British Policy, 1933–1940* (Cambridge, 1975).
54. See Stuchtey, '"Not by Law but by Sentiment"', pp. 255–70 (quotations of Fisher and the Canadian pp. 263 and 267).
55. Franklin Reid Gannon, *The British Press and Germany, 1936–1939* (Oxford, 1971).
56. Quoted in Rolf-Dieter Müller, *Enemy in the East. Hitler's Secret Plans to Invade the Soviet Union* (London, 2015), p. 120.
57. Quoted in G. Bruce Strang, 'Britain's Guarantee to Poland, March 1939', *Journal of Contemporary* History, 31 (1996), pp. 735–6.
58. See Anna M. Ciencala, 'Poland in British and French Policy in 1939. Determination to Fight – or Avoid War?', *Polish Review,* XXXIV, (1989), pp. 199–226, especially pp. 203–6.
59. *The Times*, 25.8.1939.
60. *The Times*, 8.11.1939.
61. Patrick R. Osborn, *Operation Pike. Britain versus the Soviet Union, 1939–1941* (Westport, CT, and London, 2000).
62. Thus Roger Moorhouse, *The Devil's Alliance. Hitler's Pact with Stalin, 1939–1941* (New York, 2014).
63. Daniel Todman, *Britain's War. Into Battle, 1937–1941* (London, 2016), p. 195.
64. For the contrast between the British and French war economies in this respect see Talbot C. Imlay, *Facing the Second World War. Strategy, Politics and Economics in Britain and France, 1938–1940* (Oxford, 2003).

65. Quoted in Rowbotham, *A Century of Women*, p. 247.
66. William Manchester, *The Last Lion. Churchill*, (London, 1983–2012), p. 637.
67. Avi Shlaim, 'Prelude to Downfall: The British Offer of Union to France, June 1940', *Journal of Contemporary History* 9 (1974), pp. 27–63.
68. Thus Anthony J. Cumming, 'The Warship as the Ultimate Guarantor of Britain's Freedom in 1940', *Historical Research*, 83 (2010), pp. 165–88.
69. See Robin Prior, *When Britain saved the West. The Story of 1940* (New Haven and London, 2015).
70. Quoted in Jeremy Black, 'Introduction', in Jeremy Black (ed.), *The Tory World. Deep History and the Tory Theme in British Foreign Policy, 1679–2014* (Farnham, 2015), pp. 13–14.
71. See David Edgerton's *Britain's War Machine. Weapons, Resources and Experts in the Second World War* (London, 2011), especially pp. 47–8, 124–5.
72. David Killingray, Fighting for Britain. *African Soldiers in the Second World War* (New York, 2010). J. Lee Ready, *Forgotten Allies*, 2 vols (1985) and J. Lee Ready, *Forgotten Allies. The Military Contribution of the Colonies, Exiled Governments and Lesser Powers to the Allied Victory in World War II. Volume I. The European Theatre* (Jefferson, NC, and London, 1985).
73. See Andrew Stewart, *Empire Lost. Britain, the Dominions and the Second World War* (London, 2008), p. 106.
74. For the extent of British mobilization, metropolitan and imperial, see now David Edgerton, 'The Primacy of Foreign Policy? Britain in the Second World War', in Mulligan and Simms (eds.), *The Primacy of Foreign Policy in British History*, pp. 291–304, especially pp. 296–7.
75. Jörg Friedrich, *Der Brand. Deutschland im Bombenkrieg, 1940–1945* (Berlin, 2002).
76. M. R. D. Foot, *The Special Operations Executive 1940–1946* (London, 1999).
77. W. S. Churchill, *Blenheim* (London, 1941), p. 7.
78. See now Dan Plesch, *America, Hitler and the UN. How the Allies Won World War II and Forged a Peace* (London, 2011), especially pp. 31–57 (quotation p. 34).
79. See Phillips O'Brien, *How the War was Won. Air-sea Power and Allied Victory in World War II* (Cambridge, 2015).
80. Thus Roger Beaumont, 'The Bomber Offensive as a Second Front', *Journal of Contemporary History*, 22 (1987), pp. 3–19, especially pp. 13–15 (quotation p. 13)

81. Quoted in Klaus Larres, 'Churchill: Flawed War Leader or Charismatic Visionary?' in Simms and Urbach (eds.), *Die Rückkehr der "Grossen Männer"*, p. 154.
82. Quoted in Lothar Kettenacker, *Krieg zur Friedenssicherung. Die Deutschlandplanung der britischen Regierung während des zweiten Weltkrieges* (Göttingen and Zürich, 1989), p. 212 (Strang), p. 534 (O'Neill), pp. 538 and 537–42 (Churchill).
83. Quoted in Kettenacker, *Krieg zur Friedenssicherung*, p. 141.
84. See Patrick J. Hearden, 'Early American Views regarding European Unification', *Cambridge Review of International Affairs*, 19 (2006), pp. 67–78, especially pp. 74–5.
85. See now David Reynolds, *From World War to Cold War. Churchill, Roosevelt and the International History of the 1940s* (Oxford, 2006), pp. 121–36.
86. See Brian P. Farrell, 'Symbol of Paradox. The Casablanca Conference, 1943', *Canadian Journal of History*, 28 (1993), pp. 21–40, which puts the debate about the best strategy against Germany at the forefront.
87. See Vojtech Mastny, 'Soviet War Aims at the Moscow and Teheran Conferences of 1943', in *Journal of Modern History*, 47, 3, (1975), pp. 481–504.

8. 'OUR DESTINY HAS BEEN TO HELP SHAPE EUROPE.' BRITAIN AND THE CONTINENT IN THE AGE OF EUROPEAN INTEGRATION

1. Quoted in Anne Deighton, 'Towards a "western" Strategy: The Making of British Policy towards Germany, 1945–1946', in Anne Deighton (ed.), *Britain and the First Cold War* (Basingstoke, 1990), p. 59.
2. Quoted in Martin Schaad, 'Plan G – A "Counterblast"? British Policy towards the Messina Countries, 1956', in *Contemporary European History* 7, 1 (1995), p. 50.
3. Winston Churchill, 18.1.1945, in Charles Eade (ed.), *Victory. War Speeches by the Right Hon. Winston S. Churchill. 1945* (London, 1946), p. 3.
4. See Brendan Simms, 'Prussia, Prussianism and National Socialism, 1933–47', in Philip G. Dwyer (ed.), *Modern Prussian History 1830–1947* (Harlow, 2001), pp. 253–73, especially p. 272.
5. J. E. Farquharson, 'Anglo-American Policy on German Reparations from Yalta to Potsdam', *English Historical Review*, CXII (1997), pp. 904–26, quotation and reference to primacy of security p. 905.

6. David Weigall, 'British Ideas of European Unity and Regional Confederation', in M. L. Smith and Peter M. R. Stirk (eds.), *Making the New Europe: European Unity and the Second World War* (New York, 1990).
7. See Scott Kelly, '"The ghost of Neville Chamberlain". Guilty Men and the 1945 election', *Conservative History Journal*, 5 (autumn, 2005), pp. 18–24, especially pp. 21–2 (quotation p. 18)
8. See Corelli Barnett, *The Audit of War. The Illusion and Reality of Britain as a Great Nation* (London, 1986).
9. Jim Tomlinson, 'Balanced Accounts? Constructing the Balance of Payments Problem in Post-war Britain', *English Historical Review*, CXXIV (2009), pp. 863–84, especially pp. 883–4, and 'The Attlee Government and the Balance of Payments, 1945–1951', *Twentieth-century British History*, 2 (1991), pp. 47–66, especially p. 58.
10. Thus Thomas Hall, '"Mere Drops in the Ocean": The Politics and Planning of the Contribution of the British Commonwealth to the Final Defeat of Japan, 1944–45', *Diplomacy and Statecraft*, 16, 1 (2005), pp. 93–115, especially pp. 95, 101, 109–10.
11. Anne Deighton, '*Entente neo-coloniale?* Ernest Bevin and the Proposals for Anglo-French Third World Power, 1945–49', in Glyn Stone and T. G. Otte (eds.), *Anglo-French Relations since the Late Eighteenth Century* (London and New York, 2008), pp. 200–218 (Bevin quotation p. 208).
12. Quoted in R. W. Johnson, 'Every Club in the Bag', *London Review of Books*, 8.8.2002, p. 15.
13. Quote in Anne Deighton, 'The "Frozen Front". The Labour Government, the Division of Germany and the Origins of the Cold War, 1945–7', *International Affairs*, 63 (1987), p. 453.
14. Quoted in Deighton, p. 64.
15. Cited in Deighton (ed.), *Britain and the First Cold War*, p. 58.
16. Quoted in Dianne Kirkby, 'Divinely Sanctioned. The Anglo-American Cold War Alliance and the Defence of Western Civilization and Christianity, 1945–48', *Journal of Contemporary History* 35, (2000), pp. 385–412 (quotation p. 400). See also J. Schneer, 'Hopes Deferred or Shattered. The British Left and the Third Force Movement, 1945–9', *Journal of Modern History*, 56 (1984), pp, 197–226.
17. John Charmley, 'Duff Cooper and Western European Union, 1944–7', *Review of International Studies*, II (1985), pp. 53–63.
18. Winston Churchill, *Europe Unite. Speeches 1947 and 1948* (London, 1950). 'A Speech at Zurich University', 19.9.1946, pp. 197–202.
19. See Klaus Schwabe's 'The Cold War and European Integration, 1947–63', *Diplomacy and Statecraft*, 12 (2001), pp. 18–34.

20. Thus Avi Shlaim, *Britain and the Origins of European Unity* (Reading, 1978), pp. 114–42.
21. Thus J. W. Young, *Britain and European Unity, 1945–99* (Basingstoke, 1999), p. 18.
22. See John W. Young, *Britain, France and the Unity of Europe, 1945–1951* (Leicester, 1984), pp. 77–9 *et passim.*
23. Quoted in Young, *Britain and European Unity*, p. 34.
24. Quoted in Brian Harrison, *Seeking a Role. The United Kingdom, 1951–1970* (Oxford, 2009), p. 9.
25. Quoted in Hugo Young, *This Blessed Plot. Britain and Europe from Churchill to Blair* (Basingstoke and Oxford, 1998; 1999 edn), p. 70.
26. Quoted in Young, *Blessed Plot*, p. 113.
27. Quoted in Young, *Britain and European Unity*, p. 36.
28. Quoted in Nicholas Crowson and James Mckay, 'Britain in Europe? Conservative and Labour Attitudes to European Integration since the Second World War', in William Mulligan and Brendan Simms (eds.), *The Primacy of Foreign Policy in British History, 1660–2000. How Strategic Concerns Shaped Modern* Britain (Basingstoke, 2010), pp. 305–18, p. 306.
29. See Richard Vinen, *National Service. A Generation in Uniform, 1945–1963* (London, 2014).
30. For the impact of rearmament on the state in the 1950s see James E. Cronin, *The Politics of State Expansion. War, State and Society in Twentieth-Century Britain* (London and New York, 1991), pp. 185–6, 208–15.
31. See Hubert Zimmermann, 'The Sour Fruits of Victory: Sterling and Security in Anglo-German Relations during the 1950s and 1960s', *Contemporary European History*, 9 (2000), pp. 225–43.
32. On the centrality of Germany to British economic strategy see Geoffrey Owen, *From Empire to Europe. The Decline and Revival of British Industry since the Second World War* (London, 1999), pp. 30–56 *et passim.*
33. See Jenna Phillips, 'Don't Mention the War? History Suggests Foreign Policy Can Swing Voters', *History and Policy*, http://www.historyandpolicy.org/opinion/opinion_31.html pp. 1–2. The centrality of foreign policy is also emphasized by H. G. Nicholas, 'The British General Election of 1951', *The American Political Science Review*, 46, 2 (June, 1952), pp. 398–405, especially pp. 399–402.
34. Thus Kenneth O. Morgan, *The People's Peace. British History, 1945–1990* (Oxford, 1990), p. 103.
35. On this see Lawrence Black, '"The Bitterest Enemies of Communism". Labour Revisionists, Atlanticism and the Cold War', *Contemporary British History*, 15, 3 (2001), pp. 26–62, especially, pp. 27–8

36. Martin Ceadel, 'British Parties and the European Situation, 1952–1957', in Ennio di Nolfo (ed.), *Power in Europe? II. Great Britain, France, Germany, Italy and the Origins of the EEC, 1952–1957* (Berlin and New York, 1992).
37. See Anne Deighton, 'The Last Piece of the Jigsaw. Britain and the Creation of the Western European Union, 1954', *Contemporary European History*, 7, 2 (1998), pp. 181–96.
38. Schaad, 'Plan G – A "Counterblast"?', pp. 39–60 *et passim* (quotation p. 46).
39. Quoted in Harrison, *Seeking a Role*, p. 116.
40. Quoted in Young, *Blessed Plot*, p. 117.
41. Robert W. Heywood, 'West European Community and the Eurafrica Concept in the 1950s', *Journal of European Integration*, 4 (1981), pp. 199–210.
42. Quoted in Ralph Dietl, 'Suez 1956. A European Intervention?', *Journal of Contemporary History*, 43, 2 (2008), pp. 259–78, p. 261.
43. See John C. Campbell, 'The Soviet Union, the United States, and the Twin Crises of Hungary and Suez', in William Roger Louis and Roger Owen (eds.), *Suez 1956. The Crisis and Its Consequences* (Oxford, 1989), pp. 233–53.
44. See Diane Kunz, *The Economic Diplomacy of the Suez Crisis* (Chapel Hill and London, 1991), especially pp. 113–14, 192–3.
45. Thus Ashley Jackson, 'Empire and Beyond: The Pursuit of Overseas National Interest in the Late Twentieth Century', in *English Historical Review*, CXXII (2007), p. 1361, and W. R. Louis, 'Public Enemy Number One: The British Empire in the Dock at the United Nations, 1957–1971', in Martin Lynn (ed.), *The British Empire in the 1950s: Retreat or Revival?* (Basingstoke, 2006).
46. On this see Anthony Adamthwaite, 'Suez Revisited', *International Affairs*, 69, 3 (1988), pp. 449–64, p. 454.
47. Quoted in Morgan, *The People's Peace*, p. 158.
48. Quoted in Morgan, *The People's Peace*, pp. 173–4.
49. Quoted in Schaad, 'Plan G – A "Counterblast"?', p. 50.
50. Quoted in Tom Prendeville, 'De Valera was against European Union', *Magill 3* (2008), p. 62. (speaking in July 1955).
51. See David French, *Army, Empire and Cold War. The British Army and Military Policy, 1945–1971* (Oxford, 2012), pp. 213–15 (quotation p. 232).
52. Quoted in Young, *Blessed Plot*, p. 122.
53. See Alan Milward, *European Rescue of the Nation State* (London and New York, 1992).

54. Quoted in Young, *Blessed Plot*, p. 119.
55. See Andrea Benvenuti, *Anglo-Australian Relations and the Turn to Europe, 1961–1972* (Woodbridge, 2008), pp. 26–41.
56. Quoted in John Campbell, *Roy Jenkins. A Well-rounded life* (London, 2014), pp. 214–15.
57. See Frank Costigliola, 'The Failed Design: Kennedy, de Gaulle and the Struggle for Europe', *Diplomatic History*, 8, 3 (1984), pp. 227–52.
58. See Susanna Schrafstetter, *Die dritte Atommacht. Britische Nichtverbreitungspolitik im Dienst von Statussicherung und Deutschlandpolitik, 1952–1968* (Munich, 1999), pp. 224, 234–6.
59. Quoted in John Campbell, *Edward Heath. A Biography* (London, 1993), p. 131.
60. Quoted in Young, *Blessed Plot*, p. 195.
61. Niklas H. Rossbach, *Heath, Nixon and the Rebirth of the Special Relationship. Britain, the US and the EC, 1969–74* (Basingstoke, 2009).
62. See Jenna Phillips, 'Don't Mention the War?', pp. 2–3.
63. Quoted in Andy Beckett, *When the Lights Went Out. Britain in the Seventies* (London, 2009), p. 90.
64. Quoted in Timothy Garton Ash, 'Why Britain is in Europe. The Ben Pimlott Memorial Lecture', in *Twentieth-century British History*, 17, 4 (2005), pp. 451–63, p. 460.
65. Quoted in Campbell, *Edward Heath*, p. 397.
66. Quoted in Philip Ziegler, *Wilson. The Authorised Life of Lord Wilson of Rievaulx* (London, 1993), p. 425.
67. For the figures see Michael Vestey, 'The Nobbling Game', *Spectator*, 12.2.2000, p. 51; and Brian Harrison, *Finding a Role? The United Kingdom, 1970–1990* (Oxford, 2010), pp. 20–38.
68. Thus Campbell, *Roy Jenkins*, p. 449.
69. Douglas Wass, *Decline to Fall. The Making of British Macro-economic Policy and the 1976 IMF Crisis* (Oxford and New York, 2009)
70. Thus Eunan O'Halpin, *The Geopolitics of Republican Diplomacy in the Twentieth Century*, Institute for British-Irish Studies, University College Dublin, working paper (Dublin, 2001), pp. 8–9. Christopher Andrew and V. Mitrokhin, *Mitrokhin Archives* (2000), pp. 492, 501–3.
71. Peter Taylor, *Beating the Terrorists? Interrogation at Omagh, Gough and Castlereagh* (Harmondsworth, 1980).
72. Quoted in Young, *Blessed Plot*, p. 250.
73. Quoted in Young, *Britain and the Unity of Europe*, p. 130.
74. Quoted in Young, *Blessed Plot*, p. 310.
75. Stephen Wall, *A Stranger in Europe. Britain and the EU from Thatcher to Blair* (Oxford, 2008).

76. An early (pre-Bruges) example is Baroness Young (Minister of State at the Foreign and Commonwealth Office), Third Mackinder Lecture, printed in *Transactions of the Institute of British Geographers*, 12, 4 (1987), pp. 391–7, especially p. 393.
77. Quoted in George Urban, *Diplomacy and Disillusion at the Court of Margaret Thatcher. An Insider's View* (London, 1996), pp. 118–50, especially p. 136.
78. Quoted in Urban, *Diplomacy and Disillusion*, p. 136.
79. Quoted in Young, *Britain and the Unity of Europe*, p. 154.
80. See D. Allen, '"Wider but Weaker or the More the Merrier?"' Enlargement and Foreign Policy Cooperation in the EC/EU', in J. Redmond and G. G. Rosenthal (eds.), *The Expanding European Union: Past, Present, Future* (Boulder, CO, 1998).
81. Quoted in Young *Blessed Plot*, p. 389.
82. Stephen F. Frowen and Jens Hoelscher (eds.), *The German Currency Union of 1990. A Critical Assessment* (London, 1997).
83. Anthony Glees, 'The Diplomacy of Anglo-German Relations: A Study of the ERM Crisis of September 1992', *German Politics*, 3 (1994).
84. On the 'French alternative' see Kori Schake, 'NATO after the Cold War, 1991–1995: Institutional Competition and the Collapse of the French Alternative', *Contemporary European History*, 7, 3 (1998), pp. 379–407.
85. See Brendan Simms, *Unfinest Hour. Britain and the Destruction of Bosnia* (London, 2001), pp. 49–134.
86. See Brendan Simms, `Bosnia: The Lessons of History', in Thomas Cushman and Stjepan Mestrovic (eds.), *This Time We Knew. Western Responses to Genocide in Bosnia* (New York, 1996), pp. 65–78.
87. Quoted in Jonathan Bronitzky, *British Foreign Policy and Bosnia: The Rise of Islamism in Britain, 1992–1995. Developments in Radicalisation and Political Violence.* Published by the International Centre for the Study of Radicalisation and Political Violence (London, 2010), p. 9.
88. See Ed Husain, *The Islamist. Why I Joined Radical Islam in Britain, What I Saw Inside and Why I Left* (London, 2007), pp. 74–81 *et passim.*
89. Melanie Phillips, *Londonistan. How Britain is Creating a Terrorist State Within.*
90. Quotations in William Cash, *Against a Federal Europe. The Battle for Britain* (London, 1991), pp. 71, 80.
91. See for example Martin Fletcher and Charles Bremner, 'Tory Tirade Falls Flat as US Backs European Force', *The Times*, 11.10.2000, p. 14.
92. Report from the Embassy of the Federal Republic of Germany, London, 22.3.1999.

93. This paragraph is partly based on Brendan Simms, 'Blood, Iron and Creative Havoc', *Times Higher Education*, 25.7.2003, p. 22; and 'The Case for a European Superpower under British Leadership: Why Britain Now has the Opportunity to Become the Prussia of European Unification with Blair as its Bismarck', 7.6.2005, http:/socialaffairsunit.org.uk/blog/archives/000447.php.
94. Which this author strongly supported.
95. See Christopher Hill, *The National Interest in Question. Foreign Policy in Multicultural Societies* (Oxford, 2013), especially pp. 203–4.
96. Quoted in Jeremy Black, *The Dotted Line. Britain's Defence Policy in the Modern World* (London, 2006), p. 67.

9. BRITAIN: THE LAST EUROPEAN GREAT POWER

1. A version of this chapter was presented to the Nobel Institute in Oslo, in April 2012.
2. Quoted in Jeremy Black, 'The European Question, the National Interest and Tory Histories', in Jeremy Black (ed.), *The Tory World. Deep History and the Tory Theme in British Foreign Policy, 1679–2014* (Farnham, 2015), p. 357.
3. The best introduction here is Amrita Narlikar, *New Powers. How to Become One and How to Manage Them* (London, 2010).
4. See the figures in Geir Lundestad, *The Rise and Decline of the American 'Empire'. Power and Its Limits in Comparative Perspective* (Oxford, 2012), pp. 50 and 26. (I use his figures rather than disputing the analysis).
5. Kishore Mahbubani, *The New Asian Hemisphere: The Irresistible Shift of Global Power to the East* (New York, 2008).
6. Thus Constanze Stelzenmüller, 'The West Has Run Out of Power', *Policy Review*, April and May 2012, 172, pp. 85–94. For a less bleak but still sombre view see Ian Morris, 'Why the West Rules for Now. The Patterns of History and What They Reveal about the Future' (London, 2012), especially pp. 598–622, p. 622.
7. Fareed Zakaria, *The Post-American World* (New York, 2008).
8. Edward Luce, *Time to Start Thinking. America and the Spectre of Decline* (New York, 2012).
9. Not everybody takes this view. See Stephen G. Brooks and William Wohlforth, *World out of Balance. International Relations and the Challenge of American Primacy* (Princeton, 2008); Lundestad, *Rise and Decline*; and Robert Lieber, *Power and Willpower in the American Future. Why the United States is not Destined to Decline* (Cambridge, 2012). Predictions

of US decline have been made before, of course, and denied: Edward N. Luttwak, *The Endangered American Dream. How to Stop the United States from becoming a Third World Country and How to Win the Geo-economic Struggle for Industrial Supremacy* (New York, 1993) and Henry R. Nau, *The Myth of America's Decline. Leading the World Economy into the 1990s* (New York and Oxford, 1990).

10. See William I. Hitchcock, 'Reversal of Fortune: Britain, France and the Making of Europe', in Paul Kennedy and William I. Hitchcock (eds.), *From War to Peace. Altered Strategic Landscapes in the Twentieth Century* (New Haven, 2000), pp. 79–102.
11. On this general theme see D. Sanders, *Losing an Empire, Finding a Role: British Foreign Policy since 1945* (Basingstoke, 1990).
12. Quoted in Alan Stewart, 'A Crisis of Fate. The First Elizabethan age according to A. L. Rowse', *Times Literary Supplement*, 25.5.2012.
13. See Torbjorn L. Knutsen, *The Rise and Fall of World Orders* (Manchester, 1999) and John J. Mearsheimer, *The Tragedy of Great Power Politics* (New York and London, 2001), especially pp. 377–80.
14. See the warning by Peter Foster, *Facing Facts. Is British Power Diminishing?* Project for the Study of the 21st century (2015).
15. Quoted in Francis Elliott, 'Britain "Risks becoming New North Korea"', *The Times*, 10.3.2015, p. 8.
16. Quoted in Tracy McVeigh, 'The UN Security Council Has Lasted through Seven Turbulent Decades. But Does Britain Still Have the Clout to Justify Its Permanent Seat?', *Observer Special Report*, pp. 18–19.
17. Frank Ledwidge, *Losing Small Wars. British Military Failure in Iraq and Afghanistan* (New Haven, 2011).
18. For a contemporary discussion see James K. Wither, 'British Bulldog or Bush's Poodle? Anglo-American Relations and the Iraq War', *Parameters*, winter 2003–4, pp. 67–82.
19. See Jeremy Browne, minister of state at the Foreign and Commonwealth Office, 'British Competitiveness: Responding to the Rise of the Emerging Powers', speech to Global Strategy Forum, National Liberal Club, London, 18.4.2012.
20. Thus Jonathan Scott, *England's Troubles. Seventeenth-century English Political Instability in European Context* (Cambridge, 2000).
21. Quoted in Brendan Simms, *Three Victories and a Defeat. The Rise and Fall of the first British Empire, 1714–1783* (London, 2007), p. 635.
22. For the general context see Aaron Friedberg, *The Weary Titan. Britain and the Experience of Relative Decline, 1895–1905* (Princeton, 1988) and John Darwin, 'Fear of Failing: British Politics and Imperial Decline since 1900', *Transactions of the Royal Historical Society*, 36 (1986), pp. 27–43.

23. Thus Duncan Bell, *The Idea of Greater Britain: Empire and the Future of World Order, 1860–1900* (Princeton, 2006), and Daniel Deudney, 'Greater Britain or Greater Synthesis? Seeley, Mackinder and Wells on Britain in the Global Industrial Era', *Review of International Studies* (2001).
24. Kathleen Burk and Alec Cairncross, 'Good-bye Great Britain: The 1976 IMF Crisis' (London, 1992). For a very useful tabular summary of the decline arguments see Andrew Gamble, 'Britain in Decline. Economic Policy, Political Strategy and the British State' (Basingstoke and London, 1981; 3rd edn 1990), which has gone into multiple editions of several decades, p. 32.
25. Thus John van Wingen and Herbert K. Tillema, 'British Military Intervention after World War II: Militance in a Second-rank Power', *Journal of Peace Research*, 4 XVII, 1980, pp. 291–303.
26. Quoted in James Rogers, 'Stopping British Declinisim before It Starts', blog post, *European Geostrategy*, 19.5.2012.
27. Corelli Barnett, *Collapse of British Power* (London, 1972) and *Audit of war. The Illusion and Reality of Britain as a Great Nation* (London and Basingstoke, 1983).
28. John le Carré, *Tinker, Tailor, Soldier, Spy* (London, 1974), pp. 336–7.
29. Paul Kennedy, *The Rise and Fall of the Great Powers. Economic Change and Military Conflict from 1500 to 2000* (London and New York, 1987), p. 622.
30. For example, Andrew Gamble, *Britain in Decline.*
31. Quoted in Richard Weight, *Patriots. National Identity in Britain, 1940–2000* (London, 2002), epigraph to Part 10.
32. For a robust argument in favour of Britain's continuing great power status even at a time of supposed decline see Michael J. Turner, *Britain's International Role, 1970–1991* (Basingstoke, 2010), especially p. 1, pp. 234–5 *et passim.*
33. Quoted in Brendan Simms, *Unfinest Hour. Britain and the Destruction of Bosnia* (London, 2001), p. 5. See also Josip Glaurdic, *The Hour of Europe. Western Powers and the Break-up of Yugoslavia* (New Haven, 2011).
34. See Tony Blair, *A Journey* (London, 2010), pp. 222–49. For Blair's global stature see Philip Stephens, *Tony Blair. The Making of a World Leader* (London, 2004), p. xvii *et passim.* More critical but equally insistent on Blair's importance, see Stephen Benedict Dyson, *The Blair Identity. Leadership and Foreign Policy* (Manchester and New York, 2009), pp. 4–5 *et passim.*

35. For the prime minister's own account see Gordon Brown, *Beyond the Crash. Overcoming the First Crisis of Globalization* (London, 2010), pp. 50–66.
36. Lundestad, *Rise and Decline of the American 'Empire'*, p. 6
37. Thus 'UK Economy to Overtake Both Japan and Germany', *Daily Telegraph*, 26.12.2015.
38. The persistence of British power today is well argued by Justin Morris, 'How Great is Britain? Power, Responsibility and Britain's Future Global Role', *British Journal of Politics and International Relations*, 13 (2011), pp. 326–47, especially pp. 331–3. For a bleaker view see Christopher J. Hill, 'British Foreign Policy Priorities: Tough Choices', 66/4 (2010), pp. 11–14.
39. For the persistence of Anglo-British identity see Richard Weight, *Patriots. National Identity in Britain, 1940–2000* (London, 2002).
40. Joseph Nye, 'Soft Power', *Foreign Policy*, 80 (1990), pp. 153–71.
41. Quoted in J. S. Dunn, *The Crowe Memorandum. Sir Eyre Crowe and Foreign Office Perceptions of Germany, 1918–1925* (Newcastle, 2013), pp. 233–4.
42. Thus Andrew Gamble, 'Hegemony and Decline: Britain and the United States', in Patrick Karl O'Brien and Armand Clesse (eds.), *Two Hegemonies. Britain 1846–1914 and the United States, 1941–2001* (Aldershot, 2002), p. 133, quoting a famous phrase by Geir Lundestad.
43. For some of the resulting debates see Philip Towle, *Going to War. British Debates from Wilberforce to Blair* (Basingstoke, 2009).
44. Thus John Brewer, *The Sinews of Power. War, Money and the English State, 1688–1783* (London, 1989).
45. In what follows I concentrate on the 'Anglo-sphere' but the 'Westminster model' has been exported more widely: Arend Lijphart, *Patterns of Democracy. Government Forms and Performance in Thirty-six Countries* (New Haven, 1999).
46. See David Edgerton, *Britain's War Machine* (London, 2011).
47. Thus James Belich, *Replenishing the Earth. The Settler Revolution and the Rise of the Anglo-World, 1783–1939* (Oxford, 2009).
48. John F. Williams, *Corporal Hitler and the Great War, 1914–1918* (London and New York, 2005), p. 143.
49. Thus Carl Bridenbaugh, *Vexed and Troubled Englishmen. 1590–1642* (New York, 1968).
50. See Brendan Simms, 'Towards a Mighty Union: How to Create a Democratic European Superpower', *International Affairs*, 88, 1 (2012), pp. 49–62, especially pp. 50–2.

51. See Kathleen Burk, *Old World. New World. The Story of Britain and America* (London and New York, 2007
52. Quoted from Duncan Bell, 'The Project for a New Anglo Century: Race, Space and Global Order', in Peter Katzenstein (ed.), *Anglo-America and Its Discontents: Civilisational Identities beyond West and East* (London, 2012), pp. 33–56 (quotation p. 42)
53. See D. Cameron Watt, *Succeeding John Bull. America in Britain's Place, 1900–1975. A Study of the Anglo-American Relationship in the Context of British and American Foreign-policy Making in the Twentieth Century* (Cambridge, 1984).
54. See Srdjan Vucetic, *The Anglosphere: A Genealogy of a Racialized Identity in International Relations*, and 'Bound to Follow? The Anglosphere and US-led Coalitions of the Willing, 1950–2001', *European Journal of International Relations*, 17, 1 (2011), pp. 27–49.
55. See Catherine Philp, 'Britain Sends Warships to Counter Russian Threat', *The Times*, 10.2.2016, p. 6.

10. A EUROPEAN BRITAIN OR A BRITISH EUROPE? THE UNITED KINGDOM AND CONTINENTAL UNION

1. This chapter uses material from Brendan Simms, 'Scotland, the British Question and the European Problem: A Churchillian Solution', *Journal for Comparative Government and European Policy*, 12 (2014), pp. 456–83, and Brendan Simms, 'The Churchillian Solution. Why We Need a British Europe rather than a European Britain', *New Statesman*, 3–9 July 2015, pp. 25–9.
2. See Hugo Young, *This Blessed Plot. Britain and Europe from Churchill to Blair* (London, 1998). For a recent assessment see A. Geddes, *Britain and the European Union* (Basingstoke, 2013).
3. See the debate between Will Hutton and Ruth Lea in 'Does Britain's Destiny Lie in the Heart of Europe?', *Observer*, 27.1.2013. There is an excellent cross-section of the various positions in the proceedings of a conference held at the British Academy on 9.10.2014: *Britain and the EU. New Perspectives* (Oxford, 2014).
4. Ian Traynor et al., 'David Cameron Blocks EU Treaty with Veto, Casting Britain Adrift in Europe', *Guardian*, 9.12.2011.
5. D. Davis, 'The European Arrest Warrant Leaves Britain in Handcuffs', *Sunday Times*, 9.11.2014.
6. C. Hope, 'EU Red Tape is Damaging Britain's Economy', *Sunday Telegraph*, 9.11.2014.

7. L. Fisher and C. Bremner, 'Cameron Puts His Foot Down over Move to Raise EU Budget', *The Times*, 23.10.2014. For an analysis see I. Begg, '£1.7bn EU Bill Puts UK One Step Closer to "Brexit"', Chatham House Expert Comment, 29.10.2014.
8. L. Pitel, '"We Must Threaten to Leave the EU over Migrants," Says Boris', *The Times*, 13.10.2014.
9. S. Coates, '"We Will Not Stick with Europe if it Doesn't Work for Us," Says Cameron', *The Times*, 11.11.2014.
10. Thus Denis MacShane, *Brexit. How Britain Will Leave Europe* (London, 2015).
11. For the broader historical context see L. Colley, *Acts of Union and Disunion. What has Held the UK Together – and What is Dividing It?* (London, 2014), qualified by my reflections later on in this chapter, and T. M. Devine, *Independence or Union. Scotland's Past and Scotland's Present* (London, 2016).
12. See the short but penetrating analysis in D. Runciman, 'Reflections on the Independence Referendum, *London Review of Books*, 36/17, 11.9.2014, and 'After the Referendum', *London Review of Books*, 36/19, 9.10.2014.
13. V. Bogdanor et al., *The Future of the Union* (London, 2014).
14. E.g. Will Hutton, 'Cameron's Attempt to Manipulate the Constitution is Crudely Cynical', *Observer*, 21.9.2014.
15. Robert Tombs, *The English and Their History* (London, 2014). For the early modern roots of Anglo-British power see David Scott, *Leviathan. The Rise of Britain as a World Power* (London, 2013), especially pp. 7–203.
16. On the benefits of staying and the costs of leaving see Philip. Whyte, 'Do Britain's European Ties Damage Its Prosperity?' (Centre for European Reform, 2013).
17. Matthew Parris, 'We Can't let Germany be *über alles* in Europe', *The Times*, 15.11.2014.
18. Thus Almut Möller and Tim Oliver, *The United Kingdom and the European Union: What Would a "Brexit" Mean for the EU and Other States around the World?* (Deutsche Gesellschaft für Auswärtige Politik, 2014), p. 108.
19. See Brendan Simms and Torsten Riotte (eds.), *The Hanoverian Dimension in British History, 1714–1837* (Cambridge, 2007).
20. Thus Allan I. Macinnes, 'Anglo-Scottish Union and the War of the Spanish Succession', in William Mulligan and Brendan Simms (eds.), *The Primacy of Foreign Policy in British History, 1660–2000. How*

Strategic Concerns Shaped Modern Britain (Basingstoke, 2010), pp. 49–64. For the broader context see Brendan Simms, *Three Victories and a Defeat. The Rise and Fall of the First British Empire, 1714–1783* (London, 2007).

21. See J. Pole (ed.), *The Federalist Papers* (Indianapolis and Cambridge, 2005), pp. 17–18.
22. C. Hulverscheidt, '*Was Mister Europa Rät*', *Süddeutsche Zeitung*, 28.11.2014.
23. Thus C. Mortera-Martinez, 'Free Movement. Why Britain Does not Need to Change the Rules' (Centre for European Reform, 2014).
24. D. Leppard, 'UK Must Quit EU to Dodge Rights Charter', *Sunday Times*, 17.8.2014.
25. Text at gov.uk: EU speech at Bloomberg, 23.1.2013.
26. Thus T. Valasek, 'What Central Europe Thinks of Britain and Why' (Centre of European Reform Insight, 2012).
27. Thus the persuasive analysis of Walter Münchau, 'On the Way Out? Britain's Relation with the Rest of Europe are Unsustainable', *Prospect*, August 2014, pp. 40–43.
28. As set out in Brendan Simms, 'Towards a Mighty Union: How to Create a Democratic European Superpower', *International Affairs*, 88/1 (January, 2012), pp. 49–62. The author is President of the Project for Democratic Union (PDU), a start-up think tank which seeks to make this vision a reality: http://www.democraticunion.eu/. The manifesto of the PDU, which elaborates some of the themes of this chapter, is so far only available in German, though editions in other languages, including English, are planned: Brendan Simms and Benjamin Zeeb, *Europa am Abgrund. Plädoyer für die Vereinigten Staaten von Europa* (Munich, 2016).
29. Mr Winston Churchill speaking in Zurich, 19 September 1946 (The Churchill Society. London: http://www.churchill-society-london.org.uk/astonish.html). There is a lively and very fair-minded discussion of Churchill's engagement in Europe in Boris Johnson, *The Churchill Factor. How One Man Make History* (London, 2014), pp. 295–310.
30. Quoted in A. Lemaire, 'Keep Britain within the EU' in A. Hug, *Renegotiation, Reform and Referendum: Does Britain Have an EU Future?* (The Foreign Policy Centre, 2014), p. 59.
31. See Bruno Waterfield and Francis Waterfield, 'Poland Will Support EU Benefit Curbs in Return for NATO Base', *The Times*, 5.1.2016, p. 14.

Acknowledgements

The author draws on the works of many colleagues, some of it cited in the notes, others of which have seeped into his brain by osmosis. It would be invidious to single any of them out by name, not least because they may not approve of the use to which their work has been put. At the same, time it would be churlish not to thank those who read and commented on draft chapters at very short notice: Johanna Dale, Gabriel Glickman, Edward Hicks, Tom Hooper, Ralph Houlbrooke, Roger Lovatt, John Maddicott, Scott Mandelbrote, Maire Ni Mhaonaigh, William Mulligan, Keith Robbins, Magnus Ryan, Constance Simms and Nicholas Vincent. Needless to say, none of my colleagues bears any responsibility for the views expressed here, which are the author's own. I would also like to thank my publisher, Simon Winder, and my agent, Bill Hamilton, who both believed in this book at an early stage. The greatest debt, however, is to my wife, Anita, without whose love and support I would have achieved nothing. This book is for her.